FORD COUNTRY

By David L. Lewis

Published by Amos Press, Inc.,
911 Vandemark Road, Sidney, Ohio 45365

Amos Press, Inc.

First Edition Copyright 1999

Dedication

To Yuri

Introduction

Cars & Parts' "Ford Country" column first appeared in June 1974. A quarter of the stories appearing in the column between 1974 and 1986 were reprinted in 1987 in the first volume of *Ford Country*. This second volume, almost a third longer than the first, contains half new material, half post-1986 reprints.

Both books present stories on the Ford family, company, and products. Many items are based on my research and interviews, many others on news stories and letters and printed materials from readers and former students. They have my profound gratitude, and will have that of future historians and Ford history enthusiasts as well. Their names are cited in the text and also in the Acknowledgments section.

Many items in the columns and books relate the present to the past and vice versa. There is some editorializing, perhaps to be expected of a lifelong student of Ford history. Occasionally I ruffle a reader's feathers. When that happens, I am comforted by Editor Bob Stevens' words, "you can't please everyone."

Most "Ford Country" items permit quick in-and-out reading, especially important to non-Fordists, of whom there are a goodly number. Robert Voss, Montgomery, Texas, and Lorin Jacobson, Littleton, Colo., speak for them. "I've been a subscriber to *Cars & Parts* for over 20 years," Voss remarks. "I have enjoyed your 'Ford Country' column very much, although I am not a Fordophile." "I have never owned a Ford," echoes Jacobson, "but I find all your material interesting since there are colorful personalities involved, and the commentary reaches into so many areas of human endeavor with information and insights."

I enjoy writing "Ford Country," just as I enjoy teaching, which is why at age 72 I continue to do both. Occasionally I am asked, "When will the well run dry?" Not in my lifetime, I reply, nor that of my successor, given the subject's breadth and depth. Come along with me, for the best is yet to be.

Acknowledgements

Scores of readers and others have contributed to "Ford Country," forwarding letters, e-mail, fax messages, clippings, photographs, and miscellany. Among them, Michael Skinner, St. Clair Shores, Mich. stands out. Constantly in motion throughout Southeastern Michigan, camera in hand, Mike has forwarded voluminous monthly packets of Ford/auto-related materials since the 1970s. A guide at Henry Ford Estate-Fair Lane for more than 20 years, Mike is an officer of the Henry Ford Heritage Association and ex-president of the Dearborn Historical Society and Grosse Pointe Historical Society. Thirty years younger than I, he is a logical choice to write this column in the years ahead.

Two other longtime contributors also deserve special thanks. One is Richard B. Folsom, Livonia, Mich., a veteran Henry Ford Estate guide who is president of the Henry Ford Heritage Association and ex-president of the Dearborn Historical Society. Dick, too, has forwarded Ford data since the 1970s. The second contributor is a former student, who "in appreciation of your teaching," has forwarded Ford/auto/business history-related items since 1968. He prefers anonymity.

Special thanks, too, to my wife Yuri who, in addition to having edited every word I've published over the past 46 years, has provided sound advice every step of the way.

I am hesitant to list contributors for fear of omitting some. But the following names are readily recalled.

Edward A. Abercrombie, Statesboro, Ga.; James and Joan Aberts, West Chester, Pa.; Rick Aguilar, Hansford, W. Va.; Leandro Apolloni, Windsor, Ont.; Elmer Art, Montrose, Calif.; the late David R. Babb, Belvidere, Ill.; "Bud" Baker, Pawnee, Tex.; William O. Barnes, Hilton Head, S.C.; W.T. Basore, Tulsa, Okla.; John von Batchelder, Detroit; Harold Beauman, Monroe, Mich.; Kenneth R. Belland, Fargo, N.D.; Jim Benjaminson, Cavalier, N.D.; Herman Bennett, Brownwood, Tex.; Tom Blinn, Greenville, Mich.; W. Boissevain, Los Altos, Calif.; William Borntraeger, Scotia, N.Y.; Scott Breithaupt, Rome, Ga.; Don Brewer, Dearborn, Mich.; Jim Brierly, Temecula, Calif.; D. Briggs, Arcadia, Calif.; J.D. Brookhart, St. Marys, Ohio; Robert C. Brown, Plano, Tex.; Robert L. Brown, Battle Creek, Mich.; Ford Richardson Bryan, Dearborn, Mich.; Michael Bukovac, Britt, Minn.; Mike Byrnes, Philadelphia; Philip C. Campbell, Kaiserslautern, Germany; Scott Campbell, Medina, Ohio; Jerry Capizzi, Chicago; Jeff Caplan, Omaha; Sherrie Casad-Lodge, Sidney, Ohio; Kent B. Casstevens, Sun City West, Ariz.; David Cavey, Baltimore, Md.; Bob Cawley, Kenthurst, New South Wales, Australia; Pablo Antonio Porras Chacon, Bucaramanga, Colombia; Patricia E. Chappell, Wilmington, Del.; Mel Chase, Newark, Del.; Harrison Church, Lebanon, Ill.; David E. Clower, Richmond, Va.; John A. Conde, Bloomfield Hills, Mich.; James Cranick,

Harbor Springs, Mich.; Kevin M. Crowe, Takapuna, New Zealand; Donald M. Currie, Millersburg, Mich.; Gary Custer, Harrisonburg, Va.; Bill Cuthbert, Santa Maria, Calif.; Whitman C. Daly, Berkley, Mich.; Malcolm L. Denise, Grosse Pointe, Mich.; Florence Diamond, Georgetown, Ky.; Don Doody, Vancouver, B.C.; Tom Downs, Lansing, Mich.; Robert C. Drew, Ontario, Calif.; Phil Dumka, Carlisle, Mass.; Dick Duncan, Rochester, Mich.; Ralph H. Dunwoodie, Sun Valley, Nev.; Cheryl Easley, Berrien Springs, Mich.; Jim Edison, Indianapolis; Craig Edmonds, Granada Hills, Calif.; Charles D. Edmonson, Hampton, Va.; Howard Emmert, Tulsa, Okla.; Laurent d'Entremont, Lower West Pubnico, Yarmouth County, N.S.; Carroll G. Fader, Ketchikan, Alaska; Dale R. Fairfax, Indianapolis; Andres M. Flanegin, Aruba; Leonard Fleshman, Columbus, Ohio; Dorman R. Ford, Latham, Ill.; Gary Henry Ford, Alsip, Ill.; Steve Ford, Birmingham, Mich.; Christopher G. "Kit" Foster, Gales Ferry, Conn.; Fred K. Fox, Delhi, Calif.; William Friel, Harwood Heights, Ill.; E.R. Gardner, Boyne City, Mich.; Gasiorek, Carleton, Mich.; Walter Geistler, Livonia, Mich.; Jody Glancy, Ann Arbor, Mich.; Allen Grahl, Sandusky, Ohio; William. F. Grohonski, New Hampton, N.Y.; Bill Haines, Laguna Hills, Calif.; Vernon Hales, Kearney, Mo.; Noel Hamer, Roblin, Ont.; George L. Hamlin, Clarksville, Md.; George P. and Stacey P. Hanley, Rochester Hills, Mich.; Jack Hassen, Glenview, Ill.; David O. Hayward, Southampton, U.K.; Robert G. Heinfeld, Ada, Ohio; David L. Higgins, San Pedro, Calif.; Dr. Iden Hill, Glen Ellyn, Ill.; Douglas Hughes, Waterloo, Ont.; Charles E. Hulse, Flint, Mich.; Charles K. Hyde, Royal Oak, Mich.; David Hyde, Memphis; Fernando Irigoyen, Guatemala City, Guatemala; Lorin Ironside, Almont, Mich.; John Jackson, San Jose, Calif.; Lorin Jacobson, Littleton, Colo.; Joseph E. Jankovic, Three Lakes, Wis.; Arthur C. Johnson, Spokane, Wash.; Dale Johnson, Owatonna, Minn.; Victor S. Johnson Jr., Nashville, Tenn.; Charles A. Jones, Nashville, Ga.; Burr Joslin, Sturgis, Mich.; Margaret D. Judy, Richmond Hill, Ga.; C.D. "Chet" Kass, Mountain Home, Ark.; Walter C. Kaufman, Colgate, Wis.; Dan Keller, South Whitley, Ind.; David B. Kelley, Sarnia, Ont.; Robert B. Kennedy, Klamath Falls, Ore.; Carl Klosinski, Niles, Mich.; Robert J. Koenig, Greenfield, Wis.; Tom Konop, Terrace Park, Ohio; Ric Kruse, Batavia, Ohio; Kubancik, Hendersonville, N.C.; Andrew LaBorde, Milwaukee, Wis.; Michael Lamm, Stockton, Calif.; Joe Lawson, Calhan, Colo.; Ronald C. and Linda Leggitt, Dearborn, Mich.; Vic Lenstrom, Comstock, Nev.; Robert Lenz, San Leandro, Calif.; Wade Leonard, Clinton Township, Mich.; William J. Lewis, Anaheim, Calif.; Rick Lindner, Columbus, Ohio; Tom Link, Kernersville, N.C.; Frank Loucka, Avon Lake, Ohio; Gerald A. Lundy, Cincinnati; Patrick Martin, Palatine, Ill.; Keith Marvin, Menands, N.Y.; Robert B. Marvin, Jasper, Fla.; Randy Mason, Dearborn, Mich.; Terry W. Mason, Seattle; John F. Masters, Wichita; Verna Massura, Lincoln Park, Mich.; Don Mates, Midlothian, Ill.; Leo L. Matthews, West Hartford, Conn.; Keith Mayne, Bayport, N.Y.; Robert E. McClure, Worthington, Ohio; Dallas McCormick, East Tawas, Mich.; Jil McIntosh, Oshawa, Ont.; William R.

McLaughlin, Hartford, Mich.; Cheryl McMahon, Gaines, Mich.; John Meinelt, De Land, Fla.; Bill Michaels, Syracuse, N.Y.; Frank J. Mike, Tustin, Calif.; David H. Miller, Cleveland, Ohio; Jerald A. Mitchell, Detroit; Ken Morris, Newhall, Calif.; Bill Mott, Dallas; Jack Mueller, Wauwatosa, Wis.; Floyd Murphy, Morgan Hill, Calif.; Marshall Naul, Granville, Ohio; William B. Nedobity, Higganum, Conn.; Bill Nickels, Ypsilanti, Mich.; Tim O'Callaghan, Northville, Mich.; Richard E. Osborne, Indianapolis; Herm Ovind, Yucca Valley, Calif.; Bill Parker, Lorain, Ohio; Russell H. Peebles, Grosse Pointe, Mich.; Murvin H. Perry, Johnson City, Tenn.; the late James F. Petrik, Madeira, Ohio; Steve Pratt, Mesquite, Tex.; John Preston, South Croydon, Surrey, England; the late Ronald Putz, Bay City, Mich.; Don Redbruch, Sagle, Idaho; the late Walter F. Robinson Jr., Bellevue, Wash.; Bob Rockman, Arlington, Va.; M.L. "Pete" Rodgers, Bullhead City, Ariz.; Frederick D. Roe, Holliston, Mass.; Alan Roth, Lakewood, Ohio; Robert S. Runk, Cincinnati; Tom Russell, Standish, Mich.; Terje Saethre, Lillestrom, Norway; Walter Schan, Mich.; Richard P. Scharchburg, Gland Blanc, Mich.; James J. Schild, Columbia, Ill.; George W. Schuleter, Grapevine, Tex.; Richard V. Schweitzer, Akron, Ohio; Robert Scoon, Arcadia, Calif.; David M. Scott, Wells, Maine; Will Scott, Birmingham, Mich.; Howard Segal, Orono, Maine; Michael Shields, Flat Rock, Mich.; Bruce Simpson, Dearborn, Mich.; Phil Skinner, Fullerton, Calif.; J.F. Sledge, Richmond, Va.; Cecil A. Smith, Tucson, Ariz.; Gus Stefanow Jr., Battle Creek, Mich.; Twyla Stemple, St. George, W.Va.; Carlyle V. Stewart Jr., Falls Church, Va.; Tom Stock, Grosse Pointe Farms, Mich.; James B. Stoney, Whitestone, N.Y.; Bob Thatcher, Export, Pa.; Stewart Thompson, Toronto, Ont.; Robert A. Tonnies, Cincinnati; T.J. Totushek, Severna Park, Md.; Mark R. Tuban, Mountain View, Calif.; David E. Turner, Palmerston, Ont.; James Ullery, Westland, Mich.; William Vicary, Dearborn, Mich.; Taylor Z. Vinson, Alexandria, Va.; Robert K. Voss, Montgomery, Tex.; James K. Wagner, Plymouth, Mich.; Lani Walczak, Farmington Hills, Mich.; Debra Wake-Williams, Wayne, Mich.; John Wallin, Manteca, Calif.; Timothy Wallin, Swanton, Ohio; Gayle Warnock, Scottsdale, Ariz.; Bill Watson, Burnaby, B.C.; Pete Webb, Mooers, N.Y.; Dr. Peter C. Weber, Olney, Ill.; Chuck Welch, Corydon, Ind.; Glen Whitt, Plano, Tex.; Nick Wilkens, Charlotte, N.C.; Bruce S. Williams, Canton, Ohio; Ferguson L. Willis, Madison, Wis.; Malcolm Willits, Hollywood, Calif.; C. Bud Wilson; Peter Winnewisser, Cazenovia, N.Y.; Russell S. Wollman, Fairfield, Iowa; James A. Wren, West Bloomfield, Mich.; R. Perry Zavitz, London, Ont.; Frank Zelinka, Coral Gables, Fla.; Bob Zenter, Baldwinsville, N.Y.; H. Arthur Zimmerman, Port Washington, Wis.

I also wish to express my deep gratitude to Walt Reed and Bob Stevens, publisher and editor, respectively, of *Cars & Parts* for their longtime warm support of the column and book series. Similarly I am most appreciative to art director Ken New and administrative assistant Sherry Fair for their splendid contributions to both column and books.

Contents

I

THE FORD FAMILY

Henry Ford and his wife, Clara, have 52 descendants, as noted in a 1998 advertisement congratulating the present family patriarch, "Uncle Bill" – William Clay Ford Sr. – on his 50 years as a Ford board member.

The founding Fords had one son, Edsel, who, although president of the company from 1918 until his death in 1943, was dominated by his father. Edsel and his wife, Eleanor, had four children, Henry II, Benson, Josephine, 76, and Bill, 74. Henry II headed the company from 1945 until his death at 70 in 1987. Benson, overshadowed by Henry II, nominally headed Lincoln-Mercury Division and the Ford Dealer Council. His trouble, as HFII said, is that he "could never get his arms around anything." He died at age 59 in 1978. Bill also lived in HFII's shadow. After reviving the Continental Mark II only to see it abandoned, his primary interest became the Detroit Lions football team, of which he acquired ownership in 1964. Still, he retired as a company vice-chairman in 1989 and served as chairman of the board's finance committee from 1987-95.

There are 13 fourth-generation Fords. Henry's children are Charlotte, 58, Anne, 56, and Edsel II, 51; Benson's are Benson Jr., 50, and Lynn, 48. Josephine's children are Walter Buhl III, 56; Eleanor C., 53; Josephine, 51; Alfred Brush, 49; William Clay Sr.'s are Martha (Muff), 51; Sheila, 48, William Clay Jr., 42; and Elizabeth (Lisa), 38.

Edsel II, named a company vice president in 1993, retired as president of Ford Motor Credit Company in 1998. He remains a board member, serves on selected committees, is the company's liaison with dealers, and oversees the company's 2003 centennial celebration. Three months after retirement, he joined the board of Penske Motorsports, Inc.

William Clay Ford Jr. succeeded his father as chairman of the board's finance committee in 1995, and will become chairman in 1999. Treasurer of the Detroit Lions, he is active in the team's management.

Buhl and Benson worked briefly for the company, and Elizabeth's husband, Charles Kontulis, is a Ford executive. Sheila's husband, Steve Hamp, is president of Henry Ford Museum & Greenfield Village.

One of 18 fifth-generation Fords, Charlotte's daughter, Elena, 32, works for the company – in Marketing. Most watched Generation Xer is Edsel II's oldest son, Henry III, 19, a Dartmouth College freshman. He physically resembles his great-great-grandfather.

There are 18 sixth-generation Fords, all small fry. Most of the fifth- and sixth-generation children bear popular contemporary names – Briget, Lindsey, Wendy, Allison, Ricky, Michael, Jason, Kate, Lisa, Peter, Will, Nicholas, and Jeffrey. In addition, there are Allegra, Amrita, Anisha, Kiff, and Be-Be (some go by nicknames).

A few names/nicknames bespeak a Ford heritage – Callie (Henry Ford's pet name for Clara), Clay (Mrs. Edsel Ford's maiden name), of whom there are two, plus Eleanor, Jody and Josie (for Josephine), and Charlotte. Henry III is called Sonny, and an Edsel III has yet to arrive.

The closely-knit Fords are becoming almost as abundant as Vanderbilts, du Ponts, and Rockefellers. Thanks to their large block of voting stock, they will control the Ford Company for the foreseeable future. Some likely will join the company. Those who do cannot escape being influenced by the Ford legacy. As Edsel II succinctly puts it, "People expect things of you."

Fords Visit Ireland

Three of Henry Ford's distant American cousins recently visited an Irish cousin – perhaps the first meeting of Dearborn Fords and an Irish relative in 145 years.

The American trio was comprised of Ford R. Bryan and Rylma and Roxanne LaChance. Their Irish cousin is Hazel Ford Bultimer, who lives on a farm at Crohane, near the coastal town of Clonakilty. Upon his return, Bryan wrote an account of the Americans' visit for the newsletter of the Henry Ford Heritage Association.

The Ford ancestral homesite, three miles inland from Clonakilty, is now grown up in weeds, writes Bryan, "the small, dry-stone cottage having been snitched stone-by-stone by souvenir hunters. Henry Ford's ancestors lived for nearly 300 years on land owned by the Starvell family, who were granted thousands of acres in southwest Ireland by Queen Elizabeth I. The Fords, including Henry Ford's father, grandfather, and great-grandparents, leased the little stone cottage and 23 acres – in sharp contrast to the huge manor house and estate of their landlord Jonas Starvell, centered 10 miles east at Kilbrittain where the Starvell 'castle' still stands in royal dignity.

"The Ford ancestral burial plot in Kilnagross churchyard was located. This ancient church is still in use. In 1922, Henry Ford had architectural drawings and material specifications for this church prepared by Cork architects apparently in anticipation of building an exact replica somewhere in the United States. These drawings and specifications now reside in the Research Center of Henry Ford Museum & Greenfield Village.

"The Dearborn Fords visiting Ireland thought it would be nice to have a marker placed at the abandoned Ford homesite, which is located on an ungraded public road just a hundred or so yards from the main Cork-to-Clonakilty highway. But the land on which the stone cottage stood is now owned by an Englishman named Blackburn who is said to be a member of the board of directors of Mitsubishi Motors and is responsible for distribution of Mitsubishi products in England and Ireland. Permission to publicize the Ford name at that spot may be difficult to obtain, Bryan surmises.

"Hazel Bultimer and her husband," reports Bryan, "recently were legally enabled to purchase land, and have acquired sufficient acreage to pasture 200 head of cattle, of which 90 are milked twice daily in the family's 'dairy parlor.'

"The spirit of Henry Ford lives on at the Henry Ford Tavern," continues Bryan, "in the little village of Ballinascarty, four miles from Clonakilty and about a mile from the Ford ancestral homesite. The little tavern is handsomely decorated with Ford memorabilia – pictures of Henry Ford, Henry's father, William; and a variety of British Ford automobiles.

"The well-known Gaelic Athletic Association in 1983 named their playing field near Ballinascarty the 'Henry Ford GAA Park,' " concludes Bryan. "Plans of the Ballinascarty Community Council are to convert a three-story creamery building on the main road just east of the village into the 'Ford Centre' – a museum project which is to interpret both the period in Irish history during which the Ford ancestors lived in Ireland and also the exploits of Henry Ford. Plans for this museum are well underway with considerable help in financing expected from Ford Motor Company."

Membership in the Henry Ford Heritage Association is open to anyone who sends annual dues of $10 (plus address and phone number) to Henry Ford Estate-Ford Heritage Association, 4903 Evergreen Road, Dearborn, MI 48128-1491.

Home Sweet Home

As of 1993, three of the four most expensive homes in the Detroit metropolitan area belong to members of the Ford family. All are on Lake Shore Road in Grosse Pointe Farms.

The priciest of the region's residences is Edsel Ford II's cedar-shingled $4.9 million place on Lake Shore Road, overlooking Lake St. Clair. Just up the road, hidden behind a brick wall and a thick stand of trees is the second-most expensive in the area. The owner is Edsel II's uncle, William Clay Ford, owner of the Detroit Lions and a former Ford vice-chairman. Bill's house is valued at $4.1 million. Fourth on the list is a $2.3 million home owned by Lynn Ford Alandt, daughter of the late Benson and Eleanor Ford.

Two of the 10 most expensive digs in the metro Detroit area belong to auto dealers, the others to real-estate developers, a furniture magnate, a beer distributor, and Bruce Kresge, grandson of the founder of the Kresge/Kmart stores.

The Place To Live

For wealth and tradition, according to the *Detroit Free Press*, the "most truly highfalutin addresses (in the Detroit area) may be on Provencal Road in Grosse Pointe Farms," east of the city of Detroit on Lake St. Clair.

Most of the road is off limits, notes the *Free Press*, giving it a special allure. The few who gain entry for cocktail parties or Federal Express deliveries are said to hold the memory dear, for they have had a glimpse into the lives of Detroit's rich and famous.

Henry Ford II lived on the road twice – with his first wife, Anne, and then with his third wife, Kathy DuRoss. His widow still owns the house under a company name, KDF Properties, Inc., although she spends most of her time away from Michigan.

Henry II's youngest brother, William Clay, had a house at the end of the road before moving to a larger estate along the lake. His sister, Dodie Ford, still lives on Provencal, pronounced with the emphasis in the middle, "pro-Von-sal."

In 1992, William Clay Ford Jr. bought a Provencal house, signing a $1.1-million mortgage on the property.

Lee Iacocca, never a full-fledged member of Detroit high society, almost lived on the street. In 1986 he and his second wife, Peggy, purchased a Provencal house previously owned by Henry Ford II and by his son, Edsel Ford II. Peggy, however, declared that New York was where she would rather stay. When her husband ordered her to move to the Farms or else, she opted for Park Avenue. The Iacoccas were divorced that year and sold the home after having held title for less than five months.

As for the road itself, once past the guard, one finds oneself on a winding lane of graceful elms and stately manors. The atmosphere is 19th century pastoral, a far cry from battered Detroit a few miles to the west. The road is lined with a mix of Tudor and colonial homes, most of them dating from the 1920s and valued at more than $1 million. There are ivy-covered gates, swimming pools, courtyards, and architectural details salvaged from demolished nearby estates. Several houses boast art collections much more valuable than the buildings themselves.

As stomping grounds for prominent bankers, lawyers and industrialists, the neighborhood takes up several pages of the social register, the Fords being among the most prominent of the registrants.

"Ford Row"

A "Ford Row" has sprung up in Detroit's Woodlawn Cemetery, in which many leading auto figures are buried.

Three near-identical Ford tombs may be found east of the cemetery's lagoon. One marks the graves of Edsel Ford and his wife, Eleanor, interred in

1943 and 1976, respectively; another those of their second son, Benson, and his wife, Edith, buried in 1978 and 1980, respectively. The third tomb awaits the Fords' third son William Clay and his wife, Martha.

Established in 1895 at the dawn of the auto age, Woodlawn boasts more automotive pioneers and greats than any other burying ground in the country. Among them are John and Horace Dodge, James Couzens, Ford's No. 2 man between 1903-15; C. Harold Wills, who helped develop the Model T and built his own Wills-Ste. Claire car; Roy D. Chapin Sr., who talked department store magnate J.L. Hudson (also buried in Woodlawn) into backing an auto venture; Bill Metzger, the "M" in E-M-F, who also made a car under his own name; Robert C. Hupp, founder of Hupmobile in 1908; Harry Jewett, who introduced a namesake car in 1923, George M. Holley, the carburetor manufacturer, and K.T. Keller, successor to Walter P. Chrysler as Chrysler president.

Visitors are welcome to drive through and walk about the cemetery, located at 19975 Woodward Avenue, midway between downtown Detroit and Birmingham/Bloomfield Hills, where most of today's auto leaders reside. Gates are closed at 5 p.m. After that time cars (at least) must stay the night – unless the solitary watchman can be intercepted while making his rounds.

Henry's Mother

"Can you show us a picture of Henry Ford's mother?" writes reader Ancel Robinson of Provo, Utah. Mary Ford, above, died of childbirth at age 37 in 1876, when Henry was 12 years old. Without his mother, Henry said later, the house was like a watch without a mainspring. (Photo courtesy Michael Skinner, St. Clair Shores, Mich.)

Henry's Sister Speaks

Henry Ford's younger sister, Margaret Ford Ruddiman, wrote the foreword for a catalogue of the Henry Ford Museum's Henry Ford Personal History Exhibition, a feature of the institution for several decades after 1953. Her brief tribute reads as follows:

"During my lifetime I have been privileged to observe in the making many of the things which have so completely changed our way of life and our habits of thought.

"My brother, Henry Ford, contributed much to the changed world in which we now live. I have always been very proud of my brother. I realize the great temptation to give such a life as my brother's some mystical beginning – to find some early sign that such a person is one 'set apart' for some special work in the world. If such were the case with my brother, these signs escaped all of us who were closest to him. We, who grew up with him, agree upon the fact that his outstanding characteristic was his naturalness.

"As a younger sister, I have had the opportunity to see him at work as a country-boy mechanic and later as a world figure. Herein the Henry Ford Room are gathered both objects and papers that mark the milestones on his road to success. Yet each of these objects from his first handmade tools to his office as a successful manufacturer tell the same story of a natural simplicity.

"Like every boy he was a 'dreamer,' but unlike most boys who grow older he never ceased to be a 'dreamer.' From his first sight of a steam traction engine he dreamed of ways to lighten the chores of farm life. As a mature man he constantly dreamed of ways to make the burdens of life lighter that man might have more time for a better life."

Many people have tried to determine the wellsprings of Ford's "genius," to figure out what made him tick. Sister Margaret and others close to Ford could only point to his "naturalness" and "simplicity." Many people, however, are "natural" and "simple," yet leave no mark. Ford's genius, elusive to Margaret, remains so to this day.

Will Ford

We don't know all we'd like to know about Henry Ford, but we know quite a bit, thanks to the nearly hundred books and thousands of articles written about him. But we know very little about Henry's brother, William, and have hankered for more information.

An article, "Will Ford and Family," in the Autumn, 1992, edition of the *Dearborn Historian*, by Ford R. Bryan, helps fill the gap.

William Ford Jr., eight years Henry's junior, lived in his older brother's shadow. But Will, states Bryan, was anything but a shadowy figure ... "he was considered to be an upright, straightforward gentleman, less glorified, but perhaps better liked by many locals than was Henry."

Will was born July 14, 1871 on the Ford homestead at the corner of Ford and Greenfield roads – in the house Henry moved to Greenfield Village in 1941. He was the youngest of the five children of William Ford Sr. and Mary (Litogot) Ford, and he lived at the homestead fully twice as long as Henry did.

Will farmed with his father until 1897, when William, Sr. moved into a Detroit apartment. While at the homestead, the younger Ford operated a farm machinery business. He left the farm in 1903, when the house had to be moved several hundred feet to the east to allow Greenfield Road to be extended southward to Michigan Avenue. At that time, Henry took possession of the house and farm, and Will and his wife, Frances, moved to the corner of what is now Tireman and Scotten avenues, Detroit .... Some of the homestead's furniture accompanied the Will Fords to their new address.

Between 1903-14, Will continued to sell farm implements, and also worked at the Detroit Lubricator Company, first as a machinist, then in sales. In addition, he operated two or three threshing crews. As Henry resumed farming in the Dearborn area, Will threshed for him, and by 1914 had sold his equipment to Henry and had become Henry's farm superintendent, which position he held until 1921.

Along with his farm superintendency, Will had charge of the service department at his brother's tractor plant on Dearborn's Elm Street, and Will's son, Lewis, became a tractor test driver. Later, Will served as the plant's employment manager for two years. Meantime, the family returned to Dearborn in 1916.

At the end of World War I, Will and Lewis obtained the Fordson tractor distributorship for sections of Michigan, Ohio, and Indiana. Their business was the William Ford Tractor Sales Company with headquarters on Monroe Avenue in Dearborn.

In 1919, Lewis, 19, died, presumably from influenza. Lewis's brother, Burnham, 16, that year joined his father in the tractor distribution business as a delivery boy. Will distributed tractor implements as well as tractors inasmuch as Fordsons were sold without accompanying equipment.

By 1922 Will was Dearborn's mayor and chief of police, and was described by a local newspaper as being "the biggest man in town and the best liked." It was said that he knew all of Dearborn's 2,000 residents and "calls everybody by his first name and never gets puffed up over his brother's riches."

In 1924, Burnham Ford, in partnership with a close friend, and with the help of his father, bought the Ford dealership in Flat Rock, Mich. Burnham operated the dealership until 1933, when he could not meet payments due on a mortgage held by Dearborn State Bank, owned by Henry Ford. The dealership was lost, and Burnham became sales manager for the Wayne (Mich.) Ford dealer.

In 1926, Will, with assurances by Henry that tractor production would remain steady for many years, organized an expanded operation in Highland Park, Mich., near Ford Motor Company's big plant. The new business, Universal Power Shovel Company, made and sold Wilford power shovels, clam shells, and cranes, all designed for use with Fordson tractors.

In 1928, however, with little forewarning, Ford tractor production was transferred to Cork, Ireland. Without Fordson power for its products, Universal Power went bankrupt in 1929, and so did Will, who defaulted on debts to some of his best friends.

In 1931, Edsel, possibly at Henry's suggestion, came to Will's rescue, arranging for financing for a new William Ford Tractor Sales Company at 6405 Schaefer Road, Dearborn. Will is said to have repaid his bank loan within two years. But the tractor business was slow during the depths of the Depression, and by 1934 Dearborn's city directory listed Will as crew manager at a nephew's Ford dealership, Robert W. Ford Sales, said at the time to be the largest Ford dealership in the world. Burnham was a salesman at the same agency.

The William Ford Sales Company became the Ford-Allen Company – Tractor and Implement Distributors." Meantime, in 1937, Will and Frances had moved from Dearborn to a 500-acre farm on Pleasant Road near Brighton, Mich. The Ford-Allen Company was still operating in 1948 with William H. Breech, the son of Ford's executive vice-president, Ernest R. Breech, as president.

Will was moved into a nursing home in 1958 and died in Brighton's Whitehall Convalescent Home on May 6, 1959 at age 87. Frances died in 1965, followed by Burnham in 1978 and a daughter, Edith, in 1986. All are buried in the northwest corner of the Ford Cemetery on Detroit's Joy Road, just west of Greenfield Road.

Will and Frances were never close to Henry and his wife, Clara, except when Henry sought to acquire their homestead furniture to restore his and Will's birthplace. Then he often visited the Will Fords. Otherwise, as Bryan notes, contact between the brothers generally was limited to sightings at weddings and funerals.

It's often been said that Henry Ford was a failure as a father. It would appear that he also left something to be desired as a brother, at least to Will. He did better by his sister, Margaret, but that's another story.

The Lady in J-205

Not every Floridian lives in the same building as a niece of Henry Ford's. But those who live in St. Andrews Estates South in Boca Raton do, as attested in an article, "How Well Do You Know Catherine Ruddiman J-205?" by the Estate's roving reporter, Vivian Karn.

"Catherine Ruddiman's mother," the article leads off, "was a sister of Henry Ford. When Catherine was seven years old she and her mother spent the winter in Detroit with Aunt Clara and Uncle Henry. That Christmas of 1909 Catherine received roller skates. Learning to skate was a real adventure. Many a winter evening cousin Edsel and the whole family were 'picking up' or 'holding up' Catherine so that when spring arrived she would be ready for her sidewalk adventures.

"Some of Catherine's childhood memories include the small greenhouse which Aunt Clara loved so much, where there was a plant that folded its leaves when touched and one with blossoms that looked like tiny pocketbooks; the sunken garden that was the beginning of the famous Fair Lane Rose Gardens; Edsel's drawings from his mechanical drawing class that lined the walls of his room – long sleek cars, reflecting the trend and design of the future in contrast to the Model T his father was building.

"After dinner Uncle Henry would often take the family to the Highland Park Plant where Catherine was awed by the huge wheels, the cranes, the noise of a factory at work, the greasy floors which always prompted a reminder to 'clean the soles of your shoes' when leaving. Uncle Henry would greet with warmth the workmen and foremen by name.

"Catherine recalls the 1920s when the Fords became interested in the restoration of the Wayside Inn in South Sudbury, Mass., which was made famous by Henry Wadsworth Longfellow's poem, "Tales of the Wayside Inn." Here the Fords often hosted costume parties of early American dancing. On one occasion when Catherine and her mother attended, Alice Longfellow, with her two sisters, came in gowns their father had bought for them in Paris. Catherine was impressed by Miss Alice's ring which contained perfume. These girls were mentioned in their father's poem, "The Children's Hour."

"By the time Catherine and her mother returned to Detroit to live, Uncle Henry was experimenting with the soybean to determine its food and industrial value. Her uncle, Dr. Edsel Ruddiman, was chief chemist in soybean research at the Ford Experimental Laboratory, and often brought little packages of soybean flour and dehydrated spinach for Catherine to experiment with in baking cakes and cookies.

"Following Henry's death, Mrs. Ford visited Catherine's mother as she was working on a 'true story of the life of the Ford family' as they were growing up. This article was published in 1953 in *Michigan History* under the title, "Memories of My Brother, Henry Ford." Later, Catherine coauthored a children's book, *Henry Ford: Boy with Ideas*.

"Catherine is able to share her memories with her two cousins from the Ruddiman side of the family, Evelyn Davis and Mildred McKinley, sisters who reside close to her in J-319."

Your commentator interviewed Miss Ruddiman during the tea hour in her stately Dearborn home a decade ago. Such a pleasant memory - chatting with her about Uncle Henry, Aunt Clara, Cousin Edsel, other Fords, and their neighbors and friends in days of yore.

Somewhere In Time

Mary Catherine Ruddiman, 90, a niece of Henry Ford, and Edith Payne, 104, who claims to have ridden in Henry Ford's quadricycle in 1896, were guests at Ford's Dearborn home, Fair Lane, on November 10, 1992. Both women submitted to questions from Fair Lane's volunteer guides and others, including your commentator.

Ford's niece fielded every question with aplomb. If she didn't have an answer, she was frank to say so. She was equally willing to say that she hadn't met this or that celebrity friend of her uncle's. Not every "old-timer" is so inclined.

Miss Ruddiman and her mother, Margaret, Henry's sister, lived with her uncle and Aunt Clara in Detroit during the winter of 1908-09, following the death of M.C.'s father, James Ruddiman. During that stay Mary Catherine recalls having been taught to roller skate by the Fords' son, Edsel, and remembers her aunt calling newfangled Jell-O "nervous pudding."

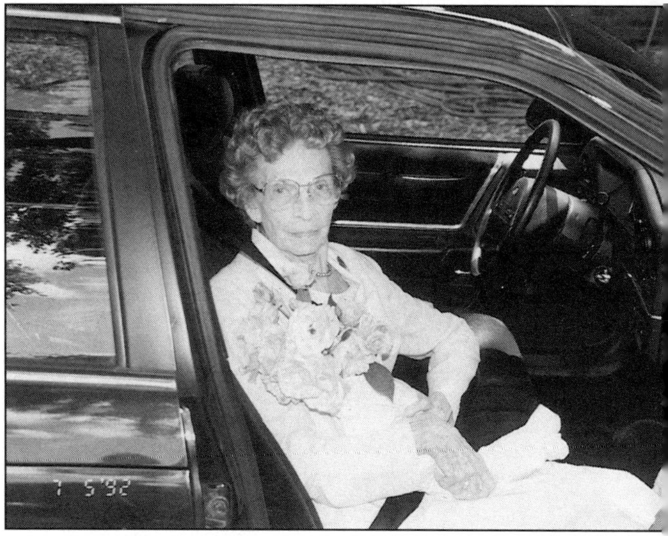

Reflecting Uncle Edsel A. Ruddiman's interest in soybeans, Mary Catherine recalls having made soybean cake, cookies, bread, biscuits, and muffins, and giving "prototype" pastries to family members. Asked to describe Aunt Clara, she replied, "very determined."

In response to questioning, Mary Catherine noted that she is the oldest member of her family, prompting Mrs. Payne to chime in with "so am I."

Mrs. Payne's girlhood was spent in downtown Detroit – on Porter Street, near Bagley Avenue, where the Fords resided. When eight years of age, she says, she rode in Henry's quadricycle. Asked how it felt to ride in Ford's first car, she replied, "Boy we felt big."

A voluble woman, Mrs. Payne, after "Happy Birthday" was sung to Mary Catherine, intoned, "And many more." Laughing, she said she sometimes can be a "Payne."

Also in attendance was Ford Richardson Bryan, a distant cousin of Henry Ford, the "Grandma Moses of Ford history." Bryan worked in Ford's Rouge Plant for 10 years and the company's Scientific Laboratory for 23 years before retiring at age 62 in 1974. That year, he became a Henry Ford Museum and Greenfield Village volunteer, and to date has logged more than 10,000 hours in that capacity.

Bryan published his first article on the Ford family/Ford Company history in 1978, and since then has authored articles and books (starting with *The Fords of Dearborn* in 1987) at an accelerating pace.

Ford Relative Dies

Frances Bryant ImOberstag, 78, daughter of Henry Ford's brother-in-law, Edgar LeRoy Bryant, died in Dearborn on July 14, 1993.

Mrs. ImOberstag was instrumental in providing funds for the restoration of the Field Room in her uncle's mansion, Fair Lane.

She also appeared on a 1993 Public Broadcasting System program, "The Great Depression: A Job at Ford's," in which she recalled that her uncle and aunt, inasmuch as their lifestyle was unchanged by the Depression, were little aware of the impact of the era on the lives of ordinary people. Throughout the program, Mrs. ImOberstag's comments on her famous uncle struck me as being evenhanded and credible, whereas some of his critics, having nothing good to say about him, were far less so.

Ford Cousin

Henry Ford's cousin, Mrs. Nellie Williams, of Eveleth, Minn., was publicized in the July 15, 1915 issue of the *Virginia* (Minn.) *Daily Enterprise*, following announcement of the auto king's intent to purchase Mesabi Range ore property and acquire a fleet to carry ore to Detroit.

A photocopy of an article on Mrs. Williams, forwarded by reader Michael Bukovac, of Britt, Minn., states that the Minnesotan had often visited her famous cousin's Detroit home and also the Brighton, Mich. farm of Henry's younger brother, William. Mrs. Williams, continues the article, discussed the Mesabi Range's mines with her cousins. William said that he preferred his farm to the best mine in the country.

Mrs. Williams told the *Enterprise* that she had been a resident of the Range country "for several years," and that her son, Cyril Williams, was Eveleth's city clerk. Another Ford cousin, E. Bothnen, who resided on the Range six years earlier, was said by Mrs. Williams to be the only Ford relative employed by the Ford Company. [Ford's son, Edsel, seems to have slipped Mrs. William's mind.]

Henry visited Duluth in 1914, according to Mrs. Williams, and met with his Range relatives at the time. Mrs. Williams noted that wealth had not changed her cousin, and he remained "genial company." Only Ford's relatives and a few other persons had the magnate's private phone number, the Minnesotan added.

It would be interesting to know if any Williams family members still reside in the Eveleth area. I recently put the question to Henry Ford's niece, Catherine Ruddiman, 90. She knew of none.

Ford Relative?

"First of all," writes Patrick Martin, of Palatine, Ill., "let me tell you that I just love your column and look forward to it every month. What I'm really writing about, however, is this:

My family and I are trying to find out who our ancestors may be and we have reason to believe that a family member may have been a brother to either Henry Ford or to Henry Ford's father. Could you please tell me if either of these men had a brother and, if so, what their names were?"

Okay. Henry Ford had four brothers, two of whom lived to adulthood. John (1865-1927) and William Jr. (1871-1959). John married Mary Ward, and they had children named Ethel, Robert, and Clarence. William married Frances Reed and their children were named Lewis, Burnham, Myra, Edith and Mary Ellen.

Henry Ford's father, William had two brothers, Henry (1830-1901) and Samuel (1832-1884). Henry married Katherine O'Leary and they had eight children who grew up in California. Samuel married Nancy Kennedy and their children were named Wallace, John, Albert, Henry, Howard, plus an unnamed infant son.

After referring Martin to the Ford Archives for additional information, he reported that it was unable to furnish any help beyond that which I had provided. "Unfortunately," he added, "I have not been able to definitely find a relationship with Henry Ford ... [but] I have not been able to prove that I'm definitely not related to him either. At least I can say that the possibility exists."

All In The Family

Upon marrying Mike Flaherty in 1980, Darleen Flaherty, head of Ford's Industrial Archives, heard a rumor about her husband's family being related to Henry Ford.

"I was very skeptical," Darleen recently informed a Ford publication, "but went ahead gathering names along with birth and death dates. After exchanging some correspondence with Mr. Ford R. Bryan, family genealogy expert at the Henry Ford Museum, I was told that 'yes,' the rumor was true."

Mike Flaherty's great-grandfather, Richard Flaherty, was a son of a first cousin of Henry Ford's. Mike's grandfather, Richard Cleveland Flaherty, was an hourly employee at Ford's Rouge Plant in the 1930s. For years Richard rebuffed friends' suggestions that he capitalize on his family connection. But during the Great Depression, after losing his job and failing to find another, he wrote to second cousin Henry Ford, and got his job back. "That is the last connection between the Fords and the Flahertys," says Darleen.

Mike Flaherty is a 23-year employee of Ford Car Product Development. Darleen, a 26-year Ford veteran, ably presides over the company's premier archival collection, located in Redford Township, Mich. The Redford archives are distinct from the better known Henry Ford Museum and Greenfield Village (Ford) archives.

Tip's Favorite Story

The late speaker of the House of Representatives, Tip O'Neill, was a great storyteller, and his favorite story concerned Henry Ford.

"It seems," Tip would start out, "that after making his fortune Henry Ford traveled to Ireland to visit his mother's ancestral home. There, the great industrialist was met by a contingent of local leaders who elicited from him a $5,000 contribution toward construction of a new hospital.

"Ford was surprised, therefore, to see a headline in the local newspaper the following day: 'Ford to Donate $50,000 for Hospital.' And he began to smell a rat when the same local leaders called up to apologize for the paper's mistake and promised to get a correction, with the $5,000 figure printed prominently the next day.

"How much, Ford asked ruefully, would it take to finish construction on the hospital? About $75,000, they told him. And he agreed to pay the $75,000 if he could have a motto written on an arch above the entrance.

"Of course, the Irish said. And so Ford ordered the motto written: 'I came amongst you and you took me in.'"

This chestnut is apocryphal, and has been told in multiple versions. But Ford, whose forebears came from Ireland, did have a soft spot for the Irish, and built a tractor plant in Cork in 1917. One of Ireland's largest factories, the facility, converted to car and truck assembly in 1932, employed approximately 1,200 workers. Ford, in turn, was Ireland's market leader for more than 60 years.

In 1984, however, the plant was closed, Ford blaming the shutdown on the small size of the plant which, it said, was uncompetitive compared with larger facilities elsewhere in Europe. Also, the company said that the end of protection for Irish car assemblers after 1984 meant that the plant would have to continue "with one hand tied behind its back." Until that year, vehicles assembled in Ireland enjoyed significant tax concessions over cars imported in built-up form.

After the closure was announced, an Irish government delegation visited Dearborn in a last-ditch effort to plead for the plant's continuance. The delegates were cordially received, but their pleas came to naught. Ford no longer is Ireland's market leader.

Henry's Uncle Henry

Dick Folsom, of Canton, Mich., president of the Dearborn Historical Society, stands behind the grave marker of the Henry Ford, for whom the auto magnate is believed to have been named. Folsom took the picture in 1993 in Foresthill, Calif., population 900, where Ford's Uncle Henry, who left Michigan in 1851, died in 1901 at age 66. The cemetery, Folsom writes, is "pretty run down." The scenery around Foresthill, located midway between Sacramento and Lake Tahoe, is impressive, as indicated by the above photo.

Henry Ford is often said to have been named after his "Uncle Henry." But which Uncle Henry is open to question, as noted in Ford Richardson Bryan's book, *The Fords of Dearborn.*

Ford had two Uncle Henrys: one was his father's younger brother; the other was his father's sister's husband. Bryan, himself a distant relative of Henry Ford, discusses the uncle most often believed to be the Henry Ford for which the magnate was named, while warning that the question is by no means incontestably resolved.

Henry Ford, the younger brother of *the* Henry Ford's father, William, emigrated at age 17 from Ireland to Dearborn in 1847. Unlike the 21-year-old William, Henry was restless and in 1851 left for California's gold fields. His descendants – he had 10 children – don't know for sure whether he reached California by foot or by ship via Panama, but the former seems more likely.

In California, Henry reportedly settled in 1856 at Iowa Hill in Placer County, a gold mining district in the foothills of the Sierra Nevada range. About this time he acquired a mining claim in the settlement of Bath on the Foresthill Divide, also in Placer County. Henry's family stayed in that area, although Henry himself later prospected for gold in Idaho.

In 1864, after being asked by his brother William whether he planned to return to Michigan, Henry responded from Idaho in prose not unlike that written by his celebrated nephew.

"Dear brother you wanted to Know if i was going Back to See you All any more but there is no brother in the world that would like any better to go Back and see you All than i would but the winters is so Cold Back there and long and i like the Climate in Californe So well an a Count of no Snow in the winter and Pleasant in the summer i Shall not be able to give you a disid Answer until i see my wife this Fall i am getting old and tired of mining and Shall Settle Down Pretty Soon ... and (hope) to go Back to michigan to See you once more."

Henry also inquired about his father and offered to send money to him, if needed. Henry died in Foresthill in 1901, and some of his descendants still live in the area.

Nice Lad

A little yarn about Henry Ford as a boy was called to our attention by reader John von Batchelder, of Detroit. The story appears in a book, *I Remember Detroit*, written in 1949 by John C. Lodge in collaboration with M.M. Quaife, and bought by Batchelder, a self-confessed bookaholic, at a recent Detroit Public Library book fair.

In the 1870s, Lodge – who was born in 1862, a year before Henry Ford – and two friends drove a horse and light wagon west from their Detroit homes until they came to a clump of hickory trees.

"Nearby was a neat-looking farmhouse," recalled Lodge, "and a boy of about my age out in front. We stopped the horse and asked him if we could gather some of the nuts. He said we could, and turned in and helped us, working so fast that he shelled more nuts than we did.

"Presently the dinner bell rang, and we decided we had enough and started to leave. He told us we would have to go into dinner, and when we hung back he said his mother wouldn't like it if we didn't. So we went in, and such a dinner – chicken with dumplings, green apple pie, and a lot of other dishes. It was a wonderful meal, and I can remember it yet.

"On the way into the house we mentioned that he hadn't told us his name. He said, 'Henry Ford.' About 20 years later when I was working on the *[Detroit] Free Press*, I called one day on Alex Dow, who was boss of The Detroit Edison Company ... A man in overalls came in, and Mr. Dow said to me that this was his chief engineer. I said to him, 'I remember you. You are Henry Ford.' He replied, 'I remember you, too.'

"After Mr. Ford left the room Mr. Dow told me about Ford's fussing with an old buggy in which he had put an engine. He drove it around evenings and the loafers at the Majestic Building corner spoke of him as 'Crazy Ford.' Mr. Dow said, 'He is a genius. I hope he has got something.' "

Lodge later became mayor of Detroit, and one of the city's major expressways is named for him.

Ford Accident

Henry Ford's sole auto accident was reported in an April 2, 1927 *Automotive Industries*' article forwarded by noted historian Ralph Dunwoodie, of Sun Valley, Nev.

Ford was hospitalized after his Model T coupe was crowded from the road by a larger car while driving from Dearborn Engineering Laboratory to his home. The identity of the larger vehicle was being sought by police, who also were investigating the possibility of deliberative intent.

The accident occurred shortly after dusk. After being forced over narrow curbing, the auto king said he plunged down an embankment. The car crashed into a tree and overturned, Ford being knocked unconscious. Snow and rain beating through the broken window of the vehicle revived him. After turning off the car's engine, he made his way to the gatehouse of his estate. Several times, he reported, he had to stop and rest, despite the falling sleet.

Ford initially was treated at his home by his doctor, R.D. McClure. Not recovering satisfactorily, he was removed by ambulance to Henry Ford Hospital. A hospital bulletin reported that Ford had suffered a slight concussion, severe contusions over the ribs and back, and considerable strain of back muscles. Prior to the accident, *Automotive Industries* reported, Ford had been "singularly free from any periods of illness or injury."

To safeguard Ford, plans were being made to have him accompanied or followed by a companion when he resumed driving. For years, the article noted, "Ford has persisted in going about unaccompanied particularly in and about his plants. When traveling he usually has a retinue."

News of Ford's accident was delayed until a statement was made by his representatives in Detroit's Federal Court, where he was a defendant in an "anti-Semitic" suit for $1 million brought by Aaron Sapiro. The magnate had been summoned as a witness. The suit was settled out of court shortly thereafter.

In his later years Ford usually rode in cars driven by chauffeurs (he called them drivers) and his chief aide, Harry Bennett.

Ford And Drug Administration

Most of us are aware that Henry Ford tried to rehabilitate alcoholics and cigarette addicts. But his efforts to reform drug addicts is less well known. A September 1915 article in a British publication, *American Ford Owners Association "Official" Monthly*, is in fact, the only published account of the subject I have seen.

"Mr. Ford," states the magazine, "has never discharged a man from his factory because he was a victim of alcoholism. He believes that the men who crave for liquor are almost hopelessly handicapped by their craving. The habitual drug users present the same problem and so Mr. Ford, while building the Henry Ford Hospital in Detroit, decided to send several of the drug and alcoholic victims to a hospital in New York with a physician to observe their treatment ... (with the thought) of devoting one of the units of his new institution to curing other drug and alcoholic victims.

"One of the two drug users sent to New York was not employed in the Ford factory. Mr. Ford got him out of a prison in Detroit, where he was placed for stealing morphine from a drugstore in that city...

"When the victims were taken to New York they were in the most desperate state that can be imagined. The two morphine victims wanted morphine on the train." But, added the magazine, "when the three alcoholics and two drug addicts returned to Detroit, they were said to look like 'new men.'

"This new method of handling men, formerly considered as derelicts, is going to solve one of the biggest economic problems of the day," rhapsodized the article. "Mr. Ford is establishing a precedent that in the end will show all of the big industrial corporations of this country the best method by which they can reclaim the percentage of their men ... which, if turned loose on society, would constitute a most serious menace."

The article then noted that the Ford Co.'s 19,000 employees harbored fewer "alcoholics and drug fiends than the average in other large industrial centres on account of Mr. Ford's Investigating Department. (This department) keeps close touch with the men and is informed as to how each man spends even his spare time."

"When a man gets drunk," declared Dr. Eisman, the physician who accompanied the addicts to New York, "the investigators seek the cause instead of having him discharged. The next step is to remove the cause, whenever possible."

The Investigating Department, more precisely the Sociological Department, was organized after the announcement of the five-dollar day. It did investigate workers, as the above indicates, but had its good side, too. Eventually, however, it was discarded along with most of the business paternalism of the first two decades of this century.

Ford's alcohol/drug rehabilitation efforts proved visionary, and have come full circle, inasmuch as Ford and many other large employers today expend large sums trying to rehabilitate substance abusers, as alcoholics and drug and tobacco addicts are now called.

Thanks to Keith Marvin, of Menands, N.Y., for forwarding the *Ford Owners* article.

Barbier And Fords

A.R. Barbier (second from right) with Edsel Ford (right) and Henry Ford (in straw hat slightly left of center) inspecting construction of the company's Dearborn Engine Plant in 1940. Barbier gave this photo to your commentator in 1963. The engine plant is still in use.

A.R. Barbier

"Henry Ford was reluctant to admit that he had an advertising department," A.R. Barbier, once Ford's advertising chief, states in a quarter-century-old letter recently unearthed in my study.

"His was the famous 'mousetrap' theory," said Barbier, "although it is questionable as to whether he was actually building a better mousetrap as the 1930s wore on. Even so, Edsel Ford, under whose direct supervision I worked, freely referred to me as 'Ford Adv. Mgr.'

"Constructive advertising progress under this setup was extremely difficult because of the H.F. philosophy and by interferences by his own key men – always maneuvering to keep his good graces. Under these conditions, I carried on until Ford abandoned car production in the interest of war work. Then, in November, 1941, while Edsel Ford was on leave of absence because of ill health, I was unceremoniously released. The timing of this was precipitated by Harry Bennett with whom I had consistently refused to cooperate over the years.

"In the spring of 1942, I joined a small (advertising) agency in Buffalo as (account executive) on the Bell Aircraft account. Not satisfied with this connection, and interested in getting back to my hometown, Detroit, I resigned in the fall of 1942 to join MacManus, John & Adams, Inc. as Cadillac account executive, a position I held until my retirement in the fall of 1958, after having been appointed a vice president of the company in the fall of the previous year."

Roy Barbier was one of the decent and honorable men who worked for Ford during its "years of darkness" – the Depression and World War II years when Henry Ford largely neglected his business and Harry Bennett increasingly ran it. I met Barbier when researching my book, *The Public Image of Henry Ford*, in the early 1960s. He, and later his widow and his daughter,

Florence Diamond, also were very helpful to me; and the latter gave me many books from her father's valuable library, some Ford-related, others rare and classic.

Henry Ford TV Ads

Ford Motor Co., according to an October 25, 1995 *Detroit News* article, "finally feels comfortable enough to use its famous founder in national television advertisements.

"For the past year," the *News* continues, "the automaker has been airing commercials featuring a black-and-white image of Ford along with sequences of the company's new vehicles. To the sound of drumbeats, a voice sounding like it comes from the distant past claims, 'I want to build a motor car for the great multitude ... Any person making a good salary will be able to own one and enjoy with his family the blessing of hours of pleasure in God's great open spaces.'

"As far as anyone can remember," the *News* adds, "it's the first time the company has used Henry Ford to sell cars."

We have news for the *News*: Henry Ford signed or otherwise was the focal point of Ford ads on several occasions. During the company's first two years, ads emphasized that Ford was "the same genius which conceived the world's record maker – the 999 (racing car)" and proclaimed that "Our Mr. Ford made the first Gasoline Automobile in Detroit and the third in the United States" (both claims untrue). In 1927 Ford signed the first ad in the Model A introductory campaign, and in 1933 his signed "personal message" ads extolled the Ford organization's virtues. In 1944 the company's "Henry Ford" campaign, based on events in the founder's life, pointed up the sources from which "sprang the genius and success of the Ford Motor Company." These ads illustrated Ford as a youthful watch repairer, at his first meeting with Thomas A. Edison, demonstrating one of his early cars to a reporter in 1900, participating in the New York-to-Seattle race of 1909, etc.

The *News* reasons that Ford has been fearful of featuring Ford in ads because of his anti-Semitism. "If this was 20 years ago, maybe it would be a factor," Hal Augustine, Ford's corporate advertising manager, rebuts. "The anti-Semitism is something that's there, no doubt about, it, but it's something that's in the very distant past. Heritage is one facet of the business that we want to communicate."

Detroit-area Jewish groups do not regard the Ford Company's image as offensive. "The Ford Motor Co. has long since lived down the bigotry of Henry Ford," Richard Lobenthal director of Michigan's Anti-Defamation League, observes. "I have not received any complaints about (the ads). While somebody's memory may jump back to the old man's anti-Semitism, it is not a stumbling block. One can't deny Ford was founded by Henry Ford."

When the U.S. government proposed to honor Henry Ford with a 13-cent stamp on his centennial in 1963, Jewish protests blocked issuance of the stamp.

Contemporary Henry Ford-related TV commercials use a voice-over approved by the Ford family. The commercials are running on such cable channels as CNN, A&E, and Discovery and such network programs as "Meet the Press" and "Face the Nation."

"I would probably not be enthusiastic about the use of Henry Ford as a symbol," remarks Jay Houghton, a senior consultant at Automotive Marketing Consultants Inc., Warren, Mich., who added that he had seen the Ford commercials. "If you have to rely on history, then you are not doing your job. The past is the past, let's invent the future."

I disagree with Houghton. Ford isn't so much relying on history as in taking advantage of it. Unlike GM's founder, William C. Durant, or leading executive, Alfred P. Sloan Jr., Henry Ford's name is known to almost everyone who knows anything. Moreover, the magnate's image is generally favorable except to liberal professors, a certain number of Jews, socialists, and aging unionists. If a company has a Henry Ford in its past, that company would be shortsighted in not trotting him out now and then for marketing and public relations purposes.

Jewish Boycott

"Even as a young boy, I was aware that Jews weren't buying Ford products in the early 1930s," recalls reader John C. Jackson, of San Jose, Calif.

"Detroit's Jewish population seems to have had its own private boycott," states Jackson. "During 1930-33, I lived (in a mostly Jewish neighborhood) on Vicksburg near Linwood, and attended the seventh through ninth grades at Hutchins Intermediate School at Blaine and Woodrow Wilson. I walked to school, and remember the absence of Model Ts and Model As parked along the way. Lots of Chevrolets and other makes, but no Fords."

Jackson's recollections are valid. During the 1930s, especially after 1938 – when Henry Ford accepted a medal from the German government – Jews largely ignored, if not completely boycotted, Ford vehicles.

Franklin Exhibit

The life and achievements of Rabbi Leo M. Franklin, neighbor and friend of Henry Ford, was celebrated in a mid-1998 exhibit at Temple Beth El, Bloomfield Hills, Mich., over which Rabbi Franklin presided from 1899-1941.

"Dr. Franklin," a Temple Beth El brochure states, "in the 1920s and 1930s worked to combat the anti-Semitism of Henry Ford and Father Charles Coughlin."

Until Ford launched an anti-Semitic crusade in 1920, Rabbi Franklin annually accepted a complimentary Model T from the automaker. The campaign prompted the rabbi to terminate the friendship. Following Ford's apology to Jews in 1927, Rabbi Franklin congratulated the magnate on his "courageous stand" and expressed hope of resuming "those fine friendly relationships which through so many years it was mine to enjoy."

The Leo M. Franklin Collection is housed in Temple Beth El's Rabbi Leo M. Franklin Archive, 7400 Telegraph Road at 14 Mile Road, Bloomfield Hills.

Thanks to reader Mike Skinner, St. Clair Shores, Mich., for forwarding the Archive's brochure and exhibit literature.

Science Trailblazer

Henry Ford is one of 14 persons awarded a Science Trailblazer Award by the Detroit Science Center. The award honors science pioneers who have lived, worked, or been educated in Michigan, and whose contributions have been of international significance.

Ford was one of several auto figures honored, another being Walter P. Chrysler. Although Ford and Chrysler may be more properly regarded as self-trained, hands-on engineers, rather than as scientists, they funded many scientific research projects; and, in Ford's case, nonautomotive as well as automotive.

75th Birthday

Memories of Henry Ford's 75th birthday in 1938 were recalled in an heretofore unpublished September 28, 1973 letter from Robert A. Boyer, head of the auto king's Soybean Extraction Laboratory from 1929-43.

"I remember that day quite vividly," Boyer recalls, "because Mr. Ford spent the first half of the morning with me at the lab. He had his personal photographer, George Ebling, take pictures of him reading one of our lab reports *without glasses*. He was proud of this. He also challenged me to race him across the street to our soybean extraction plant about 75 yards away. I could hardly keep up with him although I was about 45 years younger than he."

Boyer's letter was prompted by a visit to Greenfield Village, at which time he spent considerable time in the former soybean lab located therein. This building, he reported, "is now being used as a receiving station for the Edison Institute. I could not help but think that this laboratory should be restored to the same conditions when our soybean activity was at its peak. This would be about the time of Mr. Ford's 75th birthday. The widespread interest currently being shown by the public in the soybean would make the lab an interesting and educational exhibit."

In 1973 Boyer was a "textured vegetable protein industry" consultant.

"Essential" Ford Library

"Ten Ford biographies that should be included in every Fordophile's library" are cited by Richard Folsom, president of the Henry Ford Heritage Assn., in the association's Summer 1995 newsletter. Brief comments accompany some of the books, which "are not presented in any specific order." The biographies and comments are: 1. *Ford: The Times, the Man, the Company*, by Allan Nevins. 2. *Ford: Expansion and Challenge, 1915-1933*, by Allan Nevins and Frank Ernest Hill. 3. *Ford: Decline and Rebirth 1933-1962*, by Allan Nevins and Frank Ernest Hill. (1, 2, and 3 are considered the Ford trilogy. Together they are highly informative and scholarly.) 4. *Young Henry Ford: A Picture History of the First Forty Years*, by Sidney Olson. (If you want to understand Henry Ford after 1903, you must read this book to learn about the events that shaped his life before 1903.) 5. *The Public Image of Henry Ford: An American Folk Hero and His Company*, by David L. Lewis. (A gentleman who actually knew Henry Ford once told me that this book captured, better than any other, the true spirit of Henry Ford and his influence within Ford Motor Co. and southeast Michigan.) 6. *The Last Billionaire: Henry Ford*, by William C. Richards. 7. *Henry Ford: His Life - His Work - His Genius*, by William A. Simonds. 8. *Henry Ford and Grass-roots America*, by Reynold M. Wik. (Captures the essence of why the average American admired Henry Ford.) 9. *Henry Ford's Own Story*, by Rose Wilder Lane. (The first biography of Henry Ford is fascinating just because it was the first.) 10. *Henry Ford: An Interpretation*, by Samuel S. Marquis. (Written at the height of Ford's popularity, this book was one of the first to decipher what Henry Ford was all about.)

What do I think of the list? It's excellent.

Fords In Books

"I read your 'Ford Country' article about songs with Fords in them," writes reader Jil McIntosh, of Oshawa, Ont. "I'm more of a reader than a music fan, and so your article got me thinking about Fords in books. Not car books, but regular stories where Fords are part of the plot. Naturally I couldn't dig up as many as you could of songs, but here's some for your collection.

"1) *Brave New World* by Aldous Huxley. Surely the grand-daddy of all this genre. The action takes place around 600 A.F. (After Ford) and genuflecting takes the form of making the Sign of the T, for the Model T. Naturally 'Ford!' is the expletive of choice. (Although I will admit it got tiring after the first few chapters.)

"*Lake Wobegon Days* by Garrison Keillor. The book is filled with references to Fords, but right at the beginning we're introduced to the mayor's business, namely, 'Bunsen Motors - Ford - New & Used - Sales & Service.' How could you not vote for him, especially when he's the guy doing the oil changes.

"*The Candy-Kolored Tangerine-Flake Streamline Baby* by Tom Wolfe. Wolfe went to a hot rod show in Burbank and wrote about the 'Ford Custom Car Caravan,' a display of hot-rodded and customized Fords designed, as Wolfe writes, to catch the kids now and turn them into lifelong buyers.

"*Contact by Carl Sagan*. I loved this one. The story is about a scientist who discovers a message from outer space and astronomer Sagan describes binary pulsars and the 1667 megahertz hydroxyl line (you can bet I copied that one straight from the page) with ease. He also describes the scientist's one extravagance, a carefully maintained 1957 Thunderbird with removable hardtop and little glass portholes flanking the rear seat. Obviously it's a UFO: Unidentified Fourseating Object.

"That's all I could come up with. I'm sure there's many more out there. One I wondered about is John Steinbeck's *Travels with Charley*, in which he drives around the country talking to people. He writes, 'I wrote to the head office of a great corporation, which manufactures trucks. I specified my purpose and my needs.' The truck is only referred to as 'the truck' or 'Rocinante,' the name he chose for it after Don Quixote's horse. Although I have a number of books on Steinbeck (my favorite author), I don't know what kind of truck made this historic journey.

"I was also surprised that, although the Okies migrating to California were so often shown in Fords, *The Grapes of Wrath* used a Dodge and a Hudson Super Six; I don't believe the identity of their pickup truck is ever given. In one conversation between two unidentified men, one says he would never buy a product of Henry Ford's, for his brother works in the plant and tells stories about it."

"Please keep up 'Ford Country,' one of the features I always look for first whenever my new issue arrives."

I too was surprised, when viewing the film version of *The Grapes of Wrath*, to see the migrating Joad family aboard a Dodge truck, bought for $75. Considering the number of people and amount of goods transported, a vehicle larger than a Model T (TT) truck certainly was needed.

Ford Bibliography

Henry Ford's *My Life and Work* (Garden City, N.Y.: Doubleday, Page & Company, 1922): "probably been translated into more languages than any book since the Bible, according to William T. Kelley's manuscript, 'A Comprehensive Annotated Bibliography of Automotive Marketing, Distribution and History,' prepared at the University of Pennsylvania in 1962.

Kelley's manuscript has the following to say about other Ford books:

Harry Bennett's *We Never Called*

Him Henry (New York: Fawcett Publications, 1951, 180 pp.): "Personal reminiscences of a lieutenant of Henry Ford. Anecdotal accounts of Ford the man and of his system of management and industrial espionage. Extremely critical." Kelley might have added "extremely inaccurate."

Ford Motor Company's *Ford at Fifty, 1903-1953* (New York: Simon & Schuster, Inc., 1953, 108 pp.): "A popularized public relations history of the Ford Company to celebrate its Golden Anniversary. Mainly pictorial treatment (has) some material on early history of the Company, but nothing unique."

Garet Garrett's *The Wild Wheel* (New York: Pantheon Books, 1952, 220 pp.): "An appraisal of the contributions of Henry Ford by one who knew him .... Concludes that in view of the decline of laissez faire in the present-day society, Ford could not have duplicated his accomplishments in our generation."

Rose Wilder Lane's *Henry Ford's Own Story* (New York: Ellis O. Jones, 1917, 184 pp.): "An early [actually the first] popularized biography of Ford. Laudatory and uncritical. Seems to have no documentation whatever."

Allan Nevins' *Ford, the Times, the Man, the Company* (New York: Charles Scribner's Sons, 1954, 688 pp.): "An exhaustive study of the social and economic setting within which the automotive industry developed, Ford's biography, and a definitive history of the Ford Motor Company to 1915. A brilliant piece of industrial history writing."

Allan Nevins' and Frank Ernest Hill's *Ford, Expansion and Challenge, 1915-1933* (New York: Charles Scribner's Sons, 1957, 714 pp.: "A continuation of Nevins early history of Ford. A brilliant and definitive history of Ford the man and of his company up to the shift to the Model A [actually the V-8] in 1932."

William Adams Simonds' *Henry Ford, His Life – His Work – His Genius* (New York: Bobbs-Merrill Co., 1943, 365 pp.): "A popularized biography of Ford. Contains information of interest about the development of the Ford car. Uncritical evaluation of the personality and philosophy of Ford." Simonds was a Ford employee for many years.

Upton Sinclair's *The Flivver King, A Study of Ford-America* (Pasadena, Calif.: Upton Sinclair, 1937, 256 pp.): "A popularly written account of Henry Ford by an outstanding novelist. Tends to be very critical of the man, and is extremely so of his policies toward labor."

Charles E. Sorensen's *My Forty Years with Ford* (New York: W.W. Norton & Co., Inc., 1956, 345 pp.): "Personal recollections by a key Ford executive during the early days of the development of the industry. A good description of Ford's production methods and business philosophy. Particularly useful is Chapter 10, the Birth of Mass Production, by one who took an active part in the process." This book grew out of Sorensen's participation in Ford's Oral History Program of the 1950s.

Keith Sward's *The Legend of Henry Ford* (New York: Rinehart & Co., Inc., 1948, 550 pp.): "A well-documented analysis of Ford and the operations of his company. Takes a rather hostile point of view." Neither the book nor Kelley notes that Sward was the UAW's public relations director.

Ford Bryan

Ford R. Bryan, 86, poses in 1998 at the entrance to the vault in Ford's 96-year-old Piquette Plant, Detroit. Bryan's grandmother, Emma Ford, was a cousin of Henry Ford's. A retired Ford Company scientist, Bryan began researching the family in 1978, and since then has written numerous excellent articles and books on Ford history.

Ford Sketch

Today we read much of books and seminars which help prepare students for college entrance exams. But such aids are not new, as evidenced by a 1931 paperback, *Biographical Sketches in American History*, authored by Lucian Lamm and published by the Collegiate Entrance Book Company, Inc., of New York.

In the preface, the book states that it is written "as an aid to students who are preparing for the College Entrance and Regents' examinations, and particularly for the questions of biography which will appear on these examinations."

The book presents biographical sketches of 131 prominent Americans, Henry Ford among them. Ford is one of only 10 "Great Industrialists and Financiers" covered by the volume, the others being John Jacob Astor, Andrew Carnegie, Cornelius Vanderbilt, Jay Gould, Edward Henry Harriman, James Jerome Hill, John D. Rockefeller, John Pierpont Morgan Sr., and John Pierpont Morgan Jr.

The book also provides a number of questions asked on recent Regents' Examinations. Among them is one which includes Ford: "State briefly the importance in history of each of five of the following: John Jacob Astor, Clara Barton, Susan B. Anthony, James R. Lowell, Orville Wright, Mary Lyon, Henry Ford, Cornelius Vanderbilt."

In 1931, many college-bound students could answer such questions satisfactorily. Today, few such students, or even university students, could do so; and I say this from my vantage point as a professor of business history in one of the better business schools in one of the nation's better universities.

Thanks to Mike Skinner, of Dearborn, Mich., for forwarding a copy of the Lamm book.

"Ford" Funeral Home

"I recently found the former William Hamilton Funeral Home building in Detroit," writes Fordophile Dick Folsom, of Canton, Mich. "It was to this building that the body of Henry Ford was taken on the morning of April 8, 1947. If I'm not mistaken, this is also where Edsel was taken when he died."

The funeral home is located in a run-down area south of the Wayne State University campus. The area is so bad, Folsom added, that he did not get out of his car to look around.

Folsom's fears are justified. For years I roamed the inner city of Detroit, taking and gathering Ford-related pictures and information about the Fords, without a thought of personal safety. By the 1970s, however, I began to make sure that my camera and I could get to my car before anyone else could.

Ford's Mourners

"I've got a bet on," says reader William R. Taylor, of Philadelphia. "I say that a quarter-million people viewed Henry Ford's body when it lay in state. A friend of mine says 100,000. Who's right?"

Taylor's friend is closer to the mark, with Ford's mourners having been estimated at 30,000 by the *Montgomery* (Ala.) *Advertiser*; 70,000 by the *New York Times*, 100,000 by *Newsweek*, and 105,000 by *Time*. In any event, the queue to view Ford's body at times was a mile long, as suggested by the above aerial view. Ford's bier was located in the Recreation Building (also called the Education Building and Lovett Hall) at top of photo. The building in the foreground was the gateway to Greenfield Village.

Recalls Ford's Funeral

Henry Ford's funeral procession wended its way from midtown Detroit to the west side of the city on Apr. 10, 1947. One of those who watched the procession was Leonard W. Williams, then a 12-year-old west-sider. Now a resident of Sunnyvale, Calif., Williams recalled the procession as follows in an issue of the *Professional Car Society Journal*:

"Even though I was still a boy, I knew that a very important man had died. Mr. Ford lay in state in ... Dearborn. My father had taken me out there to see this great man laid out in his massive bronze casket.

"The day of the funeral was a typically mild April day. There was a light overcast. The route of the funeral procession had been published in all of the Detroit newspapers, and it would pass by on a street not far from my home. I was standing at the corner of Scotten and Tireman. The route of the procession was from St. Paul's Episcopal Cathedral on Woodward Avenue, west on Grand Boulevard (past the GM Building) to Tireman, then out to Joy Road to the family cemetery next to St. Martha's Episcopal Church.

"It was late morning. Crowds lined the entire funeral route. The first vehicles to pass by were two Dodge

Henry Ford's funeral procession vehicles are shown after the ceremony at Detroit's tiny Ford Cemetery on Joy Road, west of Evergreen. Motorcycle policemen who led the procession are in the foreground; mounted officers keep back the crowd at left. It's been raining; the pavement's wet; Joy Road's shoulder is muddy. (Photo from the Collections of Henry Ford Museum and Greenfield Village.)

panel trucks loaded with flowers. About five minutes later, we could see the main procession coming, led by a police escort. The hearse was first. It was a gleaming 1942 Henney Packard. Immediately behind it were half a dozen of the Ford family's custom-built limousines - all Lincolns. Then there were more standard Lincolns, then dozens of Mercurys, then Fords. I don't remember any Cadillacs."

The *Journal* also noted that in May 1943, Edsel B. Ford's body was carried from church to cemetery in an "extremely rare 1937-39 K-Series V-12 Lincoln hearse."

Thanks to reader Richard V. Schweitzer, of Akron, Ohio, for forwarding the *Journal*'s article.

Henry Ford's Grave

"What, if anything," inquires reader Walter Schan, of Southfield, Mich., "do you know about a rumor/story that circulated during the fifties that Henry Ford was buried in the Ford Cemetery on Detroit's Joy Road 'à la Pullman' style?"

"I know," Schan continues, "that for several years after Henry Ford was buried 'in ground' at the Ford Cemetery that there was a 24-hour-a-day, seven-days-a-week security guard, sitting in a tiny booth, and that he stayed there until tourists/viewers stopped coming."

Graves of the wealthy, Schan explains, were commonly robbed during the late 19th century, and "this is why George Pullman, the railroad sleeping car magnate, had himself buried in a vault encased in concrete surrounded by crossed railroad rails."

Here are the facts as I know them:

Ford is interred with his wife, Clara, his parents, other Fords, and a handful of farm neighbors in the Ford's 19th century burying ground now situated on the front lawn of St. Martha's Episcopal Church. By my pacing, the cemetery, 300 yards west of Greenfield Road, is 33 yards long, 20 yards wide.

Eight steps from the highway, the plot is surrounded by a green cast iron fence 3-1/2 feet high at the road, 2 to 3 feet high elsewhere. The fence's three gates usually are locked, but visitors can step over the iron work without difficulty. Once inside, they can stroll amid the tombstones, find shade under the evergreens, or rest on one of four wooden benches.

Ford's grave is near the center of the cemetery. Above the $14,935 bronze coffin and $824 copper vault in which he is buried is a low white marble stone, 3-1/2 feet by 7 feet, upon which is engraved a large cross and the inscription:

HENRY FORD
July 30, 1863
April 7, 1947

Henry's and Clara's graves initially were guarded around the clock to prevent desecration. "People," said Ford's niece, Catherine Ruddiman, a cemetery trustee, "were taking grass, dirt, branches, anything that could be moved. To eliminate the need for a guard and guardhouse and to provide permanent protection against vandalism, the Fords' bodies were exhumed, then reburied in a concrete vault to which a metal grille rising 19 inches above the ground is anchored. The grille is unlocked only for grass cutting as well as on the anniversary of Ford's death. For more than two decades, children from Greenfield Village schools placed flowers on the Fords' graves on or near the anniversary of Henry's death. After the last of the schools closed in 1969, officials of the village continued the tradition for a time.

Upon first arriving at St. Martha's, the Rev. Edwin A. Griswold, "couldn't fully understand the need for such security arrangements. But," he added, "after being repeatedly asked by visitors if Ford were buried in a solid gold coffin or if he and his wife had been buried with their valuables [including a Stradivarius violin], I could better appreciate the Ford family's concern."

For many decades the Ford Cemetery was surrounded by family farmlands. Following her husband's burial, Clara provided $1 million for the construction of St. Martha's to prevent the property from falling into developers' hands.

Ford's grave is visited by a mere handful of people. I have visited the cemetery many times, and seldom see anyone there. In contrast, Ford's birthplace, removed from Dearborn's Greenfield and Ford roads to Greenfield Village in 1944, has been visited by millions.

Probably not one in 1,000 Detroiters knows where Ford is buried. Indeed, only a handful of people in the vicinity of Joy and Greenfield likely are aware that Ford is buried within a few hundred yards of them.

Some historians have said, with reference to the tombs of Presidents, the bigger the monument, the smaller the man. If this adage has any reverse truth, Henry Ford perhaps is an even greater person than he has been made out to be.

Grave Visitor

Mr. Honda, a Japanese visitor, pays his respects at Henry Ford's grave in Detroit's Ford Cemetery. St. Martha's Episcopal Church, endowed by Ford's wife, Clara, is in the background. (Photo by Michael Skinner, St. Clair Shores, Mich.)

Ford's Orchestra

Musical instruments and musicians in Henry Ford's old-fashioned dance orchestra are the subjects of a paper by Martha Burns, Lincoln, Mass.

"The orchestra that played for Ford's parties and classes was one of his own curious concoctions," writes Martha. "When first described to the public (in 1925), his orchestra was a four-piece group consisting of violin, dulcimer, string bass, and cymbalum.

"The 'fiddle' had always been the mainstay of country dance orchestras throughout the United States. The dulcimer, a trapezoidal instrument with course of strings which were struck with small mallets, or 'hammers,' was also found fairly commonly in American dance orchestras, particularly among the northern states. The string bass was a somewhat unexpected instrument to find in a dance orchestra at the time, but the cymbalum was even more of a surprise.

"The cymbalum is an instrument somewhat similar to the dulcimer except that it is tuned chromatically and it has damper pedals akin to those on a piano. What made the cymbalum an unusual choice for Ford's orchestra is that it is a native Hungarian instrument. But said Ford, 'I like its sound and its flavor. It's old and mellow and fine.'

Henry Ford, right, listens attentively as his old-fashioned dance orchestra plays one of his favorite tunes. Left to right, the instruments consist of a dulcimer, string bass, fiddle, and cymbalum. (Photos from the Collections of the Henry Ford Museum and Greenfield Village.)

"Ford also employed a sousaphone instead of a string bass to boom out bass lines. It is the sousaphone that plays the bass lines on the phonograph recordings that were made during this period. This too was a very curious instrument to be found in an orchestra like Ford's. The orchestra also occasionally employed piano, the guitar, the mandolin, and other instruments.

"The musicians' backgrounds were as varied as their instruments," continues Martha. "Clayton Perry, the fiddler, was originally from Ashtabula,

Ohio, and had picked up old-time fiddling from his grandfather, though he seems to have had some degree of formal training.

"Edwin Baxter, the dulcimer player, was a former interurban bus driver who had also worked in Michigan lumber camps in which he no doubt picked up much of his skill and repertoire. He had learned to play the dulcimer from his father, and his grandfather also had played the instrument. Baxter was the only member of the Ford orchestra who could not read music.

"Much of the orchestra's repertoire was gathered from early collections of printed dance music. Baxter picked up the tunes by ear from the other musicians. One member recalled that Baxter had an excellent ear.

"William Hallup, the cymbalum player was Hungarian by birth. He learned that Ford had acquired a cymbalum, and was looking for someone who could play it. Hallup was by all accounts an excellent musician. In addition, he was well versed in old-time American dance music and Hungarian and classical music as well.

"Maurice Castel, the bass player and sousaphone player, was also a clockmaker. In addition to playing in the orchestra, he maintained all of the clocks in Ford's home, and also cleaned and repaired watches which Ford gave away as gifts.

"In 1937, Gino Caporali joined the orchestra, taking Castel's place on the bass fiddle. Caporali was born in Florence, Italy, but had moved to Pittsburgh as a child. Though most of his musical background was classical, he had played the fiddle at frequent old-time dances as a youth.

"All of the musicians in the Ford orchestra were employed on a full-time basis," concludes Martha. "When not playing for Ford's dance parties or classes, they were loaned to schools and organizations for their dances, or practicing in the old engineering laboratory."

Martha, one of my former students, is an accomplished guitarist. In the 1970s she was a member of the Pigtown Flingers, a group patterned after Ford's orchestra. The Flingers often played at Greenfield Village and elsewhere in the Detroit area. Listening to them play some of Ford's favorites – "Turkey in the Straw," "Old Zip Coon," "Weevily Wheat," "Speed the Plow" – it was easy to understand why the automaker for two decades had his very own orchestra. If I had his money, I would too.

Henry Ford's Fiddler

"I doubt if you have seen this story on Mellie Dunham," writes reader Jim Pearsall, of Zarephath, N.J., of an article on Henry Ford's favorite fiddler in the March 1968 issue of *Down East: The Magazine of Maine*.

Pearsall was right. I hadn't seen the article, and it's a dandy, the best I've seen on Norway, Maine's most famous citizen. The author is Vic Whitman, a part-time Norway resident, who became friends with Dunham in 1924 after driving over one of his hens while a college student.

In addition to being a fiddler, Dunham, born in 1853, was the nation's premier maker of snowshoes, having fashioned the footwear worn by Admiral Peary on his discovery of the North Pole. In 1925 Dunham became Maine's champion old-time fiddler, prompting an invitation from Henry Ford to play for him in Dearborn.

Dunham made an instant hit with Ford, possibly because he liked the auto king and showed it; also because he didn't stand in awe of the magnate. On meeting Ford, Mellie bobbed his head, shook hands and inquired after Ford's health as if he had known him all his life.

Ford also liked Dunham's fiddling. "He plays well," he told Mellie's wife, Gram. "It's a pleasure to listen to him instead of all this rubbish they call jazz. The "Rippling Waves" waltz he composed is as easy for Clara and me to dance to as any tune I ever heard. And when he plays and calls those contra dances he reminds me of a rubber ball the way he bounces around."

At the end of the Dunhams' two-week visit with the Fords, Henry asked Mellie how much he owed him for his music. Dunham scratched his head. Finally, he said, 'When I play away from Norway, I get three dollars. But it's a long way out here – I shall have to ask you five.'

Having heard about Dunham's regular fees, Ford smiled and handed him an envelope. It contained a rare three-dollar gold piece – and a thousand-dollar bill.

Because of widespread publicity, Dunham was offered a tour on the Keith-Albee vaudeville circuit for more money than he had made in a lifetime of fiddling and making snowshoes. He was a smash hit on stage, being held over in Boston, New York, Newark, and Philadelphia. He also made four phonograph records for RCA-Victor in New York and Camden, N.J.

When Dunham's Philadelphia stint ended, he visited the Peary exhibit in Washington's Smithsonian Institution. There he was permitted to reexamine the explorer's snowshoes, the making of which he considered his life's greatest achievement.

After completing his vaudeville tour, Mellie returned to Norway and resumed fiddling for local folk. I don't know how long he lived, but on my next trip through Maine I plan to visit Norway to find out.

Violin Lesson

Bruce Simpson, Dearborn, Mich., may be the only person who received a violin lesson from Henry Ford.

A student at Ford's Greenfield Village schools during the 1930s, Simpson played the violin during chapel services attended by the auto king.

"One day after service," Simpson informed *USAuto Scene*, "Henry Ford told me, 'Bruce you have a problem with your bowing. Let me show you.' " And then he taught the nine-year-old how to play in a more fluid manner. Later, Ford loaned Simpson a 200-year-old Gagliano violin for four years.

Ford, according to Simpson, was a humble, down-to-earth, friendly, spontaneous man "who had good ways with children" and often took them to his farm near Milan. "And that was not just to ride the tractor," Simpson said. "He gave us real work to do."

Simpson's father, Howard, *USAuto Scene* reports, created a three-speed automatic transmission while a Ford employee. Bruce, also a Ford careerist, was involved in the design of the company's first sealed cooling system in 1949. In addition, he worked on the 1956 Ford, known for its safety advances, and served as executive engineer for fuel economy and emissions during the 1970s. Retiring in 1986, Simpson now is a vice-president for quality standards for an Allen Park, Mich. consulting firm – and first violinist with the Dearborn Symphony Orchestra. In 1998 he played to a most appreciative audience at Henry Ford's 135th birthday party at Henry Ford Estate-Fair Lane.

Henry Ford's Chef

Jan Willemse, one of Henry Ford's chefs, is the subject of an article, "Cooking for Henry," by Eleanor Eaton in the May/June 1995 issue of *Michigan History*.

Willemse, 96, attributes his good health partly to his Dutch genes, but mostly to his introduction to soybeans by Ford in the 1930s. "I've been eating soybeans ever since," he told Eaton.

Willemse acquired his cooking skills in Holland while apprenticing for an uncle who was a caterer. After coming to America in 1919 he served as a cook in hotels in Boston and Miami Beach. At the latter city's Nautilus Hotel he was discovered by Edsel Ford, whose yacht was moored at the hostelry's marina. Edsel's recommendation to his father eventually brought the Dutchman to Dearborn.

Willemse first worked as pastry chef at the Dearborn Inn, then as a party chef for Henry and Clara Ford in Greenfield Village, where he was asked to develop soybean recipes. When Willemse began experimenting with soybean recipes, Robert Smith, a Ford food chemist, created a substitute for milk and ice cream from the beans. Although the ice cream proved unpopular, the soymilk and a topping called DelSoy (Delicious Soybean) are still in demand. Willemse also was acquainted with researchers R.H. McCarroll, Harold Joyce, and Robert Boyer, who created the first plastic auto parts from soybeans.

During his years with Ford, Willemse grew very fond of the Fords. He saw Henry almost daily, Clara several times a month when she visited him at work. "They were family," he informed Eaton. "Mrs. Ford was like a mother to me. She even looked like my mother, though she was a little heavier. Both of them were strict but fair, just like my own parents .... [Henry] enrolled our sons in the Greenfield Village schools and also invited us to old-time dances and other affairs at the village that he and Clara hosted. I provided refreshments for the dances .... Usually they were finger sandwiches, punch, and cocoa. There was soy in everything I made, though the guests didn't know it. At that time many people still considered soybeans suitable only as animal food."

Dr. Edsel Ruddiman, Ford's chief food chemist, was Willemse's advisor. When the chef began experimenting with soy recipes, Ruddiman gave him soybean flour from which he made soft rolls. "Mr. Ford kept wanting more and more soybean foods," Willemse says. "Everything I made had to have soy in it. And he liked everything I made. But one thing I never served him was soybean coffee. I don't know why."

A favorite of Ford's, Willemse recalls, was the Model T cracker, named by the automaker after being told that a Model T hubcap had been used to cut the cracker "because I couldn't find a cutter of the right size in the kitchen." Clara especially enjoyed white-chocolate chip cookies and soy bread, which Willemse daily sent to the Fords' home.

In 1934 Willemse created an all-soy dinner at the Ford Pavilion at Chicago's A Century of Progress Exposition.

After Ford's retirement, Willemse owned a catering business for several years, then joined Miesel Sysco, a food wholesaler, of which he eventually became executive chef. He retired at 92 because of a company takeover. Until then he drove to work daily in an Escort. "I wouldn't think of owning anything other than a Ford," he declared.

In 1992 Willemse and Eaton coauthored a book, *Cooking for Henry: Memories and Recipes of Chef Jan Willemse.* A section is devoted to soybean recipes.

Soy For Health

Henry Ford passionately believed that soybeans were a health panacea and ate meals consisting of only soybean derivatives. But even he might be surprised by present-day claims for the legume.

An article, "Have Great Sex Every Day Until You Die," in the March 1998 issue of *Men's Health*, states that men in their 40s should "start loading up on one of the world's greatest sex foods: soy .... More than 200 studies have found that genistein – a crystalline compound found only in soy – wards off prostate cancer, shrinks enlarged prostates, and increases fertility. It also promotes firmer erections by lowering cholesterol levels and cleaning your arteries. So find a way to work it in, okay?"

Poland Spring Water

"I read somewhere that Henry Ford liked Poland Spring Water," writes reader Keith Wilson, of Birmingham, Mich. "Is that the same Poland Water that can be bought today?"

It is. Poland Spring Natural Spring Water (the trademark), has been shipped around the world from Poland, Maine, since mid-19th century. It won top honors at Chicago's 1893 World's Colombian Exposition and the 1904 St. Louis World's Fair, prospered for decades, then faltered, and was acquired by Perrier in 1980.

Enjoying Poland Spring Water himself, Ford gave bottles to others. Unopened bottles of the beverage, with labels in mint condition, were sold at a mid-1970s Dearborn auction of the household effects of Evangeline Dahlinger, mother of John Dahlinger, who claimed to be Henry Ford's son.

Deer Hunters

A 1908 photo of Henry Ford and his son, Edsel, then 15, appears in *American Rifleman*, published by the National Rifleman Assn.

The picture appears in an article on a Michigan hunter/guide, Harold O. Davidson, 93. As a 15-year-old, Davidson led the Fords on a deer hunting expedition in an 18,000-acre preserve near Sylvania, Mich.

The article is of special interest in that it depicts the elder Ford as a deer hunter, rather than a protector of wildlife, for which he was nationally acclaimed. In fact, his estate, Fair Lane, was a wildlife sanctuary before he and his wife made their home there. Most of the property remained in a natural state throughout the Fords' lives, offering a haven for wildlife, including numerous deer.

Friend Of The Cypress

Henry Ford tried to save one of Florida's greatest natural resources – some of the world's finest virgin bald cypress trees – according to the July 16, 1995 issue of *Florida Magazine*.

In 1913 thousands of the centuries-old cypresses, many as high as 130 feet tall, stood in a 50-mile-wide area of Collier County. That year, business interests paid $1.4 million for 100,000 acres of the cypress swamp, which contained two-thirds of all the country's cypresses. The purchase price was only $14 per acre.

A few years later, a Ford agent acquired an option to buy much of the land. The automaker impressed with the area's beauty, sought to acquire the property, then give it to the state. But the state, concerned about the cost of maintaining the area, declined the gift.

Lumber companies then moved into high gear, cutting down the huge, beautiful trees as quickly as possible. Soon most of the cypresses were gone. But some remained at Corkscrew Swamp, which derived its name from a nearby winding river, which had been called the Corkscrew River before its name was changed to the Imperial River.

In 1954, an association raised money and bought the Corkscrew land from a variety of sources. Almost half of the funds were provided by the Ford Foundation. Thus Ford-derived money finally went to buy a part of the property the industrialist had offered the state four decades earlier. Today the land, owned by the National Audubon Society, contains some of the most beautiful cypress trees to be found anywhere.

Thanks to daughter Lani Walczak, a transplanted Floridian, for forwarding the article.

Waste Not, Want Not

Most readers know that Henry Ford converted wooden shipping containers into Model T floorboards.

But fewer readers may know, as reported by *Automotive Industries* in 1928 and 1996, that the industrialist fed into his steel furnaces all scrap from his rolling mills, plus trimmers and crate nails. He also converted old paint cans into mop pails, and was among the first to stamp small parts from offal. Car rattles and squeaks were muffled by worn conveyor belt material.

Mr. Clean

"I've read that Henry Ford kept his plants very clean," writes Kevin Jordan, of Morristown, N.Y. "How much of a stickler was he?"

A good example of Ford's passion for cleanliness appears in a speech, "Motown on the Menominee: The Ford Motor Company in Iron Mountain," given at the 1990 annual meeting of the Historical Society of Michigan by Kenneth G. Hafeli.

In August 1926, Hafeli states, Ford visited his Iron Mountain (Mich.) Chemical Plant, of which T.C. Albin was superintendent. Upon inspecting the plant's sawmill with his son, Edsel, and manufacturing boss, Charles Sorensen, the auto king was appalled by the mill's unsightliness. Declaring "This is not my building," he walked out. Shortly thereafter the embarrassed and offended Albin resigned.

Henry Ford Biography

Henry Ford was the subject of an hourlong "Biography" program on the Arts and Entertainment television channel on July 21, 1994.

Superlatives were not spared by host Peter Graves and narrator Jack Perkins as they introduced the program. To them, Ford was the man who "gave the car to America," "invented the modern age," and "changed the world."

Among the program's interviewees were Ford's oldest great-granddaughter, Charlotte, and his great-grandson, Edsel II, a Ford Company vice president. Charlotte, six at the time of the auto king's death, observed that "if I remember my great-grandfather at all, I remember that he had a hard handshake. He'd shake hands first, then give me a kiss."

Other "talking heads" included Robert Casey, research archivist at the Henry Ford Museum and Greenfield Village, who described Ford as "the most influential man of the 20th Century," and Robert Lacey, author of *Ford: The Men and the Machine*," who noted that the Ford "changed the way we live." Also appearing was David Moore, a participant and observer of the Detroit labor scene since the 1930s. Moore, who heartily dislikes employers, has appeared in several films relating to Ford and the 1930s, and has yet to utter a kind word about Ford or his company.

Ford is shown with his friends, Thomas Edison and Harvey Firestone, on a radio broadcast. Ill at ease, the Dearbornite in a series of platitudes exhorts young men to take advantage of the opportunities available to them.

The film also shows scenes from the so-called "Hunger March" on the Rouge Plant in 1932, during which four participants were killed and a fifth died later. Typically, the impression is left that the march was inspired by Ford workers, rather than by the communists, who organized such marches for reasons of their own in many cities in 1932.

Ford And Royalty

"How did Henry Ford act around royalty?" writes reader Keith Boyd, of Phoenix. "I read somewhere that he treated them just like anyone else."

Ford, according to an aide, Fred L. Black, whose memoirs are deposited at Henry Ford Museum & Greenfield Village, was opposed to undue ceremony around anybody. "He never called royalty 'Your Highness' or anything like that," Black recalled. "It was always 'Prince This' or 'Prince that.' I always understood that he called King George V 'King.'

" ... He was at ease with people because he just didn't worry about whether he said the right thing or not .... Had he made an effort to do and say the proper things, such as 'Your Royal Highness,' or consider just what he should do, I think he would have been very ill at ease."

Some royal visitors were more in awe of Ford than vice versa, especially those from deposed families or countries that the magnate had the money to buy.

Ford And McCormick

Battling between Henry Ford and Robert R. McCormick, publisher of the *Chicago Tribune*, is discussed at length in Richard Norton Smith's 1997 book, *The Colonel: The Life and Legend of Robert R. McCormick 1880-1955.*

In 1916 McCormick, misinformed that pacifist Ford would deny leaves to employees sent with National Guard units to pacify the Mexican border, editorialized that the industrialist was "an ignorant idealist" and an "anarchistic enemy of the nation which protects him in his wealth."

Ford's denial of the *Tribune*'s charges was printed by the newspaper, which stood by its characterizations of the magnate. Ford filed a $1 million libel suit, culminating in the first of many "trials of the century." Dragging on for three years, the suit also richly documented the plaintiff's ignorance of American history.

Jurors decided that Ford had been libeled, while absolving the *Tribune* of malicious intent. Damages were assessed at a humiliating six cents.

McCormick continued to attack Ford. In 1923, in opposition to the industrialist's efforts to acquire an unfinished government dam on the Tennessee River, the publisher wrote Secretary of War John W. Weeks that "Henry Ford is an unscrupulous, rapacious hypocrite."

By the 1930s both Ford and McCormick had found someone they disliked even more than each other: President Franklin D. Roosevelt.

In December 1943 the old antagonists came full circle. Visiting Detroit, McCormick staged a very public reconciliation with his former foe. As photos were taken of the seated pair, the shorter Ford, age 80, was propped up on "several pillows" so as to appear at a height level with McCormick. Afterward, the publisher expressed his delight.

"Ford's a great little guy," he remarked to a *Tribune* executive .... "He wants me to run for President of the United States ... and furthermore he'd back me with every penny – every cent he has he'd put on me if I'd run for President."

McCormick would have felt less flattered had he known that Ford also told Harry Bennett's wife that tough guy Harry "should be President of the United States."

Romney's Challenge

American Motors Chairman George Romney once challenged Henry Ford II to a highway game of "chicken," ex-AMC public relations executive John Conde recently told the *Detroit News.*

Michigan Governor George Romney at the wheel of an experimental sports car called Allegro in the Ford Pavilion at the New York World's Fair in 1964.

When Romney's Rambler adopted unibody construction – now an industry standard – the car was criticized by Henry Ford II and others as being weak. Stung, Romney publicly challenged HFII to meet him in a head-on crash. "We cautioned him against it," Conde recalls, "but he issued the challenge anyway. If Ford had accepted, he probably would have wet his pants."

Romney later served as Michigan's governor. He lived until 1995.

Mickey Rooney thoroughly captivated Henry Ford (right) and his son, Edsel (left), as attested to in this photo of Rooney with the auto tycoons in the Henry Ford Museum on Feb. 9, 1940. Rooney had the title role in Young Tom Edison, *which had its world premiere that week in Port Huron, Mich., Edison's boyhood home.*

Mickey And Company

Diminutive Mickey Rooney's friendship with Henry Ford is discussed in the actor's recently-published book, *Life Is Too Short*.

Rooney recalls his Feb. 9, 1940 visit to Dearborn, at which time Ford and his son, Edsel, with Harvey Firestone, guided him through the Henry Ford Museum and took him to lunch in the company's executive dining room. Ford also showed the 20-year-old Rooney one of the first Lincoln Continentals. When Rooney expressed admiration for the car, Ford said he'd give him one, and a few months later dispatched a blue Continental to the young actor in Hollywood.

One of the admirers of Rooney's car was Clark Gable, who, after taking the car for a 15-minute spin, placed an order. Rooney said he was flattered by Gable's interest in his vehicle, and even more pleased that his (Rooney's) Continental was a gift.

Maritime Hall

Henry Ford was elected to the Maritime Hall of Fame in 1988, reports the Spring 1998 issue of Henry Ford Heritage Association's publication, *Ford Legend*.

The hall is the only U.S. museum honoring ships and seafarers who have contributed to the nation's maritime heritage. It is part of the American Merchant Marine Academy, Kings Point, N.Y.

Ford was honored on several counts – as a shipowner, shipbuilder, and maritime pioneer. "By choosing watersites for many of his major car factories," the hall says of him, "he greatly bolstered shipping on the Great Lakes and Erie Canal. By connecting his docking facilities to rail lines, he anticipated intermodal transportation. During World War I, he built and sold 199 small wooden tugs and minesweepers. After the Great War, he bought hundreds of surplus ships, converting many to barges and the rest to scrap. He was one of the first U.S. owners to adopt diesel propulsion to his fleet, when the *Henry Ford II* and *Benson Ford* sailed in 1924."

The *Legend*'s article excerpts from the September 1988 edition of the Great Lakes Maritime Institute's *Telescope*.

Auto Hall

"How many Ford people are honored in Dearborn's Automotive Hall of Fame?" asks reader Clyde Shoebert, Tampa, Fla.

Those who spent careers with Ford Motor Company are Henry Ford, Edsel Ford, Henry Ford II, and Philip Caldwell. Those identified with Ford for part of their careers are John and Horace Dodge, C. Harold Wills, William S. Knudsen, Ernest R. Breech, and Lee A. Iacocca. Barney Oldfield, another honoree, was a Ford racing driver.

Golden Ax Hall

Henry Ford and Lee Iacocca are among those included in the "Golden Ax Hall of Fame" created by Bob McCarthy, a Los Angeles employment counselor.

"Ford," says McCarthy, "was fired from an engineering job in Detroit in 1895 because he spent too much time fiddling with a horseless vehicle equipped with an internal combustion engine.

"More than 70 years later," McCarthy adds, "Ford's grandson fired auto whiz Iacocca for 'personal reasons,' thus freeing Iacocca to lead Chrysler out of bankruptcy and write his best-selling memoirs."

Ford wasn't exactly fired by his employer, the Detroit Illuminating Co. But, he was asked by his boss to choose between his job and working on his car, and opted for the latter.

Other members of the Golden Ax Hall include Albert Einstein, Benjamin Franklin, Winston Churchill, David Letterman, Dr. Ruth Westheimer, R. Buckminster Fuller, and Billy Martin. McCarthy's point is that his Hall's members survived being axed, and so can his clients.

Poor Timing

I've always thought it unfortunate timing that the Hall of Fame for Great Americans discontinued elections before Henry Ford's inclusion (honorees must have been deceased at least 25 years before being eligible for induction). A recent Associated Press article on the hall agrees, noting that "certifiably famous Americans such as Henry Ford were never elected."

The hall, founded in 1900, went out of business in the late 1970s. It is located on the campus of Bronx Community College, formerly the Bronx campus of New York University. One of the nation's greatest collections of portrait sculpture reposes in the outdoor hall. But the 102 bronze busts of the honorees are slowly disintegrating because of exposure to the elements and neglect.

Henry A Yardstick

For decades leading figures in one field or another field have been referred to in the press and elsewhere as "the Henry Ford of" one thing or another.

Even so, it's surprising to find Carlos Lehder Rivas, the biggest foreign drug smuggler ever brought to trial in the U.S., described by U.S. Attorney General Robert Merkle as the "Henry Ford of the cocaine trade." Rivas was so described because he is "the pioneer of the mass transportation of cocaine for the American consumer."

Among others recently linked in the press with Henry Ford are McDonald's Ray Kroc, the "Henry Ford of the hamburger" and "the service sector's equivalent of Henry Ford"; Powell Crosley Jr., the "Henry Ford of radio"; Louis Marx Sr., the "Henry Ford of toymaking"; William J. Levitt, the "Henry Ford of housing"; Henry J. Kaiser, the "Henry Ford of the West"; E. Haldeman – Julius, the "Henry Ford of literature"; J.P. Seeburg, the "Henry Ford of jukeboxes"; cosmetics queen Elizabeth Arden, who "was to the personal beauty business what Henry

Ford was to the automobile industry"; and Detroit science whiz Matthew Tait, 18, wants to do for the robotics business what Henry Ford did for the automobile; make a lot of them and make them affordable for everyone."

Ford Of Gambling

Mirage Resorts, Inc., considered the gambling industry's most forward-thinking enterprise, was rebuffed in its recent bid to participate in Detroit casino gambling.

"It was just not to be," Mirage attorney Melvin Hollowell told the *Detroit Free Press*, "even though Mirage owner Steve Wynn is the 'Henry Ford' of the gambling industry." Known for its glitzy resorts with spewing volcanoes and exotic animals, Mirage offered the Motor City an $800-million casino and luxury hotel reminiscent of 19th century Paris.

Thanks to reader Mike Skinner, St. Clair Shores, Detroit, for forwarding the *Free Press* story.

Levitt Compared To Ford

The death of William J. Levitt in 1994 evoked comparisons of the "father of suburbia" to Henry Ford.

"Levitt was to suburbs as Henry Ford was to the auto," historian Kenneth T. Jackson, author of *Crabgrass Frontier*, told *Newsday*. "Just as Ford made it possible for average workers to make the automobile a routine part of their life style, Levitt made the suburban detached home a normal expectation for the middle class."

"But access to the two men's contributions was quite different," Les Payne, an African-American columnist at the *Syracuse Post-Standard*, reports. "The Model T and what followed was reasonably accessible to all Americans who could pony up the money. Levitt tolerated no such equality. Levitt's housing changed the course of American housing. Would not that change have been even better, if Levitt, like Ford, had made his housing dream available to all Americans who could afford it?"

Thanks to reader Peter Winnewisser, of Cazenovia, N.Y., for forwarding the *Post-Standard*'s article.

Ford of Fast Food

White Castle's cofounder is called "the Henry Ford of fast food" in David Hogan's 1997 book, *Selling 'em by the Sack: White Castle and the Creation of American Food*.

"What Henry Ford did for the automobile, Billy Ingram did for fast food in America," Hogan says. "The hamburger chain played a key role in selling Middle America on fast food," he adds, and the larger McDonald's, Wendy's, and Burger King are greatly in its debt.

Thanks to Rick Lindner, Columbus, Ohio, for forwarding a *Columbus Dispatch* story on White Castle.

Gates, God, Ford

"Gates Isn't God (or Even Henry Ford)" sings out a *Washington Post* headline over a story on Microsoft Chairman, Bill Gates.

After cataloging Gates' achievements, the *Post*'s story observes that the software king's "business triumphs do not yet qualify him as an innovator in the mold of, say, Edison or Ford. Ford is the best comparison, and the similarities – and differences – are revealing. Both were early enthusiasts for a new technology. Ford tinkered in a woodshed to build his first car in 1896. Gates wrote software as a teenager. Ford didn't personally invent any critical technical improvement to the car; the story is similar for Gates and the computer. What separates the two is that Ford pioneered a system of mass production that altered all industry and the face of America.

"Before the Model T in 1908," the article continues, "cars were costly and scarce. Ford's decision to make only one model and his streamlining of production – including the adoption of the assembly line – changed that. Between 1908 and 1913, Ford's output went from 10,202 to 202,667 cars; by 1923, it was 1.8 million. His approach was widely copied. By contrast, the PC explosion has been driven by the growing power of chips to make computers more versatile and user-friendly. Microsoft may have slightly speeded the process by creating a dominant and recognizable software that hastened consumer acceptance. But it would still have proceeded rapidly, as the Internet shows. Gates was late to see its importance; it grew anyway."

The article also states that the personal computer's "social significance still falls short of that of many past technologies: the railroad (which created a national market); the automobile (which transformed living and working patterns); the TV (which became the greatest form of mass entertainment); antibiotics (which tamed many deadly infections); and the harnessing of electricity."

Thanks to Dr. Peter Weber, Olney, Ill., for forwarding the *Post*'s article.

Grand Boulevard Home

Henry, Clara, and Edsel Ford ushered in the 20th Century in this two-story home with attic at 582 W. Grand Boulevard, Detroit, having moved there in the fall of 1900 to acquire additional space to accommodate Henry's 74-year-old father, William, and sister, Jane. The house was razed some years ago. (Photo from Henry Ford Museum and Greenfield Village, Dearborn, Mich.)

Ford Residences

The fifteen homes in which Henry and Clara Ford resided between 1888 and 1947 are discussed in an article in the Fall 1993 edition of the Henry Ford Heritage Association's newsletter. The author, Dick Folsom, of Canton, Mich., is president of both the association and the Dearborn Historical Society and a volunteer guide at Ford's former estate, Fair Lane.

The Ford's first home, Folsom observes, is not the "Square House" or "Honeymoon House," as many think. Rather, it is the Moir House, a small dwelling located on the 40 acres of land given to Henry by his father in 1886. After spending the first 13 months of their marriage in this home, the Fords moved into the "Honeymoon House" in

Hendrie Avenue Residence

The Fords moved to a spacious apartment at 332 Hendrie Avenue, Detroit, between Hastings and Rivard, in the fall of 1901, about the time of the organization of the Henry Ford Company, the second of Ford's three automotive enterprises. While living in the center unit of this three-apartment building, Henry helped organize Ford Motor Company in 1903 and his father, William, died in 1905. Arched doorways were in vogue at the turn of the century just as they are today. The building no longer stands. (Photo from Henry Ford Museum and Greenfield Village, Dearborn, Mich.)

May 1889. In that home in 1891 Ford sketched a plan for adapting an internal combustion engine to a carriage.

The Moir House is long gone, but the "Honeymoon House," removed to Garden City, Mich. in 1953, still stands, guarded by a State of Michigan historical marker.

After spending three years of married life in Dearborn, Folsom notes that the Fords moved to 618 John R Street in Detroit in September 1891. While living in this duplex, recently razed, Henry began nine years of employment by Detroit's Edison Iluminating Company. Thenceforth, he tended to move each time he got a pay raise.

The Fords moved to an apartment at 7 Washington Boulevard in the spring of 1892, and then to a small flat at 162 Cass Avenue not long thereafter. They moved to 570 West Forest Avenue in May 1893, and there the Fords' only child, Edsel, was born on November 6, 1893.

Shortly thereafter, the family moved to a duplex at 58 Bagley Avenue, where Ford on Christmas Eve, 1893, ran his first internal combustion gasoline engine and in 1896 built his first car.

Spending three and a half years on Bagley, whose site is designated by an historical marker, the Fords moved in July 1897 to their eighth residence, 72 E. Alexandrine Avenue, the first single-family home they had known since leaving Dearborn.

After Ford resigned from the electric company to devote himself to his first auto venture, the Detroit Automobile

Harper Avenue Home

Moving up, Henry, Clara, and Edsel Ford in the fall of 1905 moved to this flat in the 400 block of Harper Ave., Detroit, not far from the Ford Company's new Piquette Plant. Here the Fords enjoyed their first taste of upper-middle-class living. The Fords lived in this home until 1908 when they moved to 66 Edison Avenue (now 140 Edison) in 1908. When I first photographed the Harper home in 1972, the owner rushed out and asked, "Why are you taking pictures of my building?" I replied, "because Henry Ford once lived in it." "Is that so," he mused. "I'm going to raise the rent." The building was torn down to provide parking space for the nearby Oakland Avenue Baptist Church. (Photo from Henry Ford Museum and Greenfield Village, Dearborn, Mich.)

Company, the family moved to 1292 Second Boulevard. They moved again to 582 W. Grand Boulevard during the fall of 1900 to acquire space to accommodate Henry's 74-year-old father, William, and sister, Jane.

In the fall of 1901, about the time Henry helped organize the Henry Ford Company, the Fords moved to an apartment at 332 Hendrie Avenue. While there, the Ford Company was formed on June 16, 1903, and in that apartment William died in 1905.

Prospering, the Fords in the fall of 1905 moved to a flat at 145 Harper Avenue, where they enjoyed their first taste of upper-middle-class living. They remained on Harper Avenue until moving into a spacious house at 66 Edison because of the lack of privacy brought on by Henry's skyrocketing fame. A state marker has been placed in front of the residence, now owned by a Wayne State University professor, Jerald Mitchell, and his wife.

Early in 1915 the Fords took up residence in the "Ten Eyck House," a rustic dwelling located on the property where their mansion, Fair Lane, was being built. Clara and Edsel moved into the mansion in November 1915, and Henry – then preoccupied with the ship he had chartered in the hope of mediating an end to World War I – arrived shortly thereafter.

The Fords, Folsom calculated, moved an average of once every 1.8 years during their 59 years of marriage.

Membership in the Henry Ford Heritage Association is open to any Ford family history enthusiast. Annual dues of $5 should be sent to HFHA, Henry Ford Estate, 4901 Evergreen Road, Dearborn, MI 48126.

Fords' Florida Home

"Mangoes," the winter home of Henry and Clara Ford, recently was opened to the public by the city of Ft. Myers, Fla. The "Today" show's Willard Scott served as master of ceremonies at the "champagne debut," which was attended by Edsel Ford II, a great-grandson of Henry Ford, and Morgan Firestone, a great-grandson of Harvey Firestone Sr.

The program for the debut describes the setting and provides a few historical details:

"Majestic palms sway gently, the fragrance of the tropical fruits and flowers waft by on the breeze, and the welcome mat is out at the 'Mangoes' inviting visitors to experience a unique glimpse into the private life of the world's first billionaire, Henry Ford, and his wife, Clara."

The fruition of efforts started by local real estate developer Jim Newton (personal friend of both Ford and Thomas Edison) ... and a loosely formed committee in the early 1980s, the city's acquisition of the Ford home became a reality July 1, 1988 when city officials signed a purchase agreement for $1.5 million ... Plans were approved for a $350,000 restoration program in the spring of 1989.

"The three-acre estate, nestled along the banks of the Caloosahatchee River, overlooks McGregor Boulevard, and was bought by the Fords in 1916 ... The Fords' home reflects their Midwestern homegrown values, as well as the effect of extraordinary wealth. Though simply built, the house has unusual grace, and is furnished authentically to the historical period and taste of the Fords. Much of the furniture was acquired locally, including wicker furniture and a wardrobe, which was original to the house."

The brochure contains photos and descriptions of the house's features and rooms including Ford's study. The study contains the magnate's telescope for birdwatching, books by favorite authors, and an early 19th century globe. The living room is said to have been used for square dancing, for which a cranked gramophone furnished the music. The program also notes that the Ford Motor Co. Fund contributed $50,000 toward the house's restoration.

Ford wintered in Ft. Myers in order to spend more time with his idol, Thomas A. Edison, whose next-door home has long been a tourist attraction.

A frontal view of Henry and Clara Fords' Ft. Myers, Fla., winter home. The photo was taken early in the Fords' residency inasmuch as the trees, now fully grown, were newly planted at the time. (Photo from the Collections of the Henry Ford Museum and Greenfield Village.)

Admission to the Ford home is $3; to the Edison home/museum $5; to both $7.

Mayor Wilbur Smith is exuberant about the combined attraction, predicting that it will double tourist visitation and bring the city "$1 million in profits."

A plaque near the two homes notes that the site is "The only spot in history where two of the world's greatest men had their homes – side by side."

Thanks to Dearborn's Mike Skinner, who attended the house opening, for forwarding information and photos of the setting and ceremony.

Huron Mountain Club

The summer retreat of Henry and Clara Ford in Northern Michigan's Huron Mountains is discussed in an article by Ford R. Bryan in the Summer 1992 edition of the *Dearborn Historian*.

The Fords "cabin" was located within the exclusive Huron Mountain Club, approximately 40 miles north of Marquette, several miles beyond the small town of Big Bay. The club, which dates to 1889, is bordered by Lake Superior and (by 1929) 12,400 acres of primeval forest interspersed with lakes and streams. The Huron Mountains are rugged, but not lofty.

By 1929, as Bryan notes, the majority of the club's 74 member families were Detroiters with almost as many from Chicago. Most of the cabins were passed from generation to generation. But that year the Fords, no doubt abetted by their great wealth and the fact that Henry was the largest private employer in Northern Michigan, joined the club.

The Fords' cabin, accommodating 12 people, was ready for occupancy by August, 1930. The lumber was supplied by the magnate's nearby Pequaming sawmill.

The Fords most often visited their cabin in late summer, traveling between Dearborn and Marquette on one of their large iron ore boats. The ships had luxurious passenger quarters; and, in addition to their owners, often accommodated the couple's guests, most numerous among them Henry Ford Hospital nurses.

While "up north," Henry also spent time in Big Bay, and, at age 80 in 1943, he bought the town, including its large lumber mill, hotel, and 52 houses. Ford spent several millions restoring the mill and employee homes, plus another half million on the hotel, in which he maintained a seldom used private suite for himself and Clara. The hotel also served as a vacation headquarters for numerous friends who worked at the Ford Company and Ford Hospital.

After Clara Ford's death in 1950 (she survived her husband by three years), the Fords' Huron Mountain Club membership and cabin were transferred to John W. O'Boyle, a wealthy Dallas oil man.

Your commentator visited the club in 1973, when leading a Greenfield Village tour group. The only means of gaining entry was to obtain permission from a club member, in our case O'Boyle's widow. Permission was obtained via an appeal to the Marquette attorney who administers the club. He radioed (there was no phone line into the club) the resident manager, Tom Jernstad, who, after getting Mrs. O'Boyle's okay, arranged for our group to pass through the gates.

At that time the club, open only summers, had 48 members. One of the last preserves of the wealthy, it had never been publicized in a national magazine, although I was told that *Fortune* and other publications had tried for years to gain access. I was requested to photograph only the ex-Ford cabin, and, of course, complied.

The O'Boyle dwelling commands a beautiful view of Lake Superior; and to the rear is a waterway which berths the yachts of club members. Pine trees surround the handsome two-story building. Inside, the first floor is dominated by a huge open-ceiling living room. At the time of my visit, Mrs. O'Boyle's son, William, a Harvard graduate student, and his wife, were occupying the cabin, and showed us around.

The club now owns more than 24,000 acres, which team with naturalists from universities investigating forest and wildlife conditions in perhaps the most pristine environment in Michigan. At times the U.S. government has recommended that the area be converted into a national park, but members have been able to resist incursion by convincing others that the area is too cool, has too few beaches, and is too remote from centers of population to make it worthwhile. This viewpoint is self-serving, of course, but has kept the feds at bay.

The Big Bay properties also were sold in 1951. The mill, set afire by a workman's cutting torch as machinery was being removed, is now a windowless shell. The hotel still operates as the Thunder Bay Inn. In 1973, I noted that most of the original furnishings and fixtures had been removed, an exception being a brass fireplace screen and a solid brass andiron which once belonged to Pittsburgh financier Andrew Mellon.

"The lobby and dining rooms give a hint of their former splendor," according to my two-decade-old notes, "and the kitchen remains superbly equipped. Bedrooms remain as in Ford's day, sans furniture. The Fords' magnificent solid wash basins and tubs are still here, attesting to Henry's insistence on going first-class even when "roughing it" in the north country."

Readers who tour Northern Michigan will wish to visit Big Bay, along with Ford's other Northern Michigan properties. They may also wish to visit the Huron Mountain Club, but that will take some doing, unless they do as one of my students once did. He backpacked along the shore of Lake Superior, and, as he later told me, walked as "pretty as I pleased" right through the community.

Spruce Tree

In 1942 or 1943 young Fred Rydholm, an employee of Northern Michigan's Huron Mountain Club, got word that members Henry and Clara Ford wanted a spruce tree planted next to their cabin.

Rydholm and a fellow employee dug up a spruce about four or five feet high, along with a ball of earth the size of a bushel basket. Upon taking the tree to the Fords' cabin, they were told by a maid that the couple wished to inspect the tree in their living room.

"It's out in the truck," Rydholm said.

"Just take it out of the truck and bring it in where they can see it," the maid insisted.

Thinking the maid did not understand, Rydholm explained, "It's quite large and very heavy and kind of dirty."

"That's all right. Mr. and Mrs. Ford want to see it, just bring it in."

Rydholm could hardly believe his ears, but he and his companion lugged the tree into the living room and set it in the middle of the floor.

"That's a nice one," Mrs. Ford said. "Turn it around," Henry added. "Now let's see the other side again."

Afterwards the workers planted the tree "on a little rise outside the Fords' bedroom window .... "It's still there, nearly 50 feet high," the author recalls in his 1989 book, *Superior Heartland: A Backwoods History*. "In fact its present owners recently suggested that it cuts out too much light and that it may have to be cut down."

Later Rydholm, while on naval leave, was assured by Ford that the spruce "was doing fine." On that occasion the magnate also introduced Rydholm to his houseguests, eldest grandson, Henry Ford II, and his wife, Anne.

Ford's Country Home

Henry and Clara Fords' former country home in Macon, Mich., is on the market for $299,000.

The 125-acre estate, listed in the National Register of Historic Places, was described as follows in a sale brochure prepared by Lenawee Properties, Inc., 118 West Chicago Blvd., Tecumseh, Mich. 49286.

"This century-old Greek Revival farmhouse located in the Village of Macon (about 50 miles southwest of Dearborn) was auto king Henry Ford's country seat and enjoys the same rural setting and is in as good condition as it was in Ford's heyday. Ford also built and operated in Macon a sawmill, general store, and schools and erected a chapel. The village of approximately 100 people, located in the center of Ford's vast rural holdings, thus became the magnate's farm capital.

"The house was built in approximately 1830 and was completely restored by Henry Ford in 1932. The old-fashionedness was preserved by electric switchplates hidden in the walls, pegged oak floors, documentary wallpaper, and woodwork painted in Williamsburg colors. The kitchen continues the effect with a brick chimney housing a modern oven and a reproduction of an old woodburning stove equipped for cooking with electricity. There is a large woodburning fireplace in the dining room. The windows retain much of the original glass. Black walnut woodwork, including the windows, and the basement floor of brick over flagstone are some of the extravagant features of this showplace.

"The 'Summer Kitchen' is a separate outside building in back of the house which is connected to the main house by an underground tunnel. It has a large brick fireplace and rough wood paneling. Other outside buildings built at the approximate time of the house include the carriage house, the horse barn, the cow barn, and the corn crib. When Henry Ford restored the house, he also rebuilt these buildings which are of wood construction and have paneled barn siding exteriors. The floors are wood. Three smaller outbuildings reminiscent of days gone by have also been preserved. They are the brick smokehouse, the nut house (used for drying nuts) and the outhouse constructed of black walnut siding.

Henry and Clara Fords' Macon, Mich. country home, as it looked in 1976, and still looks today.

"The highly productive vast farmlands surrounding this handsome site were responsible for growing the soybeans with which Ford experimented during the 1930s and 1940s.

"The total picture is that of a beautifully restored country estate perched on productive farmlands. The elegance of the stately home is enhanced by the spacious front lawn and white decorative fence in front of the house."

The brochure also mentions the Delicious, Jonathan, and McIntosh apple trees from which your commentator plucked fruit (with the permission of the owner, let it be added) in autumns of yore.

Thanks to reader Mike Skinner of Dearborn for forwarding Lenawee Properties' sale literature.

Henry Ford's columned summer cottage, "The Bungalow," is now a bed-and-breakfast inn.

The Bungalow

Henry Ford's Pequaming, Mich. summer home, "The Bungalow," is featured in a recent *Milwaukee Journal* article on bed-and-breakfast places in and around Wisconsin.

Ford and his wife, Clara, occupied "The Bungalow" from the time the magnate bought the entire sawmill town in 1923 until the mid-1940s. After the Fords' deaths, the house became a one-family home, later converted into an inn by Lora Westberg, the present innkeeper.

"The Bungalow," according to the *Journal*, "provides elegant lodging in eight rooms, including a two-room suite, all with antique furnishings. A full breakfast is served in the huge dining room paneled in knotty pine and bird's-eye maple. In the center of the adjacent living room is a roaring fireplace, creating a setting where lodgers can sit back and ponder the beauty and splendor of the North. Rates range from $65 to $85. Contact: The Bungalow, Route 1, Box 123, L'Anse, Mich. 49946; phone 906-524-7595."

In addition to "The Bungalow," another Pequaming landmark harks back to the Ford era – a big water tower with the Ford logo looming over the abandoned village like an ancient totem of a civilization lost.

Thanks to Walter C. Kaufman, of Colgate, Wis., for forwarding the *Journal*'s article.

Ford/Pharaon Plantation

The Richmond Hill, Ga. plantation once owned by Henry Ford and now owned by Saudi multimillionaire Ghaith R. Pharaon has been in the news, Pharaon having been described as the leading frontman in the U.S. for the Bank of Credit and Commerce International (B.C.C.I.). The bank has been accused of bank fraud, money laundering, and bribery around the world.

Pharaon bought the Ford estate in 1982, restored it to its former grandeur, and entertained the rich and the famous ranging from Saudi princes, Pakistani financiers, Chinese television stars, and U.S. politicians such as ex-Secretary of State Alexander Haig and ex-Atlanta mayor Andrew Young.

The 50-year-old Pharaon, who spends much of his time globe trotting, has not been in his Georgia mansion since the spring of 1991, and local residents think that his brief, glittering residency may be a thing of the past. If so, the fate of the mansion, built in 1936, once more will be in question.

Ford and his wife, Clara, wintered at Richmond Hill until their deaths in 1947 and 1950, respectively. The Ford Foundation, to which the property had been bequeathed, sold the estate to the International Paper Company in 1951. The property had a series of owners before being acquired by Pharaon.

Richmond Hill, Ga's Ford-built Community House as it looked when sparkling new in the late 1930s. Few, if any, small southern communities could boast such a facility. (Photo from Henry Ford Museum & Greenfield Village.)

Henry Ford's Richmond Hill, Ga. Community House had greatly deteriorated by the time this photo was taken in 1972, and it looked little better when I last saw it in January 1995. The building is now being restored by new owners who are converting it into a mortuary.

Community House

"Funeral Home in Richmond Hill Is a Dream Come True" trumpets a March 22, 1995 headline in the *Richmond Hill-Bryan County News* (Ga.). The headline refers to the conversion of a Henry Ford-built Community House into a mortuary.

The 18-room structure was built in the 1930s for residents of Richmond Hill, the locale of a plantation on which Ford and his wife wintered in the 1930s and 1940s. The building and an accompanying four acres recently were bought by morticians Freddie and Ronnie Stewart, of Vidalia, Ga., from a family which had lived in the house for more than 20 years. During those years, the place's exterior visibly deteriorated, although the structure itself, according to Freddie Stewart, is "very sound. Good materials were used," he adds.

In the 1930s and 1940s the house, staffed by a resident hostess and a home economics teacher, served as a dormitory for girls attending a Ford-financed high school in Richmond Hill. The students cooked and served their own meals and learned table etiquette. Also, they were given dancing lessons in a large second-story ballroom. The ballroom will become a casket display area.

The new owners also plan to remove building walls to provide a 150-seat chapel and two "layout rooms." The back wing will be made into two apartments for staff members.

Thanks to Margaret Judy, of Richmond Hill, for forwarding the *News*' article.

Lab Founder Dies

Harry G. Ukkelberg, 88, an agricultural chemist and founder of the laboratory at Henry Ford's Richmond Hill, Ga. plantation, has died in Savannah.

Ukkelberg, born in Minnesota and a graduate of the University of Minnesota, was employed by Thomas Edison in Ft. Myers, Fla. where he met Ford in the early 1930s. Ford had a winter home next door to Edison's winter residence. After Edison's death, the automaker decided to winter in Georgia. His Richmond Hill mansion was under construction when Ukkelberg joined the plantation staff on July 1, 1936.

Ukkelberg's reminiscences, taped by the Ford Archives in the early 1950s, were furnished to the *Richmond Hill Area News* by Mrs. Mildred Hughes, Richmond Hill, Ga.

"Mr. Ford was interested in finding a new crop that could be grown in this section," Ukkelberg said in his memoir. "We received seed from various countries in the world through the Ford organization such as perilla and chia, both oil producing plants, which grew well.

"Another crop Ford was interested in was ramie. Ramie has a very strong bast fiber and was used by the Egyptians and others for many centuries. Ford said the fiber is stronger than steel which is doubtful. He told me to plant 200 acres. There was not enough planting material in North America to plant 200 acres. It grew fairly well, but was not a crop that would be a commercial business.

"Mr. Ford was interested in trying to make use of all waste materials such as sawdust, bark, and cull vegetables. Some of the projects he suggested included making fertilizer from sawdust, since sawdust has no fertilizer value there was no chance for success.

"He also asked us to make bricks from sawdust using various amounts of cement, but that was a failure too.

"In 1937, a laboratory was built for trying his various suggestions in which he had some equipment to make plastics. We made plastics from sawdust which was quite good. We also made from sawdust rayon from which a pair of socks was knitted.

"Among other things, we made flour from cull sweet potatoes which was sold in the [local] commissary. We also made alcohol from cull sweet potatoes which we used as fuel mixed with gasoline in a pickup truck. That may have been the first time alcohol had been used as a fuel in a motor vehicle. In 1940 the laboratory burned down, and that ended our laboratory experiments."

The plantation itself was sold to the Southern Kraft Timber Corp. in 1951, following the deaths of Henry Ford in 1947 and his wife, Clara, in 1950.

Ukkelberg served as a horticulturist for the Southeastern Tidewater Experiment Station in Fleming, Ga. from 1950-65.

Thanks to Jerry Lundy, Cincinnati, Ohio, for forwarding the *Richmond Hill Area News*'s article on Ukkelberg.

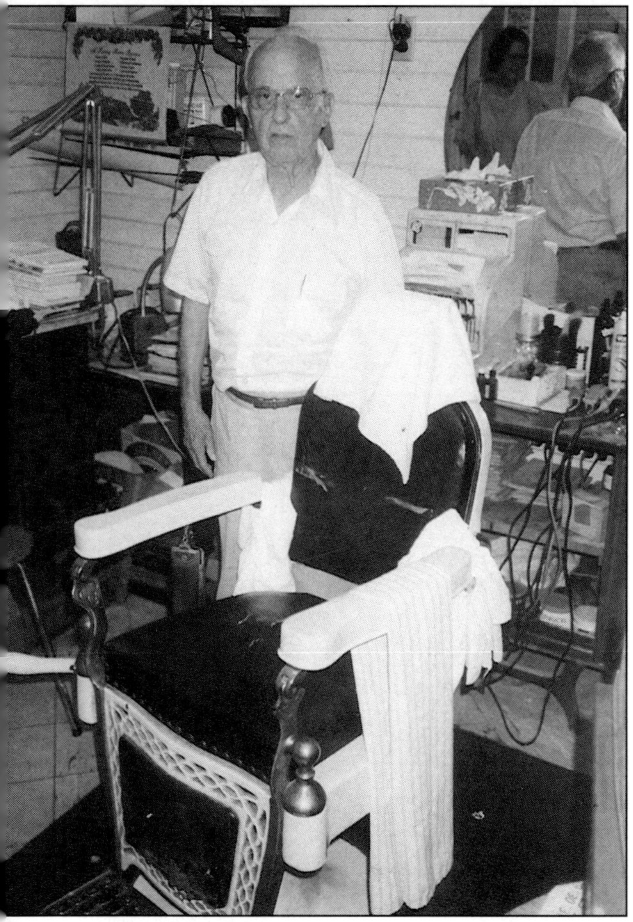

Ford's Barber

Bailey Carpenter, 86, stands beside the chair in which he barbered Henry Ford when the auto king visited his Richmond Hill, Ga. plantation in the 1930s and 1940s. Carpenter still cuts hair in a small shop behind his home. He told me in 1973 that his chair and the straight razor used to shave Ford were for sale at the "right price," and repeated the statement when this photo was taken in August 1997.

Ford As Humanitarian

"Is it true that Henry Ford, like Elvis Presley, often gave people things upon impulse?" asks reader Jocelyn Arnet, of Sheboygan, Wis.

Yes, although unlike Presley, who gave away Cadillacs, Ford provided Ford cars, jobs, and, above all, hope and help to the needy. The automaker's sister, Margaret Ruddiman, wrote eloquently of such gifts in an article "Memories of My Brother Henry Ford" in the September 1953 issue of *Michigan History*.

[My brother], she writes, "was warm-hearted, sentimental, and generous. There are many people living in the areas where he was active who will vouch for the fact that when life seemed darkest for them and when their burdens seemed too much to bear, he was the then unknown benefactor who provided them with a job, or a home, or the best of hospital and medical care if necessary to set them on their feet so that they might again stand alone as self-reliant citizens ... It was the type of good neighborliness we had learned as children ...

"A crippled child, even though a perfect stranger, always interested Henry," Mrs. Ruddiman added. "Seeing such a child on the street, he frequently would give orders to one of his men to locate the child's home and provide the necessary medical treatments to repair the crippled body. Those of his personal staff can tell many stories of this spontaneous outpouring of his generous spirit."

Much evidence corroborates Mrs. Ruddiman's remarks. Ford's spontaneous generosity was one of the most attractive sides of the multifaceted industrialist.

Helping Hand

Henry Ford's fondness for children was revealed in his numerous late 1930s-early 1940s visits to a Big Bay, Mich. children's camp, Bay Cliff, which accommodated 200 children. Ford and his wife, Clara, summered in the nearby Huron Mountain Club.

"He loved to talk to the children and would play the mouth organ or Jew's harp for them," states C. Fred Rydholm in his 1989 book, *Superior Heartland: A Backwoods History*.

The camp's director, Miss Morse, invariably presented Ford with a list of children who needed medical attention. On one occasion Ford was informed of 10 children who needed their tonsils removed.

"Send them to Ford Hospital [in Detroit almost 500 miles away] and have it done," the magnate replied.

"Well, they can't go alone," Morse answered. "How will they get there?"

"Or have it done here and send me the bill, if that is easier," Ford answered.

On another occasion Morse introduced to Ford a little girl in a wheelchair. When the rickets-stricken girl stood with the aid of crutches, her legs were revealed as terribly bowed.

"Send her to Ford Hospital and have her stay there 'til she's cured," Ford directed.

"But she can't go down to Detroit alone and be away from her family that long," the magnate was told.

"Send her mother with her or whoever needs to go ... we'll take care of it," was the response.

Rydholm, who listened to such conversations, thought to himself, "We aren't going to see Mr. Ford around here anymore .... But he didn't seem to mind," and the industrialist's visits and largesse continued.

Ford Aid Pays Off

A *Detroit Free Press* story on the Herrick family of Tecumseh, Mich. recalls Henry Ford's assistance to the founder of the family fortune, Ray Herrick.

Herrick, after starting a machine and tool company in Hillsdale, Mich., in 1934 at Ford's suggestion moved the firm to Tecumseh, renaming it Tecumseh Products. The following year, the auto magnate, upon hearing that the enterprise needed financial assistance, provided a $60,000 line of credit.

Making the most of its Ford connection, the company, which produces refrigeration units and small engines, raised its sales to $1 million within two years. Herrick, at his death in 1973, left an estate of more than $16 million. His firm, still controlled by his family, now has annual sales in excess of $1 billion.

Paternalism

Being a Good Samaritan did not pay off for Henry Ford, suggests reader Robert Tonnies, Cincinnati, who explains as follows:

"The winter of 1916-17 was one of the coldest ever recorded in the Ohio Valley. The Ohio River froze over from bank to bank crushing hundreds of steamboats and ending the passenger steamboat era on the Ohio for good .... Unfortunately, virtually all of the coal was brought to Cincinnati on river barges. Almost every house in the city was heated with coal, and it did not take long for a coal shortage to develop.

"Henry Ford, hearing of the plight of the city, diverted a trainload of coal en route to his Detroit factories to Cincinnati and had five tons of coal delivered free of charge to the homes of all of his employees. Henry Ford was virtually a father to his employees in those days. He was always interested in improving their lives such as when he instituted the $5 daily wage. I think the reason he fought unions so fiercely later in his life was because he felt betrayed by the employees that he had taken such good care earlier on."

Camp Legion

"We liked each other," recalls Professor Charles M. Westie of Henry Ford, whom Westie met in 1938 while attending the magnate's Camp Legion. The Dearborn farm camp was established to assist underprivileged boys, most of them sons of deceased or disabled veterans.

Henry Ford's Camp Legion as it looked before, during, and after World War II. The buildings were located near Ford's present World Headquarters. Your commentator worked in one of the structures in 1952, the company's News Department being located therein. The buildings were razed a few years later. (Photo from the Collections of Henry Ford Museum and Greenfield Village.)

"The Great Depression was just winding down in 1938," Westie recently told the *Detroit Free Press*, "and I needed a job in order to get to college. I had graduated from Dearborn's Fordson High School in January, and was working for a drugstore for 35 cents an hour.

"One day, a fellow who had been in my Boy Scout troop asked me if my father was a veteran. When I said, 'Yes,' he told me to get my father's discharge papers and see our scoutmaster. In a few weeks, I was sitting in a barn at Greenfield and Ford roads cutting seed potatoes, making sure there was at least one eye in each chunk of potato. It was a rainy and cold spring for the first 35 boys of Henry Ford's Camp Legion.

"Henry Ford believed that 'with one foot in the soil and one in industry, America will be safe.' He established a camp on the site of the original Ford farm acreage, roughly bounded by Greenfield, Southfield, Michigan and Ford roads. We lived in Army tents, first clearing the brush in the woods, then helping to build a mess hall, shower room, and a 'powerhouse' containing a couple of V-8 engines and a generator. Camp Legion grew from 35 young men to 100.

"One day as I was trying to cut a two-by-four, Mr. Ford came along. We had been told that if we encountered the Old Man we were to let him speak first and always call him Mr. Ford.

"I was not doing very well, despite a class in manual training. 'Having trouble, son?' he asked.

" 'Yes Mr. Ford. I need a crosscut saw, and this is a ripsaw.'

"He reached for the saw and examined the teeth. He then put his left knee on the board and sawed through it in five or six strokes. I was awestruck to see this 75-year-old man do what I could not do. He said to me, 'You were chopping the board. A saw is not a hatchet; you have to use the entire length of the saw.' I mumbled, 'Thank you, Mr. Ford.' As the Old Man turned away, he called back, 'So long, Ripsaw.'

"Mr. Ford would join us for breakfast in the mess hall occasionally. He would praise Dr. George Washington Carver, who developed uses for the soybean, including small parts for Ford cars made of soybean plastic. At Camp Legion, we had soybean pancakes, soybean milk, soybean patties, and soybean bread. We even had soybean ice cream on occasion. This was not our favorite fare, but we were young men who worked quite hard and would eat anything.

"Wherever Mr. Ford was, there was Harry Bennett. On one occasion, the Old Man climbed over the wall of Fair Lane, his home about two miles away, and gleefully told us Harry did not know where he was. Soon after a frantic phone call, three black V-8s went barreling along the dusty lane in a hurried search.

"Another time, some photographers were trying to line us up for a picture-taking session. Finally Mr. Ford hollered out, 'Harry you are always telling other people what to do; you line them up!' Like a drill sergeant, Bennett got us all in rows in front of our tents.

"Now that I am approaching the age of the Old Man," concludes Westie, "and having been a professor of sociology for some 30 years, I am aware that some of Henry Ford's statements reflected narrow views. But, as a young man, I felt that he and I were somehow friends. As I look back 50 years, he is a significant part of my Michigan memories."

Thanks to Mike Skinner of Dearborn, for forwarding the *Free Press* article in which Westie's reminiscences were published.

Ford Kept Family Alive

Tom Nemet, a former chairman of the American International Automobile Dealers Assn., says that Henry Ford kept his family alive in Nazi-controlled Romania during World War II.

Before the war, Nemet's father, a Jew, worked for Ford. Although the senior Nemet was interned by the Germans, his family was kept alive by Henry Ford – details are not provided – while other Jews in his neighborhood disappeared never to be seen again. They say Henry Ford was an anti-Semite, Nemet says, "but I wouldn't be here today if it hadn't been for him."

Nemet adds that Ford set up his father with a dealership less than a week after the family returned to New York after the war.

Thanks to reader William S. Synder, of Orange, Calif., for forwarding *Automotive News*' story on Nemet.

Top Personality

"Rummaging through my souvenirs I recently found a 1976 Associated Press story which rated "Henry Ford, the Model T, and the rise of the automobile" as the 10th top story of two centuries of U.S. history," writes reader Clements Wilson, Fresno, Calif. "The ratings were based on an AP poll of newspaper editors and radio and television news directors."

"What hit me," Wilson continues, is that Henry Ford's name is one of only seven personalities included among the top 20 choices. The others whose names are mentioned are No. 8, "Watergate scandal and the resignation of President Richard M. Nixon," No. 11, "Assassination of President Abraham Lincoln," No. 12, "Assassination of President John F. Kennedy," No. 14, "Thomas Edison and the electrification of the nation," No. 16, "Franklin Roosevelt's New Deal, and No. 18, "The Wright brothers and the growth of aviation."

"Ford and the Model T are the leading symbols of the auto age," Wilson continues, so it seems fitting that they should be mentioned by name."

Other top stories are: No. 1, "American Revolution," No. 2, "Drafting of the Constitution," No.3, "Civil War," No. 4, "World War II," No. 5, "American moon landings," No. 6, "Development of the atomic bomb," No. 7, "1929 crash and ensuing Great Depression," No. 9, "World War I," No. 12, "Development of television," No. 15, "Vietnam," No. 19, "Louisiana Purchase," and No. 10, "Supreme Court decision outlawing segregation."

Other stories receiving a considerable number of votes included the establishment of judicial review of the Constitution by the Supreme Court under Chief Justice John Marshall, the waves of immigration into the United States in the 19th and early 20th centuries, the continuing agricultural revolution beginning with Eli Whitney's cotton gin, John Deere's plow, and Cyrus H. McCormick's reaper, the development of the computer, and the emergence of the U.S. as a world power.

The development of the computer and/or electronics might be ranked more highly in a 1999 survey. Henry Ford, the Model T, and the rise of the automobile could be expected to maintain their ranking.

The Model T is the only car mentioned in the survey. In your commentator's view, it is the "Car of the Century."

Time's Covers

Time covers are "the mirror of a remarkable century," the magazine states. "Here are the great individuals: Einstein and Churchill, Truman and Mandela, Picasso and Freud and Ford."

Henry Ford has appeared on *Time*'s cover five times, Lee Iacocca four times, Henry Ford II thrice, and his brothers, Benson and William Clay, once each

(the brothers were shown together on May 18, 1993, a month before the Ford Company's 50th anniversary observance). Walter P. Chrysler and GM President/CEO Harlow H. Curtice each made the cover three times, GM's Alfred P. Sloan Jr. and William S. Knudsen, twice each.

Henry Ford was on the cover on July 27, 1925, Jan. 14, 1935, March 17, 1941, March 23, 1942 and Dec. 7, 1998. Slated to have been named *Time*'s "Man of the Year" in 1941, he was sidetracked after America's entry into World War II focused attention on President Franklin D. Roosevelt.

Iacocca made the cover on April 17, 1964 in conjunction with the Mustang's introduction, and also on Sept. 8, 1980, March 31, 1983, and April 1, 1985. Henry Ford II was the cover subject on February 4, 1946, May 18, 1953, and July 20, 1970.

Chrysler was depicted on April 20, 1925, Jan. 7, 1929, and Jan. 8, 1934, Curtice on Nov. 1, 1954, Jan. 1, 1956, and May 12, 1958. Sloan was shown on Dec. 27, 1926, and Sept. 24, 1945; Knudsen, Jan. 18, 1937 and Oct. 7, 1940; GM Chairman Fred Donner, May 18, 1962; GM scientist Charles F. Kettering, Jan. 9, 1933; and ex-GM executive John De Lorean, Nov. 1, 1982. AMC Chairman George Romney made four covers, thrice as Michigan's governor.

As a member of GM's Public Relations Staff, I was among those assigned to come up with "warm, human anecdotes" for *Time*'s coverage of Donner. We could think of none. Moreover, the cover sketch made it appear as if Donner was smelling something regrettable.

Heroic Henry

Henry Ford is one of 11 persons cited as a "hero worthy of lasting appreciation" by *Detroit Free Press* columnist Judd Arnett.

"Today's heroes," says Arnett, are largely designated by the media, which "must have a new one every whipstitch in order to keep the presses rolling, the cameras clicking, the box offices jingling. In rapid succession we have been presented with athletes, TV personalities, authors overflowing with four-letter words and visions of sex, politicians with pretty faces and empty noggins."

In addition to Ford, Arnett names as authentic heroes Jesus Christ, Presidents Theodore and Franklin D. Roosevelt, Eisenhower, Truman, and Reagan, Adlai Stevenson, Charles Lindbergh, Albert Einstein, and Bobby Jones.

"Henry Ford, the original," says Arnett, "was a hero up until he got rich and about 50 years old and fell in with some evil influences. Then he became a national pain in the posterior. But during his early years, when he was struggling with the great notion of putting the nation on wheels by perfecting mass production, he did more to change America, to get it out of the mud and the prairie dumbness that had dominated it, than any other force of his tenure.

"Ford had the idea that the combustion engine should work to the advantage of the average citizen, whereas the steam engine had benefited mostly the wealthy. That concept revolutionized the Republic and caused the industrialized world to follow suit. Given today's technology, Ford would be driving the Japanese bonkers, instead of vice versa."

I would argue that Ford was heroic until 57 years of age in 1920, when he launched his misguided campaign of anti-Semitism, and that he retained heroic qualities in diminishing degree for almost as long as he lived. Getting rich had nothing to do with the lessening of his heroism. Falling in with some evil influences did, but Ford was too much his own man to be led down paths that he hadn't already started upon.

Ford Cult Celebrity?

"Was Henry Ford ever 'sighted' after his death, as Elvis Presley and Amelia Earhart have been?" asks Barbara Malnak, Kansas City, Mo.

Insofar as I know, American popular culture never bestowed on Ford that rarest of accolades. Perhaps it is because an estimated 100,000 people trooped past the auto king's well-photographed bier. Also, an estimated 30,000 people milled around the cathedral at which his funeral services were held and more than 20,000 persons gathered around the cemetery in which he was buried. Elvis and another "sightee," 1950s actor James Dean, also had highly-publicized funerals. Conversely, some other "sightees," including Earhart, John Wilkes Booth, confederate raider William Clark Quantrill, and Adolf Hitler, all died in obscure and/or controversial circumstances.

Most Influential

Henry Ford's greatness may be measured by a *Life* magazine list of the 100 most influential Americans of the 20th century. Ford was one of only three people unanimously named to the list by the more than 60 historians and other authorities consulted by *Life*.

Orville and Wilbur Wright were the other unanimous choices. The only other automotive figure named to the list was Alfred P. Sloan Jr.

"It's a list of the most influential people of the past 100 years," says Mary Steinbauer, editor of the special issue. "In making our selection we looked at how our lives would be different if each of our honorees didn't live."

Henry One Of Greatest

Time's editorial staff named Henry Ford one of the 20th Century's 10 greatest people in its Fall 1992 special issue, "The Millennium."

Ford was ranked second on the list, headed by Sigmund Freud. Others named, in order of listing, are Mohandas "Mahatma" Gandhi, Sir Winston Churchill, Pablo Picasso, Pope John XXIII, Franklin D. Roosevelt, Margaret Sanger, Mother Teresa, and Martin Luther King Jr.

The issue also presents the 10 most famous quotes of the millennium. Henry's "History is more or less bunk," isn't on the list, but presumably was considered, along with "The public can have any color of car it wants, so long as it's black."

Technological breakthroughs also were cited; among them were mass-produced Model T Fords; Lindbergh's solo flight across the Atlantic; the atom bomb; and moon landings. Henry is pictured standing beside a flivver.

In addition, the magazine carries a feature entitled, "1,000 Years at a Glance," which lists "the events, inventions and political movements, the conflicts, heroes and villains, that shaped our world during the past millennium." Ford's moving assembly line/mass production methods aren't cited, nor is the Model T or the $5 day, all likely candidates in your commentator's ever humble opinion. Instead, in the years framing Ford's greatest achievements, the list includes "1907 Picasso and Braque create Cubism" and "1914 World War I follows the assassination of Austrian Archduke Ferdinand" – the former scarcely in the same league as Ford's exploits, the latter very much so.

20th Century Shapers

Henry Ford, among many others, has been nominated for *Time* magazine's "Man or Woman of the Twentieth Century."

The magazine is asking the public to suggest candidates. Slotted into five categories, the list of nominees already includes the following broken into five categories:

Builders and Titans: Thomas Edison, Henry Ford, Steve Jobs, and Bill Gates.

Warriors and Statesmen: Franklin D. Roosevelt, Ronald Reagan, Mahatma Gandhi.

Scientists and Healers: Wilbur and Orville Wright, Albert Einstein, Jonas Salk.

One Of Century's Greatest

Henry Ford was among those depicted in a 1993 television documentary on the 20th century's greatest figures. The program was prepared and presented by Clive Jones, a prominent British TV personality.

Ford, shown strolling the garden of his estate, Fair Lane, was described as a "genius" and as the "Lenin of the West" in tribute to his popularity with the masses. "He put his name on the century like no one else," Jones declared. "Ford Motor Company," he added, "was the new America."

Ford also was shown chopping trees while camping with Thomas Edison, Harvey Firestone and other friends, and while speaking on radio in support of President Hoover" 1932 re-election bid. The speech was wooden, prompting Jones to remark that Ford's voice from the 19th century and his personality did not have to match his achievements.

Ford's anti-Semitism also was mentioned.

Henry Ford Among Top 100

Henry Ford is ranked as the 91st most influential person in history in the revised 1992 edition of Dr. Michael H. Hart's book, *The 100: A Ranking of the Most Influential Persons*, reprinted in 1996 by the Carol Publishing Group, Secaucus, N.J. Initially published in 1978, the book's first edition sold 60,000 copies.

A scientist with a Ph.D. in astronomy from Princeton University, Dr. Hart notes that he has designated the most influential persons, not the greatest. The selectees, he adds, "had the greatest affect on history and on the course of the world" ... (and) are based on the "total amount of influence that each of them had in human history and on the everyday lives of other human beings."

In the book's first edition, Ford was not named to the top 100 list, rather was cited in an "honorable mention" category. He was one of three persons promoted to the second edition's 100 list, and in its preface Dr. Hart explains why:

"Many readers wrote in, claiming that I had underestimated (Ford's) importance, and presented reasons why he should have been included in the first one hundred. On reconsidering the matter, I have concluded that the critics were right, and I have altered this edition accordingly.

"One must not infer," Dr. Hart continues, "that the revised edition is simply the result of a poll. It was not the number of objective letters which caused me to change my mind about Ford – indeed, I received more objections on some other points – but the soundness of the reasoning in those letters."

Along with Ford, Mikhail Gorbachev and Ernest Rutherford were added to the second edition's 100. To make room for them, Niels Bohr, Pablo Picasso, and Antoine Henri Becquerel were demoted to honorable mention status.

The second edition's rankings, one through 30, are Muhammad, Isaac Newton, Jesus Christ, Buddha, Confucius, St. Paul, Ta'ai Lun, Johannes Gutenberg, Christopher Columbus, Albert Einstein, Louis Pasteur, Galileo Galilei, Aristotle, Euclid, Moses, Charles Darwin, Shih Huang Ti, Augustus Caesar, Nicolaus Copernicus, Antoine Laurent, Lavoisier, Constantine the Great, James Watt, Michael Faraday, Karl Marx, Wilbur and Orville Wright, James Clerk Maxwell, Martin Luther, George Washington, Genghis Kahn, Adam Smith, Edward de Vere (Shakespeare), and John Dalton ...

Ford, the only industrialist named to the list of 100, ranked ahead of Queen Elizabeth I, 94; Mikhail Gorbachev, 97; Charlemagne, 98; and Homer, 99.

The honorable mention list includes some notable figures such as Winston Churchill, Marie Curie, Gottlieb Daimler, Benjamin Franklin, Gandhi, Martin Luther King Jr., Lenoir, Abraham Lincoln, Samuel F.B. Morse, Mozart, Marco Polo, Franklin D. Roosevelt, Socrates, Sun Yat-sen, Harry Truman, and Frank Lloyd Wright.

The top 100 list includes three persons who lived before 600 B.C.; 13 between 600 and 201 B.C.; 16 between 200 B.C. and 1400 A.D.; four in the 15th century; nine each in the 16th and 17th centuries; 12 in the 19th century; 18 in the 19th century; and 16 in the 20th century, Ford being rated this century's 16th most influential person.

Of the 100, 36 were scientists and inventors, 31 politicians and military leaders, 14 secular philosophers, 11 religious leaders, five artistic and literary figures, two explorers, plus Ford.

The five-page chapter on Ford emphasizes his contributions relative to mass production, wage-price theories and practices, and the Model T. It was noted that he was "eager to publicize (his mass production methods) – resulting in a tremendous increase in productivity throughout the world."

Famous Michiganians

Henry Ford is one of 11 Michiganians listed in the famous people section of the *World Almanac.* Others are George Custer, Paul de Kruif, Thomas Dewey, Edna Ferber, Edgar A. Guest, Betty Hutton, Robert Ingersoll, Will Kellogg, Danny Thomas, and Stewart Edward White.

Movers and Shakers

Henry Ford is cited as one of the "movers & shakers" who have written articles for or been discussed in *Popular Science*, the magazine reported when celebrating 125 years of publication in January 1997.

Other major figures named by the magazine are Alexander Graham Bell, Jacques Cousteau, Madame Curie, Charles Darwin, George Eastman, Thomas A. Edison, Albert Einstein, Bill Gates, Stephen W. Hawking, and Orville Wright. Lesser persons cited were Sylvia Earle, Guglielmo Marconi, Nikola Tesla, Heinrich Hertz, Burt Rutan, Igor Sikorsky, and Buckminster Fuller.

Ford wrote in *Popular Science* about one of his favorite topics, "pastoral living." His July 1922 article was forwarded by Dr. Peter Weber, Olney, Ill., assisted by the Olney Public Library and Shawnee Library System.

Ford proposed the establishment of "agricultural-industrial villages ... wherever hydroelectric power is available and the land tillable." Residents were to devote a few weeks in the spring and fall to agrarian pursuits and the remainder of the year to industrial work.

Increased use of tractors and power machinery, Ford believed, would improve people's health and provide more happiness and prosperity than ever before.

Some of Ford's thoughts were practical, others utopian, if not incredible.

"Suppose, for the sake of argument," he said, "we should actually exhaust our oil resources, exhaust even our vast shale deposits. What then? ... When we have need of alcohol for fuel purposes, it will be produced commercially in sufficient quantity to meet all requirements. There is enough alcohol in an acre of Michigan potatoes to plow the acre of ground that raises them for a hundred years!"

One wonders if Henry and his ghostwriter imbibed some potato juice before making this assertion.

Technology Innovators

Henry Ford is listed among America's "technology innovators" in a May 1997 *Scientific American* editorial by Editor-in-Chief John Rennie.

Others cited included Benjamin Franklin, Thomas Jefferson, Thomas A. Edison, Alexander Graham Bell, George Washington Carver, Eli Whitney, Orville and Wilbur Wright, Robert Fulton, Buckminster Fuller, Charles Goodyear, Samuel F.B. Morse, Elias Howe, George Eastman, Elmer Ambrose Sperry, Charles A. Lindbergh, Edwin H. Land, Grace Murray Hopper, Jack Kilby, Robert Noyce, Jonas Salk, Robert H. Goddard and Vannevar Bush.

"The country," Rennie notes, "could barely have survived, let alone flourished, without their genius."

Thanks to Dr. Peter C. Weber, Olney, Ill., for forwarding Rennie's editorial. An avid reader of scientific and medical journals, Dr. Weber over the years has sent along many Ford-related articles which otherwise would have been overlooked by this column.

Ford And Technology

Henry Ford's importance in U.S. technology may be measured by counting the number of index references to the auto king in Alan I. Marcus' and Howard P. Segal's excellent 380-page 1989 paperback, *Technology in America: A Brief History*.

Ford has 13 references, second only to Thomas Edison's 20. George Westinghouse has nine references; Cyrus H. McCormick and Alexander Graham Bell seven; Oliver Evans and Samuel F.B. Morse six. Thomas Jefferson, Robert Fulton, Isaac Singer, Henry A. Wallace, and William J. Hale (chemurgy) are referred to four times; Benjamin Franklin, John Fitch, George Eastman, the Wright Brothers, and Hiram Maxim, and Alfred P. Sloan Jr.

three; Eli Whitney and Frederick W. Taylor two; and Charles F. Kettering once.

Among industries, agriculture rates 58 index mentions, electricity 43, mills 38, weapons 29, textiles and automobiles 28, spaceflight 22, radio 19, iron 18, and aircraft and computers 16.

Ford is discussed in the context of chemurgy, Eagle boats, industrial sociology, "systematic techniques" including the moving assembly line, and his village industries.

Great Man Theory

The Great Man Theory has long fascinated those seeking to define the elusive quality of leadership. The theory contends that leaders are born not made, and that luck and fate play an important role in bringing out leadership qualities.

Proponents of the Great Man Theory, according to Prof. David L. Cawthon, writing in the May/June 1996 issue of *Business Horizons*, "point to Lee Iacocca, John F. Kennedy, Martin Luther King Jr., and Douglas MacArthur as examples of great men whose innate abilities are connected with situational forces."

Without Hitler, so the theory goes, Churchill would not have achieved greatness; without racial tension in the U.S., Martin Luther King Jr. would not have gained his stature.

At age 40 Henry Ford seemed an unlikely leader. Indeed, he had made two false starts as an auto manufacturer before founding the Ford Motor Company in 1903. But within a decade he had acquired wealth, become the auto industry's dominant figure, and gained a measure of national prominence. In 1914, at age 50, he became an overnight international celebrity by more than doubling the wages of most of his workers. During the teens he also acquired full ownership of his firm, and since that decade has generally been recognized as the auto industry's leading figure.

Was Ford a *born* leader? Who can say? If so, it was not revealed during the first four decades of his life. But then fate, destiny, or providence, call it what one will, came into play. The timing of Ford's entry into auto making and the introduction of his Model T were perfectly timed. Also, by chance, he was teamed with a business manager, James Couzens, who contributed as much as Ford himself to their firm's early success.

Many others launched auto companies and cars at the same time as Ford. But none assembled such a strong management team, none so inspired people to do their best, plus things that others said could not be done, and none had Ford's phenomenal success. In the end the Dearbornite proved himself a remarkable catalyst/leader. That is why he remained neither a farmer, mechanic, nor powerhouse engineer, rather became one of the century's greatest movers and shakers.

Genius/Crackpot

Henry Ford was "the original model for what has since become a familiar American character type: the multimillionaire as both genius and crackpot," states the 1997 book, *Creating Modern Capitalism*, edited by Thomas K. McCraw.

GM's Alfred P. Sloan Jr. is described as the "prototypical organization man: calculating but never callous, and supremely effective as a business manager.

I think of Ford as a genius/ignoramus, rather than as a genius/crackpot. Sloan was the administrator I'd wish to have in charge of my business were I to take a yearlong cruise. He could be callous, however. In late 1945, he spurned ex-GM President William S. "Big Bill" Knudsen when the latter sought to rejoin GM following wartime service as the nation's production chief. In addition, he rebuked Knudsen for having resigned GM's presidency to accept a $1 a year job with the government, an offer which Knudsen, a Danish immigrant, did not believe he could not honorably refuse. Sloan's rejection, Knudsen's daughter told me, broke her father's heart.

Ford's Image

Henry Ford's public image is discussed in two business books of the 1980s, Jonathan Hughes' *The Vital Few: The Entrepreneur and American Economic Progress* (New York: Oxford University Press, 1986), and Jeffrey Sonnenfeld's *The Hero's Farewell: What Happens When CEO's Retire?* (New York: Oxford University Press, 1988).

"The growth of the Ford 'image,' " Hughes observes, "is in itself one of the prodigies of American communications history. The singular thing about Ford's self-apotheosis is that a great many believed it all and Ford achieved a fame and esteem nearer to Lincoln's than Edison's. In Ford's prime, in the early 1920s, he must have been more widely known than any other American."

Sonnenfeld, in describing Ford as "an authentic folk hero," describes the magnate's image as "that of an appealing popular folk hero and a ruthless tyrant whose imagination and record of accomplishment became symbolic of the American dream of unbounded opportunity. Ford's rise from humble origins, his effective self-promotion, his entrepreneurial genius, and his sweeping social visions catapulted him into heroic status."

Hughes is correct with respect to Ford's visibility during the 1920s. During that decade the industrialist received more publicity than any other American except President Calvin Coolidge. Today little is remembered about Coolidge's administration whereas most people continue to associate Ford with much around them, e.g., a motorized society, mass production, and a fourth of America's cars and trucks.

School Of Hard Knocks

Film dialogue of 1930s films often referred to Henry Ford, then one of the country's richest and best known figures.

The most recent such movie I've seen is *Hold That Coed*, a campus spoof starring John Barrymore, George Murphy, Joan Davis, and Jack Haley. Barrymore played a state governor who was disinterested in financing higher education. "Henry Ford never went to college," he bellowed to his aides. "Neither did Thomas Edison, and, come to think of it, neither did I."

Time was when many self-made men prided themselves on not being college-bred. Their knowledge, they said, didn't come from any "kollege" – it came from the School of Hard Knocks. Henry Ford was indeed a graduate of the latter school.

Ford The Greatest

"I recently ran across a reference to a 1971 book, *Economics and Capitalism*, in which you authored a chapter on Henry Ford being the greatest businessman in American history," writes University of Minnesota's Prof. Scott Helmsley. "How do you justify your assessment, if I may ask?"

The assessment was based on a survey of 423 business people attending executive development seminars at the University of Michigan in 1967-68. By a wide margin Ford was ranked as America's greatest businessman, followed by Andrew Carnegie, Thomas A. Edison, John D. Rockefeller, Alfred P. Sloan Jr., Bernard M. Baruch, Alexander Graham Bell, E.I. du Pont, Walter P. Chrysler, Harvey S. Firestone, George Eastman, Marshall Field, Walt Disney, J. Pierpont Morgan, Andrew W. Mellon, Thomas J. Watson Sr., Frank W. Woolworth, Cyrus H. McCormick, William Randolph Hearst, Sebastian S. Kresge, Richard W. Sears, Charles Goodyear, George Westinghouse, Eli Whitney, and Cornelius Vanderbilt.

Although most of these men belong on the list, some do not. This was to be expected since study participants' impressions and opinions – as well as their sure knowledge of entrepreneurs' achievements – were mirrored in the balloting. Businessmen who bequeathed consumer products and large companies bearing their names undoubtedly received more consideration than those whose legacies do not include self-named products or firms.

Edison and Westinghouse, for example, were great inventors, but not great businessmen. Edison looked upon business as an adjunct to invention. Westinghouse was a poor administrator; his electric firm went into receivership after the Panic of 1907. Disney was highly creative, but his brother Roy was the business brains of Walt Disney Productions. Sears was a great promoter, but his lack of administrative and financial ability almost drove the company to the wall during the mid-1880s.

Do I agree with Henry Ford's No. 1 ranking? Yes.

Most Interesting

Of all the people interviewed by *Detroit News* columnist Walter W. Fuller – and they included Presidents Hoover, Roosevelt, Truman, and Eisenhower, Admiral Nimitz, and William S. Knudsen – Henry Ford was deemed the most interesting.

Writing in 1963, Fuller recalled one of the half-dozen times he talked with Ford. The setting was a summer afternoon tour of Ford's outdoor museum, Greenfield Village. The guest of honor was the elderly Luren D. Dickinson, Michigan's governor in 1939-40.

As Ford's son, Edsel, showed the governor through the village, Ford lagged behind and joined step with Fuller, who was reporting on the tiny tour group.

"Mr. Ford was easy to talk with," Fuller recalled. "He was as spry as a young man that day, and once or twice referred to the governor, who was just four years his senior, as 'the old man.' ... He told me that he was in tiptop physical condition. His eyes shone as he told me he could beat me in a race 'any old day' – which wouldn't have been too difficult, I'm sure. He also told me that he rode a bicycle around his Dearborn estate everyday.

"We were leaning against a wooden railing built to keep visitors away from [Edison's laboratory] equipment. He patted the top of the railing, then looked at me. 'How high do you judge this railing to be?' he asked. I judged it at three feet. 'You're about right,' he said, 'and I can jump over it from where I stand, without touching it.'

"It appeared he was just about set to make the leap when Edsel and the group returned [from the other end of the laboratory]. Then, he softly said: 'I really can do it, but not now ... it might shock the old man.'

"Later we attended services at Martha-Mary Chapel [within the village]. Mr. Ford asked me to sit next to him in the first row balcony, from where we looked down on the youngsters who filled the main floor.

"A male organist was playing soft music. Mr. Ford leaned close to me, and whispered: 'Just by raising my hand I can get him to play my favorite number. Watch.'

"Soon the organist looked toward the balcony. Mr. Ford raised his right hand to his chin, and stuck up two fingers. At this the organist switched tunes and started playing 'I'll Take You Home Again, Kathleen.'

"Mr. Ford smiled broadly, appearing as happy as a kid with a new toy. 'See, what'd I tell you?' He chuckled, and so did I. A little later he bade me a warm good-bye."

Thanks to Mike Skinner, of St. Clair Shores, Mich., for forwarding Fuller's column.

Service, Not Greed

Greedy – and nongreedy – people were featured in an article in *USA Weekend.*

Ford Motor Company's founder was one of those singled out for nongreed. "Henry Ford didn't begin Ford Motor Company for greed," said publisher Malcolm Forbes, one of the nation's richest persons, who added that "the incidental part of Ford's ambition was wealth."

So true, as revealed in Ford's testimony during a 1916-17 lawsuit in which the auto king defended himself against the Dodge brothers. The Dodges insisted that Ford, as the Ford Company's major shareholder, agree to distribute company dividends to shareholders (including the Dodges) rather than use profits for plant expansion.

"What is the purpose of the company?" the Dodges' trial lawyer asked Ford at one point.

"To do as much as possible for everybody concerned," responded Ford, "to make money and use it, give employment, and send out the car where the people can use it ... and incidentally to make money .... Business is a service not a bonanza."

"Incidentally make money?" queried the attorney.

"Yes, sir."

"But your controlling feature ... is to employ a great army of men at high wages, to reduce the selling price of your car, so that a lot of people can buy it at a cheap price, and give everybody a car that wants one."

"If you give all that," replied Ford, who must have felt that the lawyer had admirably stated his policies, "the money will fall into your hands; you can't get out of it."

With a viewpoint like that, simply stated and honestly felt, is there any wonder that Ford was one of the most popular Americans of his day? And today, as we assess greed on Wall Street and other places, could we not use a few more Henry Fords?

Ford No. 1

Henry Ford's importance during the years between Sarajevo and the Great Crash is illustrated in J.C. Furnas' excellent 1974 book, *Great Times: An Informal Social History of the United States 1914-29*.

The book mentions Ford on 30 pages, William Jennings Bryan 25, Woodrow Wilson, William Randolph Hearst, and John Dos Passos 24, the Rev. Billy Sunday 23, Sigmund Freud 21, David Wark Griffith 18, Sinclair Lewis 16, Herbert Hoover and Walter Lippmann 12, and Calvin Coolidge eight.

As the author said, "One can no more keep Henry Ford from popping up constantly in this book than Dickens' Mr. Dick could keep Charles I's head from popping up in his."

Cutting a wide swath, Ford is discussed in contexts ranging from his campaigns against cigarettes and on behalf of pacifism to his five-dollar day and moving assembly line, plus his Model T, Model A, World War I record, anti-Semitism, Greenfield Village, and his exhibit at San Francisco's 1915 Pan-Pacific Exposition.

In addition to social histories, Ford also pops up in technological, economic, political and even military accounts of the period.

Ferrari, Not Ford

Enzo Ferrari, not Henry Ford, has been named Autocar Man of the Century by the British weekly magazine, *Autocar*, and the Morris Mini, not the Model T or Volkswagen beetle, has been named Autocar Car of the Century.

The magazine made its selections "after polling many in the industry as well as readers of the publication."

Setting Record Straight

Enzo Ferrari and the Morris Mini were named as the Autocar Man of the Century and Autocar Car of the Century, respectively, by Britain's *Autocar* magazine.

My 31-member University of Michigan Business School class, composed of 13 foreign students, questioned the selections and sent the following letter to the editor:

"May we venture the opinion that Henry Ford is the 20th century's greatest auto figure and that his Model T had a greater impact on the century than any other vehicle. If we were voting on this subject, we would be more inclined to think of Mr. Ferrari as one of the greatest motorsports figures, perhaps the greatest, and of the Mini as one of the most significant of vehicles.

The class also took issue with *Automotive Engineering*'s February 1996 ranking of "the top 10 significant events in the history of the automobile." Developed by the SAE's Fellows Committee, the list includes the following in order of rank:

"Automotive electronics, automatic transmission, pneumatic tire, electric self-starter motor, emission control systems, hydraulic brakes, safety restraint systems, fuel injection, air conditioning, and mass production."

The class wrote the editor that "mass production exceeds in significance any of the other events listed. Also, the list seems remarkably narrow inasmuch as it cites only engineering/manufacturing-related events. As important as these developments are, we believe that there are others outside the engineering/manufacturing sphere which have had an equal, if not greater influence on the auto, the auto industry, motorists and the nation itself. Among these developments are Henry Ford's wage/price policies and practices, the Model T, foreign competition, government regulation, the rise of the truck market, and the belated focus on quality and safety.

"It appears as if the fellows were wearing blinders when they were preparing their list," the class added. "May we suggest that the list would have been improved – and earned a higher grade than the B- we assigned it – if the fellows had been educated more liberally and otherwise expanded their horizons beyond the engineering profession. In the latter regard may we heartily recommend nonfiction books-on-tape for those fellows who have little spare time to sit with books, but are commuters or exercisers."

Overrated Americans

American Heritage asked select journalists, politicians, and historians to choose the single most overrated figure in all American history. Henry Ford was among those nominated.

Ford was selected by Bernard Weisberger, who noted that Ford, "despite popular misconceptions, did not invent the automobile, the assembly line, vertical integration, or mass ownership of cars."

True. But it was Ford who capitalized on the above "inventions" to far greater degree than anyone else, just as U.S. steel makers capitalized on European steel making advances and the Japanese have reaped the harvest of Western creativity.

The moral: Innovations are fine, but of what use are they to innovators unless they can exploit them satisfactorily?

Ford was in good company among *American Heritage*'s overrated figures. Others nominated were Benjamin Franklin, Patrick Henry, Thomas Jefferson, Woodrow Wilson, General George Armstrong Custer, and John F. Kennedy.

Henry Ford? Who's He?

Readers of this column may assume that Henry Ford's name remains a household term everywhere.

Not so in France, according to sportswriter Joe Falls of the *Detroit News*, who recently asked a literate 20-year-old Frenchwoman to identify Ford and 24 other prominent North

American people and well-known names. The woman, a student of English, German, and tourism in Chambery, France, near the site of the Winter Olympics, said of Ford, "We see many Ford signs in our country, so I will say he was a politician."

Ford's closest friend, Thomas A. Edison, fared better; the woman said he "found electricity." She also correctly identified Mickey Mouse, Mike Tyson, Elvis Presley, Butch Cassidy and the Sundance Kid, Abraham Lincoln, Dwight D. Eisenhower, Elizabeth Taylor, Frank Sinatra, George Gershwin, Santa Claus, Marilyn Monroe, Lee Harvey Oswald, John F. Kennedy, the New York Yankees, and the Statue of Liberty.

Lee Iacocca was said to be "an Indian who fights for the rights of his people." Other misidentified or unknown included Dan Quayle, Michael Jordan, Babe Ruth, Charles Lindbergh, Donald Trump, Jonas Salk, and the Montreal Canadiens."

Sprinkler Pioneer

The automatic lawn sprinkler system you've installed, or still yearn for, may have been pioneered by Henry Ford. At the least, Ford installed one of the country's first residential sprinkler systems on the grounds of his Dearborn estate, Fair Lane.

Before the system was installed, Fair Lane's gardeners dragged hoses to water peonies and roses and grass close to the mansion, but neglected the outlying premises. Ford devised a system whereby water could be pumped from the River Rouge through a gargantuan matrix of underground steel pipes, and delivered through pop-up sprinkler heads to a sizable portion of the estate's 1,210 acres.

Fair Lane's system is being restored at a cost of $26,000.

Ford Homes

Henry Ford deserves more credit than he has received as a pioneer in production-line house construction.

In 1919, when Ford began to build 250 homes for workers in his Henry Ford & Son Tractor Plant, houses generally were built by a single construction crew. Ford-built houses employed a crew to dig basements with Fordson tractors, another to lay foundations, another to build outside frames, another to finish interiors, and still another to finish exteriors and to landscape.

The houses were built by Ford factory artisans. Still standing on Dearborn's Beech, Military, Edison, Gregory, and Francis streets, they comprise the Ford Homes Historic District.

The above information is from an article published by Joseph Oldenberg in the Spring 1980 issue of the *Dearborn Historian*. Thanks to reader Mike Skinner, St. Clair Shores, Mich., for forwarding it.

Brush With History

"When I attended high school in St. Paris, Ohio during the 1930s," the late Frank Knull, of West Liberty, Ohio, told a friend and reader Bernard R. DeRemer, "I spent a lot of time at Henry Ford's Detroit, Toledo & Ironton depot learning telegraph code.

"One day the door opened and who should walk in but Henry Ford. A billionaire in 1924, he had bought the DT&I; it was a toy for him. He had a '23 Ford Tudor equipped with flange wheels to run on railroad tracks – one of his favorite ways to travel.

"He was dressed in a conservative business suit – no flashy jewelry or other signs of ostentation. Addressing the station agent, he asked, 'Mr. Ginn, are you satisfied with the way things are going?'

" 'Oh yes, Mr. Ford,' Ginn replied.

"Ford examined the books carefully to assure himself that all was well. Noticing me, he said, 'Evidently that young chap is not satisfied because he is trying to improve himself. People should always try to achieve more!' "

"That chance meeting was so memorable," Knull added, "that it's almost as vivid today as it was nearly six decades ago."

Henry's Gift

Maurice LaVelle was a veteran Ford supervisor on the verge of retirement. Shortly before retiring, he was asked by Henry Ford to go for a drive. The men drove to a newly-constructed house, and Ford asked LaVelle how he liked it. LaVelle replied that it was a fine house, whereupon Ford gave it to him in appreciation of his many years of loyal service to the company.

This story was passed on by reader W.E. Mott, of Dallas, who got it from the son of H.W. Campbell, LaVelle's brother-in-law. Campbell had worked with Ford at Detroit's Edison Illuminating Company in the 1890s, later moving to Dallas for health reasons and opening a suburban Dallas Ford dealership.

Although Mott got the story thirdhand, it rings true, for Ford gave a number of houses, as well as many cars, to favored employees and friends. These homes occasionally are on the market, and often are advertised as houses built by Henry Ford and given to so-and-so. Such an association, one presumes, enhances their value.

Believe It Or Not

Many a story has been told about Henry Ford, some true, some not. Here's one told about him by his grandson, Henry Ford II, to a *Detroit News* columnist, Nickie McWhirter:

"Early in Ford Motor Co. history, it was not unusual for Henry Ford to appear among his workers up to his elbows in axle grease. On one such day, Ford was concerned about some mechanical problem in the design of his car, a problem said to have been licked by engineers at a competing car company. Oil smudged and reeking of gasoline, Ford set out unaccompanied and unannounced for the sales showroom of that competing company.

"He walked into the showroom floor looking 'somewhat destitute' and was ignored by the sales staff. His approaches were rebuffed. All the salesmen were seemingly very busy with paperwork or with a few well-dressed, presumably well-heeled, sales prospects.

"Finally a young man, perhaps not even a salesman at all, but some clerk, asked Ford if he had any questions about the cars. Ford had a million questions. The young man answered them as best he could.

"Ford wanted to see the engines, lay his hands on them, fiddle with this and that, do everything short of crawling under the cars on his back, wrenches in hand.

"Finally this disheveled-appearing stranger told the young man he would buy three of these cars. Ford reached into his grease-stained trousers, pulled out a roll of currency and began peeling off $100 bills.

"Of course, salesmen came running now. Ford waved them off. He'd do business with the 'young fella,' he said. 'And if you want a good job, young fella, come see me tomorrow. My name's Ford. Henry Ford.'

"Gasps all around.

"According to Henry II, his granddad sent drivers to pick up the cars within the hour and had all three cars broken down to parts on the Ford factory floor shortly thereafter.

"The Deuce said it was true."

Concern For People

Henry Ford's concern for people is spotlighted in Bruce Simpson's reminiscences, which appeared in a publication of the University of Michigan-Dearborn's Fair Lane Estate.

"As a boy I attended the Greenfield Village Schools, starting the initial class in 1929," recalls Simpson. "The following year we started having a short, nondenominational chapel service before each school day, held in the Martha-Mary Chapel. Mr. Henry Ford usually attended these chapel services, so we saw him almost every school day. Our chapel services usually consisted of a hymn or two, a popular song ('Home on the Range' was a favorite), the Lord's Prayer, a responsive reading from the Bible and a special number. The special number might be a vocal solo (Susan Alderdyce, Catherine Miller, and Margaret Voorhees were Mr. Ford's favorites), an instrumental solo, or a reading. And so it was at these chapel services that I played the violin on many occasions when Mr. Ford was present.

"One such occasion I'll never forget. After a service at which I played, Mr. Ford came up to me and said he had a suggestion about my violin playing. It had to do with the way I changed the direction of the bow. To make his point clear, he borrowed my violin and showed me just what he meant. (Actually, smooth bow changing is a rather sophisticated part of violin technique.) At any rate, I'm probably the only person in the world who had a 'violin lesson' from Mr. Henry Ford.

"And Mr. Ford was very supportive of my efforts on the violin. When I progressed to the point where I could appreciate a really good violin, Mr. Ford loaned me a beautiful Gagliano violin from his collection. I played this violin for four years, and it was a great inspiration for me. This violin is now on display in the Henry Ford Museum, and I still enjoy seeing it.

"Mr. Ford provided support and encouragement for all of us in many ways. The girls were given the opportunity to learn and work at weaving, silk making, pottery, secretarial skills, photography, and homemaking; the boys at woodworking, machine shop, foundry, glass blowing (I especially enjoyed this), auto mechanics (working on Model Ts), besides everybody being involved in music, sports of all types, and, oh yes, academics. When someone showed particular interest or a flair for something, he or she was given every opportunity to pursue it. I remember my sister Charlotte, who also attended the Village Schools, was especially interested in weaving and horseback riding. She still has some very fine fabric she wove in the Village and some ribbons for her riding skills.

"I never ceased to be amazed at the scope and diversity of Mr. Ford's interests and involvements. His mechanical genius was undoubtedly his greatest talent, but close behind in my mind was his interest in and concern for people. All people – great people and common people, including kids like us. He had many famous people among his friends – statesmen, industrialists, entertainers, musicians, and movie stars. His special friends were other pioneers like himself, people like Edison, Burbank, and George Washington Carver. I remember seeing many such people who would come to our chapel services with Mr. Ford.

"In spite of his great fame and fortune, Mr. Ford always impressed me as a very natural, even humble, person. He also enjoyed having a good time, whether square dancing or showing us a newly restored steam engine – he really enjoyed himself. And he enjoyed doing things for other people, which he did in many ways. Mr. Ford was, without a doubt, a truly great man, and he left the world a much better place than when he found it. I shall always be grateful for the opportunity I had of knowing him."

Ford Stories

"I am an avid reader of your 'Ford Country' column each month," writes Walter Geistner, of Livonia, Mich. "Recently my father loaned me several old issues of the *Detroit News*. One issue is a special edition of May 29, 1946 entitled, 'The Automotive Golden Jubilee.' I found several interesting articles concerning Henry Ford and the Ford Motor Company that I thought would make for some good reading material in your column."

Here is the first of the three stories:

"While Henry Ford and Harvey Firestone were watching qualifying trials for the 1932 Indianapolis 500-mile race they witnessed a near-accident on the southwest turn when Pete Kreis went into a spin. His car whirled a couple of times but remained upright and stayed on the track.

" 'Those damn Firestone tires,' remarked Kreis, who evidently hadn't caught the name of the tire maker as he was being introduced to him and Ford immediately after the mishap. 'Those plys split easier than a locust's back,' he added.

"While Ford was laughing heartily, Kreis was reminded that Firestone was present. Kreis stuck to his views and told Firestone what was wrong with the tires.

"For six months after that Firestone technicians worked on the construction of a racing tire that would stand the strain of the bricks on the Indianapolis track at high speed. The result is the tire that has been in use since."

Second story: "Back in 1933 a strike at the Briggs Manufacturing Co. was holding up production of bodies for the Ford Motor Company. A newsman asked the late Judge William F. Connolly, then general counsel for the Briggs company, if such delays, due to strikes, were covered in the Briggs contract with Ford. 'Contract?' Judge Connolly answered. 'We have no contract. We have been doing business with the Ford Motor Co. for 23 years without a scratch of a pen.' "

Third story: "One of the oldest automobile dealers in the country is William L. Hughson, of San Francisco, who has been selling Fords for 43 years. He reports he has sold 87,000 Fords. Hughson came to Detroit in January, 1903, and signed a dealer contract with Henry Ford almost six months before the Ford Motor Co. was incorporated. 'I had a check for $5,000 and I got six cars from Mr. Ford,' he explained.

"In San Francisco, Hughson put on a show for the people who lined the steep hills to watch the cars perform. But the spectators were skeptical and would not buy. Hughson then started a taxi service. Some months later the public changed its mind and the Fords began to sell.

"During the San Francisco earthquake and fire Hughson's place of business was destroyed. 'But I saved my automobiles,' he said, 'and we used them to place dynamite to blast fire lanes until the fire finally was under control.' "

Postscript: Harvey Firestone's company, bought by Japan's Bridgestone Tire, now is called Bridgestone-Firestone, and it seems only a matter of time until the "Firestone" will be dropped. Hughson, Ford's first dealer, remained a Ford agent until his death in 1969, and his store remained in business until 1979.

The first Henry Ford had many "handshake agreements." One backfired mightily, namely his 1938 deal with tractorman Harry Ferguson, whose $251,000,000 lawsuit against the Ford Company, Dearborn Motors, and the chief officers of both companies, was settled out of court for $9,250,000 in 1952. After Old Henry's retirement in 1945, all suppliers had written contracts with Ford Motor Company.

Brief Encounters

Brief encounters with Henry Ford were recounted by Greenfield Village guide Jerome S. Wilford in the February 28, 1988 issue of the *Detroit News*, recently uncovered in my files.

One of 18-year-old Wilford's duties in 1933 was writing a daily journal about the village's and Henry Ford Museum's visitors, craftsmen, and construction. The journal circulated among only a dozen people including Henry and Edsel Ford and the half-dozen other men who ran the Ford Company.

The writing assignment led to a variety of contacts with the auto magnate. On one occasion, Ford told

Wilford how to obtain lubricating oil for watches: put a handful of black walnut shells in a can of water atop a fence post, then let the sun's warmth gently extract a light fine oil from the shells.

"How did you think of that?" Wilford asked, expecting some privileged insight.

"Read about it. In a book," was the reply.

Wilford sometimes thought Ford was testing his character. Early in his reporting experience, the magnate picked up the youth in his car. "It was a wintry Saturday morning," Wilford recalled, "and, as on most weekends when his regular driver was off, he drove himself – often across lawns, commons, and fields. In no more than 15 or 20 minutes, he drove me around to three or four building projects, stopping at each to talk briefly about the building's history and how it was acquired. He also told me to get certain construction information at each site from the carpenters on Monday.

"At the last stop," Wilford continues, "the car bogged down in snow ... Spinning the wheel at top speed generated enough heat from friction to melt the snow and underlying ice ... and warmed up the topsoil as well. The result, as the car lurched forward, was mud all over a newly painted outbuilding, a condition that [Ford said] would 'give the workmen something to do.' ....

"Come Monday morning, I set out to talk to the carpenters. But Mr. Ford already had visited each of the designated projects and told the workmen that if I came around asking questions, they were not to tell me anything!

"As it turned out, simple observation, some puzzling over the prints, and bits of information from workers who told other workers what they thought I needed to know provided enough for a detailed report.

"Mr. Ford's reaction? He never told me."

Ford, it seems, wished to test Wilford's initiative and see whether he would follow instructions come what may. No doubt he was satisfied by the youngster's performance and believed that a worthwhile lesson, requiring no comment, had been learned.

Ford's "energy and enthusiasms," Wilford adds, "did not produce verbosity. Talk was spare. He was sometimes hesitant, shy; manner and idiom reflected his rural background. But his meaning – if not always his purpose – was usually quite clear and to the point."

Ford's Flower Girl

When Great Britain's King and Queen visited Windsor, Ontario, Canada in the 1930s, Henry Ford recited a poem to a five-year-old girl who gave him flowers on the occasion. Reader Verna Masura tells the story:

"My father, Avreh LaLonde, worked for Hiram Walker in Windsor. The train of the King and Queen made a brief stop next to the plant. Henry Ford was there to meet the royal couple and I was chosen, because my father worked at Hiram Walker, to be a flower girl and present flowers to him. I don't recall who gave flowers to the King and Queen. I was a dainty little thing and Mr. Ford, as he sat waiting, put me on his knee. He asked if I knew how to make a Ford car, and I replied, 'No.' Then he told me this little poem, which has always been treasured by me.

'A little gas, a little oil
A little spark, a little coil
A piece of tin and a 10-inch board
will make you a brand new Ford.'

"It is a pleasure to know," Ms. Masura adds, "that Mr. Ford, being such a busy man, had time for little ones and also knew how to handle them."

Quite true. Ford liked children as much as they liked him, and always found time for them.

Henry's Orders

Henry Ford expected his subordinates to obey orders, as noted by Bob Smith, who worked in the industrialist's soybean labs a half-century ago.

"One day Mr. Ford came into the Moir House Lab" (in Dearborn), Smith recently informed me. "He said he wanted to take some exercise in the woods. He told Rufus Wilson, his driver, to stay put until he got back.

"After Mr. Ford had been gone about 15 minutes, it started to rain. Wilson thought he better find Mr. Ford, and keep him from getting wet. Wilson jumped into his car, and went looking for Mr. Ford. He had to drive about half-a-mile around the end of a ditch in order to cross over to get into the woods.

"Just about the time Wilson left, Mr. Ford came back. Finding his car missing, he asked, 'Where's Wilson?' I told Mr. Ford that Wilson had gone looking for him because it had started to rain. He replied, 'I told Wilson to stay here until I got back,' and added, 'Napoleon used to shoot his generals when they didn't obey orders.'

"He then said, 'I'm going upstairs. Don't tell Wilson where I am.' So he went upstairs, where he had some beds, and I suppose, took a nap. Shortly afterwards, Wilson came back, and wanted to know if we'd seen the boss. Of course, we had been told not to tell Wilson anything so we said 'No.' He drove off, and said he'd come back later.

"Finally, after an hour, Mr. Ford came down, found Wilson, and told him, 'After this, when I give orders, obey them.' "

At least Rufus wasn't shot.

Fastball

Henry Ford was so sure of the strength of his car's windshield that he asked a Detroit Tigers pitcher, Art Herring, to see if he could throw a baseball through it. Herring's experiment is recalled in Richard Bak's 1991 book, *Ty Cobb Would Have Caught It: The Golden Age of Baseball.*

The book does not say whether Herring, who pitched for the Tigers between 1929 and 1933, threw against a Model A or a V-8. "I had a good fastball," he reminisced. "They clocked me at 94 miles an hour ... I could make the windshield crack, but I couldn't throw a ball through it. Henry Ford gave me a dime. Boy, I treasured that. Had it in a steamer trunk in my barn until it burned down a few years ago."

After leaving baseball, Herring worked as a carpenter. He was interviewed by Bak in his Gas City, Ind. mobile home.

Olds And Ford

"The time was in 1901 or 1902," writes reader/historian Charles E. Hulse, Flint, Mich. "The Olds Motor Works was booming and could not make enough of its little curved-dash cars.

"One day after the shift had ended R.E. Olds was alone in his office busy with paperwork. The night watchman stuck his head in and said, 'Mr. Olds, Henry Ford is out in the plant nosing around. Shall I boot him out?' R.E. grinned and said, 'No, let him look around. He can't hurt anything.' "

Hulse, who chatted with Olds several times, asked the auto pioneer if he recalled anything else about Ford. "He told me," states Hulse, "he had helped Ford out by giving him an Olds front axle, a set of Weston-Mott wire wheels, and some other minor parts. One can see that these parts were used by Ford in his 1902 tiller-steered model, which is in the Henry Ford Museum.

Henry Ford Admirer

The following essay, submitted by Mark R. Tuban, whose connection to Ford as an employee and dealer dates to 1913, and who now is president of Tuban Industrial Products Co., of Mountain View, Calif., speaks for itself:

"Perhaps once in a lifetime," writes

Tuban, "it happens to a Ford dealer or salesman that he sells 22 cars at one time. It happened to me this way.

"Before World War II one of the best combat groups of the United States Army Air Force was transferred from El Paso, Texas, to Moffett Field in Mountain View, Calif., where I had my Ford dealership. The group was under the command of Colonel Horace Kenyon, a fine leader concerned with the well-being of his pilots. Many of the pilots owned Chrysler Airflows, and they were having a great deal of trouble with them.

"When I learned about the trouble the Chrysler owners were having, I spoke to Colonel Kenyon during social hours at Moffett Field and to some of the owners. The pilots were interested in Lincoln Zephyrs, the hot car at that time. We talked about the situation – what to do with the high-priced used cars and about financing, different models and colors, insurance, etc.

"The aviators set up a committee to decide where, when, and how to buy Zephyrs. It was finally decided that the new cars should be picked up at the Lincoln plant in Detroit. The flyers assumed responsibility to pick up their cars there. They were to fly across the country on Army planes since the freight charge for delivery of a Lincoln car to San Francisco was then $300, and the hitchhiking would provide a substantial savings.

"I arrived in Detroit by bus a day early, and as the aviators came in I introduced the people on both sides of the transaction. Those who arrived on schedule took trips through the Ford plant. Some of the group straggled in because of bad weather, and the official delivery was postponed several days. (The Army did not fly at night at that time.) The attention and courtesies the military people received from Ford Motor Company made it obvious that someone higher up was taking an interest in the affair.

"Some members of the group had their own schedules, but they all liked to meet at the Lincoln plant for an excellent lunch. Henry Ford joined them on two occasions. Mr. Ford knew all about the transaction, and was warmly interested in talking with the pilots, whose homes were scattered throughout the United States.

"One day after lunch, Mr. Ford said he had a surprise for us, and ordered the waiter to bring in a bowl of Michigan cherries, a treat, he said, such as we had never experienced. After tasting the sour, wretched little specimens of that fruit, I, being somewhat aggressive, said that if I could get back to California before the cherry season was over, I would send him some Bing cherries which were many times larger and much sweeter.

"When I returned to the Santa Clara Valley, the season was almost over, but I had two five-pound boxes of cherries carefully packed and shipped by railway express to Fair Lane.

"In a few days I received a telephone call from Mr. Ford's secretary who thanked me for the cherries, and said that Mr. Ford had asked for me to ship to him two boxes of cherries every day during the annual season which lasts several weeks. He added that Mr. Ford would prefer that the cherries be riper.

"Thus started a period of my supplying Fair Lane with cherries. The outcome was that while the cherries cost about thirty cents a pound, the air express charge was over a dollar a pound – but who sent a bill to Henry Ford!

"When Mr. Ford died, I continued to send the cherries to Fair Lane. I am attaching a photocopy of a letter from Mrs. Ford."

The letter, in Mrs. Ford's handwriting, and on Fair Lane stationery, is dated June 16, and, although the year is not mentioned, it had to be written during one of the summers following Mr. Ford's death – 1948, 1949, or 1950. The letter reads as follows:

"Dear Mr. Tuban – A delicious box of cherries came this morning, and I know the office will thank you for them. I want to thank you myself. You have been so generous in past years, always sending them while Mr. Ford was here, and he enjoyed them so much. Very Sincerely, Clara Ford."

"I hope," states Tuban in his cover letter, "you will find my essay sufficient proof that Mr. and Mrs. Henry Ford were warm people, if you could get to them. Mr. Ford is generally considered as having been a difficult person to get along with, but I found that dealing with Mr. Ford was quite easy as long as one delivered on what was required. One of the things that has bothered me for many years is that Mr. Ford's reputation of being very cantankerous overshadowed his kindness, humaneness, and generosity."

Henry Comes To Town

Henry Ford's visit to Dillon, S.C. in 1939 was recently recalled by centenarian Gordon G. McLaurin, still "lawyering" in Dillon.

A town resident, Joe Cavell Davis, according to McLaurin, "was so taken with Ford's reputation that she sent him one of her cakes every year for his birthday. Ford finally invited the Davises to Detroit for a visit, and when the Davises in turn invited him to Dillon, he accepted, arriving in his private rail car."

The story smacks of truth. From the mid-1930s until the year of Ford's death in 1947, the auto king and his wife, Clara, annually traveled to and from their Georgia plantation in their private railroad car, and could easily have made a side trip to Dillon.

Thanks to reader William O. Barnes III, Frogmore, S.C., for forwarding the *Columbia* (S.C.) *State*'s article on McLaurin.

Chance Encounter With HF

A chance encounter with Henry Ford recently was recalled in the *Detroit Free Press* by Franklyn Maxey, a retired Berkley, Mich., teacher.

"One early summer evening in the 1930s," remembers Maxey, "Dad and I were returning from Detroit to our home in Northville. Dad turned the car from Plymouth Road onto Ann Arbor Trail. We stopped alongside a large cultivated field and waved at a farmer on a tractor. The farmer, who was wearing a straw hat, stopped, climbed down, and walked over to meet us at the fence. It was Mr. Henry Ford. The field was one of his first soybean adventures."

Ford delighted in waving to and chatting with people, and, of course, those on the receiving end have told and retold their tale all the years of their lives.

Bob Boyer Recalls Ford

An article on Henry Ford and soybeans prompted a June 6, 1973 letter from Robert A. Boyer, who headed the auto king's Soybean Extraction Laboratory from 1929-43. At the time I simply acknowledged and filed this interesting letter, but now let's see what the little-publicized Boyer, with whom Ford spent a lot of time, had to say about his boss.

"I first met Henry Ford in the winter of 1925 at the millpond behind Mr. Ford's Wayside Inn in South Sudbury, Mass.," Boyer began. "It was my habit to ice skate on this pond after attending high school during the day. One day Mr. Ford appeared with skates and we soon had an impromptu hockey scrimmage. This was a frequent occurrence until my graduation from high school in 1927.

"It was then that Mr. Ford suggested that instead of enrolling at Dartmouth, I spend a year or two in Dearborn at the Rouge Plant to get a variety of experiences in order to determine what career to pursue. It was during this time that Mr. Ford built the laboratory in Greenfield Village and put me in charge. Since that time I have been actively involved with the soybean industry and it is my plan to continue to be active in it.

"My assessment of Henry Ford's

Henry Ford swings an ax on the dent-resistant plastic trunk lid of a 1941 Ford. In the presence of Walter P. Chrysler, he performed this feat one time too many – the lid fractured. (Photo from the Research Center of the Henry Ford Museum and Greenfield Village.)

strengths and weaknesses are biased," Boyer continues. "We had a very close and warm relationship and I suppose he was my hero. One of his greatest strengths, in my opinion, was his ability to motivate and inspire men to great accomplishments in areas that were entirely new to them.

"Many times I was with him when he would decide to start a new project such as one of his Village Industries. He would usually select a man with no previous experience and then over the years one could see that man grow, develop, and do things of which he had no idea he was capable. There were many examples of this throughout the Ford Empire, particularly in the Production Departments.

"In other areas," Boyer adds, "Mr. Ford was less successful. The 'Peace Ship' episode, his political activities, and his relationship with the Jewish community are examples. His almost fanatical support of Harry Bennett distressed me very much and caused a great deal of trouble during his later years. Bennett's Service Department scandal reminds me very much of the story now unfolding in Washington concerning Watergate. It is another story of misplaced trust and support of aides who misused that trust."

Boyer also comments on Ford's axing of a plastic trunk lid in 1940. "Mr. Ford's personal car was equipped with one of these lids," he noted. "It was his custom to keep an ax in the car and whenever he had a guest with him he would swing the blunt edge of the ax on the door. The day he partially ruptured the door, his guest was Walter P. Chrysler himself. That particular trunk lid had borne the brunt of many blows and probably some minute fractures had already occurred. This time a visible fracture occurred similar to splintering in a piece of green wood. It was not a clean break and the lid was still functional. Mr. Ford was astute enough to carry off the situation by praising the ability of the plastic lid to absorb this extreme impact energy."

After leaving Ford, Boyer worked six years for Cincinnati's Bracket Co., which bought Ford's plastic business in 1943. He then served as a consultant for Swift, Lever Bros., Unilever (in

England), General Mills, Ralston, Purina, Nabisco, and was retained by Miles Laboratories' Worthington Food, Inc., of Worthington, Ohio, when he wrote me. He also lived in Worthington.

I do not know what became of Boyer after he wrote me (he was 63 at the time), but I seem to recall having read of his death. By any reckoning he was a plastics pioneer, and undoubtedly would have contributed much more to Ford Motor Co.'s work in this sphere had not the 80-year-old Henry Ford sold his plastics business in 1943.

Ford Inspires

Stories about Henry Ford, Ray Kroc, and Stanley Marcus inspired orphan Tom Monaghan, founder and chairman of Domino's Pizza, according to a book, *Rediscovering American Values: The Foundation of Our Freedom for the 21st Century*, by Dick DeVos, president of Amway.

Monaghan's sister, Mary Bernarda, read the stories to young Monaghan to show that it didn't matter where one came from or how little one has to start with. Among statements taken to heart by Monaghan was Ford's "Whether you believe you will succeed or fail, you are right." Monaghan, DeVos states, understood that one's outlook on life has a lot to do with what one does with life.

Gathered around a 1932 Lincoln V-12 convertible at the Indianapolis 500 track are, left to right, Capt. Edward V. "Eddie" Rickenbacker, Henry Ford, Edsel Ford, seated in car, Harvey Firestone Jr., Henry Ford II, Benson Ford, and Harvey Firestone Sr. The Ford grandchildren appear well fed.

"Indy" With Henry

When two teenagers sneaked into the Indianapolis 500 race, they found themselves in some unexpected company – that of Henry Ford. Let Richard Palmer, of Cortaro, Ariz., tell the story as he related it in the May/June 1995 edition of *Reminisce*.

"My friend Wally and I often played hooky from Shortridge High School in Indianapolis during the month of May so we could go to the track and watch the race cars. But our most memorable trip to the track was on a school holiday – Memorial Day 1932.

"Wally's grandfather was a

contributor to the Speedway, and he had a 'distinguished pass' for entry through the front gate and admission to the 'pagoda,' a five-story structure reserved for the press and VIPs.

That year, Wally's grandpa wasn't able to attend the race, so he offered the pass to Wally, who eagerly accepted it. At the track, Wally entered through the main gate, then met me at the fence and slipped the pass to me.

"The pagoda was more of a challenge – each level had a guard at the door. But since each floor had a balcony, Wally could get up to one level, lean out over the railing and lob the pass down to me.

"By noon, we'd made our way to the top floor, where about 20 people were congregated in a small area.

"And what a congregation it was! The host was Capt. Eddie Rickenbacker, World War I ace, former '500' driver and owner of the Speedway. His guests included Harvey Firestone and his son, and Edsel Ford and his sons, Henry Ford II and Benson.

"Around 12:30, I heard a guard's voice boom, 'Good afternoon, Mr. Ford,' as Henry Ford himself ascended the final steps to the top of the pagoda and tipped his hat to the guard.

"Nearly 69 then, Mr. Ford was the picture of health. His keen blue eyes stopped on Wally and me.

"Capt. Rickenbacker stood, greeted Mr. Ford grandly and offered his seat. But Mr. Ford replied, 'Eddie, you go ahead and enjoy the race. I'm going over there and talk with these two young men.'

"I detected a disappointed look on Capt. Rickenbacker's face as Mr. Ford approached us, removed his straw hat and stuck out his hand. 'Good afternoon,' he said politely. 'My name is Henry Ford.'

"His first question was how we got to the top floor of the pagoda. When we explained how we'd dropped our one pass from floor to floor, Mr. Ford laughed heartily and said, 'It's a good thing it isn't a windy day.'

"The three of us chatted for two hours! Mr. Ford especially liked the story I told about seeing an old Model T 'Tin Lizzie' motoring right past newer cars stalled by muddy ruts on a country road.

"Every so often during our conversation, Capt. Rickenbacker would rise and offer Mr. Ford his seat. But each time Mr. Ford politely refused, saying he was enjoying himself. Capt. Rickenbacker would turn back with a glum look on his face, and disappointment showed clearly on the faces of his other guests.

"When the race was almost over, Capt. Rickenbacker suggested Mr. Ford join him in the winner's circle. Wally and I shook hands with Mr. Ford and sincerely thanked him for the great visit. Capt. Rickenbacker gave us a cold stare.

"I've often reflected on that day and wondered what motivated the greatest self-made industrialist of his time to spend two hours talking to two ordinary teenagers."

Years later, Palmer returned to the Speedway legally and officially. He and his father built and owned cars that raced there.

As to why Ford devoted himself to the teenagers and ignored his host, only he could have explained. In any event, his behavior was in character. He genuinely liked being around young people, and seldom lost a chance to talk with them. Rickenbacker, who deserved more from his guest, paid the price.

Thanks to readers Mike Skinner, St. Clair Shores, Mich., and Jim and Joan Aberts, West Chester, Pa., for forwarding Palmer's reminiscences.

Ford A Murderer?

Are you ready for this?

Henry Ford may have murdered John and Horace Dodge, according to the book, *The Dodge Dynasty*, by Caroline Latham and David Agresta.

John died of respiratory problems Jan. 14, 1920. Horace died of hemorrhaging, with the added complications of cirrhosis of the liver, on Dec. 10, 1920.

"There were those who believed that the death of the Dodge brothers was more than an unfortunate chain of events, but was actually due to foul play," note the authors. "Rumors flew throughout Detroit that they had both been served lethal liquor ... and it was noted that the symptoms of their illnesses were very similar to those caused by certain types of poison ...

"Right up to the present day, in fact, there are people in Detroit who are convinced that John and Horace Dodge were murdered. Perhaps also the gossip was kept alive by a feeling of animosity toward the punitive arranger of the murder; none other than Henry Ford!

"Certainly, the deaths could be viewed as fortuitous for Henry, constituting in one stroke a revenge for his loss in court (the Dodges forced Ford to pay dividends on Ford Co. profits – of which Ford received 58.5 percent, the Dodges 10 percent – rather than plow all income back into the business) and the removal of one of the most serious competitive threats to Ford's dominance of the auto market. That dominance had been eroding year by year, and the Dodge was one of the reasons. The Dodge car had zoomed to the number three sales position in the industry within a few years, and most observers felt the Dodge brothers were ready to give Henry Ford a run for the lead. With the large amount of capital John and Horace had collected from their lawsuit against Henry, and the sale of their Ford stock, they had plenty of funds to invest in a battle for the lead. The death of the Dodge brothers effectively eliminated their company as a competitive threat to take over the number one position ...

"Certainly Henry Ford was a ruthless competitor, and just as certainly by 1920 he had reasons for hating the Dodge brothers. Yet, the Dodge family apparently disregarded the rumors. Dodges and Fords continued to have a limited but amicable social relationship, and both Henry Ford and his son, Edsel, were asked to serve as honorary pallbearers at Horace's funeral – an unlikely honor if the family thought Henry was Horace's murderer."

It's poppycock to think that Ford murdered the Dodges. He didn't hate them; and, in retrospect, had good reason to thank them for suing him, considering the marvelous publicity that arose from the "Dodge suit."

As for the two cars, Model T sales and market share grew steadily through the teens, along with the growth of the fine medium-price Dodge. The Dodges never indicated any desire to challenge the low-price Model T.

Henry Ford And TVA

Henry Ford's face is among those shown in a 36-foot mural in the lobby of the Tennessee Valley Authority's headquarters building in Knoxville. The mural, which chronicles TVA's history, was created in 1969 by TVA artist Robert Birdwell. Initially hung in the visitors area at Wilson Dam, Muscle Shoals, Ala., it was moved to Knoxville in 1982.

Among those featured in the mural are: forester Gifford Pinchot, who pioneered the concept of unified resource development; Sen. George Norris, of Nebraska, who shaped TVA legislation; and President Franklin D. Roosevelt, who signed the TVA Act.

An article on the mural recently was forwarded to your commentator by TVA Chairman Marvin Runyon, a former Ford vice president (body and assembly operations) and ex-chairman of Nissan of America, whom I visited in Knoxville. Runyon's accompanying letter included a history lesson.

"Your spotting Henry Ford in the mural in our lobby was very perceptive. He was included in the mural because at one time the residents of Muscle Shoals thought of Henry Ford as more of a savior than TVA.

"When World War I ended, Congress put Wilson Dam and the nitrate plants

Cecil Whitlock, production superintendent of Ford's Sheffield (Ala.) Aluminum Castings Plant in 1972, examines a six-decades-old street marker within a "city that never was" adjacent to present-day Muscle Shoals, Ala. Michigan and Jefferson are two of Detroit's major avenues, although they do not intersect in the Motor City.

Wilson Dam and nearby nitrate plants on the Tennessee River at Muscle Shoals, Ala., in 1924, when Henry Ford was seeking to buy the government-owned complex for $5 million. (Photo from the Collections of the Henry Ford Museum and Greenfield Village.)

in Muscle Shoals up for sale. Henry Ford bid $5 million for the facilities, and the local residents dreamed of his building a 'Ford City' that would bring industry and jobs into the region.

"Conservationists opposed the sale, however, and three years later Ford withdrew his offer. The facilities stood idle for almost 10 years until Congress created TVA to make sure of the Muscle Shoals facilities and develop the resources of the Tennessee Valley.

A history of the TVA sent by Runyon elaborates on Ford's offer:

"In 1921," stated the booklet, "Congress put its World War I-built Muscle Shoals hydroelectric dam and two nitrate plants up for sale. Henry Ford, the leading industrialist, bid $5 million for the properties that had cost $130 million to build. Because Congress had intended that Muscle Shoals would produce fertilizers during peacetime, the purchase bids came before the Senate Committee on Agriculture and Forestry, headed by Sen. George Norris of Nebraska. Norris said that if Ford's low bid were accepted, it would amount to 'the greatest gift ever bestowed upon mortal man since salvation was made free to the human race.'

"Norris was not alone in his opposition to Ford's proposal. A photograph of Gifford Pinchot standing in the middle of the Tennessee River at Muscle Shoals with his fist clenched above his head in protest to 'the rape of this great national heritage by Henry Ford' illustrated the opposition of leading conservationists to the sale.

"But local residents of this northwest Alabama farm country had a much different opinion of the Ford proposal. For them it meant industry, development – badly needed jobs. When Ford talked, somewhat vaguely, of a city near Muscle Shoals where industrial employment would reach one million, developers began paving streets through cornfields, pouring sidewalks, and erecting lampposts. Congress debated the sale, and debated. Three years later Ford withdrew his bid because 'a single affair of business that should have been decided in a week has become a complicated political affair.' 'Ford City' was never built, and for years useless sidewalks, complete with fire hydrants, remained in the undeveloped countryside near Muscle Shoals."

Your commentator visited Muscle Shoals in 1974, and was struck by the prevalence of street names familiar to Detroiters: Michigan, Jefferson, Woodward, Puritan, Pilgrim, Fort, etc., plus Fordsway, and businesses with names reminiscent of the Detroit area – Woodward Avenue Shoe Mart, Dearborn Town House, Highland Park Electric Co. Ghost towns we have seen, but a ghost town of a "city that never was" – that was different.

Henrys And Edsels

An obituary of a Harrisonburg, Va. man, Henry Franklin Ford, born 1918, has been forwarded by reader Gary Custer, of the same community, who writes, "There are a lot of people here around Mr. Ford's age named Henry Ford so-and-so or Edsel so-and-so, but here is a Henry Ford."

Custer adds that Henry F. Ford sold him a '31 truck many years ago, saying "it was the last one Henry Ford sold. Ha ha."

As Custer says, numerous persons have been named for Henry and Edsel Ford. In 1930 in Detroit alone there were 12 Henry Fords, although not all may have been named for the automaker. Namesakes with whom I've corresponded or read about include Edsel Henry Ford, cofounder and ex-president of the Edsel Owners Club of America; Cincinnati twins Henry Ford Pugh and the Rev. Edsel Ford Pugh, born in 1923; Henry Ford Hubbard (born 1942), fifth child of former Dearborn Mayor Orville L. Hubbard; Edsel Ford Tucker Sr., who worked for Ford for 40 years and never missed a day of work, and his son, Edsel Ford Tucker Jr.; Henry Ford Rust, Zanesville, Ohio, and Edsel Ford Fong, a San Francisco waiter.

Film director Francis Ford Coppola, a Detroiter, has offered two explanations for his middle name, noting that he was born in Henry Ford Hospital and that his father was a musician on radio's "Ford Sunday Evening Hour."

Ford Drive

There's a Ford Drive in Colby, Kan., also streets named Mercury, Lincoln, Packard, Franklin, Stutz, Duesenberg, Overland, Hudson, Nash, De Soto, Chevrolet, Plymouth, Dodge, Chrysler, and Cadillac.

The streets were named by subdivision developer C.D. Murray, a former Ford, Plymouth/De Soto, and Nash dealer.

Stadium Name

"What will Ford name the new Detroit Lions stadium?" inquires reader Ben Hawthorne, Fayetteville, N.C.

A name has yet to be announced. Ford bought naming rights for the 70,000-seat downtown Detroit football stadium – yet to be built – for $40 million in 1996. It plans to display vehicles on the premises and to use the facility for Ford-related events.

In recent years many stadiums and arenas have been named for companies and products including TWA Dome in St. Louis, Target Center in Minneapolis, and General Motors Place in Vancouver, B.C. Ford Chairman Alex Trotman has said that Ford's name will appear in the name of the Lions stadium.

Meantime, the Detroit press has suggested such names as Ford Dome, Taurus Dome, Mustang Dome, Thunderbird Dome, Henry Dome, Edsel Dome, Billy (son of Lions owner William Clay Ford Sr.) Dome, Michidome, Motor Dome, Motown Dome, Comeback Dome, and Soul Dome.

Ford has Ford Centers for the Performing Arts (theaters) in Chicago, Toronto, and New York.

Peace Ship Secretary

Irving Caesar, perhaps the last survivor of Henry Ford's 1915 Peace Ship, died at age 101 on December 17, 1996.

Born on Manhattan's Lower East Side on July 4, 1895, Caesar, after answering a newspaper advertisement, found himself appointed secretary to the Peace Ship, whose ill-fated mission sought to stop the European war. While on the mission, Caesar wrote little songs telling the Germans to stop behaving so badly. He urged Ford to have the lyrics translated into German and dropped into German trenches. His suggestion went unheeded.

Later Caesar, a Tin Pan Alley lyricist, put words to such enduring musical standards as "Tea for Two," "Swanee," "Is It True What They Say About Dixie?" and "Sometimes I'm Happy." He collaborated on songs and Broadway shows with George Gershwin, Vincent Youmans, Rudolf Friml, George M. Cohan, and others.

Secret Of Success

"All the lessons of success are contained in Longfellow's 'Psalm of Life,' " Henry Ford once told a Boston reporter at South Sudbury's Wayside Inn, where the magnate was vacationing. "And the real secret is in the last few lines," added Ford, who then read them as follows from a book in hand:

"Let us, then, be up and doing,
With a heart for any fate;
Still achieving, still pursuing
Learn to labor and to wait."

After reading the entire nine-stanza poem, Ford shut the book with a snap. "That," he said, "contains all the lessons of success. Let any man sit down and ponder those lines that Longfellow wrote and he will find the lessons in them far better than any other advice that was given by any man. I know of no better lesson for success."

Ford, a doer as well as thinker, also must have particularly liked the third, seventh, and eighth stanzas: They read as follows:

"Not enjoyment, and not sorrow
Is our destined end or way;
But to act, that each tomorrow
Find us farther than today."

"Lives of great men all remind us
We can make our lives, sublime
And departing, leave behind us
Footprints on the sands of time."

"Footprints that perhaps another
Sailing o'er life's solemn main,
A forlorn and shipwrecked brother,
Seeing, shall take heart again."

It is significant, too, that Ford read the entire poem, for to this day some people question whether the industrialist could read. On July 1, 1995, for example, when being interviewed by the Arts & Entertainment television channel for a program on the homes of America's "auto barons," my interviewer blithely informed me that Ford could not read. Perhaps this myth will have to be added to the one insisting that all Model Ts were painted black.

Thanks to reader Mike Skinner, of St. Clair Shores, Mich., for forwarding a clipping on the Ford interview.

Chesterton Poem

"There seems to be no shortage of material for "Ford Country," writes reader Leigh Styan, Forest Park, Ill., "but just in case, here's a poem I found while browsing through *The Collected Poems of G.K. Chesterton* (London: Methaen, 1942, 9th ed.).

The poem, entitled "The Peace of Petrol," is, according to Chesterton's subtitle, "to be sung to the air of 'Kabul River' on the conclusion of an English peace brought about by American intervention." The first of three representative stanzas reads:

He has many a car and chuffer
(Still the bugle, sheathe the sword),
so I left my mates to suffer
All because of Mr. Ford.
Ford, Ford, Ford of many millions,
Ford of many motors in the Park;
And our lord will laugh like thunder
at the Good Cause going under
When we stab it, to oblige him, in the dark.

Styan is puzzled as to Chesterton's precise reference to Ford, and so am I. But I suspect it has to do with Ford's unsuccessful attempt in 1915 to end World War I through continuous neutral mediation which, if carried out, likely would have given neither side a clear-cut win. Many Britons, reasoning that only complete victory could vindicate their sacrifice of life and treasure, opposed Ford's efforts.

Tin Lizzie

A recent letter to the editor of *This England* recalls a 1924 trip in a Model T between Wembley and Oxford.

"We must have met only about 50 cars," recalls S.J. Hobbs, Chadlington, Oxfordshire. "The journey was dark and cold and I could see the exhaust pipe of the car glowing through the floorboards.

"Henry Ford and his cars were a big joke to us children. We called them 'Tin Lizzies' and sang this little ditty.

There was a little man,
His name was Henry Ford,
He got a bit of rubber
and a little bit of board,
A little drop of petrol,
and an old tin can.
He put the thing together,
and the darned thing ran.

"Recently a friend called on me in his 1916 Model T. The original cost 140 – now it is valued at 15,000! ... The car's ignition system always is packed with cigarette cartons to stop vibration."

Thanks to reader Carlyle V. Stewart Jr., Falls Church, Va. for forwarding a copy of *This England*, which justifiably bills itself as "Britain's Loveliest Magazine."

Getting Even

"I've run across references to Henry Ford's race for a Michigan Senate seat against Truman H. Newberry in 1918," writes reader

Stanley Lawton, of Rochester, N.Y. "But where can I find the full story about the election and Ford's postelection efforts to deny Newberry the seat that he narrowly won."

The most comprehensive treatment of the subject is S. Ervin's 1935 book, *Henry Ford vs. Truman H. Newberry*, which discusses both the election and its aftermath. The treatise is a strongly argued defense of Newberry's legal and moral blamelessness.

A more manageable and highly readable account of the episode is a 30-page article, "Campaign on Trial: The Unnecessary Ordeal of Truman Newberry," appearing in the 1987 edition of the *Wayne Law Review*. The author is Prof. Maurice Kelman of Wayne State University.

Ford ran for the Senate at the suggestion of President Woodrow Wilson, who was impressed with the industrialist's tremendous wartime popularity and belief that Ford was the only Wilson and League of Nations' man capable of being elected to the Senate from traditionally Republican Michigan. Reluctantly, Ford entered the race, adopting the attitude, "If they want to elect me let them do so, but I won't make a penny's investment."

As a nominal nonpartisan independent, Ford was entered in both the Democratic and Republican primaries. Most Democratic papers, identifying Ford with Wilson, were enthusiastic about his candidacy. The Republican and independent press, however, was tartly critical. The *New York Times* – in one of my favorite quotes about Ford – remarked that Ford's election "would create a vacancy in both the Senate and in the automobile business and from the latter Mr. Ford cannot be spared."

Ford, who campaigned in neither the primary or general elections, easily won the Democratic primary and finished a respectable second to Newberry in the Republican primary. Campaigning vigorously and spending lavishly, the wealthy Newberry won the general election by a vote of 217,088 to 212,751.

During the campaign, Ford's political opponents placed special emphasis on Edsel Ford's draft deferment. "Why not send the indispensable Edsel to the Senate?" asked one Republican newspaper. A cartoon in the *Grand Rapids Press* showed Quentin Roosevelt's grave (Theodore Roosevelt's son had been killed in action) and the younger Ford with a golf club in hand. In answering these gibes, Ford took full responsibility for retaining Edsel at his Highland Park Plant and remarked that if Edsel did serve he would be found "fighting," and not sticking his spurs into a mahogany desk in Washington," an obvious slap at Newberry's son, an Army officer stationed in Washington during the war.

After the election, Ford, humiliated and bitter, embarked upon a costly, sustained, and intensely vindictive effort to block Newberry's Senate seating, and even to put his adversary behind bars for alleged campaign illegalities. In response to Ford's charges and those made by other political enemies, Newberry was indicted by the Justice Department on charges of having violated the Federal Corrupt Practices Act. The litigation and repeated demands for the senator's expulsion from the Senate so embarrassed Newberry that he resigned from the Senate on Nov. 18, 1922. Although Ford had not won a Senate seat, neither in the end had his rival.

Newberry resumed a quiet private life in Detroit, never again straying from the world of boardrooms and private clubs. He died in 1945, two years before Henry Ford.

Ford A Populist?

"Was Henry Ford a populist?" asks Merrill Jamerson, of Chattanooga, Tenn. "Thinking about his life, it seems to me he might have been?"

He qualifies, if one accepts *Webster's Dictionary*'s definition of a populist as one who "represents the views, interests, etc. of the common people." In a 1982 book, *Profiles in Populism*, edited by Willis Carto, Ford was chronicled as one of "thirteen leading American populists." Others of the book's populists were Thomas Jefferson, Andrew Jackson, Charles A. Lindbergh, and Father Charles Coughlin.

Down On The Farm

Henry Ford was a lifelong prankster, recalls a distant cousin, Ford R. Bryan, in a publication of the University of Michigan-Dearborn's Fair Lane Estate.

"As a boy," recalls Bryan, "Henry was said to have had his share of fun at the expense of his younger brothers, John and Will. However, there was at least one case, as told by Will to his son, Burnham, where Henry came out the loser.

"It seems that the boys' father, William, had a rule that the first one of the boys to arrive outside after breakfast was given preference in the chores. Henry could usually beat the others to the barn and get the choice assignment.

"But one morning things were different. When Henry grabbed his boots to race for the barn he stuck his feet into hot applesauce. Will had spotted the applesauce on the kitchen stove and got it into the boots just before Henry had come leaping down the stairs from his bedroom. That morning, for certain, Henry did not especially enjoy doing his chores, and was no doubt already plotting a way to get even with the rascal who outwitted him that morning."

Wrong About Booze

Henry Ford didn't spend much time in wishful thinking. But he did so with respect to the legalized prohibition of liquor. He thought the Prohibition Amendment, which took effect in 1920, sealed the doom of alcohol in the U.S., and he continued to think so as late as 1929, mountainous evidence to the contrary.

In his book, *My Philosophy of Industry*, published in 1929, Ford stated: "The United States is dry not only legally but by moral conviction .... There are a million boys growing up in the United States who have never seen a saloon, and who will never know the handicap of liquor, either in themselves or their relatives; and this excellent condition will go on spreading itself over the country when the wet press and the paid propaganda of booze are forgotten.

"There should be no mistake about it. The abolition of the commercialized liquor trade in this country is as final as the abolition of slavery. These are the two great reforms to which moral America committed itself from the beginning of its history."

The 21st Amendment of 1933 dashed Ford's dreams of a liquorless society. The magnate also crusaded against tobacco, banning its use in Ford plants for as long as he headed his company.

Blame It On Henry

Henry Ford was partly responsible for the Volstead [Prohibition] Act of 1919 which banned alcohol, according to the newsletter of a new Northern Ohio car club.

The act was passed for two reasons, the newsletter states: "(1) Anti-German bias following World War I against brewmeisters of German descent (2) Henry Ford didn't drink and his assembly line worked great except on Fridays and Mondays when absenteeism caused significant problems and financial losses to his company. Henry Ford prevailed on the Du Ponts, who owned General Motors, and together they 'financed' the lobbying effort which would never have succeeded without their financial support."

Ford welcomed the Volstead Act, but to say that he contributed importantly to its passage credits him with power that neither he nor the Du Ponts possessed. Still, it's fun to read such things.

Thanks to reader Bob Thatcher, Export, Pa., for forwarding the club's newsletter, sent to enlist his membership.

Unique Introduction

A brown jug of corn liquor enabled Woody McKay to meet Henry Ford, as recalled by McKay's son, also named Woody McKay, in the July-August 1995 issue of *Antique Automobile*.

In 1915, the article states, the senior McKay, a Davidson College dropout, was a fledgling salesman attached to Ford's Charlotte district. From his boss he learned that Henry Ford, then vacationing in Asheville, was unable to obtain corn liquor for fuel-experimentation.

"I can get Mr. Ford a train load of corn liquor," McKay informed his boss. After being put in touch with Ford's traveling secretary, the youth arranged to obtain a jug of corn liquor from the Asheville office of the U.S. Treasury's Revenue Department. This done, he delivered the liquor to Grove Park Inn where Ford, the article states, was staying with Thomas Edison, Harvey Firestone, Calvin Coolidge, William Jennings Bryan, and Charles R. Crane, ex-ambassador to Russia. McKay, a South Carolina orphan was, in his son's words, in "high cotton."

A grateful Ford invited McKay to dinner with himself and his friends. Bryan, saying he had "heard of this stuff all my life" asked to smell the liquor. McKay removed the cork, Bryan sniffed and said nothing.

After the dinner, McKay says, Ford answered questions about his "recent peace mission to Europe." When the magnate returned to his suite, he asked McKay about moonshiners and mountain people for almost two hours. Finally, Mrs. Ford interrupted the meeting about one o'clock by saying, "Gentlemen, it's Mr. Ford's bedtime. Maybe we can hear more of these tales another time."

"Woody," Ford said, "what are your plans for tomorrow?"

"I plan to drive back to Charlotte. I've got my job there and I have to return the Model T."

"Well, I would like for you to stay up here with me a few days. Is that a possibility?"

"But I have a job to do at Ford Motor Company."

Ford was said to have paused for a moment, then remarked, "Tell you what. You call home tomorrow and tell them to send you some clothes and you stay up here. I'll try to run the Ford Motor Company a few days without you."

McKay, recalled his son, soon had a new position with a self-styled title, "Director of Special Services," although others called him "the playboy" of Ford Motor Company. "For the next few years, interrupted only by service in World War I in France," the younger McKay adds, "Dad did whatever Mr. Ford wanted him to do. Because of the fertile and ubiquitous mind of this engineering genius, Dad maintained a busy and varied existence."

It's an interesting and mostly plausible story. But the timing and cast of characters are off. Ford, Edison, Firestone, and Burroughs, visited Asheville in 1918, not 1915. They were not accompanied by Coolidge, Bryan, or Crane.

Henry Ford Psychic?

"Henry Ford was clairvoyant," states *Psychic News*. The industrialist, according to psychic Edgar J. Hochauswer, "used his psychic powers to peer into the future and determine what the demands of the consumers would be. And, he built his line of cars to specifically fill those needs!"

Ford, the article continues, "used to amuse his friends and family with his 'magic' tricks, but many people felt he relied upon his highly developed psychic skills to perform his stunts." Ford, adds Hochauswer, "was a conservative businessman who never came to terms with his extraordinary psychic ability.

He would do anything to disguise his psychic gifts, although he received great pleasure in utilizing them. It was an easy task for Ford to plan ahead. All he had to do was to direct his psychic forces to a future time and observe what the customer was driving."

The article notes that Ford made several drawings "in the early 1900s that resemble Ford's current line of cars." Unfortunately, the article isn't illustrated with these drawings, nor does it say where they are.

In addition to Ford, *Psychic News* credits the Wright brothers with having psychic abilities to "show them the way."

Ford's Publicity

"I wonder if we will ever see Henry Ford's likes again," writes reader Malcolm Willits, of Hollywood, Calif., "or could it only have happened in the 1910-35 period, how a person like him could so dominate the news.

"It probably helped," Willits continues, "that he had a private corporation and was accountable to no board of directors who might not have liked some of the things he did, or chances he took. Of course, I feel Henry Ford was 95 percent great, and Edsel was 100 percent. Owning a 1934 V-12 KB Lincoln Judkins 7-passenger limo and a 1928 Lincoln 7-passenger sedan makes me a bit prejudiced toward them."

As Willits suggests, Ford received a remarkable amount of publicity starting with the announcement of his five-dollar day in 1914. During the 1920s he received more publicity than any other American except Calvin Coolidge; and Coolidge received a bigger press only because he occupied the Presidency nearly two-thirds of this time.

Busted Billionaire Act

Henry Ford, a natural-born publicist, had many ways of generating self-publicity. One of them was his "busted billionaire" act, whose script appeared to be written especially for reporters.

In 1929 the industrialist had to borrow two cents in order to buy a commemorative Edison stamp at a Jubilee of Light celebration in Atlantic City. A few weeks later he engineered another national wire story by sending the lender a two-cent check.

In 1933, the *New York Times* informed its readers that "at the moment (Ford) has in his pocket just a $1 bill, and it is all he has carried for months." The bill, the *Times* added, had been presented to Ford by an appreciative youth to whom the industrialist had given a job.

In 1934, at Gettysburg, Ford found himself without funds after he had accepted a twenty-five cent pamphlet from a vendor. His statement, "I haven't any money," made the nation smile.

In 1939, T.E. Webster, who was inspired by another of Ford's financially embarrassing moments, drew one of his famous "The Thrill That Comes Once in a Lifetime" cartoons, showing the manufacturing magnate standing next to a phone booth and asking a youngster, "Could you lend me a nickel?"

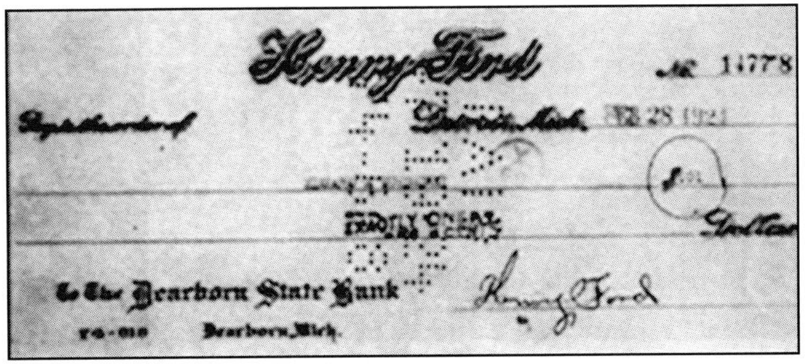

This check for one cent, written on Feb. 28, 1924 to Edward A. Huebener, created publicity for both Henry Ford and the recipient. The photo was found by Don Brewer, of Dearborn, in a drawer of a jeweler's bench he bought in Detroit in the mid-1960s.

Borrows Two Cents

Henry Ford, left, buys the first Thomas Edison Commemorative Stamp after borrowing two cents to pay for it. The stamp was issued on June 7, 1929 in Atlantic City in conjunction with Light's Golden Jubilee celebration. Others pictured are Atlantic City municipal and General Electric officials. Borrowing of a pittance was part of Ford's "busted billionaire" act which invariably generated publicity and evoked a public smile. (United Press International photo.)

Ford Quotation

Henry Ford's enigmatic statement, "Whether you think you can or you think you can't, you're right," appears in a booklet, "Your Attitude Determines Your Attitude," published by Successories Publishing, Lombard, Ill.

Among the booklet's other quotations are Thomas Jefferson's "The glow of one warm thought is, to me, worth more than money," Charles Dickens' "Reflect upon your present blessings, of which every man has plenty; not on your past misfortunes, of which all men have some," Abraham Lincoln's "A person will be just about as happy as they make up their minds to be," Winston Churchill's "The pessimist sees difficulty in every opportunity. The optimist sees opportunity in every difficulty," Clint Eastwood's "I don't believe in pessimism. If something doesn't come up the way you want, forge ahead. If you think it's going to rain, it will," and that old standby, "Whether the glass is half-full or half-empty depends on the attitude of the person looking at it."

Thanks to reader Michael Skinner, St. Clair Shores, Mich., for forwarding the booklet.

Quotations

One measure of a person's legacy is the number of memorable quotations he has left behind. By this yardstick Henry Ford left a substantial legacy. He is quoted 18 times in the newly-published *The New York Public Library Book of Twentieth-Century American Quotations*. The voluble Lee Iacocca is quoted only twice.

Several of Ford's statements are familiar: "History is bunk," which should read "History is more or less bunk"; "Money is like an arm or a leg – use it or lose it"; "These really are good times, but only a few know it" [stated in 1930]; and "It is all one to me if a man comes from Sing Sing or Harvard. We hire a man, not his history."

But most of the Ford quotations are obscure, unworthy of the subject, and not worth quoting here. No fewer than five statements came from Ford's 1928 *Forum* article on success. One or two came from the auto king's autobiography, *My Life and Work*, none from his equally memorable autobiographical work, *Today and Tomorrow*. The editors even attributed to Ford a 1973 statement made by his grandson Henry Ford II: "New York is a different country. Maybe it ought to have a separate government. Everybody thinks differently, acts differently. They just don't know what the hell the rest of the United States is." Thus HFII, although unlisted in the index, is unknowingly cited.

Dissatisfied with the New York Public Library's compilation of Ford quotations, your commentator hereby submits his own list of Henry's 25 most memorable quotes:

1. History is more or less bunk.
2. The public can have any color of car it wants so long as it's black.
3. Thinking is the hardest work there is, which is probably the reason why so few engage in it.
4. With one foot in industry and one foot in agriculture, America is safe.
5. Money is like an arm or a leg – use it or lose it.
6. I'm glad to see you all here. (Sing Sing Prison, 1915)
7. "Harry, they're [reporters] all skunks, and you know what happens to people who play with skunks."
8. Help the other fellow. (personal motto)
9. A bore is a fellow who opens his mouth and puts his feats (sic) in it.
10. The best thing one man can do for another is get off his back.
11. Out of the trenches by Christmas, never to return!
12. The average man won't really do a day's work unless he is caught and can't get out of it. (March, 1931)
13. The question, "Who ought to be boss?" is like asking who ought to be the tenor in the quartet. Obviously, the man who can sing tenor.
14. These are really good times, but only a few know it. (March, 1931)
15. Opportunity will not overlook you because you wear overalls.
16. It is all the one to me if a man comes from Sing Sing or Harvard. We hire a man, not his history.
17. I've no use for a car that has more spark plugs than a cow has teats.
18. Any place is a good place to start from.
19. You can't build a reputation on what you're going to do.
20. Before everything else, getting ready is the secret of success.
21. Nothing is particularly hard if you divide it into small jobs.
22. Gentlemen, a million of anything is a great many (entire speech at banquet celebrating the production of the one millionth Ford, 1915)
23. It is pretty well understood that a man in the Ford plant works.
24. The cow must go.
25. There are only two good things in the book [the Bible] worth a damn.

Touring The *Fairlane*

Henry Ford's former railcar, the *Fairlane*, was toured by members of the Henry Ford Heritage Association on November 2, 1996.

Owned by Michiganians Mr. and Mrs. Richard Kughn, the 82-foot-long, 100-ton all steel *Fairlane* is parked adjacent to the police station on Maple Road in Saline, Mich., approximately a half-mile north of U.S. 12.

The *Fairlane*'s name emblazons both sides of the car. The spelling inexplicably differs from that of Henry Ford's estate, Fair Lane. Curtained at each window, the khaki-colored car sports gold stripes and a black top.

The *Fairlane* has 10 sections. Off the open, brass-railed observation platform is a radio telephone-equipped "observation room" containing two comfortable arm chairs and a sofa. Forward is a small compartment, followed by a bedroom with wash basin, dresser, and closet.

A fourth room accommodates a double bed, dresser. And toilet. Next is a connecting bathroom with tub-shower, then another bedroom with toilet.

Ford Railcar

Henry Ford's railcar parked behind the Henry Ford Museum shortly before its sale to the St. Louis Southwestern Railway Lines in 1942. At that time the car's name was spelled *Fair Lane*; now it's *Fairlane*. (Photo from Henry Ford Museum and Greenfield Village, Dearborn, Mich.)

The eight-seat dining room is adorned with a large, handsome breakfront. Beyond is a storage room containing two fold-down bunks for crew members, then a galley with stove, oven, grill, and microwave. A small vestibule is built into the front of the car.

Built for the Fords in 1920-21, the *Fairlane* was sold to the St. Louis Southwestern Railway Lines ("Cotton Belt") in 1942. The Cotton Belt donated the vehicle to the Cherokee Nation, headquartered in Tahlequah, Okla., in 1973. The Cherokees, which used the car as a tourist office, sold the vehicle to the Kughns in 1982, sale price undisclosed.

Built by Pullman Company at a cost of $159,000, the *Fairlane* was one of the longest and most luxurious private cars of its day.

The Fords made extensive use of their home on rails. In July 1921 they took it to Boston, in September to Iron Mountain in Michigan's Upper Peninsula. In mid-October Henry's son Edsel, the Ford Company's president, and three other executives rode the car while inspecting the firm's newly-acquired railroad, the Detroit, Toledo & Ironton. They also made side trips to Ford's coal mines in West Virginia and Kentucky.

Through the years the *Fairlane* logged regular trips to the Fords' winter homes in Ft. Myers, Fla., and Richmond Hill, Ga.; to their summer homes in Northern Michigan's Huron Mountains and in Pequaming; to the Wayside Inn in South Sudbury, Mass., which the Fords had restored; and to New York City for Clara's shopping expeditions. The car also made many other trips, among them runs to West Orange, N.J., home of Ford's best friend, Thomas A. Edison; to Indianapolis for the Indy "500" race; to Dayton for an inspection of the Wright Brothers' birthplace and bicycle shop; to Southampton, Long Island, for grandson Henry II's wedding; and for repeated visits to the Chicago and New York world's fairs. Many important figures were guests aboard the car including Presidents Warren G. Harding and Calvin Coolidge.

The Fords generally hitched the *Fairlane* onto regularly scheduled trains, easily arranged in a train-filled era. They shared the car for the last time on March 19-21, 1942, when returning from their Georgia plantation. Clara boarded the car for a final time from April 26-29 for a New York shopping trip. In total, the car was used nearly 400 times by the Fords or their families or guests.

In mid-1942 the government ordered a stop to private-car haulage for the duration of World War II. The *Fairlane* was sold for $30,000, of which the Fords pocketed $25,000, a broker $5,000. The Fords continued to use private cars for rail travel, renting them from the New York Central and other lines.

Henry Ford's Railcar

Dick Folsom, left, president of the Henry Ford Heritage Association, and member Rick Lindner, of Columbus, Ohio aboard the observation platform of Henry Ford's former railcar, *Fairlane*. The association's November 2, 1996 tour marked the car's first public viewing.

Ford On Reincarnation

Henry Ford is cited in a recent *People* magazine article on prominent figures who believed in reincarnation.

"Work is futile if we cannot utilize the experience we collect in one life in the next," Ford is quoted as saying. The article also maintains that the automaker attributed his pacifism to the fact that he was born on July 30, shortly after the Battle of Gettysburg, in which he believes he was a soldier felled in battle.

Ford frequently stated his belief in reincarnation. He claimed that he had accepted the theory as a young man, after reading a book entitled, *A Short View of Great Quotations*, by Orlando J. Smith. As proof of validity of his thesis, Ford would cite a chicken's behavior:

"When the automobile was new and one of them came down the road, a chicken would run straight for home –

and usually be killed. But today when a car comes along, a chicken will run for the nearest side of the road. That chicken has been hit in the ass in a previous life."

This view and Ford's insistence that the body had a "queen cell," which could never be destroyed naturally, astounded many listeners. On the other hand, Ford often was quoted in the press regarding his religious activities and his belief in God and in Jesus Christ.

Thanks to Mike Skinner, Detroit, Mich., for the *People* magazine article.

Ford Servant

Any number of servants have spilled the beans about their employers, most of them for money, and consequently their remarks tend to be sensationalist.

Rosa Buhler, maid servant to Henry Ford's wife, Clara, also talked about her former employers, but circumspectly. She was interviewed three times in 1981 and 1982 by Dick Folsom, of Canton, Mich., now president of the Henry Ford Heritage Association, who published some of her reminiscences in the Spring 1995 issue of the association's *Newsletter*.

Buhler, a German immigrant, was a Grosse Pointe, Mich. maid for three years before being hired by Mrs. Ford in March 1933. Sent to Dearborn by an employment agency, she did not know that she was headed for the Ford estate.

"I took the bus on my day off to Southfield Road [Dearborn]," she told Folsom, "and walked to the Gate House where they told me to go. The chauffeur had the day off ... it was a Sunday ... so the man at the gate told me I would have to walk to the house. It was about one mile. I fell in love with Fair Lane [the Ford's home] then. It was so beautiful ... all the flowers were in bloom alongside of the driveway."

Buhler was met by "a very proper butler, Thompson," who took her to the library to be interviewed by Mrs. Ford. Quickly hired, she was instructed to return to Detroit on the bus to buy a uniform – at her expense – and return. She was called by her last name since there was a cook also named Rosa.

Buhler lived on the mansion's second floor, near the servants' staircase. Her door had louvers so that she could hear a call-board when Mrs. Ford called. "It was a very nice room" she recalled. "I had a window seat and my own bath."

As Mrs. Ford's maid, Buhler took care of Mrs. Ford's clothing and sewed, and also had Henry's suits cleaned after each wearing.

Each day, she remembered, Ford's secretary, Frank Campsall sent to the mansion an envelope containing $200. Buhler put the envelope in Ford's coat pocket. "Almost everyday when I would take Mr. Ford's suit from the day before, the envelope would still be unopened in his coat pocket .... Every week I would send the envelopes back to Mr. Campsall's office .... but they always sent a new envelope everyday just in case he needed it."

Buhler liked to walk on the estate at sunrise. "Mr. Ford liked to get up early too," she observed. "I would see him walking in the gardens at the same time I was there. I would say 'Good Morning' and he would wave back. He really enjoyed that time of day. He used to chop wood with an ax in the woods .... [Also] he loved to ride his bike along the driveway. He usually did that after dinner every evening."

Buhler met all of the Ford's famous guests. "One day," she remembered, "Mrs. Ford said to me, 'We're having an overnight guest but it's quite a secret. His name is Mr. Kane.' When he came to the front door I knew who he was - Charles Lindbergh. I went to carry his suitcase, but he wouldn't let me .... He stayed in the Colonial Room." She also met the Duke of Windsor.

The Fords had one gun in the house, the maid noted, "in the night stand between their beds. Mr. Ford told me where it was."

Every morning Mrs. Ford, according

to Rosa, put out her husband's pills on a small plate next to his breakfast dish. "Once when she left the room, I saw Mr. Ford open the window ... near the Blue Garden ... and throw out the pills. He told me not to tell Mrs. Ford. When Mrs. Ford returned, she asked him if he took his pills. He looked at me, and with a smile on his face held up the plate and said to Mrs. Ford, 'The plate's empty, see?' I didn't say a thing to Mrs. Ford. Once, Mr. Ford made friends with a mouse. He used to feed it little crumbs from his toast. He asked me to keep that a secret too."

The Fords, Buhler said, "lived a very quiet life. They would often sit and listen to the radio in the evening, or Mrs. Ford would read to Mr. Ford in the library. He liked that. They both loved the gardens and their birds ... they loved to watch birds."

The Henry Ford Heritage Association, P.O. Box 2313, Dearborn, MI 48123, has 303 memberships including 419 individuals. Annual dues are a modest $10, making membership one of North America's best bargains.

Ford Chauffeur

George Burch, 85, who occasionally chauffeured the Ford family, recently was interviewed by the *Dearborn Press & Guide*.

Burch worked for Ford Motor Co. from 1925 until 1967. By virtue of having a chauffeur's license, he now and then drove Henry Ford's wife, Clara, and her grandchildren around Dearborn. "One Sunday," he cites as an example, "I drove the grandchildren from the Ford mansion to the Ford farm at Ford and Southfield roads. They wanted to see the animals." Henry Ford II was 12 to 14 years of age at the time, Burch recalls.

Burch often ran errands for company officials, and was assigned to drive Prince Ferdinand of Germany when the last Kaiser's grandson visited Dearborn.

The driver frequently saw Henry Ford, but talked with him only once. The episode involved an engine Burch had transported from Indiana for the Henry Ford Museum. Ford wanted to examine the engine after it was disassembled and laid out for inspection. Burch was asked to show Ford the engine.

Burch's Ford career was interrupted in 1932, when he was told to get married, or be laid off. Unready for marriage, Burch accepted the layoff, but was reinstated the next year with full seniority. He eventually married.

Thanks to Mike Skinner, of Dearborn, Mich., for forwarding the *Press & Guide*'s story.

Ford Driver Dies

Dolph L. Thorne, 83, of Ypsilanti, Mich., who claimed to have been Henry Ford's driver, died recently.

After starting to work as a young man in a Ford factory, according to an *Ann Arbor News* obituary, Thorne was assigned to drive Ford's car. "Mr. Thorne talked about how Old Henry always thought every boy should go skinny-dipping at water holes," recalls Foster Fletcher, a friend of Thorne's. "But, Mrs. Ford didn't want her son being seen like that in public. So Dolph would sneak the car out of the garage, so Old Henry and Edsel could drive out to a water hole."

May we put a question mark on that yarn? Edsel was born in 1893. Thorne joined Ford in 1923. That'd mean that Edsel, by then four years into the presidency of Ford Motor Co., was sneaking out at age 30 with his father to go skinny-dipping.

Thorne also, according to Fletcher, recalled the day Ford notified his pilots he was getting out of the flying business. Ford, said Thorne, "blamed the decision on too much governmental regulation of the airlines." But, that wasn't the problem. Ford sold only four airplanes in 1932, and couldn't sustain aviation activities at a time when the auto business also had gone to pot.

Floyd A. Apple, left, and Apple's biographer, Dick Folsom, at Henry Ford's 122nd birthday party (1985) in Dearborn.

Apple, according to his biographer, Dick Folsom, was a "marvelous man. He was just pleasant and cheerful, always cracking a joke here and there. He had nothing but praise for Henry Ford and the family. He said that Henry Ford never said a bad word to him."

Fair Lane Workman Dies

Floyd A. Apple, one of the last persons to talk with Henry Ford before the latter's death on April 7, 1947, died on January 29, 1988 in Garden City, Mich.

Apple, 85, felt that fate was responsible for his employment on Henry Ford's estate, Fair Lane. A driver of experimental dump trucks for the Ford Company in 1925, Apple was asked to take a load of topsoil to the estate. The truck broke down in the rose garden. While awaiting help, he was asked by Fair Lane's powerhouse supervisor if he knew anything about boilers. He did, and worked the next quarter-century in the powerhouse. Often he was accompanied on his rounds by the master of the estate, who had a special fondness for generating equipment and those who tended it.

In addition to Henry Ford, Fair Lane's powerhouse was visited by other luminaries, among them Thomas Edison, Harvey Firestone, and President Herbert Hoover, the latter in 1929 when in Dearborn for the dedication of the Edison Institute.

Apple, a native Ohioan, retired from Fair Lane in 1950, the year Clara Ford, Henry's wife, died. He then worked as a refrigeration expert at the Ford Research and Engineering Center in Dearborn until 1964. A volunteer Fair Lane tour guide for many years, he continued to attend guide meetings until the summer of 1987.

Ford Waitress

Garnet (Pat) Jacques, one of Henry Ford's favorite waitresses, died at age 62 in 1990.

The former Garnet Davis quit high school in 1944 to become a Dearborn Inn waitress. She lived on the premises in a dormitory-like setting from 1944-47.

Henry Ford often asked to be seated at one of Pat's tables. "It didn't matter if it was breakfast, lunch, or dinner," said husband Warren Jacques, "he would always tip Pat 16 cents. Always .... I think it was because she was 16 at the time. She thought he was terrific."

A 16-cent tip was more than adequate in an era of 10 percent tips. In 1947-48, as a waiter in the University of Illinois' Illini Union dining room, I was pleased with a 10-cent tip on a 90-cent luncheon.

Rare Inscription

Among the rarest of books inscribed by Henry Ford are those signed before he became world famous in 1914. Among them are two copies of *Land Birds Bird Guide: Song and Insectivorous Birds East of the Rockies, From Parrots to Bluebirds*, published in 1912.

One of the books was given by Ford to a Canadian bird lover and naturalist Jack Miner. This book is displayed at the Jack Miner Museum, of Kingsville, Ontario, Canada. Another is owned by the Henry Ford Estate – Fair Lane, having been purchased in 1980 from a Romeo, Michigan, woman whose bird-loving uncle worked with Henry Ford on mechanical projects.

In the Miner book, Ford wrote, "I am your friend Henry Ford." In the other volume he inscribed, "My Friend John from Henry Ford."

$1,500 Photos?

A photo of Henry Ford, inscribed and signed by the auto king, has been priced at $1,500 by John K. King Used & Rare Books, Detroit, Mich.

"Michigan's Largest Bookstore," as King describes itself, reproduces the Ford photo on the cover of its "Catalogue 59." Inside, it describes the item as follows:

"FORD, HENRY, INSCRIBED & SIGNED PHOTOGRAPH. 12x8" (image 8x6"), portrait by C.M. Hayes & Co. Detroit n.p.n.d. [no place no date] (1920s).

"Very important inscription to Albert Kahn, the world famous architect responsible for many buildings at major Ford complexes such as Highland Park, Rouge, Willow Run Bomber Plant (WWII), etc. The inscription reads 'To Albert Kahn, Your best friend is the one who can bring out the best that is in you. Henry Ford.' Ford's anti-Semitism is well known and his association with Kahn and this inscription seems to ring of irony. Photo is dry mounted to still board, margins have ink spots, some soiling, one corner with minor crease. A mat & frame would preserve this significant & rare association piece. $1500.00."

"I figure this photo is worth $750-$1,000," writes Mike Skinner, of Dearborn, who forwarded a photocopy of the catalog cover and advertisement. "What do you think?"

I agree with Mike's estimate. There's no question that the inscription is excellent, and that it is addressed to an important figure in his own right. Still, I question whether it's worth approximately four times Ford's signature alone. That said, if anyone thinks the item is worth $1,500 he/she can write King at 901 W. Lafayette, Detroit, or phone (313) 961-0622.

Valuable Letter

Can a letter signed by Henry Ford be worth from $6,000 to $9,000? An auction house thinks so, having attached that value to a letter from the industrialist to journalist Herman Bernstein.

The two-page typed letter, datelined Detroit, 23 July, 1927, reiterated Ford's apology for a series of anti-Semitic articles appearing in 1920-22 in Ford's national newspaper, the *Dearborn Independent*. The letter apologizes for "the alleged interview with me assailing you," disclaims any responsibility for the "translations, publications, or distribution" of a book, *The International Jew*, based on the articles, and acknowledges and expresses regret for the damage done by the articles.

Ford met Bernstein on the so-called Peace Ship chartered by the auto king in 1915, in an effort to mediate an end to World War I. Bernstein denied Ford's allegation that he was an informant on Jewish wrongdoings and filed a $200,000 libel suit. The suit was settled out of court, after which Ford apologized both to Bernstein and the Jewish people at large.

Henry/Clara Signatures

An indenture bearing the signatures of Henry Ford and his wife, Clara, has come into the possession of Dick Folsom, Canton, Mich.

The document, dated Nov. 9, 1944, provides for Henry's sister, Margaret Ruddiman, and her daughter, Catherine, to buy for $1 the Ford-owned house (plus contents and land) in which they were living at 154 River Lane, Dearborn. The Fords' signatures were witnessed by two of Henry Ford's secretaries, Frank Campsall and Charles Schweitzer.

Margaret was one of Ford's two sisters, the other being Jane, who died in 1906. Margaret lived in the River Lane house until her death in 1960. Catherine, 90, now lives in Florida.

Catherine and Folsom are friends, and Catherine gave the document to her friend. Inasmuch as asking prices for Henry Ford's signature now range up to $2,500, Folsom's document – containing the signatures of both Henry and Clara, and being the kind of instrument it is – probably is worth $4,000 to $5,000.

Henry Ford Signatures

Several of Henry Ford's signatures were auctioned late last year by California Book Auction Galleries, of San Francisco, from the Henry Ford Collection of the Early Aviation Library of Harold W. Jensen.

The auction house suggested bid ranges for the autographs; the sums they actually brought I don't know. But the suggested figures make it clear that the asking price – and presumably the value – of Ford's signature has increased markedly in recent years. Some of the autographed items offered for sale were described as follows:

"Torn-out section of the *Dearborn Independent* with typed statement at bottom signed in ink by Ford ... Marked with red ink is a story about James Couzens, who was an original and important Ford employee. The typed note states: 'While I have bought this paper (*Dearborn Independent*), I am not taking active management of it until Jan. 1st, 1919. I do not agree with this article in any way. My sentiments are to help you (at the time Couzens was mayor of Detroit) in every possible manner ...' This item was apparently sent or given to Couzens ($1,000/$1,500)."

"New First, Second, Third, and Fourth McGuffey's readers ... each inscribed and signed by Ford on front free endpaper: 'Compliments of Henry Ford of Dearborn, Mich.' Each is a reprint copy from the original, issued by Ford in 1928 ($4,000/$5,000)."

"Ford & Harry Ferguson, signed by both. Original silver print photograph of Henry Ford and Harry Ferguson sitting outdoors across a table with the model of a tractor between them. 11 x 14. Signed by Ford and Ferguson below their positions in the photograph ($2,000/$3,000.)"

"Ford and the Fordson Tractor. Original silver print photograph of Henry Ford, Lord Northcliffe, and a group of men looking at a demonstration of a prototype Fordson tractor, 8 x 10, double matted with complete printed description below. Signed by Ford in lower left corner of photograph. During the third year of World War I, the British had put an order in for the first 6,000 Fordson tractors and this official entourage headed by Lord Northcliffe was checking up on the Ford operation to see how production was coming along. This is an official photo of the event ($3,000/$4,000)."

"Signed by Henry and Edsel Ford. Original silver print photograph of Henry & Edsel Ford & nine other men in what appears to be a large warehouse space. 8 x 10. Signed by Henry & Edsel Ford below their positions in the photograph ($2,000/$3,000)."

"Important Document Signed by Henry & Edsel. One-page T.D.s by Henry Ford and Edsel B. Ford on Ford Motor Company letterhead stationery, addressed to stockholder James Couzens. 11 x 8. Detroit: January 28, 1916. The document, signed by Henry Ford as President and Edsel Ford as Secretary, concerns the quit claiming of all Tractor business to Henry Ford for the sum of $46,810.76. The document is rubber-stamped at top 'Received January 29, 1915,' James Couzens, apparently forgetting to change the year. In upper-right hand corner is the pencil notation: 'Gave proxy to Liebold,' (Henry Ford's secretary) with 3/25/1916 written in ink ($3,000/$4,000)."

Thanks to Mike Skinner, Dearborn Mich., for forwarding the auction's catalog.

Me 'n Henry

A signed photograph of Henry Ford posing with St. Louis Cardinals stars Dizzy and Paul Dean and Pepper Martin and comedian Joe E. Brown recently was sold for $1,400 by Detroit's John K. King Books. The photo was taken in front of Greenfield Village's Martha-Mary Chapel on October 4, 1934, when the Cardinals were in Detroit to play the Tigers in the World Series.

Everyone in the photo including one of the Deans' wives, Patricia, A.F. Ruppenthal, and Kathryn F. Brown, autographed the photo. Purchased in California, the print was sold to a Detroit area collector who, in conformance with King policy, was not identified.

Your commentator is struck by the height and bulk of the Dean brothers, who stood more than half a head taller than the 5-foot, 9-inch Ford. The photo also recalls mid-1930s St. Louis area advertising which carried pictures of the Dean boys and the words, "Me 'n Paul," Dizzy being the more colorful and talented of the brothers.

Ford Signatures

Henry Ford's signature is worth considerable money partly because the industrialist seldom signed letters sent in his name. But as many as 200 Ford signatures may be tucked away in the Big Bay/Marquette area of Northern Michigan. Here's why:

In 1940 Ford and his wife were invited to a square dance at Bay Cliff, a Big Bay youth camp. At a camp social a few days earlier more than 200 children had received attractive autograph books with padded leather covers.

During the dance, recalls Fred Rydholm in his 1989 book, *Superior Heartland: A Backwoods History*, "one little crippled youngster went back to his dormitory, picked up the autograph book, and brought it to Mr. Ford for his signature. While he was signing the book, several other children saw what was going on and left the dance for the same purpose. Soon they were all rushing off to get their books and a line was rapidly forming, pushing, and shoving in front of Mr. Ford. Suddenly, as if by signal, all the rest of the campers ran off to get their books and the dance was over.

"Mr. Ford stood up and looked at the line of coverall-clad children, then told an aide 'to get a box to put all these books in so I can take them up to Huron Mountain [Ford's club]. I'll sign them up there and send them back in a few days.' " Ford kept his promise; and my guess is that most of the autograph books are extant, gathering dust in attics or storerooms.

On a subsequent visit to the camp, one of the counselors asked Ford if she could take his picture. He stopped and posed. Some people thought the counselor was nervy to make such a request, but Ford, according to Rydholm, "didn't seem to mind."

Last Autograph

Henry Ford's "last known documented autograph" appears on a photo obtained by Joseph Hadda, a pre-World War II employee of Ford's Chemical Research Laboratory, located within Greenfield Village.

Hadda, who lives in Detroit, related how he obtained the autograph in a letter on file at Oak Hill & the Martha Berry Museum, Rome, Georgia. Henry Ford and his wife, Clara, were major Berry College benefactors.

Hadda's letter reads as follows:

"I took this picture to the Christmas play in the [Henry] Ford Museum auditorium in December, 1946 to have Mr. Ford sign it for me after the program. I chatted with him briefly in the lobby. He appeared to be a little tired so I did not want to bother him with it at that time.

"A week or so later, I gave the picture to Ed Litogot [a descendant of a brother of Henry Ford's mother, Mary Litogot, called Mary O'Hern after adoption at age three] and asked him to have 'the boss' (Mr. Ford) sign it for me when he saw him. Ed called me a few weeks later and brought it over to me.

"Later on, Robert Rankin, Mr. Ford's chauffeur, told Ed Litogot that this was Mr. Ford's last signature. It was signed on January 23, 1947 in the Greenfield Village print shop .... According to Rankin, after Mr. Ford signed it he said, 'I wonder where Ed (Litogot) got that picture?' Mr. Ford died a little more than two months later on April 7, 1947."

Thanks to Scott Breithaupt, director of Oak Hill & the Martha Berry Museum, for furnishing the text of the letter and to Dearborn's Ford Richardson Bryan, leading authority on the extended Ford family, for information on Messrs. Hadda and Litogot.

Little White Slaver

Henry Ford's 1914 anti-cigarette book, *The Case Against the Little White Slaver*, has been reprinted by the Historical Society of Michigan, with support from Blue Cross-Blue Shield of Michigan.

Your commentator wrote the introduction to the 76-page softcover reprint, and perhaps can best acquaint "Ford Country" readers with it by presenting the following excerpts from the introduction:

"Ford's dislike of cigarettes first found expression in sales literature sent to his company's dealerships in 1908. 'Don't get yourself up like some young sport whose chief aim in life is to "smoke up" a half-dozen packs and take his lady friends joyriding,' salesmen were admonished. 'Selling cars is a dignified profession; act the part.' In 1911 Ford went further, permitting no one, including customers and visitors to smoke in his sales branches, located in the nation's largest cities.

"In early 1914, Ford, vacationing in Florida with his idol, Thomas A. Edison, learned that the inventor shared his views on the evil effects of cigarette smoking. Asked to put his opinions in writing, Edison responded with the famous letter reprinted in *Little White Slaver*. Ford, delighted with the missive, presented framed copies to the schools of Detroit and Highland Park, home of his huge factory, and publicly announced his opposition to cigarette smoking.

"The automaker then decided to publish anti-smoking pamphlets aimed at young males. Girls, few of whom smoked, and smokers over age 25, believed beyond redemption, were not to be targeted. The project was assigned to Ford's capable, blunt secretary, Ernest G. Liebold, who doubled as the magnate's chief of staff.

"Liebold turned for assistance to a *Detroit Free Press* feature writer, Len G. Shaw. The newsman invited scores of educators, physicians, judges, youth workers, athletes, and employers to comment on cigarette smoking. Some of their letters appear in Ford's book, along with a vigorous rebuttal by Percival I. Hill, president of the American Tobacco Co. (The book) went through three printings, as thousands of copies were distributed to students through high schools and colleges and to new Ford hires.

"Edison's remarkable letter set the tone of Ford's crusade. The inventor, who indicated the burning paper wrapper of cigarettes, rather than tobacco itself, claimed that this 'injurious agent' had a 'violent action on the nerve centers, producing degeneration of the cells of the brain, which is quite rapid among boys.'

"The sage of Menlo Park, who himself enjoyed cigars and an occasional chew of plug tobacco, added that he employed no cigarette smokers. Taking Edison's cue, Ford similarly focused on the adverse effects of cigarette smoking, ignoring cigars, pipe smoking, and chewing tobacco.

"Going beyond Edison's letter, Ford emphasized the moral aspects of cigarette smoking, claiming that 'almost every criminal is an inveterate cigarette smoker.' Both men were outdone by compatriots who condemned not only cigarettes, but tobacco in general, and also emphasized tobacco's deleterious physical effects. Interestingly, in the light of present-day discussion, no one advocated smoking bans in restaurants, public buildings, trains, and the like.

"Ford's anti-smoking campaign would have attracted little attention had it not followed in the immediate wake of the magnate's '$5 day,' which more than doubled Ford Co. male workers' wages. This 'shot heard around the world' immediately made Ford one of the globe's most admired and respected figures. His view on the subject carried weight, and he could not be dismissed by the tobacco industry as yet another crank ....

"Ford, a highly paternalistic employer, expected his workers to practice what he preached; and he banned tobacco of all kinds from his plants for decades. Thousands of foremen smoked anyway, and company lore is replete with stories of employees swallowing cigarettes or flushing butts down toilets when pounced upon by security guards.

"The ban remained in effect until November, 1947, seven months after Ford's death. It was lifted – for male employees only – by the founder's grandson and successor, Henry Ford II, himself a cigarette and cigar smoker. Tobacco companies, which had protested Ford's opposition to tobacco by boycotting Ford products in the 1930s, were jubilant ....

"In the long-run, Ford's vision and common sense were vindicated. If he and his friends stopped smoking for some of the wrong reasons, their major thrust – that cigarettes were harmful – was three generations ahead of its time. In the late 1980s, many employers, Ford among them, bowing to ever-mounting evidence of the harmfulness of smoking on smokers and nonsmokers alike, banned smoking on their premises except in limited, designated areas. Several of the nation's major health organizations have called for a smoking ban in homes.

"Ford's campaign may or may not have deterred many boys from smoking cigarettes; likely we'll never know. What is known is that cigarette consumption, partly because of increased smoking by females, accelerated during Ford's lifetime from 16 billion cigarettes in 1914 to 367 billion in 1945. By that yardstick, Ford's crusade, as one of his biographers put it, had 'all the success of a butterfly trying to heel the *Queen Elizabeth* by doing handsprings on its stack deck.'

"Nonetheless, *The Case Against the Little White Slaver* stands as a courageous effort to save youths from themselves; and it blazed a trail which many would follow – eventually. Its original editions being scarce collector's items, it is fitting that this delightful little book should be reprinted by the Historical Society of Michigan."

The book may be obtained by sending $10, plus four percent sales tax for Michigan residents, to the Society, whose address is 2117 Washtenaw, Ann Arbor, Mich. 48104; phone (734) 769-1828.

Edsel Ford (1893-1943), a camera enthusiast, took countless pictures of family members and friends. He also appears in many snapshots. This is a formal photograph, taken by Pirie MacDonald, Photographer of Men, N.Y. Date is unknown, but Edsel's appearance places him in his 40s, near the end of his all-too-brief life. (Photo from Henry Ford Museum and Greenfield Village, Dearborn, Mich.)

Anniversary Year

Edsel Ford, unsung during his lifetime, remains unsung, if the July 26 edition of *USAuto Scene*, a Detroit area tabloid, is any indication.

The publication noted that "1993 is quadruply monumental in the automotive world. It marks the 100th anniversary of the automobile in America, the 90th anniversary of the Ford Motor Co., the 75th anniversary of the Ford Rouge Plant, and the 130th anniversary of the birth of Henry Ford."

The year 1993, the tabloid might be reminded, also marked the centennial of Edsel Ford's birth. Edsel's lack of recognition stems partly from his desire to remain unpublicized. Throughout his life, in fact, Edsel shunned publicity as much as his father sought it: and was no less successful in avoiding the spotlight than Henry was in bathing in it. The younger Ford usually turned down requests for biographical data; almost always refused requests for written expressions of opinion; granted interviews only for compelling business reasons; even banned the use of the pronoun "I" in company statements in which his name appeared.

When asked by company publicists to pose for pictures at business functions, his usual reply was, "See if you can get Father to do that. He likes that sort of thing. I don't." His reputation for shunting newsmen to the elder Ford provoked the *Philadelphia Inquirer* to grumble in 1942 that his longest statement to the press had been, "See Father."

During interviews, Edsel was pleasant, but said very little. "When he spoke," stated the *Detroit News*, "it was not with the picturesque flourish that would make a tale to be told and retold, but with quiet understanding and reserve." Edsel, although president of the world's most-publicized company for a quarter-century, never conducted a business press conference.

The younger Ford remained in the background for several reasons. According to noted industrial designer, Walter Dorwin Teague, who worked closely with Edsel during the 1930s, the main reason was: "An unselfconscious modesty that left no need for the kind of compensations publicity has to offer."

Edsel also valued privacy. "I don't want to be in the position that Father's in," he told an associate, "... to be set upon by autograph hunters and people trying to sell me some idea." Edsel also knew that his father resented sharing the limelight with anyone – including his son.

Edsel sought anonymity and he achieved it. In 1922, as he stood in front of the Senate Office Building with members of the Senate Banking and Currency Committee, before which he had just testified, he was waved out of camera range by a press photographer:

"Bud, would you mind – this is just for big shots." In 1935, to his delight he was able to visit San Diego's California-Pacific Exposition 19 times without being recognized by newsmen or any other visitors.

In retrospect, it is clear that Edsel was more than talented; he was creative. He was more than hard-working; he had an extraordinary sense of responsibility to his company and community. He was an excellent administrator, and he commanded the affection, respect, and loyalty of his associates. Had he lived beyond 1943 and led Ford Motor Co. into the post-World War II era, he would have revived the firm no less surely than did his eldest son, Henry II, and HFII's mentor, Ernest R. Breech.

Dr. Edsel A. Ruddiman

A biographical sketch of Dr. Edsel A. Ruddiman, for whom Henry Ford's son, Edsel, was named, appears in the Winter 1995 issue of the *Dearborn Historian*, quarterly publication of the Dearborn Historical Commission.

Dr. Ruddiman, editor/author Winfield H. Arneson states, was born on a Dearborn Township farm near Warren Avenue and Southfield Road on Dec. 27, 1864, a half-year after Henry Ford's birth about a mile away. Both boys attended a one-room school in the nearby "Scotch Settlement." Later the auto king moved the schoolhouse to Greenfield Village, complete with the last-row desk on which the initials "H.F." and "E.A.R." were carved. Village visitors can sit at this desk today.

After attending school in Detroit (Henry quit after completing the eighth grade), Dr. Ruddiman earned bachelor's and master's degrees in pharmacy from the University of Michigan in 1886 and 1887, respectively. He received a medical degree from Vanderbilt University in 1893, and served as a professor of pharmacy at that institution from 1890-1920, being a dean part of that time.

Dr. Ruddiman served as chief chemist for several Michigan companies between 1920-26. In the latter year he was hired by Ford to conduct nutritional research on the soybean, and continued in that endeavor for as long as his former schoolmate was active.

In 1943 Dr. Ruddiman was one of nine men named in a codicil to Henry Ford's will to serve on a board of trustees which was to have administered the Ford Company for 10 years after the founder's death. The codicil subsequently was nullified.

Dr. Ruddiman died on March 21, 1954 at his Long Boulevard, Dearborn residence. He is buried in Evergreen (Scotch Settlement) Cemetery. His name, like that of his namesake, Edsel Ford, lives on in Ford's greatest marketing disaster.

Edsel's Wedding House

The house in which Edsel B. Ford, only son of Henry Ford, and Eleanor Clay were married on November 2, 1916 was open to the public during a tour of homes in Detroit's Historic Boston-Edison Homes District.

The house from 1906-11 was the home of Alex Malcomson, one of Ford Motor Company's principal charter shareholders. At the time of Edsel's wedding it was the residence of Eleanor's mother, a sister of Joseph L. Hudson, owner of Detroit's largest department store.

A veritable who's who of autodom attended the wedding, among them the Dodge brothers, who owned 10 percent of Ford Company stock. The brothers, after chatting pleasantly with Ford at the reception, the next day slapped him with a lawsuit in protest against his one-man control of the Ford Company and his diversion of profits into the Rouge Plant and other expansion projects. The Dodges wanted profits converted into dividends, so they could expand their own new auto firm.

The nuptial site, called the Joseph R.

McLaughlin House for the attorney and state senator who built it in 1900, is located at 121 E. Boston Boulevard.

Thanks to reader Mike Skinner, of Dearborn, Mich., for forwarding the district's home tours brochure.

Ford House

Sign on the premises of Edsel & Eleanor Ford House, Grosse Pointe Shores, Mich. A pleasant tea room, located in the building from which guided tours begin, is open Wednesdays through Saturdays from 11:30-3:30 p.m. (Photo by Michael Skinner, St. Clair Shores, Mich.)

Signage for Edsel Ford Court at Lakeshore Drive, St. Clair Shores, Mich. The court is a three-block thoroughfare lined with moderately-priced apartment buildings.

Edsel Ford Court

Many streets have been named for Henry Ford, and now we learn of a second one named for his son, Edsel – Edsel Ford Court in St. Clair Shores, Mich. The community is adjacent to Grosse Pointe Shores, where Edsel and his wife, Eleanor, resided from the late 1920s until their deaths in 1943 and 1976, respectively.

The Edsel Ford Expressway, part of I-94, has been Detroit's principal east-west thoroughfare since 1955.

Thanks to Mike Skinner, of St. Clair Shores, Mich., for forwarding a copy of a *Grosse Pointe News & Connection* advertisement on a residential site on Edsel Ford Court.

Edsel Ford Fong

A recent article in *Image*, the Sunday magazine of the *San Francisco Examiner*, describes a local waiter named Edsel Ford Fong as "The Rudest Waiter in the World."

Fong worked 20 years ago in Sam Wah, a restaurant in the heart of Chinatown. The article's author, Gary Kamiya, says "the provenance of (Fong's) ludicrous name is uncertain." On the contrary, it seems fairly certain that it could have derived only from the name of the former president of Ford Motor Co.

Edsel Ford House

"Where can I get information on Edsel Ford's home, which I understand is open to the public?" inquired reader Paul Mariana, of Jersey City, N.J.

Best bet is from the Edsel and Eleanor Ford House, 1100 Lake Shore Road, Grosse Pointe Shores, MI 48236; phone 313-884-3400 for tour information.

A handsome, highly illustrated 104-page book on the home, *Edsel and Eleanor Ford House*, by James A. Bridenstine, was published in 1988 by the Wayne State University Press. Excerpts from the *Detroit Free Press*' review of the book follows:

"This book is a stunning tribute to the creation of Edsel and Eleanor Ford House, a house that was both home and exhibit hall, a place that integrated the arts of the architect, the decorator, and the landscaper.

"With luxuriant photography, most of it in color, and a text that describes the home and its treasures in rich detail, 'Edsel and Eleanor Ford House' is pure pleasure. Whether you treat it as a wish book or as a guide to the Albert Kahn-designed 60-room Cotswold cottage-style house on the shores of Lake St. Clair, this volume will have you picking out your favorite rooms and furnishings."

The house is one of four historic homes of auto figures open to the public; the others being Henry Ford's Dearborn home, Fair Lane; Lawrence Fisher's Detroit residence; and the estate of John Dodge's widow on Rochester's Oakland University campus.

Haven Hill Vandalized

Edsel Ford's Haven Hill Lodge, located in the Highland State Recreation Area in northwest Oakland County, has become a haven for vandals.

The lodge was built of white cedar logs cut from Ford Company timber holdings in Michigan's Upper Peninsula. Sandstone used in six massive chimneys came from Vermont and blue clay for the tennis courts from Spain, while hardware on doors and windows was forged at the company's Rouge Plant. The lodge, plus a stable, gatehouse, and sheep barn, cost $1.4 million.

Haven Hill was used as a Ford family getaway until Edsel's death in 1943. During the 1930s, when kidnapping was much in the news, Edsel's four children sometimes were sent there as a protective measure.

The lodge and its accompanying 1,200 acres were sold to the State of Michigan's Department of Natural Resources (DNR) in 1946 for $307,500. The dwelling served as a conference center until 1972, and as an environmental education center until closed in 1980 because of Michigan's financial stringencies.

Today, most of the lodge's windows are boarded, or broken, and its plaster is crumbling. The floor is littered with scraps of charred paper and the walls are covered with graffiti. Break-ins are commonplace. It would take $1 million to restore the lodge, according to Park Superintendent Ron Lounsbery. [Editor's note: The lodge was destroyed by a fire set by three teenagers on Jan. 22, 1999.]

Lincoln Highway

After attending the second annual meeting of the Lincoln Highway Association in Boone, Iowa, in 1994, reader David Babb, Belvidere, Ill., wrote the following about Edsel Ford's disillusionment with the promoters of the highway's "Ideal Section":

"The 'Ideal Section' was located near Dyer, Ind. It was just over one mile long and had been designed with width, thickness, landscaping and other features expected to be the highway of the future. We saw photos showing repair before it even opened because the expansion joints were improper. All of this was in the 1920s.

"Edsel Ford contributed substantial

funding for the project and was also going to contribute to a 40-acre campground which was also to be part of the 'Ideal Section.' Apparently the promoters kept raising the costs and Edsel eventually withdrew thinking that they were taking advantage of his deep pockets. Also mentioned was the fact that Henry Ford opposed funding of the project, thinking that public roads should be funded at public expense."

Boone meeting participants saw a video in which the late George Preston, Belle Plaine, Iowa, recalled a visit by Henry Ford and Thomas Edison to Preston's filling station. The station is now a roadside museum.

Fringe Benefit

"Edsel Ford had a hard time working for his old man," writes reader Russell S. Wollman, Fairfield, Iowa. "But oh boy, the fringes. Once a year he'd have the Ford Works build a one-off to his specs. This is all the health insurance I'd need."

Edsel's Mistress's Car?

"My eye was caught today by the following ad in [an old-car magazine]," writes ex-Ford executive Malcolm L. Denise, of Grosse Pointe, Mich.:

"1936 Ford roadster. V-8, supposedly Edsel Ford's mistress's car, newly restored, blue, $35,000."

"Edsel?" asks Denise. "One has to allow for advertiser's hype ... a top quality restoration of that model is worth two-thirds the price asked in the ad."

Quite true, at the time. Just as any car allegedly or actually linked to Hitler, Presley, Liberace, etc. fetches an inflated price, so would one allegedly belonging to "Edsel's mistress."

Did Edsel have a mistress? I've heard an unfounded comment or two suggesting that he did, while hearing a great deal more about him which suggested that he did not.

Edsel Ford's Yachts

Two of Edsel Ford's yachts are discussed in C. Philip Moore's recently published *Yachts in a Hurry: An Illustrated History of the Great Commuter Yachts.*

The first of the yachts, the *Greyhound*, 58 feet long and 10 feet, 5 inches wide, was built in 1916 in New York. The craft's two Liberty V-12 engines pushed its speed to 33 mph.

Edsel sold the *Greyhound* to E.L. Richards for $30,000 before taking delivery of his next boat, the *Marlin*. Renamed *Get There*, the former *Greyhound*'s present whereabouts and owner are unknown.

The *Marlin*, built for Ford in Maine in 1930, was designed as a dual-purpose commuter and sportfishing boat. Bought sight unseen and commissioned in Miami, the ship, 51'6" in length and with a beam of 16'6", was powered by twin 145-Sterling Dolphin engines for a top speed of 28 mph. Notable features included a large forward cockpit, cabin amidships with sleeping accommodations for four people, a larger aft cockpit arranged for fishing with chairs, and a fish well and bait well under the cockpit. *Marlin* originally carried an 8-foot skiff on the aft part of the house, and a swordfishing-style pulpit extended several feet from her plumb bow.

Ownership of the *Marlin* after Edsel Ford's sale of the boat in 1935 is not fully documented, but it is known that she was owned in the late 1930s by Arthur Houghton of the Corning Glass Corporation, then by Schenley Distilling Company, and saw service with the Coast Guard in World War II, patrolling between Palm Beach and Fort Lauderdale. After the war she was owned by the Yellow Cab Company.

In 1952, while languishing in a boatyard in Falmouth on Cape Cod, *Marlin* was bought by Joseph P. Kennedy, father of the late President. Subsequently sold to the D. Acierno family, of Sayville, N.Y., the *Marlin* now is called the *Deama* and regularly cruises on Long Island Sound.

Thanks to Mike Skinner, Dearborn, Mich., for forwarding pertinent pages from *Yachts in a Hurry*.

Big Turnout For Edsel

"I was home on military leave in May 1943 when Edsel Ford's funeral service was held at St. Paul's Episcopal Cathedral on Detroit's Woodward Avenue," writes reader Walter Schan, of Southfield, Mich.

"My father's friend let me view the proceedings from the roof of a nearby two-story building. Far, far more people attended Edsel's funeral than that of his father, Henry Ford."

Edsel's services probably outdrew his father's because of the ages of the two at death – Edsel was 49, his father 83. Many of Edsel's friends and associates, in the prime of life, could attend his services, whereas many of Henry's contemporaries had passed from the scene. Moreover, Henry, mentally and physically impaired, had been inactive for several years.

In any event long lines of people viewed Henry Ford's body as it lay in state on the first floor of Greenfield Village's Recreation Building, now called Lovett Hall. Estimates of the mourners ranged from the *Montgomery Advertiser*'s 30,000 and the *New York Times*' 70,000 to *Newsweek*'s 100,000, and *Time*'s 105,000.

Edsel Ford Book

A biography of Edsel Ford has yet to be written, and Robert Yagley, associate editor of Barnes & Noble Books, thinks one should be.

In a recent letter, Yagley, while inviting me to write on Edsel, discussed the project as follows:

"I would be interested in proposing to my publisher and the B&N Trade Department the possibility of a book on Edsel Ford. Although he's not as well known as his father or even his son, I believe he is an immensely overlooked figure in American history. His involvement with the Rouge plant, Willow Run, and the collapse of the [Detroit] Guardian Trust, put him in the forefront of this century's most pivotal events - mass production, the Depression, and the war effort. Yet, despite his immersion in these seminal events of an increasingly mechanized society, his patronage of Rivera's murals and the Detroit Institute of Arts as well as his friendship with William Valentiner [head of the Institute] reveal a very sympathetic man with a unique vision of the early twentieth century.

"I'm sure I could generate some interest here at Barnes & Noble, if you are in the least bit intrigued with this proposal. Though I'm just speculating here, I sincerely believe there's a substantial book to be made on Edsel Ford."

I completely agree with Yagley, but declined his offer. For one thing, I've other writing commitments, and I continue to teach full-time in the University of Michigan Business School. For another, I've long been reluctant to write a book about Edsel, partly because his business life (the part that most interests me) is sad, if not tragic. That said, I have written three articles about him, the latest, "Edsel Ford: The Gentle Businessman," appearing in the May-June 1994 issue of *Michigan History*.

It may be hoped that Yagley will commission someone to write Edsel's biography. Meanwhile, Henry Dominguez, of Sacramento, Calif., who authored *The Ford Agency* in 1980, has been researching a book on Edsel since 1988, and, in addition to spending time at the Ford Archives, has interviewed many people who knew and worked with Edsel. Dominguez has worked for General Motors for 12 years, the last seven of them with Saturn.

Axing The "Playhouse"

Henry Ford II was wielding a fireman's ax the first time Rouge plant employee Walter B. Morgan saw him. It was 1945, and the 27-year-old scion was being escorted through the factory.

He arrived at a group of offices where, recalls Morgan, "some of the big bosses would bring their women. They had beds and whiskey in those offices, and we called it 'the playhouse.' Ford was being shown around by a group of Service Department men (loyalists of Harry Bennett, Henry Ford's chief aide and HFII's principal antagonist), and when he came to these offices, he wanted to know what they were for.

"The servicemen didn't want him to see the offices, so they told him nobody had a key. Ford just took an ax off the wall and tore those doors down. He later ordered them to get rid of all that."

That episode, as Morgan told the *Detroit Free Press*, was the first and only time he saw Ford up close. Morgan, 74, attended the Henry Ford Trade School and traces his company service date to 1934. He retired in 1972. Morgan has fond memories of both Fords, adding that they "have to be given a lot of credit for helping blacks. If I had my life to live all over again," he concluded, "I'd work for Ford."

Immediately after becoming company president in 1945, Ford fired Bennett and dismissed, demoted, or transferred a thousand of his cronies including, no doubt, those who denied him keys to 'the playhouse.'

Henry Ford II Stories

Your commentator seems to be favored with a Henry Ford or Henry Ford II story or two at every Ford-related meeting he attends in the Detroit area. Recently, while attending a Henry Ford Estate-Fair Lane Interpretative Planning Session, I heard the following about HFII from Edward Francis, president of William Kessler and Associates, Inc. (architects):

Henry II, giving an address in Detroit in the presence of Mayor Coleman Young and other civic leaders, was represented as being as "drunk as a loon" and swearing throughout, according to Francis' boss, Bill Kessler. The latter, expressing amazement over Ford's profanity, told his tablemates that he had never heard so many cusswords in his life. His fellow listeners, having heard Ford before, assured Kessler that the industrialist's performance was "routine."

HFII did indeed often drink too much at gatherings, and when inebriated he used foul language and also said and did a good many things that his associates and friends wished had been left unsaid and undone.

The second story concerns a swimming pool that Henry II had built as a surprise gift for his second wife, Cristina. After Kessler designed the pool, it was quickly constructed while Cristina was in Europe. Returning, she dumped all over the pool and insisted that everything but its dimensions and water be redesigned. "Fish spouting water" seemed to be of prime importance.

The Ford residence was razed some years ago, and upscale housing now graces the premises. Ironically, the sole remaining vestige of the Ford era is the swimming pool.

HFII And Telephone

"Telephone anecdotes about famous people seem to be a dime a dozen," writes Will Scott, a Ford vice president between 1968-86, who then proceeds to spin some about his ex-boss, Henry Ford II.

"Henry Ford's personal life was always fair game for the media," Scott recalls, "and one day the *Detroit News* ran a front-page article intimating that his second marriage was on the rocks. The paper hit the street about 11 a.m. and before noon Mr. Ford had tracked down his old friend, Martin Hayden, the editor of the *News*. 'Martin,' he shouted over the phone, 'couldn't you have shown the decency of talking to me first before running me down in that gossip sheet of yours?'

" 'I'm sorry, Henry, but I really did try to reach you. They told me you were in London.' There was a pause before Mr. Ford closed out the conversation. 'Martin, where in the hell do you think I'm calling you from?' "

Scott also remembers his wife, Barbara, groping for the phone one night at about 3 a.m. "I heard her protest, saying, 'He's sound asleep!' Then I could actually hear the voice on the other end of the line shout, 'Well, wake him up.' Barb gave me the phone. 'What in the hell is going on?' Mr. Ford asked. 'You're the third person I've called this morning who was still in bed.' When I asked him where he was, he reminded me that I damn well knew he was in Europe. It was, of course, already 8 a.m. in London."

Late one Sunday afternoon, Scott reminisces, "the phone rang while I was watching a Detroit Lions football game on TV. My wife answered in the kitchen and then she shouted to me in the den. 'It's for you. I think it's the painter, finally.' I picked up the phone and the voice said, 'This is not the painter but before we're through you probably are going to wish it was. This is Henry Ford ....' (His prediction was a good one)."

Hirsute Henry II

Was growing a beard one of his better ideas, I asked Henry Ford II in April 1985, two years before his death. His reply was that of a man who lived life his way and enjoyed going against the grain.

"I thought growing a beard was a super idea," he replied. "But I couldn't find many people who would go along with me. I was in Africa, and we were out in the bush. There was no running water and it was just a hell of a problem to shave. We were out there for 30 days, and we had to ask for water every time we wanted it. We got warm water a couple of times a day to wash our hands, and we could take a shower if we gave enough notice.

"I just said to hell with shaving, it wasn't worth it. That's how I grew a beard the first time. The second time I grew it because nobody liked the first one. I figured if people didn't like it, it was a good reason to have another go at it," he laughed. "I don't know whether I'll do it again or not. I might. If I went down South and just sat on a beach somewhere I might."

His second beard was his last.

Snappy Dresser

"Did Henry Ford II pay as much attention to his dress as his grandfather?" asks reader Wilson Farraday, of Anderson, Ind.

Yes, as indicated by this photo of HFII looking as if he stepped out of a bandbox. Although Ford's chairman had a bay window when this picture of him was taken by your commentator at Benson Ford's funeral in July 1978, his well-tailored suit does much to disguise his portliness.

HFII On Art

During his lifetime Henry Ford II collected much valuable art. In 1985 I asked him to discuss his art collection, and he did so as follows:

"I'm not a collector, and I've never been a collector .... I've never been a collector because (a) I'm not knowledgeable enough in any one of the specific kinds of art and (b) I've really never had enough time or total interest to get into it in a full-time way. So what I've done over a period of 40 years or so is – if I see something that looks pretty good and I like it – buy it, if I can afford it.

"I've made some pretty good choices," Ford added, "and I have sold off some stuff. I've sold off pictures basically, also some porcelains, some decorative pieces. Some haven't done very well, some have done well.

"But I'm neither in a buying mood or a selling mood. I might buy if I see something really extraordinary. But then I also think of the longevity ahead of me, and it's not very great so I figure, well, what the hell am I buying this for? I better do something else. So I don't really go after anything. I don't peruse the catalogs to the extent that one would if one was really desirous of making an effort to find something that's really nice."

HFII was right about his longevity. He died only 29 months after our discussion. He was chairman of Sotheby's the last three years of his life, 1984-87.

HFII's Renoir

"I have read that Henry Ford II was an art collector. What's the most valuable of his paintings?" inquires Rene Delacroix, of Montreal.

Answer: Renoir's 1878 "Cup of Chocolate," which was sold at auction in 1990 to an unidentified Japanese collector for $18.2 million.

Ford inherited the Renoir from his mother upon her death in 1976, then gave it to his three children, Edsel, Charlotte Ford Downe, and Anne Ford Scarborough.

Thirty-six Ford family paintings sold for $48.6 million at the 1990 auction, conducted by Sotheby's, which had estimated the artwork would fetch $66 million to $85.8 million. The next most valuable of the Ford paintings was

Cezanne's 1880's view of the Provence estate of the artist's father. It sold for $7.2 million in 1990.

A copy of the Renoir hangs in the Edsel and Eleanor Ford House in Grosse Pointe Shores, Mich., which is open to the public.

No Queenly Intervention

It's been rumored that Henry Ford II interceded with Queen Elizabeth in 1983 to enable a friend, Detroit-based real estate developer, A. Alfred Taubman, to purchase England's prestigious auction house, Sotheby's. Ford bought a piece of the firm, as did another Taubman friend, Detroit businessman Max Fisher.

Ford's widow, Kathy, scotches the rumor. "I do know," she recently told *Detroit Monthly*, "and numerous people in London keep saying to me all the time, that Henry was very instrumental in [Taubman] getting Sotheby's." Kathy, however, doesn't believe the rumor about Henry and the Queen. "If he had seen the Queen," she laughs, "I'm sure he would have said, 'Kate, I went to see the Queen today!' And I'd have said, 'Oh, darling, what *did* she have to say?' "

Taubman remains Sotheby's principal owner and chairman. HFII served as vice-chairman until his death in 1987.

Victor Lasky Dies

Victor Lasky, author of *Never Complain, Never Explain*, a 1981 unauthorized biography of Henry Ford II, died last year in Washington.

Most of Lasky's writings focused on communism, which he abhorred. He also wrote books on John F. Kennedy, Robert Kennedy, Justice Arthur Goldberg, and President Jimmy Carter.

Lasky's Ford book, his last, was panned by the *New York Times*, which accused the author of having "complied every derogatory reference made against his subject and interviewing his most vocal detractors." This technique, added the *Times*, "Is not only indefensible, but, after a while, tiresome. Not a few readers will probably finish this book feeling almost a twinge of compassion for Mr. Ford – for anyone – who has been subjected to so vituperative a pen."

Father And Son

One of the most moving obituaries of Henry Ford II was written by his son, Edsel II. The obituary appeared in the Winter 1987 issue of *University Liggett School Perspective*, published thrice yearly by the Grosse Pointe, Mich., preparatory school descended from Detroit University School, from which HFII was graduated in 1935, and Grosse Pointe University School, from which Edsel II was graduated in 1966.

Inasmuch as the obituary has a special quality, and is unlikely to be seen by our readers in its original setting or elsewhere, we are reprinting it in these pages:

"I have been reminding myself lately that the passing away of Henry Ford II is essentially a Thanksgiving. It is an occasion on which our sorrow should be equally mixed with gratitude. It's a moment in our lives when we will inevitably look back and remember what we have lost; but we must also look forward and consider what we have gained – through the life, love, service and dedication of Henry Ford II. And if we manage to do that – perhaps with a small smile in our hearts – we shall be doing what Daddy wanted. I know that, because he wrote a letter to my stepmother and me in which he made his wishes very clear.

"He wrote: 'It is my most earnest wish that I shall be remembered in an atmosphere which enables those who participate to recall the good things of my life and not to linger on the regrets that death inevitably brings in its wake.

" 'If a man is remembered properly, it can be a matter for rejoicing rather than sorrow and it is my most sincere desire that the last chapter of my life, rather than my death, shall be celebrated in this spirit.'

"Daddy didn't, of course, go around *being* famous. When somebody once asked him what it was like to be Henry Ford II, he said he didn't know how to answer the question. He had never been anybody else.

"Some people started to think of him in that way, and first saw him as the public man that he couldn't avoid being. They said his name was on the building. But there was no more to it than that. His heart was in it. He dominated the company – but the Company also dominated his life, which was essentially one of undivided service to the responsibility that had been thrust upon him in 1943 when he came out of the Navy.

"When the times settle down, and we are all a little farther away, I believe that history will see him for what he *did*. We can best think about him for what he *was*. He was a man of many contradictions – but that was to be expected. We are all shaped by the circumstances of our destiny and he had no choice but to lead a challenging and complicated life. Nobody ever said it would be easy. The buck always stopped with him and he never shirked a decision. He was the first to admit that not all his decisions were right. He also was the first to accept the responsibility when things went wrong.

"The heart that beat steadily for 70 years and 25 days was a warm heart, and it cared for those who were not famous men or women. The unsung people who worked for him knew where his heart was and what was in it. They knew it at his homes in Turville, England, and Grosse Pointe, Michigan. They knew it at Ford plants in Dagenham and the Rouge. They knew it in Detroit, and they knew it in the offices and factories all over the Ford world. His generosities were large and small, but they all were made in the same spirit. He always said "thank you." He never forgot to say "please." Sometimes he was blunt because he called a truth, a truth. He gave straight answers. He never deceived anybody, least of all himself.

"And if those of us who are his children and family have any regrets, it is that we have had to share so much of him with the many other people in that larger Ford family. And Kate, above all, knows what I mean. It didn't make the time we had with him any less precious. It merely meant that there was never *enough*. But now we *have* time. We have time to remember and recapture what he called in his letter 'the good things' of his life – and those will last us forever. We shall always see him, shan't we? We shall always hear him. We shall never forget his tremendous zest for living and the fight he put up right to the end. I hope we all shall remember – I certainly shall – that he left us a challenge.

"My father's first duty was to the tradition of the Ford family and to the company which bears the family name – a worldwide team of men and women who still depend on it as we do. Whether they call it 'Ford' or 'Ford's,' Daddy inspired in them the same sense of loyalty that he had, and that he instilled in us. As a family, we have inherited the responsibility to remember his own definition of what family meant, and to carry on – in our own way – building the vision that made him what he was. And that, in a sense, made us all – family and friends – what we are.

"There is a part of him that will forever be part of us."

Thanks to Mike Skinner, of Dearborn, Mich., the world's No. 1 Fordwatcher, for inviting our attention to Edsel's essay.

Henry Ford II's Ashes

"Where is Henry Ford II buried?" asks reader Walter Schan, of Southfield, Mich. HFII's body was cremated, and his family has yet to reveal the disposition of the ashes. A news report speculated that Ford's widow, Kathy, and Edsel II, dropped the remains from a helicopter over the

Detroit River, near the Motor City's Renaissance Center, of which HFII was the godfather. Rumor also has it that the ashes repose in a New Orleans night club, a thought not inconsistent with HFII's request – which was carried out – that a New Orleans jazz band play "When the Saints Come Marching In" at the close of his memorial service.

Ford Transition

Henry Ford II's passing of the baton to Philip Caldwell is cited as a model of corporate transition in a book on retiring executives by Harvard professor Jeffrey Sonnenfeld.

Deflating the "myth" that HFII mismanaged his succession by firing Lee Iacocca, the book instead portrays Iacocca as a jilted president who made too much noise after being fired. "It is not unusual that succession candidates are disappointed with the outcome, and certainly that was true in Iacocca's case," Sonnenfeld writes. "What was unusual was the fury of the candidate who was not selected."

Ford began planning his succession in 1976, Sonnenfeld says, and made it clear in 1977 and 1978 that Caldwell, not Iacocca, would succeed him. HFII hoped that Iacocca would quit. Since Iacocca didn't do so, he was fired in July 1978.

The Ford succession is one of many discussed in the book, which is based on Sonnenfeld's theory that a chief executive's departure style can have a profound influence on a company.

HFII Rules The Roost

Meetings with Henry Ford II and his subordinates always seemed more formal than did confabs with the chairmen of General Motors and Chrysler and their subordinates, Robben Fleming, ex-president of the University of Michigan recalls.

At Ford meetings, said Fleming, people always seemed to wait for HFII to speak before speaking themselves, then took their cues from the boss. "And they always called him 'Mr. Ford,' never Henry," added Fleming. "At GM, when Tom Murphy and Pete Estes were chairman and president, it was 'Tom and Pete,' and executives seemed to express their views more freely. At Chrysler, too, despite Chairman Lynn A. Townsend's considerable ego, subordinates seemed to speak up more than at Ford."

Surveys Are Bunk

Henry Ford regarded history as more or less bunk, and Henry Ford II viewed customer surveys in much the same way.

"We got into a frightful habit in this company of relying too much on surveys," Henry II told me in 1982, "and I'm under the impression that it still exists to a certain extent. I'm not a big survey man. I think that if you are in the (auto) business you ought to know what the hell you want to do. You can't rely on a survey to pull your bacon out of the frying pan.

"If you show people something that won't be out for three or four years, I don't think you can rely on their judgment. It's not their fault. They just haven't seen anything else; and they haven't had the benefit of seeing drawings and quarter-size models and to hear about what other people are planning to do that you find out about in different ways. A lot of people in the past, maybe even today, tend to say, well, this is what the survey says, and thereby relieve themselves of making a decision. I think that's bunk. If people don't think they know what the public is going to want they shouldn't be in the job."

If HFII's comments seem arbitrary with respect to surveys and customer relations, he at least was never heard to say, "The public can have any color it wants so long as it's black."

Down With Lawyers

"Henry Ford II didn't like lawyers," Will Scott, a Ford vice president between 1968-86 wrote in his unpublished personal history. "They think they know everything, they waste time, and they cost a lot of money," the industrialist told Scott.

"Much to the annoyance of three Ford general counsels that I knew over the years," Scott adds, "Mr. Ford never would appoint them to the Board of Directors. 'They can sit in on the meetings if they want,' he would explain, 'so why put them on the Board?'

"One day when I was in his office discussing some proposal, he asked me what Legal thought about it. I responded that I hadn't been able to get a firm position from them. Mr. Ford was inclined to go along with the proposal but he suggested touching base with the lawyers. 'Get Tisdale in here,' he barked over the intercom. Wright Tisdale, vice president and general counsel soon came in. Wright was acquainted with the proposal and talked at length, finally advising Mr. Ford that on a business judgment basis – not on legal grounds – he was against the proposal. After he left the room Mr. Ford smiled that big grin of his and said, 'That does it, let's go ahead with it!' "

That episode reminds me of another that occurred when I interviewed Henry II following his retirement. A call came from the Ford Company's general counsel, who asked Ford's secretary if he could see Henry II that afternoon. Over the intercom HFII replied yes, then told me that he disliked meeting with the counsel "because he always brings me trouble."

HFII and his grandfather shared a dislike of lawyers, and the senior Ford also had a marked distaste for accountants and bankers.

Nuisance Suit

"Did Roy Cohn have a case against Henry Ford II, or did he just file a nuisance suit?" asks reader John Wallingford, Teaneck, N.J.

He filed a nuisance suit, which paid off. Salient facts are as follows:

In 1978 Cohn, who had gained notoriety as chief counsel for Senator Joseph McCarthy's midcentury investigation committee, sued Ford's board of directors, explicitly Henry Ford II, for stealing.

Filed in behalf of the children of one of Cohn's law partners who had some Ford shares in trust, the $40 million suit alleged that Henry II had accepted $750,000 in kickbacks from a Chicago-based catering concern in return for exclusive concessions to provide food and beverages at company facilities. The suit also charged that the Ford Company had wasted more than $1 million in maintenance charges and personal expenses relative to Henry's six-room duplex apartment in New York's Carlyle Hotel.

At a press conference Henry II indignantly denied the charges, saying it was ridiculous for someone with his wealth to take a kickback. As for the apartment, he noted that when he used it for personal, as opposed to company, business, he had reimbursed the firm. Cohn's charges, he insisted, "went beyond the pale."

At Ford's 1978 Annual Meeting, attended by your commentator, Cohn attacked HFII on a variety of issues, ranging from the Pinto to an Indonesian bribe. Boos and cries for Cohn's ejection sounded throughout Detroit's Henry and Edsel Ford Auditorium.

A media darling in his own right, Cohn orchestrated a wave of anti-Ford publicity. It was the easier to do because the company and its chairman were well known and the charges were so scandalous. Spurred on by his publicity coup, Cohn filed amendments to his suit accusing HFII of additional misdeeds.

Throughout, Henry II had good reason to believe that Cohn was in league with New York "operator" Bill Fugazy, in turn a good friend of Lee

Iacocca, then under HFII's fire at Ford.

Cohn was rebuffed by a New York judge who ruled that Michigan had jurisdiction over his suit. An appeal was rejected, whereupon Cohn vowed to file suit in Michigan, then inquired whether a settlement might be possible. Ford, fearful of more unfavorable publicity, gave Cohn $100,000 for "legal fees" on the condition that he personally drop the suit. Cohn then declared that HFII was not guilty of any wrongdoing. His clients, the partner's children, got nothing, and did not resurrect the suit.

Ford's New York law firm admitted that the deal amounted to a Cohn buyoff. "It's Cohn we were interested in," a spokesman said, "and what he said he could do to us in the press .... he can get a headline in the *Wall Street Journal* or *New York Times* by picking up a phone .... These papers printed uncritical, big headline accounts of Cohn's charges."

"In many circles," *American Lawyer* noted, [Cohn's actions] "would be called extortion."

Ironically, *The Autobiography of Roy Cohn*, taped by Sidney Zion while Cohn was dying of AIDS in 1986, made no mention of Ford, the company or the man. To Cohn, the episode was just another of many shakedowns.

Smile In Your Hearts

"Henry Ford's recent memorial service in London was terribly cheerful, and I'm not saying this to be disrespectful," reported columnist William Norwich, of the *New York Daily News*. "It was the tycoon's last wish that his friends and family file out of St. George's Church 'with a smile in your hearts' to his favorite tune, 'When the Saints Come Marching In.'

"From his deathbed last September," continues Norwich, "Henry Ford conveyed his wishes to his son and heir, Edsel Ford, 38, in a sealed envelope.

" 'Nowhere in the world did my father have more friends than in this country, and that is why we are holding the memorial service here,' explained Edsel to London's top gossip columnist, Nigel Dempster.

"Henry Ford's widow, the former Kathy DuRoss, headed the congregation, which included a bevy of London swells," adds Norwich. "Our American ambassador, Charles Price, and his wife, Carol, hosted a luncheon for 40 people after the service at the American Embassy.

"Mrs. Ford, mother of the Gotham-based artist, Kimberly DuRoss, is said to be the main beneficiary of the automobile tycoon's estate, estimated at more than $200 million. Included in this legacy are splendid homes in London [actually Henley-on-Thames], Palm Beach, and Detroit [Grosse Pointe Farms]."

Journalists, authors, and others continually harp on common traits of Henry Ford and Henry Ford II. They had some commonality, to use an automotive term, but they were much more different than alike. If you doubt that, merely consider each's favorite song: "Turkey in the Straw" and "When the Saints Come Marching In."

Memorial To HFII

A memorial to Henry Ford II, in the form of a $1 million endowment, has been made to Henry Ford Hospital by Ford Motor Company. Ford died in the hospital, named for and built by his grandfather, in 1987.

The first two grants made from the endowment income were made in honor of Dr. Bruce W. Steinhauer and Dr. John Popovich Jr. Steinhauer was Ford's personal physician. Popovich led the team which cared for the industrialist during his final weeks.

"Tree Fort"

A "tree fort" built on Henry Ford's estate, Fair Lane, by four 10-year-old Detroiters figured in a 1950 police search involving Henry Ford II, according to one of the boys, Dennis Ward.

After building the fort, Ward told the *Detroit News*, his friends ran away from home. Three days later, on a Sunday afternoon, when asked by the police where the runaways might be, Ward mentioned the fort. He was whisked to the estate, whose gates were locked following the deaths of Henry Ford and his wife in 1947 and 1950, respectively.

Henry Ford II was summoned from his Grosse Pointe home to unlock the gates. Ward, seated in a police car, was given a stern look. "I think," Ward recalled, "he would have liked getting his hands on me if I hadn't been surrounded by policemen and our mothers. But after being told that our little fort was a long way from the mansion, he calmed down. While the police and I went off to the tree house, he picked several roses from his grandfather's garden and touchingly gave them to the moms. He also told them he hoped their children would be found safe and well.

"Actually," Ward added, "my friends were camped out along the tracks of the Chesapeake & Ohio Railroad. All three showed up the next morning looking none the worse for wear."

Bob Smith

All his life, Bob Smith, above, has looked like Henry Ford, which explains why Ford permitted Smith and his family to live in the so-called "Square House," or "Honeymoon House," in which Henry and his bride, Clara, resided early in their marriage. After the Fords' deaths, the Smiths moved the house from Dearborn to Garden City, Mich. (Photo taken by Fordophile Dick Folsom, Canton, Mich., on June 30, 1991.)

Impressed By HFII

"Did you ever meet Henry Ford II?" I recently asked Bob Smith, who worked in the Ford Co. soybean labs a half-century ago.

"Yes, a number of times," replied Bob. "The meeting that impressed me the most was a dinner that Mr. Ford arranged for the press about soybeans. It was shortly after he came back from the Navy (1943). He had been back about six months, and he wanted to talk about soybeans to the press – some film people, the Associated Press, and so on. They met in his dining room in the Rotunda Building.

"We prepared soybean products at the Carver Lab, and brought them to the Rotunda and set them up. I sat next to Mr. Ford, and, of course, the press asked him questions about the various dishes they were eating. Everything from soup to nuts was made from soybeans.

"They also asked Mr. Ford about many things besides soybeans. What impressed me most was that whenever a question was asked, and Mr. Ford didn't know the answer, he said he didn't know and would refer the question to somebody else. But he knew an awful lot about the business that I didn't think he knew. He knew how many factories the company had, where they were located, what their capacity was – things of that sort which I didn't think he would know. It had been my experience with other company executives that when asked a question to which they didn't know the answer, they would always make up something.

"Ray Rausch (a manufacturing boss)

used to bring a lot of visitors to the Carver Lab. People would ask him questions about the operation, and he would make up something. Very often he was wrong. We had to remember what he said to back him up in order not to make him look bad. But in the case of Henry Ford II, he always said, 'I don't know,' if he didn't know. Many questions were asked about soybeans that he couldn't answer, and he asked me to answer them for him. I thought from that day on that he was a good man for his job."

Seldom Called Henry

As Ford buffs know, few people called Henry Ford "Henry." It was the same with Henry Ford II, according to Will Scott, a Ford vice president from 1968-86, who forwarded the following comments on the subject:

"Few business acquaintances – and even fewer employees – called Henry Ford II 'Henry.' No matter how well you knew him, it just didn't seem the thing to do. I cannot conceive, however, that he ever admonished anyone for addressing him by his given name. He was too courteous to do that. But he was imperious too. I soon noticed that anyone he considered to be too familiar in an aggressive way simply found that his path and Mr. Ford's didn't cross very often anymore.

"The first person I ever heard call him Henry to his face was Ernie Breech, who was hired from GM in the early postwar days to be chairman of the company. Ted Yntema, the economist who was recruited as the vice president for finance called him Henry, too. I suppose that Jack Davis, the sales vice president, Red Duffy, who took over purchasing, and some of the other officers also called him Henry, but back in 1948 you probably could count the total within the company on the fingers of one hand. Age as much as rank seemed to establish the first name relationship. Breech and others were old enough to be Henry's father. Bob McNamara, one of Mr. Ford's favorites, who many years later was to become President Kennedy's defense secretary, never called him Henry, at least not in my presence.

"During the 1960s," Scott notes, "additional people began calling HFII 'Henry.' Arjay Miller did soon before he was named president in the 1960s," Scott recalls. "Bunkie Knudsen, who was hired form GM to replace Arjay, started out on a first-name basis on his first day on the job. Lee Iacocca considered himself a co-equal with Mr. Ford, so he had no trouble shifting into a more familiar tone of address fairly early as he started his rapid progress up the executive ladder." Scott adds that he himself "never pulled off" calling Henry II anything except "Mr. Ford."

When The Boss Stops By

Henry Ford II, in retirement, being greeted by workers in a Ford plant.

Remembering HFII

Many Detroit area people remember the little - and not as little - things about Henry Ford II, as chronicled by the *Detroit Free Press*.

***

"He and I were sitting next to each other after the Detroit riots," recalls Arthur Johnson, president of the Detroit Chapter of the NAACP. "I pulled out a cigarette. He leaned over, took out his gold lighter, and lit it for me. When I got home that evening, I called my family around and said to them, 'Can anyone guess who lit my cigarette today?' They couldn't believe it when I told them it was Henry Ford II."

***

"My brother-in-law, John Bannon, used to take care of Henry Ford II's car in the mid-fifties," remembers Leroy Brooks, a retired Ford worker. "I was visiting, and John introduced me to Ford, a fine guy who acted just like an ordinary man.

"But as far as I'm concerned, he was one of the world's great men, and nobody else was like him," continues Brooks. "He was a man who didn't look down on anyone. He sent a fleet of cars to John's funeral when he died of cancer about 10 years ago. That's the kind of guy Henry Ford II was."

***

"I saw him walk out the front door of the Navy Administration Building at the Rouge (where HFII was stationed early in World War II)" says Andrew Balog. "I reminded him he had the evening duty that night. He had forgotten. He thanked me, and said if I ever needed a job after the war to simply call him."

In June 1945, Balog wrote his former service mate, reminding him of his offer. Ford responded with a letter saying that a job was waiting for him in Dearborn. Balog worked as a data processor at the company for 35 years before retiring in 1981.

***

One of the fondest memories of Ken Bannon, head of the UAW's Ford Department from 1947-80, had to do with his retirement dinner.

"Henry was in Europe, but he made a point to fly back and be the principal speaker at my dinner," recalls Bannon. "There must have been 5,000 UAW Ford workers in the hall, and they gave him a standing ovation. Can you imagine any other executive flying back from Europe to say farewell to a union officer – and getting that type of reception?"

***

Pat Doyle, a New York crime reporter, remembers another side of Ford.

"One night in 1970 we were having dinner in Chinatown. The dinners cost $1.50 each. We'd always flip coins to see who would pay for dinners, and he invariably would win.

"This night, two characters came over to our table, and started picking the shrimp off our plates. I told them, 'Do that once more, and you're going to be sorry.' They persisted, and we got in to a fight with them. I couldn't believe Henry was going after his antagonist with such enthusiasm. The joint cleared out in a matter of seconds – nobody paying his bill. The two guys took off.

"I went back to the table, and waited for Henry. I thought he was in the john. After about five minutes, I decided to look around the neighborhood, and couldn't find him ... I called the cops. Then, I called his hotel, and he answered the phone. You couldn't believe how he answered the phone.

"I said, 'How do you feel?' He said, 'All right. I have a slight nosebleed,' and added, 'I'm leaving in the morning for headquarters for a board meeting.'

"Twenty years ago he helped save my life. I was dying in Columbia's Presbyterian Hospital. My ulcers had erupted, and I was bleeding to death. The doctors stopped the bleeding, but I refused the operation. Henry called the hospital, and also sent me a telegram telling me to get the operation. And, I did."

***

A final story, attributed to Theodore H. Mecke, Ford vice president-public relations from 1963-79, and one of Ford's closest confidants.

Mecke recalls a time when Ford was named one of the 10 best-dressed men in America. "They asked me to get a comment from Ford about the honor," remembers Mecke. "When I told him about it, he responded quickly: 'That's in the low-price field, I assume.' "

Brazilian Friends

"I am Brazilian," writes reader Fernando Costa, of Los Angeles, "and I have heard that Henry Ford II had Brazilian friends. Can you verify that?"

HFII made a number of business trips to Brazil, his principal port of call being São Paulo, Ford of Brazil's headquarters. Most of his days were spent at the plant, but some of his evenings were spent with a very wealthy couple, Mr. and Mrs. Luiz Campello, owners of auto parts firms among other enterprises.

While visiting São Paulo in 1988, I interviewed the Campellos. Their mansion was surrounded by a tall brick fence and guarded by a security force. In São Paulo, because of thievery and worse, people of means are barricaded behind walls and barred windows.

The Campellos met Henry II in the late 1950s when visiting Jack Anderson, owner of Detroit's Bundy Tubing, who lived next door to HFII in Grosse Pointe, Mich. On subsequent visits to Michigan, the Brazilians stayed with the Fords. After one of the dinners, Henry II prepared hamburgers for Campello and himself.

On one of his visits to Brazil, HFII spent a weekend at the Campellos' beach home, about an hour and a half from São Paulo. "When we were going to the beach," Mrs. Campello recalled, "the road went this way and that way, and Henry laughingly asked, "Are you taking me for a ride?" At seaside, Henry walked on the beach but did not swim.

The Campellos liked each of Henry II's three wives. Asked if Cristina had ever mentioned Imelda Marcos, widow of the Filipino dictator, Mrs. Campello replied, "I thought it was very bitchy when people said such things about her [Cristina]. All Grosse Pointe said Cristina was something or another [Imelda's lover]."

The Campellos also recalled being taken to a dinner for Michigan Governor George Romney when the ex-AMC chairman was running for President. "Everybody signed a [campaign donation] check," Mr. Campello recalled. "Why not?" Mrs. Campello added.

Mr. Campello attended HFII's memorial service in Grosse Pointe, having received a death-announcement telegram from Ford's third wife, Kathy. "I didn't say hello to the family at the service," he added. "I just wanted to be at the memorial. I didn't go there just to say that I was there. I called Kathy at her home after the memorial service. Edsel made a speech, and so did William Clay."

Mrs. Campello observed that her husband had been named Brazilian-American Chamber of Commerce "Brazilian Man of the Year" a few years earlier, and that Henry II had presented the award at New York's Plaza Hotel. "Almost 900 people were there," Mrs. Campello added. Her husband proudly produced a photo of HFII and himself at the ceremony.

When in Brazil, HFII, according to the Campellos, "never liked to invite people [to Campello parties] who worked for the company." I could see why. Ford of Brazil's American and Brazilian executives would not have mixed well with the sophisticated, jet-setting Campellos. Come to think of it, neither did I.

South African Trip

"I visited South Africa recently," writes reader James Murray, Larchmont, N.Y., "and was told that Henry Ford II had been there. Do you know anything about his trip?"

Ford visited South Africa in 1961 and 1982. Both trips were arranged by native South African C. John Roberts, a Ford public relations executive, whom I interviewed in 1989.

On the first visit, Roberts recalled, Henry II, 10 seconds after checking into his hotel suite, reemerged exclaiming, "There's a lady in my shower!" A reporter had hidden in the bathroom, and as soon as Ford entered she jumped out requesting an interview. She was "gracefully" asked to leave.

Roberts also remembers a visit to the equivalent of a state fair in Johannesburg. Arrangements had been made for Ford and his wife to have lunch in the "very swishey" Chamber of Mines pavilion. Ford demurred. Asked where he preferred to eat, the magnate inquired, "What's that over there?" "Oh," Roberts replied, "That's just a concessionary where you line up and get your hot dog and sauce and Coke and ice cream." Ford said, "I'd like to have lunch there." Roberts' remark, "What would you like?" was followed by Ford's rejoinder, "No, what would *you* like? I'm going to do this." Henry II then stood in line, bought three hot dogs and ice creams, and the trio ate their meal on a sidewalk bench. Said Ford, "God, this is a wonderful experience."

During his return trip, HFII insisted on seeing some of the same people he had met on his first trip, and also visited with government leaders and the nation's leading magnate, Harry Oppenheimer. He also took the 22-hour Blue Train ride from Capetown to Johannesburg. While enjoying the ride through the Cape countryside and mountains, he was bored by the crossing of the veldt on the concluding leg of the journey.

The second of HFII's South African visits was among the "farewell" trips taken in retirement, thus was more a holiday than a business trip.

HFII Namesakes

"While driving the expressways of Atlanta," writes reader Kent B. Casstevens, Sun City West, Ariz., "I was surprised to see the sign 'Henry Ford II Avenue.' This is the name of the street to the Ford Assembly Plant where the Taurus and Sable are built."

Henry II, who headed the Ford Company from 1945-79, also has the following namesakes:

Henry Ford II World Center (headquarters); Henry Ford II Lobby, Automotive Hall of Fame; and Henry Ford II Distinguished Awards for Excellence in Automotive Engineering, sponsored by Ford Motor Company and presented annually by the Society of Automotive Engineers, Dearborn; Henry Ford II Pavilion, Henry Ford Hospital, Detroit; Henry Ford II Kindergarten Building, University Liggett School, Grosse Pointe, Mich.; Henry Ford II High School, Sterling Heights, Mich.; Henry Ford II Scholar Award for Highest Academic Achievement, Stanford University, Palo Alto, Calif.; Henry Ford II Chair in Transportation, the Technion (Israel Institute of Technology), Haifa, Israel; and Henry Ford II Park, Yavne, Israel (sister city of Detroit Project Renewal).

HFII World Center

Ford World Headquarters, dubbed the "Glass House" since its opening in 1956, has been renamed the Henry Ford II World Center. Also part of the center are the Ford Motor Credit Building, upper right, and the Arjay Miller Arboretum, not shown, but to the northwest (upper left) of the buildings. Flags of nations in which Ford has plants are shown at bottom. The chairman's office, commanding a view of the Rouge Plant and Greenfield Village/Henry Ford Museum, is located on the top floor at right. The penthouse houses executive dining rooms and accommodations for board members and other VIPs.

Henry II And Harry

Businessmen generally welcome a chance to meet with the President. Henry Ford II, for example, arranged a personal presentation of the first post-World War II car, a gift from Henry Ford, to President Truman in front of the White House on August 29, 1945.

Conversely, the following year one of Truman's assistants, James Rowe, in a memorandum, "The Politics of 1948," reasoned that it would be politically advisable for the President to meet with Henry II.

The document, quoted in Joseph C. Goulden's *The Best Years 1945-1950* (New York: Atheneum, 1976), states that "Henry Ford II ... is often in Washington these days. The President should casually invite him to lunch to just talk over matters 'generally.' This picture of the American President and the Young Business Man together has appeal for the average reader [voter]."

Insofar as I know, Truman did not invite HFII to lunch, or even to tea.

Which reminds me that Henry Ford, when visiting the White House in 1917, was told the following limerick by President Woodrow Wilson:

I invited the duchess to tea,
  Her rumblings abdominal
Were simply phenomenal,
  And everyone thought it was me.

First Postwar Car

President Harry S. Truman obviously was pleased to accept delivery of Ford Motor Company's first post-World War II civilian car from Henry Ford II. The car – a 1946 Super Deluxe two-door sedan – came off the assembly line on July 3, 1945, two months before Japan formally surrendered.

HFII For Ike

Henry Ford II campaigned vigorously for Gen. Dwight D. Eisenhower for the 1952 Republican Presidential nomination, as revealed by telegrams sent by HFII and his associates to Michigan's national convention delegates.

On July 5 Henry II wired delegate Stanley S. Kresge, of the five-and-dime chain, "Dwight Eisenhower is the only individual under whose leadership the Republican Party can hope to achieve victory in November. I hope you ... are giving this strongest of all arguments in his favor the consideration it merits in your deliberations between now and the scheduled caucus of the Michigan delegation on Sunday morning, July 6th." Similar wires were sent by Ford vice presidents John Bugas and John R. Davis and Ford's brother-in-law and sister, Walter and Josephine Ford.

Three days earlier HFII had wired Kresge to "join me and a group of others having a more or less common interest at the apartment of Ray Johnson of Borg-Warner at 1500 Lake Shore Drive, Chicago, on Monday, July 7, for cocktails from 5 to 8 p.m." Kresge wired back, "Believe have another engagement then. Will try to be with you part time if possible."

After Ike became President, he and HFII were a golf twosome in Newport, R.I. Recalling that day in 1985, Ford told me that he was invited by the President to "ride in one of those atomic submarines."

" 'I'm terribly sorry,' Henry II replied ... 'but I have a meeting in New York this afternoon at 4' ... "It was a meeting at General Electric, of which I was a director. I've always wished I'd said, 'oh screw that meeting.' "

Thanks to Ford aviation historian Tim O'Callaghan, Plymouth, Mich., for forwarding copies of the telegrams, which he found in Kresge's papers.

Happy Birthday, LBJ

A post-Presidential (1969) birthday gift to Lyndon Baines Johnson from Henry Ford II, this mint 1910 Model T transported grandchildren and visitors around the LBJ Ranch before being put on permanent display in the Lyndon Baines Johnson Library and Museum in Austin. The car is similar to one used by the Johnson family during LBJ's boyhood.

Famous Last Words

Henry Ford II's statement, "The Edsel is here to stay," is cited in a recent *Detroit News* article on unfulfilled prophecies.

Also cited were such prophecies as "The talking motion picture will not supplant the regular silent motion picture" (Thomas A. Edison); "That's an amazing invention [the telephone], but who would ever want to use one of them" (President Rutherford B. Hayes); "It's too early for a Polish Pope" (Cardinal Karol Wojtyla two days before being elected Pope in October 1978); "A Japanese attack on Pearl Harbor is a strategic impossibility" (Major George Fielding Eliot three years before the attack on the naval base); "the best Adolf Hitler could hope for would be to head the Postal Department" (German

President Paul von Hindenberg); and "Stocks have reached what looks like a permanently high plateau" (Yale Professor Irving Fisher a week before the Great Crash of 1929).

Presidential Ballots

"You have written about Henry Ford II's opinions of various Presidents," writes Chris Taylor, of Haverhill, Mass. "Do you know which Presidential candidates he voted for in every election?"

In 1968 Ford told *Look* reporter Al Rothenberg that he had voted for Thomas E. Dewey in 1944 and 1948, Dwight D. Eisenhower in 1952 and 1956, Richard M. Nixon in 1960, and Lyndon B. Johnson in 1964.

Ford's remarks to me about later nominees and presidents suggest that he voted for Nixon in 1968 and 1972, Gerald R. Ford in 1976, and Ronald Reagan in 1980 and 1984.

Never Complain ...

Disraeli, "Death Valley Scotty," William Faulkner's grandmother, and a character in the film *Ninotchka*, among others, uttered the phrase, "Never complain. Never explain," long before Henry Ford II first publicly said them in February 1975. Yet, as reader Robert Leavenworth, Troy, Mich., correctly notes, HFII's "use of the phrase became widely circulated, admired, copied, and attributed as being original with him."

The phrase, notes Leavenworth, also was used by British Prime Minister Stanley Baldwin long before Ford's mention of it. Harold Nicholson's *Diaries and Letters: The War Years, 1939-1945*, published in 1967, provides the evidence, dated July 21, 1943. Nicholson, a conservative politician, records that he, while having a drink with two labor politicians and government critics, was viewed with angered contempt by his party's chief whip, who may have supposed that Nicholson had "joined that gang."

"I am reminded of Baldwin's words of advice, Nicholson adds. 'You will find in politics that you are much exposed to the attribution of false motive. Never complain and never explain.' " We are left to guess when Baldwin offered his advice; surely it was no later than 1943.

HFII's Catholicism

Henry Ford II was converted to Roman Catholicism before his first marriage in 1940, but fell away from the church following his 1963 divorce and remarriage. The magnate's conversion was highly publicized, while his excommunication and subsequent inattention to religion was seldom mentioned in the general press. Following Ford's death, the weekly *Michigan Catholic*, published by the Archdiocese of Detroit, summed up his Catholicism as follows:

"He was born a Methodist and memorialized at an Episcopalian ceremony, but for nearly a quarter of a century Henry Ford II symbolized the brightest and best of pre-Vatican II Catholic laity. And when he died Sept. 29 at age 70, the former chairman of the Ford Motor Company left behind a legacy of bequests and service to the Catholic Church that seemed to have faded from memory under the bright glare of his later life. Ford frequently joined his wife at weekday mass at St. Paul's-on-the-Lake in Grosse Pointe or at SS. Peter and Paul Jesuit Church in downtown Detroit."

A Knight of Malta, Ford was awarded a medal by Assumption College, Windsor, Ont., for his lay work. He and his wife were especially generous to Boysville, a Macon, Mich. home for wayward youths, located on property given to the Archdiocese by the Fords.

A revealing incident was recalled for the chronicle by Fr. William McGoldrick, of Warren, Mich., who in the 1950s had been a young associate pastor at St. Paul's. Fr. McGoldrick did not know the Fords; simply saw them at mass. But after having left St. Paul's, he received a phone call from a priest at a Cleveland hospital for the terminally ill. The Ohioan asked Fr. McGoldrick if he knew Henry II, and although told no – went on to say that he had a parishioner/patient whose late wife had been a Catholic. The dying man wanted to convert to Catholicism, and hoped Henry II would be his baptismal sponsor in absentia. Fr. McGoldrick contacted Ford, who agreed to serve; and the man died a Catholic.

Detroit Hall Of Fame

Henry Ford II – but not his grandfather, the first Henry Ford – has been named to *Detroit Monthly*'s Hall of Fame.

"Our Famers have given Detroit its character," states the magazine. "All have a common quality – an attitude, if you will. Flaws and all, they spent little time making excuses for their warts, preferring to attack in workman-like fashion the tasks at hand."

The only other auto-related people named to the publication's hall are John De Lorean and plant architect Albert Kahn. Others selected include Jimmy Hoffa, pizza king Mike Ilitch, football star Bobby Layne, and Chief Pontiac.

The list, if it's meant to be serious, is the dumbest I've seen. "Not surprising," says a well-informed Detroiter. "Most of the magazine's staff are out-of-towners, and don't have the least idea of what is and isn't important about Detroit."

The Chairman

Henry Ford II, looking every inch the chairman of Ford Motor Co., the world's largest family-controlled business firm.

Man's Man

Henry Ford II had charisma, as illustrated by the following account of a remarkable accolade:

"I liked Henry Ford II," writes reader Jack Lyndall, a Marylander. "I met him once at one of the SAE (Society of Automotive Engineers) banquets when he was one of the invited honor guests seated at the raised head table in the huge Hall A at Detroit's Cobo Hall.

"I will never forget that memorable banquet, held the evening following the highly publicized incident in the Los Angeles area when he had been charged with driving under the influence and had a young lady with him. His name was in the official program for the banquet, and before the actual start, there was a great deal of speculation among people at my table as to whether Henry would be there.

"Then, the SAE president, acting as toastmaster, started to read the names of the VIP guests at the four head tables. He asked the people attending the banquet to withhold their applause until all the guests at each table had been introduced. But, when he read, 'Chairman of the Board, Ford Motor Co., Henry Ford II,' the hall erupted in a spontaneous, thundering, standing ovation. A wonderful tribute to him."

Detroit Characters

Henry Ford and Lee Iacocca were cited by *Detroit Free Press* columnist Bob Talbert as Detroit's two "bigger-than-life" business personalities.

"They put all of the other business people to shame," states Talbert, a 28-year veteran of the newspaper. Their fame is so bright, he added, that telling friends and family about having met them enhances one's own reputation.

Readers of Talbert's column named Henry Ford II as persons who have given Detroit "a special flavor." Iacocca and ex-Dearborn Mayor Orville Hubbard also were cited. Nobody mentioned Henry Ford, Harry Bennett, or Walter Reuther, each of whom makes my list.

Farewell To Henry Ford II

Henry Ford II was one of 22 prominent Americans, and the only businessperson, pictured in *Time*'s 1987 year-end "farewell" section.

Each of the photos is accompanied by a brief comment. Underneath Ford's photo was the statement, "My name is on the building," a statement he never made. Ford's photo shows him, perhaps in his fifties, looking quizzically, as if to say, "I'm listening, but am not sure I'm believing." Such a look undoubtedly unnerved many a Ford executive.

A youthful Henry Ford II strikes an executive pose. Like his grandfather, he had more than one side.

Downsizing HFII

"Let's see if you are willing to run in 'Ford Country' the enclosed item which I dug up last week," writes reader Steve Merriman, of San Francisco, Calif. The item, written in October 1987 by columnist Donald K. White for an unidentified San Francisco newspaper, reads as follows:

"Memories of 'No One Calls Him Henry' Ford II, who died at 70, earlier this week.

"In the late 1940s at the old San Francisco Press Club on Powell Street, Ford was the host of a cocktail party arranged for the working press by a young, newly hired, company PR man. Ford was just over 30, the PR man a few years younger.

"As Ford was working the crowd, glass in hand, and acting genial, the PR man touched his shoulder and said, 'Henry, there are some reporters over there that I think you should meet.'

"Ford looked petulant, and shook off the suggestions. The next morning a company PR higher-up called the gosling West Coast PR man from Detroit.

" 'No one touches Mr. Ford,' he said. 'No one calls him Henry. You're fired.'

"A few years later Ford was at a meeting of the Business Council at Pebble Beach Lodge.

"The meetings of the nation's 100 top executives are closed to the press, but reporters are allowed, if not welcomed, at a few social gatherings.

"At one such cocktail affair, attended by the chief executives of U.S. Steel, General Motors, IBM, DuPont, Sears Roebuck, and other stars of the business world, Ford was obviously uncomfortable around his peers.

"So he had several more drinks than

they, walked over to the three-piece band, and requested that they swing into 'Hey-Bob-a-Re-Bop.'

"As they played, Ford danced between the tables, arms overhead, fingers snapping to the rhythm.

"His stern-visaged audience watched him in silence and when the song ended they did not applaud.

"Henry was never one of the corporate elite boys. He was born to be his own elitist."

The above stories have the ring of truth. They present the HFII who did not want business associates to get too close to him, and who invariably made an ass of himself when drunk. Like his grandfather, he had other sides, some quite attractive.

Henry and Johnny

Henry Ford II and Gianni Agnelli had a lot in common, being grandsons of the founders of Ford and F.I.A.T., respectively, and longtime chairmen of family firms. They also had great respect for each other.

Agnelli, at the close of a speech before the Foreign Policy Assn. in New York in 1977, was asked to comment on HFII's pessimistic views on the decline of capitalism during the Carter administration. He replied as follows:

"I know that Henry Ford is usually very outspoken, so I am going to speak just as if he were sitting there. I think Henry Ford has surely been the most significant motorcar man in the world since the war – the most significant and the most successful, the most outspoken. He has made big decisions, the greatest percentage of them right.

"I saw his letter when he retired from the Ford Foundation, and, in that letter, he said, 'I am retiring from the Ford Foundation because the principles on which the Ford Foundation have been created are being in some ways betrayed.' And, now he is saying, 'I believe that the main forces that made America strong and big are changing. I have worked successfully for 30 years in it. I don't know if I feel, if I want, if I can cope with working in a different kind of America.'

"If Ford would retire from the motorcar world, I can say that one would miss him very much."

HFII On Florida

In retirement Henry Ford II divided his time among homes in North Palm Beach, Fla., Grosse Pointe, Mich., and England.

He had a push/pull feeling toward Florida. "I don't particularly like Florida," he told me in 1985, "but I enjoy Palm Beach because I can do what I want 80 percent of the time."

But Florida presented a problem. "I like something to do in the daytime," HFII observed. "I don't play golf. I used to, but I don't anymore. There's little to do in Florida. You're not busy, really busy, and I'm not much for sitting around."

Ford's widow, Kathy, maintains the couple's Florida home. Among her close neighbors are two of her late husband's best friends, fellow "Detroiters" philanthropist Max Fisher and shopping mall magnate Alfred Taubman.

No Fun

One of Henry Ford II's perennial gripes, recalls Will Scott, a Ford vice president from 1968-86, was being forced by reason of position and name to do many things he didn't want to do.

Scott and his wife bumped into HFII at a Grand Prix reception in 1986 in the ballroom of Greenfield Village's Lovett Hall. "It was Edsel's party," Scott remembers, "and he had asked his father to attend, presumably as a drawing card. Henry was standing apart from the crowd when we walked over to him. After the hellos, he muttered something about this being Edsel's party and he didn't know why in the hell he was there.

" 'I always have to do things I don't want to do,' he said. I allowed as how I had heard that phrase many times over the years. He laughed and then he said, 'Yeah, I know. But Edsel's going to have to learn how to do these things himself.' And with that he wheeled around and marched out of the ballroom."

Died Of Boredom

Henry Ford II, his son Edsel Ford II told me in 1989, "died of boredom."

"I found him during his retirement years to be frustrated," Edsel added, ... in that he had a lot more to add, but he didn't know how to do it ... I think he was too proud a man to go back and say, 'Listen, I've got some great ideas. Give me an office, a secretary, a couple of people, and let me work on diversification strategy' .... I believe that's what he wanted, but he didn't know how to say that to the company, and the company didn't know how to go to him and say this ....

"He was very good at long-range planning," Edsel continued, ... "He had a lot of good contacts, but he just laid idle for the latter years of his life. He wanted to participate .... I truly believe that we would be a different company today, if, after he had retired, the company had allowed him to do that."

Human Touch

Henry Ford II signs his name for a worker during a post-retirement visit to a Ford plant. His appearances at Ford factories worldwide were reminiscent of royal visits, the difference being that HFII was approachable. The phrases, "I saw Mr. Ford"; "Mr. Ford asked me about my job"; and "Mr. Ford gave me his autograph" will ring down through the decades, just as sightings of and meetings with his grandfather are still recalled by those who met the magnate in days of yore.

HFII At Hotchkiss

Henry Ford II attended Hotchkiss, a preparatory school in Lakeview, Conn., from 1933-36. Fellow student and reader Bruce S. Williams, of Canton, Ohio, recently sent the following vignette which, he notes, he's been thinking of forwarding for the past "ten or twelve years":

"For about six weeks, July/August, 1933, twenty or so students, postulants for September entrance to the Hotchkiss School, attended summer school to strengthen some academic shortcomings. In this context my brother, Monte, and I became good friends with HFII. Before regular classes began, Henry and I had achieved acceptance to Hotchkiss; Monte had matriculated into the Salisbury School in Salisbury, Conn., about six miles away.

"On a sunny fall Sunday afternoon, Henry and I decided to go halves on renting a horse and buckboard to drive over to see Monte (school rules forbade riding in cars). The Salisbury kids had a good time galloping the horse a bit, so about half way home we stopped to let dobbin get a drink at the Salisbury town watering trough. Positioning himself to drink, the horse pulled the front axle hard right, front right wheel hard against the buckboard frame. When a leaf fell into the water, dobbin shied backward, crushing the front right wheel into the frame. End of wheel.

"The drive back to the stables had Henry and me taking turns, one sitting on the left rear corner of the buckboard while the other walked along the right side holding up the broken wheel corner. We had decided to go halves. Henry did his full share of the carrying. I hoped that he might go a little better than half on his share of the $8.00 cost of the wheel, considering that stopping at the water trough was his idea. But he simply paid his share [$4.00] .... We never discussed money, but I was reasonably sure that Henry could have more easily paid for the whole wheel than I could pay for my half.

"Henry's and my friendship faded to more of an acquaintance a few months after the buckboard incident," recalled Williams. "At times being associated so closely with HFII was too conspicuous.

"One of Henry's friends from Grosse Pointe must have been Phelps Newberry, his roommate that first year," continued Williams. "Phelps ran away from school with my roommate, Henry Wetter, son of the largest Ford dealer in Memphis. The mysterious disappearance of two such close companions of HFII aroused a lot of security questions. Henry and I spent a few busy days of interrogation by Connecticut State Police, FBI, and others.

Washer And Dryer

During the latter years of his retirement, Henry Ford II's office was located on the top floor of the Dearborn building at left, one of two comprising the Parklane Towers, popularly known as the "washer and dryer." From his office on the building's front side – the back is shown here – HFII had a commanding view of the World Headquarters Building, in which he also maintained an office. Ford's suite had two full-time employees, secretary Bernhard H. Bohn and driver Tommy Shields.

Henry II and Williams went on to Yale; indeed about half of Hotchkiss' graduates entered that institution. Williams was a year behind the Ford scion. "At Yale," Williams remarked, "Henry's and my paths would cross on campus occasionally. It was always a friendly 'Hi, Bruce/Hi, Henry.' His classmates almost always called him 'Model' – short for Model T. I left college before he did, and never saw him again. I saw Benson [also a Yale classmate] once on Madison Avenue in New York right after World War II. It was a very brief but friendly meeting. His bodyguards made me feel uncomfortable."

In 1980 your commentator asked

Henry II why he went to Hotchkiss. His reply:

"It was something I wanted very much to do. My family would rather have had me go to St. Paul's. But I had a couple of friends from here [Grosse Pointe Shores, Mich.] who were at Hotchkiss, and I got a lot of sales talk on Hotchkiss. So I said to my family that I'd like to go there, and I got them to agree that I could, if I could get in."

Recalling that he enjoyed his Hotchkiss years "very much," HFII added that he still felt "very close to the school. It's a marvelous school; it was a marvelous school; and it still is a marvelous school. I enjoyed every bit of time I spent there extremely." Obviously, that little problem with the horse and buckboard had receded into memory.

Got A Little Help

Henry Ford II's employment of a ghostwriter while at Yale was discussed by syndicated newspaper columnist Donald Kaul in the wake of former White House spokesman Larry Speakes's admission that he occasionally made up "quotes" for President Reagan.

Ford, recalls Kaul, was "forced to leave Yale before graduation when it was discovered that he had hired someone to write his thesis for him. (It was discovered, by the way, because he forgot to remove the bill from the manuscript before he turned it in.)

"Years later he was invited back to school to give a speech. When he stumbled over a line in the script, he looked up at the audience and said: 'I didn't write this one either.' "

Ford had a warm spot in his heart for Yale for as long as he lived. But his fondest school memories were associated with Hotchkiss, the prep school from which he and his brothers graduated.

Henry Ford II

This bust of Henry Ford II is displayed in Detroit's Renaissance Center, which owes its existence to the magnate. (Photo by Mike Skinner, Dearborn, Mich.)

HFII Center/Statue

The life-size statue of Henry Ford II which is on permanent display in the lobby of the Henry Ford II World Center.

World Headquarters was renamed the Henry Ford II World Center on June 12, 1996. A bronze statue of HFII was unveiled at the renaming ceremony.

The center consists of the "Glass

House," Ford's headquarters building since 1956, the adjacent Ford Motor Credit Building, and the Arjay Miller Arboretum to the northwest of the two buildings.

The life-size statue shows Henry II standing with one hand in his trouser pocket, the other holding his glasses. The sculptor, Richard Miller, of Bloomfield Hills, Mich., has painted most of the Ford family. The lone exception is William Clay Ford Sr., the last surviving grandson of Henry Ford.

After viewing photographs and videotapes of Henry II and interviewing people who knew him, Miller, according to the *Detroit News*, decided that his subject's most common pose, standing on both feet with his arms crossed, was "uninviting. He's enclosing himself. He was a shy man. His best pose was when he listened to you, and that's what I did ... He's almost about to talk to you."

To ensure accuracy of every detail, Miller had Grosse Pointe, Mich., tailors Antonio Rimanelli and his son, who fitted Ford during his later years, check the cut of Ford's suit and how it laid. The statue, the sculptor revealed, cost "five healthy figures, in excess of $50,000."

The statue was installed in the main lobby of the former World Headquarters Building. Of his father's effigy, Edsel II said, "He looks so much alive it gives me goose bumps."

Among those attending the ceremony were Mr. and Mrs. Edsel Ford II and their three oldest sons, including Henry III, 16; HFII's daughter, Charlotte, and her daughter, Elena, who is the company's first fifth-generation employee; HFII's brother, William Clay Ford Sr.; and Ford directors, executives, and several hundred employees.

Henry Ford II

Although sculptor Richard Miller regarded this pose of Henry Ford II as being highly characteristic, he rejected it as being "uninviting." The photo was taken in May 1979.

Wedding Of The Century

Reader Morley Andresen of Superior, Wis., asks if Henry Ford II's first wedding has been described as the "wedding of the century."

Yes, the contemporary press described HFII's 1940 marriage to Anne McDonnell of Southampton, N.Y., as the "wedding of the century." In reality, however, Henry and Anne's wedding, and all others of the 20th century, were overshadowed by the romance and marriage of King Edward VIII of Great Britain and Wallis Warfield Simpson.

The Ford wedding took place in the Church of the Sacred Hearts of Jesus and Mary in Southampton before 1,100 guests. The reception, held on the McDonnell lawn, was highlighted by a dance between Henry Ford, 77, and his new granddaughter-in-law. The wedding site later was swept out to sea in a great Northeastern storm.

Not content to have been a participant in a "wedding of the century," Henry II, a sociable man who liked to give and attend parties, tossed extravagant "coming-out" events for his daughters, Charlotte and Anne, in 1959 and 1961, respectively. The first party, featuring medieval decor, was held at the Detroit Country Club and was billed as "the party of the century." The 1,200 guests ranged from the Gary Coopers to Lord Charles Spencer-Churchill, and the event cost $250,000, a record sum for a debutante affair. Anne's debut, also described as the "party of the century," was held at her parents' Grosse Pointe Farms, Mich., estate, and was equally lavish.

Social Register

Only one Ford, Henry Ford II's first wife, Anne McDonnell Ford Johnson, is included in the 1996 edition of the *Social Register*, which lists 26,402 of America's social elite. Anne, moreover, seems to have been included because of her side of the family and her Southhampton, N.Y. upbringing rather than her tie to HFII.

Anne's daughters, Charlotte and Anne, and her son, Edsel II, did not make the cut, nor did the Ford family patriarch, William Clay. "I don't pay much attention to the *Social Register*," Charlotte commented. "The only time I ever look at it is when I need an address or phone number."

Makes one wonder how long it will be before the Fords meet the *Social Register*'s criteria for inclusion. The family now is into its sixth generation and includes, in addition to Edsel II, his son, Henry III. Maybe by the time we get to Henry VIII.

Anne Ford

The late Anne Ford, Henry Ford II's first wife.

Anne and Bob

Anne Ford, Henry Ford II's first wife, was discussed in a 1988 interview I had with Robert W. Hefty, an ex-Ford public relations executive. Hefty was "accused" both by his wife and HFII of having an affair with Anne, and the story goes as follows:

"I was fortunate enough to be asked to work with the Ford family quite a bit," Hefty recalled. "Anne Ford brought the Metropolitan Opera back to Detroit for the first time in many, many years. She was named chairman of the local Metropolitan Opera Booster Group, and I was assigned to handle publicity for her. This meant going out to the Fords' home often for press conferences, luncheons, interviews, and so forth.

"Anne Ford had a reputation – not deserved in my judgment – of being kind of aloof as far as Detroit society was concerned. She was considered an Eastern snob by some of the local matrons. No validity to that at all as far as I was concerned.

"Anyway, I would go home at night and just rave about Anne Ford. My wife said, 'I think you're falling in love with her.' I said, 'No, but I certainly admire her.'

"Not long after that we were introducing the Comet automobile at the Burning Tree Country Club in

Washington, D.C., and Mr. (Henry II) Ford was there. Mike O'Neil, with whom I had worked at United Press in Detroit, was then the head of the Washington Bureau of the *New York Daily News*. Mike came up and said, 'Bob, my dad worked for Ford tractor for 35 years and never had a chance to meet Mr. Ford, Sr. I'd like to meet Henry Ford II and be able to tell my dad that I met him.'

"I said, 'Think nothing of it,' and took Mike up to Mr. Ford, who probably had had a drink or two. I said, 'Mr. Ford, this is Mike O'Neil.' Mr. Ford stopped me cold, poked Mike in the chest, and said, 'O'Neil, don't believe a goddamn word Hefty tells you. He's in love with my wife.' I said, 'Well, as a matter of fact, Mr. Ford, you're right.' Mr. Ford then abruptly walked away and I didn't know from that moment forth whether I had a job. But I never heard another word about it. But how he arrived at his conclusion I can't imagine."

Anne Ford, Hefty continued, was a lady with class. "She sent me a gift, a gold picture frame inscribed 'To Bob from Anne.' Inside a note she sent with it, she said, 'Thanks for putting up with me for three years.' "

"What did your wife say about that?" I asked.

"It just confirmed our 'affair,' " he chuckled.

Anne Ford Johnson Dies

Anne McDonnell Ford Johnson, 76, Henry Ford II's first wife and a patron of the arts, died in New York on March 29, 1996 of stroke complications.

Mrs. Johnson, daughter of a wealthy New York stockbroker, granddaughter of inventor and utilities magnate Thomas E. Murray, met Henry II aboard ship while returning from Europe in 1936. They were married in July 1940. The Southampton, N.Y. ceremony was covered by more than 50 news photographers and generated almost as much publicity for one of the guests, Henry Ford, as for the bride and groom. If, as was reported later, the elder Ford was vexed by his grandson's conversion to Miss McDonnell's Roman Catholic faith the day before the wedding, he gave no hint of his displeasure on the day of the marriage. On the contrary, the 77-year-old magnate beamed happily throughout the festivities and danced vigorously with the bride.

The Fords were divorced in 1964 following months of rumors in which Henry II was linked romantically to the Italian-born Maria Cristina Vettore Austin, the divorced wife of a British naval officer. Cristina and HFII were married in 1965.

Shortly after her divorce, Anne, who moved from Grosse Pointe Shores, Mich. to Manhattan, was drinking coffee with a friend at the Regency Hotel. She noticed Mrs. Austin, who was with a friend at another table. "This had to happen some time," she whispered to her companion. "I think the only gracious thing is to go over and say hello. You know I've never met her." The two, according to the *New York Times*, went over, introduced themselves and shook hands. Mrs. Ford's friend later reported: "It was all very civilized, but if there were a way to bottle up the electricity in that little room it would run the Ford industries for a solid year."

Mrs. Johnson, selected by the New York Dress Institute as one of the world's 10 best-dressed women in 1956 and named to the Fashion Hall of Fame in 1956, married Deane F. Johnson, a prominent Los Angeles lawyer in 1968. Immediately she became the most prestigious hostess in L.A. The couple bought a Regency-style house that Mrs. Johnson, a connoisseur of French furniture, filled with collectibles. She eventually became the L.A. representative of Christie's, the international auction house. Later in New York, to which she and Johnson moved in 1980, she was associated with Sotheby's.

As a member of the White House Fine Arts Committee during the Eisenhower and Kennedy administrations, Anne helped to restore

Blair House, the official guest residence for state visitors, and to redecorate the executive mansion.

The thrice-wed HFII, it has been said, married for class, brass, and ass. Anne represented class. Her survivors include son Edsel II and daughters Charlotte and Anne.

Thanks to reader Ken Morris, of Newhall, Calif., for forwarding Mrs. Johnson's obituary in the *Los Angeles Times*.

Cristina's Sunshine Days

A 1971 *Life* photo feature of Henry Ford II's second wife, Cristina, has been forwarded by reader Mike Skinner, of Dearborn, Mich.

The magazine's cover depicts a smiling, T-shirted Cristina seated on a sofa in her Grosse Pointe Farms, Mich., home. Emblazoned on the cover are the words, "Rich, Impish and almost Americanized."

Inside, under the title, "The Sunshine Days of Cristina," photos show Italian-born Cristina holding a basketball, riding a bike, talking with HFII, visiting with her stepdaughter, Charlotte, and Charlotte's daughter, Elena, and playing hostess in the Fords's penthouse apartment in New York's Carlyle Hotel.

The article observes that Cristina, who married HFII in 1964, "has shed her jet-set image and become a highly effective unofficial ambassadress for the Ford Motor Co., and for Henry. When Henry gets home at about 6:30," the magazine adds, "Cristina is there. In splendidly American fashion, the two of them eat dinner alone most nights, watch a little television and go to bed early. But many days, Henry is out-of-town and she is alone, working hard at staying fit and beautiful. There are ballet lessons and daily massages. On trips with Henry, she shines, handling herself with a piquant mix of Italian-accented exuberance and the poise expected of a Ford wife – and looking like one of Henry Ford's better ideas."

When Cristina Vettore Austin Ford was married to Henry Ford II in the 1960s and 1970s, pictures of the Italian beauty were plentiful in Ford Motor Co.'s photo files. Here's one of them, depicting the Italian beauty in a kittenish pose.

Life's account, alas, was off-the-mark. Cristina did not give up jet-setting and much preferred glamorous dinner parties to quiet nights at home. Although she enlivened many of Henry's business functions, her late arrivals constantly irritated her husband. Henry fell out of love with her, and the couple divorced in 1978. Henry soon thereafter married his third and last wife, Kathy, who admirably suited The Deuce to the end of his days.

Cristina Talks

"If some astrologer could have revealed to me what troubles I would have to go through I would not have married Henry," Cristina Ford, Henry Ford II's second wife, recently informed the *Detroit News*.

Cristina, now in her early sixties, is infuriated at people who talked about her in two tell-all Ford family biographies, and also is incensed about ongoing gossip about her friendship with former Philippines first lady Imelda Marcos.

Cristina's 1980 divorce agreement

Fast Fords

Life in the fast lane for three of Edsel Ford's children, circa 1930. Josephine, born in 1923, is in the scaled-down car. Henry, born in 1917, is at the wheel of the right-hand-drive MG, with Benson, born in 1919, at his side. The picture was taken at the Fords' Grosse Pointe Shores estate, which offered plenty of roadways for nonlicensed drivers. (Photo from the Collections of the Henry Ford Museum and Greenfield Village)

prevents her from revealing intimate details of her relationship with Henry II, who died in 1987. But she can say what she thinks about people she says have lied about her morals and relationships.

"One person started the rumor that Imelda took me away from Henry," recalls Cristina. "My God! Henry pushed me to travel to the Philippines because he wanted a factory there."

The Marcoses, she added, are genuine friends. "The day [of the] divorce ... Mr. Marcos called me and said, 'You have lost your husband, you have lost your home. You come stay at Malacanang Palace. It will be your home.' Do you think I can let them go? Not until the day I die." During frequent travels, she says, she often stops for visits at the Marcoses' Hawaiian exile retreat.

A British citizen, Cristina calls home a townhouse in London's posh Grosvenor Square district. She also has a home in Rome and a beach house outside Rome.

Cristina And Imelda

"Is there any truth to the rumor that Cristina Ford and Imelda Marcos were lovers?" asks Carl Wilson, of Wichita, Kan.

For years Cristina Ford, Henry Ford II's second wife, was rumored to have had a hotly-denied lesbian affair with Imelda Marcos, widow of the Philippines president, Ferdinand Marcos. Cristina told the *Detroit News* that Joan Bugas, wife of HF's friend and ex-Ford executive, John Bugas, was the source of the rumor, Joan supposedly having leaked the story to Peter Collier and David Horowitz, authors of *The Fords: An American Epic*.

But Horowitz told the *News* that he first heard the story from Cristina. "She was the one who first brought it up," he observed .... "She complained to me that Henry was spreading the story. Joan Bugas was definitely not the source."

Lovers or not, Cristina and Imelda were very close friends when the Marcoses were in power, and Cristina was treated like royalty when visiting Meldie in Manila.

Hold The Presses

Henry Ford II's widow, Kathy, has dampened rumors that she'll write a book about her life with Henry Ford II.

"I don't think I have any intention of doing such a thing," she told the *Detroit Free Press*. "I would say it's highly unlikely and a bit premature," she added. "Maybe I'll write a cookbook!"

Since her husband's death in September, 1987, Kathy has been shuttling back and forth between her homes in Florida, England, and Michigan, and a daughter's home in California.

Asked if she plays the Michigan lottery, Mrs. Ford said she doesn't buy tickets "because I don't feel I'm in a lucky period of my life. But if I thought I even had a 5,000-to-one chance, I'd buy a few tickets ... It's just another amusement. My staff downstairs, they buy them."

HFII On Bodyguards

In 1985, two years before his death, I asked Henry Ford II to what extent he had employed bodyguards.

He replied that he had never had a bodyguard in the U.S., although he had had them in Germany and Argentina. Adding that he had just returned from Argentina, he noted that he had had three or four bodyguards there.

"But I didn't have as many as some people I was with. I want to tell you they really put on a lot of bodyguards. One woman, an Argentine, had nine on one occasion. Another guy I knew, an American, had five or six. Christ, there were more bodyguards than there were guests. But I never had them in the States. I never worried. I never worried overseas. I had more fun trying to escape from bodyguards when I was younger than anything else."

Henry II's last remark refers to the bodyguards assigned to him and his brothers and sister after the 1932 Lindbergh kidnapping. That year HFII was 15 years of age, his siblings 13, 9, and 7.

HFII's own children were protected at home by a watchman, but were not monitored when away from the premises.

Henry Ford II

Henry Ford II in his Elvis Presley phase.

HFII'S Heroes

Asked in 1979 by a Texas researcher to name his greatest boyhood hero, Henry Ford II replied that "the person who came closest to being a hero was Francis J. McCann, a coach and teacher at the former Grosse Pointe University School. Both in the classroom and on the playing field, Coach McCann insisted upon maximum effort – more than any of us thought we could produce – and he got it."

Also asked to name the person who had the greatest influence on his life, Ford replied, "my father, Edsel Ford."

In a 1980 interview with HFII, I

asked him how he remembered his father. "I felt that I was very close to my parents all the way through my life," he responded, "and that they had a great influence on everything I did. I guess they molded my thinking when I was young. We were born when they were very young so we had a sort of participative family life. We'd play baseball and tennis together, and take trips on the boat, and do things like that. My father had a rather large sailboat. We'd go off during the day and sail with him, or go out with him in the speedboat after he gave up racing.

"My father," he added, "was very modest. He was very down-to-earth. He was a very shy man. He was very artistically inclined. He had a great feeling for the arts, and was interested in them all his life. I don't think he was particularly keen about music. He liked the music of the era, but I don't think he was particularly keen about going to the opera or symphony. He set a very high moral standard for himself, and inculcated it into all of us. He was more like a friend or another brother than a father."

Thanks to Fordophile Mike Skinner, of St. Clair Shores, Mich., for the copy of HFII's letter to Mrs. Jackie L. Pruett, of Yorktown, Tex.

Benson Ford, Vice President – Chairman of the Dealer Policy Board, Ford Motor Co.

HFII On Brother Benson

Your commentator is perhaps the only journalist who asked Henry Ford II to evaluate his brother, Benson, a Ford vice president from 1948 until his death in 1978.

In a 1985 interview, HFII had the following to say about his brother:

"That's a difficult question. Ben was a very lovely fellow with a great sense of humor and a great dedication to all kinds of social activities in Detroit. But he never really got his arms around anything of significance within the company – because I don't think he wanted to. I don't think he was inclined that way.

"I think that he did a lot of damn good things. He made a lot of speeches; he did a lot of public affairs kinds of things. He did them very well. But he wasn't a manager. Put it that way. The things that he did do he did extremely well, and he was a wonderful individual. But he wasn't the kind of person who would go in, sit down, and say let's talk all this out, let's see where we are going to go, and so forth."

HFII's critique strikes me as being right on the mark. Benson, partially deaf from childhood and never in robust health, served as general manager of the Lincoln-Mercury Division from 1948-55 and as group director of the Mercury & Special Products Division in

1955-56, but never administered either with a firm hand. From 1956-78 he was chairman of the Dealer Policy Board, which required minimal effort on his part. Although a company director from 1941 to the time of his death, and a member of several important committees, he never exhibited strong leadership and, as the years rolled by, attended ever fewer meetings. But as his brother said, he was a nice guy, and never let being a Ford go to his head.

My last meeting with Benson was at the Ford Co.'s 75th anniversary celebration at Detroit's Renaissance Center in June 1978. He gave a fine speech, and less than six weeks later was dead of a heart attack.

You Gotta Be Kidding

Henry Ford's grandson, William Clay Ford, owns the Detroit Lions football team because it "gives him an identity" and allows him to "run with the big boys," according to *Detroit News* sports columnist Joe Falls.

"I hardly think Bill Ford is concerned about that," countered *News* reader Delores Dean, Dearborn Heights, Mich. "Being a Ford in this town [Detroit] is recognition enough."

Amen. The name Ford has so much magic and carries so much weight that it's "ludicrous," to use Dean's word, to suggest that one of its leading members – and a man worth an estimated $360 million – has to own a football team to acquire an identity and run with the big boys. Bill Ford has had an "identity" from the day he was born, and for decades has had to look over his shoulder to see most of the other "big boys."

Remembering Fair Lane

Henry Ford's youngest grandson, William Clay Ford Sr., 70, toured the Henry Ford Estate-Fair Lane, with *Detroit News* reporter Jon Pepper.

Ford told the newsman that he had rarely visited his grandparents' residence over the past 40 years. With the original occupants and the furniture gone, he had looked upon the place as more of "a house than a home." On this tour, however, he remarked that the mansion was more as he remembered it, thanks to the restoration of some original furniture and the grounds.

Upon seeing the bathrooms of his grandparents' bedrooms, Ford recalled that his grandfather used to put razor blades in a glass of water, let them rust, and then mix the solution with olive oil to make hair tonic. Iron, he thought, was good for hair.

Ford also reminisced about sliding down the hallway banister, and how his grandfather cured another grandson, Benson, of catching pneumonia every winter. Deciding that Ben's problem was that he was too warm and comfortable, the elder Ford rolled him down a hill into a snowbank. Ben never caught pneumonia again.

Bill Ford Retires

William Clay Ford, 64, youngest grandson of Henry Ford and brother of Henry Ford II, has retired from the family firm, after 40 years of service. He will remain a director and chairman of the finance and executive committees.

Ford joined the company's Sales and Advertising Staff in 1949. He was appointed manager of the Special Product Operations in 1952, spearheaded planning for the Continental Mark II, and headed the Continental Division from 1954-57. Although a design success, the Mark II lost favor within the company, and the Continental Division was consolidated with the Lincoln Division. Subsequently, Ford devoted less attention to company affairs, and spent more time on the Detroit Lions professional football team of which he became president in 1961 and sole owner in 1964.

Your commentator attended Ford's retirement press conference at which the present family patriarch came through as a well informed, articulate gentleman. It would be difficult to find a retired or active Ford executive who doesn't like Bill Ford; and the same can be said of his brother, Benson, if not of Henry II.

Josephine Ford

Josephine Ford, 75, Henry Ford's only great-granddaughter, recently gave $20 million to Detroit's Center for Creative Studies (CCS) and another $10 million to the Motor City's Henry Ford Health System.

The Ford gift is the largest ever given to a private college of art and design and also is the single largest gift to a private college in Michigan.

A new CCS classroom building will be named for Mrs. Ford's late husband, Walter Buhl Ford II, an architect and former Center chairman. CCS trains many of the auto industry's designers.

The Health System, of which Henry Ford Hospital is a part, recently renamed its cancer facility the Josephine Ford Cancer Center.

Thanks to reader Mike Skinner, St. Clair Shores, Mich., for forwarding articles on the gifts.

Walter Buhl Ford II Dies

Walter Buhl Ford II, 71, son-in-law of Edsel Ford, died of cancer on October 26.

The Grosse Pointe Farms, Mich. resident had been married to Josephine (Dodie) Ford since 1943. She is the daughter of Edsel and Eleanor Ford and the granddaughter of Henry and Clara Ford.

Walter Ford, an architect, was chairman and CEO of Ford & Earl Design Associates, a commercial and interior design company in Warren, Mich. His firm did a great deal of work for Ford Motor Company over the years.

Your commentator came close to interviewing Walter Ford in May, 1990, arrangements to do so having been made by the Ford family's attorney. But Ford's cancer was diagnosed about that time, and the interview was placed on hold while the architect underwent medical treatment. Alas, the interview was never to be.

Of Walter Ford, an astute observer once said, "Josephine was darn lucky to have been married to him, considering all of the fortune seekers that she might have met and married. Walter Buhl Ford, although wed into great wealth, went to work and made a place for himself in his own right."

Ford is survived by his wife, daughters Eleanor Ford Bourke, and Josephine Ford Ingle; sons Walter Buhl Ford III and Alfred; 12 grandchildren and one great-grandchild, the figures alone indicating that this branch of the Ford family is thriving. Walter Buhl III works for Lincoln-Mercury Division; Alfred is a member of Hare Krishna.

Charlotte's Debut

The debut of Charlotte Ford, Henry Ford II's eldest daughter, was recalled by the *Grosse Pointe News.*

The ball was held in the Grosse Pointe Country Club, which was transformed into a lavish 18th century setting, according to a reprint of the *News*' 1959 account. In honor of the occasion, the club built a new entrance and a Paris decorator carpeted the interior in red and lined it with white satin. Other accents included potted trees adorned with roses and rare boxwood, thousands of magnolia leaves along the walls, and a water fountain splashing into a pool of gardenias.

The 1,500 guests, many of whom wore gowns designed by Saint Laurent, Dior, Simonetta, and Givenchy, drank nearly 500 bottles of Dom Perignon and dined on baked chicken breast marguerite, fresh fruits of ice molds, tiny sautéed chicken livers, and French pancakes. The Meyer Davis Orchestra composed a song for Charlotte. In the main ballroom, couples danced to the velvety singing of Nat King Cole.

Among the high-profile guests were the Gary Coopers, the Oleg Cassinis, and Lord Charles Churchill, youngest son of the Duke of Marlborough.

Few Grosse Pointe debutante parties matched the scale of Charlotte's coming-out extravaganza, and such events disappeared about a decade later, mostly because of the cost.

Henry Ford II was criticized for spending extravagantly on Charlotte's and later daughter Anne's parties. But it was his money, and he liked a good party as much as anybody on earth, and that was that.

Who Done It?

"I have a copy of a little 1980 book, *How to Love the Car in Your Life*, by Charlotte and Anne Ford," writes reader Paul Carrington, Lowell, Mass. "It's a pretty good book, but my question is, 'did they write it themselves?' "

Ford initially indicated that Henry Ford II's daughters had done the writing. Later word was that they were assisted very considerably by Ford writer Arnold Hirsch, other company staffers, and New York freelancer Claudia Stern, who allegedly received $25,000 for her services. Ms. Stern previously helped Charlotte write her book on etiquette.

Charlotte On Manners

Charlotte Ford, Henry Ford II's eldest daughter has been promoting her best-selling paperback, *Charlotte Ford's Book of Modern Manners*.

Charlotte, some have said, would have joined Ford Motor Co. and made quite a name for herself - had she been a man. She reportedly let her father know she was interested in joining the company, but was discouraged from doing so.

Charlotte once wrote an etiquette column, "Doing It Right By Charlotte Ford," for *McCall's* magazine, and also prepared bylined articles for the magazine. Her first such article, appearing in the May 1987 issue, was on Princess Yasmin Khan's care of her late mother, Rita Hayworth, in the latter's battle with Alzheimer's Disease. Charlotte also instructs students on etiquette at two Bronx high schools, serves on several hospital boards, and is active in the Police Athletic League of New York.

Why does she keep such a pace? "I'm a driven person," she replies. "I like to be involved. I couldn't see just shopping all day."

The strongest influence in Charlotte's life: her mother, Anne. She says that her "father was away a lot." Charlotte is the only family member who acknowledges that she liked Robert Lacey's sensationalist book, *Ford: The Men and the Machine*. Charlotte is close to her brother, Edsel, and his wife, Cynthia. "I'll stay with them when I'm in Detroit," she says. She is in daily contact with her sister, Anne Scarborough. Charlotte is married to ex-publisher, noted art patron Edward Downe Jr.

"Me And My Scaasi!"

The late Henry Ford II's daughter, Charlotte, 48, is featured in a *Town & Country* advertisement by Canadian fashion designer Scaasi. The begowned, bejeweled Charlotte, not as easily recognizable as in most of her other pictures, is shown with the designer in an esoteric fashion magazine-type setting above the line, "Me and My Scaasi."

Charlotte, like her brother, Edsel II, and cousin, William Clay, Jr., has expressed a desire to see fourth-generation Fords play a more active role in Ford Motor Co. affairs.

Charlotte Ford

"Is Henry Ford II's daughter, Charlotte, still married to Ed Downe?" asks reader William Linderman, of Youngstown, Ohio.

Last word I have on Charlotte is that, after standing by Downe when he was accused of inside trading on Wall Street by the Securities and Exchange Commission, she obtained a divorce in early 1993. Downe, upon pleading guilty, was sentenced to 3,000 hours of public service. Charlotte has resumed her maiden name.

Briefing Edsel II

During preparations for daughter Anne's 1961 debut, Henry Ford II asked one of his press relations men, Robert W. Hefty, to brief his 12-year-old son, Edsel II, on "what he should and shouldn't say to the press if he's asked anything."

The briefing took place in the library of the Fords' Grosse Pointe Shores home, at which time HFII was dressed in his bathrobe. Hefty went through the usual routine, explaining, "Above all, don't tell the press how much the party cost." "You mean," Edsel ventured, "I shouldn't tell them that it cost a quarter of a million dollars." His father scowled, "See what I mean?"

At the party Edsel II refused to dance with Anne, which, Hefty remembers, became "world news." "Why did he refuse?" I asked. "Sissy stuff," Hefty replied.

Edsel II's Perspective

Henry Ford's great-grandson, Edsel Ford II, president of Ford Motor Credit Co., recently was asked for his perspective on his automotive forebears.

"Henry Ford the First," he told *Automobile*, "had a vision for providing high-quality, good-value transportation for everybody. And the word 'everybody' was what intrigued me the most, because he was really one of the first automotive giants who had a truly global vision. For instance, when he dedicated the Sydney Assembly Plant in Australia in the 1920s, he copied the Rouge Plant. The Model T was the very first global car, if you think about it.

"Henry Ford probably would be best known for his manufacturing engineering. He created the assembly line, a lasting process that will go on forever, one we're just making better. That was his legacy.

"I think (grandfather) Edsel's legacy was his impact on the design process at Ford Motor Company. The Taurus and Mustang are almost a reflection of Edsel's creativity. I think my father's (Henry II's) legacy was one of rebuilding, of taking a company that, when he picked it up in the '40s, was going broke. And he restored it to one of the great multinational, global companies."

Edsel also commented on what it means to be a Ford. "I remind myself that executives whose names are not the same as the company's can shut off at night. If a chairman was caught speeding on an expressway, the police might not know who he was. But if his license says Edsel Ford, it's like a beacon in the night. Maybe when I close my eyes at night, the Ford mantle comes off, but otherwise it's always there. There's always a certain decorum one has to practice when one's a Ford. And we have presented the right mantle to the public. There has been almost no feuding, and we're a very cohesive family. I'm proud that we don't get into a lot of bickering, and there are no family disagreements."

Asked if he thought being a Ford posed a heavy responsibility, he replied, "Sure. Because even on vacation, I'm still Edsel Ford. And one cannot let down one's guard if one is Edsel Ford or a recognized member of the Ford family. You have to always to be on your guard, and you have to be careful of how you say things. I'm very proud of my family and what my family's been able to accomplish over the years, starting with Henry Ford the First. And that's the same kind of legacy I'd like to pass on to my children."

Edsel II has made use of his great-grandfather's desk for the past "five or six years."

Favorite Car

Edsel Ford II says his favorite personal car has been "a 1964-1/2 Mustang fastback. "Got it for my 16th birthday," Henry Ford's great-grandson told *Detroit Free Press* columnist Bob Talbert. "White with a red ribbon it. It was pretty special for me and my father ... He took as much pleasure in it as I did."

Asked about the Ford product he likes most, Edsel responded, "I've been in and around Ford cars all my life. It's like asking an artist to name his favorite painting."

Buy That Tiger!

Speculation ran rampant during early 1992 that Edsel Ford II might purchase the Detroit Tigers baseball team from Domino's Pizza owner Tom Monaghan.

Edsel, 43, fueled the speculation by acknowledging that he is a "professional sports groupie" and was "very interested" in buying the team. "I think that every young kid in the world dreams that one day he'll own a baseball team," he told WJR radio host J.P. McCarthy, when asked if he'd like to buy the club.

Edsel II's grandfather, Edsel, also expressed interest during the '30s in buying a major league baseball club. Edsel II's uncle, William Clay Ford, did buy the Detroit Lions football team in 1963. Bill became a director of the Lions in 1956, after his automotive baby, the Continental Mark II, was killed by Ford. Upon acquiring the Lions, Bill devoted more time to the team than to Ford.

Edsel's fortune is estimated at $50 million by the *Detroit Free Press*, which also states that some of Edsel's cousins "are worth much more than he."

Edsel II Down Under

"Last month I visited my grandparents' home in Melbourne and heard that Edsel Ford II once was a Ford of Australia executive," writes reader Derek Wheelhouse, of Santa Barbara, Calif. "Is that true, and has he gone back for visits?"

Edsel II was assistant managing director of Ford of Australia in the late 1970s. While in that job he suggested that blue stripes be added to the Falcon Cobra, a move that helped rejuvenate the two-door Australian model's flagging sales.

Edsel II attended the America's Cup race off Perth/Fremantle in 1987 and visited the Australian company's headquarters at Broadmeadows, near Melbourne, in 1992 in his capacity as president of Ford Motor Credit Company. While in Melbourne he also attended the Ford Australian Tennis Open.

Great-Grandfather's Desk

One of Henry Ford's desks decorates the office of his great-grandson, Edsel B. Ford II, president of Ford Motor Credit Corp.

The founder had several offices and as many desks – at his Highland Park Plant, Dearborn Administration Building, and Dearborn Engineering Laboratory, among other places. Regardless of which desk Edsel has, it's likely that he logged more time behind it in a few weeks than did his great-grandfather over many years. Henry Ford had little use for offices or desks, and usually met subordinates in their offices so he could leave any time he wished. He often entertained guests by showing them his plants or Henry Ford Museum and Greenfield Village.

Misses Father

In October 1993 retired Ford public relations executive John Sattler sent a copy of his new book, *Fifty Years Ahead of the News: A Lifetime of Practical Public Relations Experience*, to Henry Ford II's son, Edsel Ford II. Seven months later Edsel responded, apologizing for the delay in his reply and stating that he "had a great time the other evening reading the parts of the book which speak to your recollections of dealing with my father.

"I have read all of the 'Henry Ford II' books," Edsel added, "and I believe your portrayal of your encounters sound exactly the way my father reacted. Thank you for describing certain circumstances in an accurate fashion. Putting all that aside, I really enjoyed the book John! You brought back many fond memories of Daddy. I do still miss him very much."

Ford Becomes Trucker

"I now have a skill I can use," joked William Clay Ford Jr. upon getting a truck driver's license. Bill, Henry Ford's nephew, added that he nearly trashed a truck stop in the process.

After becoming Ford's heavy truck engineering and manufacturing manager, Bill found that "some of the people who'd been here for years don't know how to drive a truck." He learned how to handle big rigs at Ford's Romeo (Michigan) proving ground, then took the state license test.

With an examiner in the seat next to him, Ford drove a tractor-trailer for six hours. The worst part, he said, came when the examiner told him to back the vehicle through a truck stop. "I almost took the whole truck stop with me," he laughed.

Even though he doesn't have a truck as a personal vehicle, Ford told the *Detroit Free Press* that he and his wife may acquire one. "We've got two kids," he notes, "so it's time to move up to an 18-wheeler."

Ford returned to his Grosse Pointe Shores home and Dearborn workplace in May '89. He misses the Lake Zurich mountain vista outside his Swiss office, the view from his Dearborn office not quite measuring up.

During two years in Zurich as chairman and managing director of Ford Switzerland, Ford ran his own show and his boss was hundreds of miles away in England: "Now," he notes, "my boss, Ken Smith, is next door."

Though Ford and his cousin, Edsel Ford II, have assumed a higher profile during the past year, Bill, 32 feels that he is less scrutinized than he was in Europe. "Detroit's sort of used to having members of the family around, and over there I was sort of a novelty," he observed.

Ford has distanced himself from the Palm Beach, Fla., court battle between Henry Ford II's widow, Kathleen DuRoss Ford, and other family members over administration of his uncle's trust. "Thankfully, I have nothing to do with it. I stay as far away from it as I can. It's a shame it had to go so far."

Ford Kindergarten

The William Clay Ford Jr. Kindergarten, Morelia, Michoacan, the first kindergarten built by Ford's Mexican dealers was dedicated in March 1998 by its namesake.

The school was built on the grounds of Ford School No. 165, opened the previous September. It is one of more than 160 schools built by Ford dealers since 1966, with 10 more under construction. More than a million children have finished elementary school in a Ford-built Mexican school, and this past year 124,000 students were enrolled.

At the dedication William Clay Ford Jr. quoted his great-grandfather, Henry Ford: "Education is the greatest force in civilization and the most deserving of help."

In 2160 or thereabouts, Morelian old-timers may point to a tall tree on the kindergarten grounds and say they remember when it was planted in '98 by the man for whom the school is named.

Father And Son

William Clay Ford Jr., 41, is in line to take over his father's Detroit Lions and will be the next chairman (but not CEO) of Ford Motor Company. "How can he find time to do both jobs?" he was asked by *Detroit News* sportswriter Joe Falls.

"My job at Ford comes first," Ford replied. "I wake up at 6 a.m. and work out for an hour. I do it every day. I go to my office at Ford and thank goodness for the telephone. That's how I keep in touch not only with the Lions, but the league in general. All calls, as well as my e-mail, come to my office at Ford."

Bill noted that his father, William Clay Ford Sr., 73, is recovering from his third heart bypass operation. Both men are enamored of football. The senior Ford's "burning desire" is for the Lions to win a championship for the first time in more than 40 years.

Bill added that his love of football is not shared by other franchise owners. "They're in it for self-aggrandizement and for the ego-stroking," he remarked. "I'm really appalled at our league meetings. We never talk about the game of football. That bothers me."

Steve Hamp

"What do you know about Steve Hamp, the new president of Henry Ford Museum and Greenfield Village?" asks reader Bruno Evoldi, New Brunswick, N.J. "And what happened to the former president, Harold Skramstad?"

Steven K. Hamp, 48, an 18-year-employee of the museum/village, is a great-grandson-in-law of Henry Ford, being married to William Clay Ford's daughter, Sheila. He holds a master's degree in museum studies from the University of Michigan, and has completed work toward a doctorate. I've known Steve for most of his tenure at the museum/village, and regard him as first-rate.

Skramstad, 57, resigned suddenly from the historical institutions in the summer of 1996. He was criticized for allowing small auction houses to sell vehicles and other antiques at a fraction of their value. In 1986, for example, an 18th century sofa valued at $100,000 went for $16,500. Some people also were angered that items given by their families to the museum/village were sold without their consultation.

Sheila Hamp, chairperson of the institutions' Board of Trustees from 1987-96, was succeeded in that position by her younger brother, William Clay Ford Jr., 40. Sheila remains a board member.

The museum/village annually attract about 1.1 million visitors annually.

Elena Joins Ford

Henry Ford II's granddaughter, Elena, daughter of Charlotte Ford and Stavros Niarchos, has moved from New York to Michigan to join the family firm's World Headquarters public relations staff.

As a young woman, Charlotte, 54, also thought of working for the company. But she arrived at adulthood before the women's movement opened doors for women in business.

Ford Heir Marries

Two prominent business families were united in marriage in July 1990, when Frederic Avery Bourke III, a great-great-grandson of Henry Ford, and Allison Anglesea Kent, a granddaughter of Arthur Atwater Kent, were married at the Seal Harbor, Maine summer home of Bourke's grandparents, Walter Buhl Ford II and Josephine Ford (the latter is Henry Ford's granddaughter and Henry Ford II's sister).

Bourke is the son of Nonie Ford and Frederick A. Bourke Jr., of Greenwich, Conn. Allison's grandfather, an inventor and philanthropist, also was well known for his 1940s-era Hollywood parties. In the 1920s, his radio receiver was to the radio industry what the Model T was to the car industry.

Edsel II & HFIII

Dick Folsom, president of the Henry Ford Heritage Association, left center, Henry Ford's great-grandson, Edsel Ford II, center, and Edsel's oldest son, Henry Ford III, at the 1996 centennial celebration of Henry Ford's Quadricycle at Greenfield Village, Dearborn. Many attendees were struck by the resemblance of HFIII, 16, to his great-great-grandfather. (Photo by reader James Cranick, Harbor Springs, Mich.)

Henry Ford III

Henry Ford III, 16, son of Edsel Ford II and grandson of Henry Ford II, seated in a replica of young Ford's great-great grandfather's quadricycle at Greenfield Village on June 4, 1996, the centennial of Ford's first drive. Also pictured are Dick Folsom, center, president of the Henry Ford Heritage Association, which organized the celebration with Henry Ford Museum and Greenfield Village, and George De Angelis, who built the replica, standing behind Ford. Mike Skinner, who, like Folsom, contributes many items to "Ford Country," videotapes the proceedings at right, and Nettie Seabrooks, Detroit's deputy mayor, representing the city in which Ford built his first car, is at left.

Henry III, with De Angelis at his side, drove the car through the village streets to the ceremonial site. The first family member to bear a resemblance to the first Henry Ford, Henry III was ruled off-limits to press interrogation by his father. Perhaps Edsel II remembers his great-grandfather's remark, "Reporters are skunks, and you know what happens to people who play with skunks."

II

FORD MOTOR COMPANY

Ford observes its centennial in 2003. For 95 years it has been one of the world's largest and most profitable automakers. It also has been one of the industry's tallest antennas.

The company, as noted by J.P. terHorst, press secretary to President Ford, "is just about as American as the flag, small-towns, and the U.S. overseas. Henry, Edsel, and Henry II are gone, but the Ford name lives on, branded into U.S. culture and customs and way of life in a fashion that has no equal on this side of the ocean and scarcely a parallel anywhere on earth.

"In the Smithsonian history museums," terHorst adds, "when they talk about autos, they display Fords; when they talk about mail delivery, they display Model T trucks and the Ford Trimotor airplane; when they talk about American giants of industry, they feature a man named Ford. The company thus represents the past, the present, and the future of an industry vital to America's future."

terHorst might have added that the company retains its time-honored logo, as opposed to adopting a symbol suggestive of an inkblot test. It also has resisted telescoping its name into FoMoCo or some other form of alphabetical hash.

Highly diversified and vertically integrated since the 1920s, the company decided in the 1980s to base its future on tripartite operations involving motor vehicles, finance, and aerospace. A buying spree ensued, taking in auto- and nonauto-related firms alike. Meantime, the company expanded vigorously overseas. By the mid-1990s, however, Ford had spun-off most of its nonautomotive activities. For better or worse, the company is betting its future on its core competency – the making, selling, and financing of motor vehicles.

Ford has had great continuity of leadership, Henry Ford and Henry Ford II having ruled from 1906-79. Four nonfamily executives served as chairmen for 19 years. Now a fourth-generation family member, William Clay Ford Jr., 41, steps forward as chairman. Well-educated, talented, personable, and dedicated, Bill is the answer to his family's and the company's prayer. Destined to be at the helm for the next quarter-century, he is, to paraphrase a famed slogan, "The Ford of the Future."

"Watch the Fords Go By"

Ford's famous slogan, "Watch the Fords Go By," was featured on a mammoth electric display erected on top of Detroit's Temple Theater in 1908. A similar display with the Model T sandwiched between the slogan and the company's monthly sales figure decorated a Detroit building in 1915. (Photo from Greenfield Village and Henry Ford Museum, Dearborn, Mich.)

Ford's famous advertising slogan, "Watch the Fords Go By," has been variously reported as having been originated by the company's traffic manager, W.S. Hogue, who shouted the words at a race in which Fords were whizzing by the competition, and by the firm's first advertising manager, E. LeRoy Pelletier.

Another possible source of the slogan, according to the club publication of the Volunteer (Nashville, Tenn.) Chapter of the Early Ford V-8 Club of America, was a baseball game played in 1907 (the year the slogan first was used in Ford advertising).

According to this version, a Ford factory team "was playing another Detroit outfit when a threatening thundershower sent the spectators running for cover. In the midst of the confusion, the Ford boys loaded the bases and their cleanup hitter walloped a long one to the outfield. As the men on base came scampering across home plate, a distraught umpire threw up his hands and yelled, 'Watch the Fords go by!' The phrase caught on and began to appear in company advertising."

That it did, whatever its origins, and few auto slogans have proved as durable, the phrase having been revised for ad campaigns in both the 1930s and 1940s.

Temple Theater

Question: What do Ford's first electric spectacular and George Burns have in common?

Answer: They've both played Detroit's Temple Theater.

We've long known that Ford's famous advertising slogan, "Watch the Fords Go By," appeared in a mammoth electric sign atop the theater starting in 1908. But we learned only recently that Burns, now 96, played the Temple on his first visit to Detroit in 1917. "I play Detroit every 75 years," the comedian quipped, in reference to his October 1992 appearance at the new George Burns Theater for the Performing Arts in Livonia, a Motor City suburb.

"Ford in Future"

"There's a Ford in Your Future" is one of "10 landmark auto ads and campaigns" cited in the *New York Times*' Oct. 16, 1997 edition.

Of the Ford campaign, the *Times* states, "After World War II, automakers could not work fast enough to satisfy a car-starved public's appetite, fueled by salaries earned at defense work. Not only were not cars built while the auto plants turned out tanks and airplanes during wartime, but most Americans had been unable to afford new cars during the Depression. Ford and [advertising agency] J. Walter Thompson handled this situation shrewdly, putting off customers without alienating them, by pledging that the future would bring Fords of all wondrous manner and in plentiful supply. The promise tapped deep yearnings during the war years that the postwar world would be a better place."

Launched in November 1944, "Ford in Your Future" became the immediate postwar era's best-known automobile campaign. It was prompted by an article, "Lay that Crystal Down," appearing in the July 1944 issue of the *Ford Times*. Featuring an illustration of a woman gazing into a crystal ball, the article pointed out that postwar cars would bear a close resemblance to prewar vehicles rather than the plastic, bubbletop, and autogyro-type "dream" cars envisioned by some journalists. When the story appeared, newly appointed J. Walter Thompson was reviewing Ford literature in hopes of uncovering a suitable advertising theme. Inspired by the title, illustration, and reference to postwar cars, the agency created the "Ford in Your Future" campaign.

Other ads/campaigns cited by the *Times* included Cadillac's 1915 "The Penalty of Leadership," Jordan's 1923 "Somewhere West of Laramie," Plymouth's 1928 "Look at all Three," Chevrolet's 1950s' Dinah Shores rendition of "See the U.S.A. in Your Chevrolet," Volkswagen's 1960s-1970s' Beetle advertising, Volvo's 1960s-1970s' ads stressing reliability, toughness, and value, Honda's 1974 ad theme, "We don't make a 'woman's' car," Isuzu's 1985 ads featuring a smarmy unctuous salesman named Joe Isuzu, and Saturn's emotional 1990 ads centering on Saturn's plant and promise to provide "A different kind of company. A different kind of car."

Ford's 1907-15 "Watch the Fords Go By" campaign belongs on the *Times*' list. Also used in Ford institutional advertising in the early 1940s, this slogan, along with Packard's "Ask the Man Who Owns One," long was regarded as one of the two best-known and effective automobile slogans of all time.

Ford Slogans

Ford has had some of the most memorable slogans in automotive history, ranging from "Watch the Fords Go By" through "There's a Ford in Your Future" to "Ford Has a Better Idea."

After five years, however, the company has decided that the use of its "Best-Built American Cars" slogan is no longer a good idea. Being the best in America, consumer tests show, isn't enough; customers want the world's best. Consequently, Ford's new slogan is, "Our goal is to build the highest quality cars and trucks in the world." Ford, of course, can't claim that its vehicles are the world's best made. Japanese-built cars have that distinction.

Another Ford slogan which has been around a while is "Have You Driven a Ford Lately?" The idea behind the slogan is to suggest that, if one hasn't driven a new Ford, he should, and, upon doing so, will be pleasantly surprised. That's true, if one drives a new Ford.

But during the early years of that slogan's use, I was driving a 1979 Fairmont, which had poor roadability, limited interior space, and high fuel consumption, among other deficiencies. Each time I was exposed to a "Have You Driven a Ford Lately?" ad, I'd say to myself, "Yes, this very day, and I dislike it." Finally, in January 1987, I bought a Mercury Sable, and could put such a negative connotation behind me.

Ford has had a couple of other slogans that fell short – "No Unhappy Owners," which was unbelievable, and "Ford Listens Better," which was doubtful. On the other hand, "Quality is Job One" strikes one as being believable, while Chevrolet's "Heartbeat of America" is questionable and "The Great American Road Belongs to Buick" unbelievable.

Driven a Fjord Lately

Several Ford advertising slogans, among them "Watch the Ford Go By," "There's a Ford in Your Future," and "Ford Has a Better Idea," have been incorporated into other companies' ads. Now it's the turn of "Have You Driven a Ford Lately?"

An Admiral Cruises' advertisement in a recent *National Geographic* features an aerial view of a cruise ship sailing along a blue-water Alaskan fjord, snow-capped mountains in the background. Superimposed over this picture are the words, "Have you driven a Fjord lately?"

Thanks to former student Gorden T. Totty, Dearborn, Mich., for forwarding the ad.

Nostalgia Marketing

Ford is one of many companies engaged in nostalgia marketing.

In February 1998 the company began airing a TV commercial commemorating Henry Ford's role in putting America on wheels. The spot includes what appears to be grainy, historic footage of a Model T puttering down an early 20th century Main Street. The sepia-toned scene actually was shot in 1997 on a Hollywood back lot and was given a vintage look by use of a hand-cranked 1920s camera, old emulsion films, and special editing.

Ford hopes that consumers equate longevity with quality. "People really respond to the ad," says Bruce Rooke, executive creative director at Ford's advertising agency, J. Walter Thompson Co. "They say, 'this is a company that has lasted through a couple of world wars.' "

Yes, and a Great Depression, government regulation, foreign competition, battles between Henry Ford II and Lee Iacocca, and much else as well. In June 2003 the company will celebrate its first century, and by that time Henry Ford's ghost will have been trotted out so much that he will be the year's most publicized auto figure. In fact, given the never-ending flow of Ford media references, he may be the best publicized automan of the 21st century, just as he was of the 20th.

Blimps

"I recently read that blimps advertise Sea World, Gulf Oil, and Budweiser," writes Keith Carroway, of Bethesda, Md. "Am I right in thinking that Ford also once advertised with blimps?"

Yes, Ford used an airship for advertising after World War II. The company's advertising agency, J. Walter Thompson, proposed the idea of blimp advertising after being approached in the spring of 1946 by Douglas Leigh, Inc., of New York. Before the war Leigh had designed many of the large illuminated signs which had given Broadway its sobriquet as the "Great White Way."

For Ford, Leigh proposed to convert a 265-foot surplus Navy blimp into a flying "adship." It was to cruise at 2,500 feet, day and night, over the Atlantic seaboard, ranging from Washington on the south to Hartford, Conn. on the north. Ford agreed to the proposal in July.

Leigh decorated one side of Ford's

blimp with the slogan, "Ford's Out Front"; the other side with the message, "There's a Ford in Your Future." At night, the "Ford's Out Front" side of the airship flashed the slogan and the alternating words "in style" and "in safety." The "Ford in Your Future" message was supplemented by weather reports and news bulletins. The messages, averaging 25 feet in height and ranging from 170 feet to 200 feet in length, were legible from a distance of three miles at night, five miles during the day.

Ford's dirigible flew over the eastern seaboard in late 1946 and through the spring of 1947, then spent the remainder of the year touring upstate New York, lower Ontario, New England, and the Midwest. The craft spent the early part of 1948 in Florida, the summer and fall of 1948 in the Midwest.

By 1948, however, the novelty of blimp "spectaculars" had worn thin. In 1947 Leigh had put dirigibles into the air for Ringling Bros. and Barnum & Bailey Circus, Tide Water Associated Oil Company, Mobilgas, and Wonder Bread; and by the end of that year there were few cities in the East and Midwest and on the West Coast that had not been exposed to at least one of the aircraft. Consequently, Ford was content to let its two-year contract with Leigh expire on October 15, 1948. The expenditure for the service – $496,000 – probably was the automaker's soundest advertising investment during the immediate postwar period.

1946 Annual Report

As a privately-owned firm, Ford Motor Company was under no obligation to prepare an annual report until it went public in 1955. Even so, starting in 1946 it prepared annual reports which contained much of the same information as those issued by publicly-held firms. The reports were circulated only among family members, directors (all employees), officers, and a small number of other executives.

The first report, issued on July 25, 1947, is a scarce item, and your commentator has only a photocopy. The cover, under the word, "Confidential," shows the Rotunda, moved from the Chicago World's Fair in the mid-1930s and serving as an office building in 1946. Henry Ford's picture appears on the first page over the words, "The Ford Motor Company mourns the passing of Henry Ford – its founder – its leader – its inspiration."

The third page lists directors and officers. Directors were Henry Ford II, chairman; Ernest R. Breech, executive vice president; Mead L. Bricker, John R. Davis, and William T. Gossett, vice presidents; Burt J. Craig, treasurer; and Benson Ford. Officers, in addition to HFII, Breech, Bricker, Davis, and Gossett, included vice presidents Albert J. Browning, John S. Bugas, Lewis D. Crusoe, Delmar S. Harder, and Harold T. Youngren, and Treasurer Leon E. Briggs.

A "Ford in the News" section denotes important happenings during the year. Among them were the start of construction of assembly plants in St. Louis, Atlanta, Los Angeles, and Metuchen, N.J.; announcement of plans to build a research and engineering center in Dearborn and to transfer all truck and bus production from the Rouge Plant to the Highland Park Plant; the creation of an International Division; and the sale of the Saline, Mich. soybean processing plant and appointment of a sales agent to sell 9,600 acres of Ford farmland near Macon and Tecumseh, Mich.

Dealing only with the operations of the parent company and its Western Hemisphere subsidiaries, the report reveals that the firm showed a consolidated net income of only $2,000 in 1946. That the year the company's domestic sales were 501,653 Fords, 66,273 Mercurys, 12,007 Lincolns, and 59,773 tractors. The firm had 103,486 employees, down from 205,078 in wartime 1943 and 43,729 in Depression-era 1933.

Ford Turnaround

A book, *Reinventing the Wheel*, by Alton Doody and Ron Bingaman, focuses on Ford Motor Company's 1980s turnaround and cultural transformation.

Doody, an ex-Ohio State University marketing professor, now a consultant, admits his motive for writing the book was not entirely academic. One of his clients is Mazda, 25 percent owned by Ford. Mazda, in turn, owns Autorama, a dealer network that sells Mazda-made, Ford-badged vehicles in Japan, plus American-made Ford products.

"Our problem has been how to communicate to the Japanese market that an American manufacturer has a product worthy of consideration," says Doody. "American cars have a horrible reputation in Japan." A Japanese-language edition of *Reinventing the Wheel* was published in 1988.

Ford PR Memoir

The title doesn't suggest it, but more than two-thirds of John E. Sattler's book, *Fifty Years Ahead of the News*, deals with Sattler's public relations career at Ford Motor Co.

Sattler administered the company's important New York office from 1946-68, with time out to manage the firm's New York World's Fair Pavilion in 1964. He then spent 12 years in Dearborn, where, among other duties, he supervised Ford publications, including *Ford Times*, and planned and implemented the company's 75th anniversary celebration.

Along the way, Sattler worked closely with Henry Ford II, Benson and William Clay Ford, Lee Iacocca, and many other Ford executives. These associations, plus brushes with the likes of Babe Ruth, Walt Disney, Eleanor Roosevelt, Princess Grace, and other well-known personalities, contribute to a wealth of well-told tales.

Chronologically, the stories range from Sattler's press activities at the time of Henry Ford's death in 1947, through the New York Fair and the burglary of HFII's New York apartment in 1964, to the company's 75th anniversary observance in 1978.

I first met Sattler, Ford's "Mr. New York," in 1953, after having joined Ford's News Department the year previous. We kept in touch through my postwar Ford years, and in 1988 and 1990 I interviewed him in connection with research I was doing. His experiences were so interesting that I, among others, encouraged him to write his memoirs. He has done so in a 287-page book which also recounts his early life and public relations career, the latter continuing to this day.

The well-illustrated book may be acquired for $19.95 from Sattler International, 2525 Waite Ave., Kalamazoo, MI 49008.

Shook Book

"I've seen a reference to a book called *Turnaround – the New Ford Motor Company* by Robert L. Shook," writes reader Hugh Jensen, of Long Beach, Calif. "Can you comment on it?"

Rather than comment, let me quote from the *Detroit News*' review of this 1991 book.

"Ford Motor Co.'s shifting fortunes and colorful executives have provided the plot and characters of one of America's longest-running industrial epics.

"That makes it unforgivable for a writer to produce a boring book with such rich material.

"Shook purports to tell the story of the automaker's trip from the financial brink to become the nation's most profitable automaker during the 1980s .... In fact, Shook's book reads like a pile of Ford press releases.

"Current and former executives talk about the Bad Old Days before they got religion. Then, after an unpleasant bath in the company's financial red ink, they learn that the customer is king, the union is our friend, and quality is job one.

" ... But Shook fails to capture the human drama that unfolds when a corporate empire desperately tries to save itself.

"In the early 1980s, Ford executives were frantically trying to restructure a company that was losing huge sums of money. Ford risked $3 billion on a sedan called the Taurus – more than it had ever spent on a single vehicle. Its success depended upon a then-radical aerodynamic styling that had drawn negative reviews at numerous consumer clinics.

"Yet, Shook would have us believe that Ford's executives never flinched at the prospect of such a gamble. He mentions in passing that Ford's board of directors was divided on the project – then drops the subject.

"Who was nervous about Taurus' price tag? Which Ford executives hated its jelly-bean look? Readers won't find the answers in this book."

Your commentator thinks better of the book than the *News*' reviewer, David Sedgwick, while agreeing that it isn't of the same quality as such 1980s books as David Halberstam's *The Reckoning*, Peter Collier's and David Horowitz's *The Fords, An American Epic*, or even Robert Lacey's *Ford, the Men and the Machine*.

Ford Left Out

A 1994 book, *Collision: GM., Toyota, Volkswagen and the Race to Own the 21st Century*, by Maryann Keller, cites GM, Toyota, and Volkswagen as the "new Global Big Three." Ford is excluded because, Keller says, "it has not been a innovator in this industry since the 1920s. And it is not No. 1 in any market."

Both assertions will come as a surprise to Ford's public relations people, who can reel off a string of "Ford firsts" since the 1920s and name several markets, ranging from Britain to Taiwan, in which Ford is the sales leader.

Keller also states that "GM was the first international car company with acquisitions in Germany, Britain, and Australia, and even decent export sales to Japan in the 1920s." Ford, in point of fact, preceded GM into each of these markets and in every significant way was the first international auto firm.

Keller, Wall Street's most respected auto analyst, also predicts that General Motors might again become the world's leading car company (it is, of course, still first in worldwide sales). Indeed, she says that GM, because it is the automaker that "has most recently overcome great problems," is the "best car company in the world."

Not a Bestseller

The 1987 book, *The Fords: An American Epic*, by Peter Collier and David Horowitz, was not a sales success in Horowitz's view.

In his 1997 autobiography, *Radical Son: A Generational Odyssey*, Horowitz states that "the Ford book never made the bestseller lists, and though 70,000 hardback copies were sold, it didn't earn back its advance, and we (the authors) didn't receive a dime for our efforts after it was published.

The book's sales suffered, Horowitz adds, because it was published in the wake of Robert Lacey's best-selling *Ford: The Men and the Machine*. In addition, *American Epic*, although favorably reviewed by the *New York Times* and the *Los Angeles Times*, was panned by the even more influential *New York Times Book Review*.

Aware that the Collier-Horowitz book was in the offing, Lacey's publisher, Little, Brown, pressured its man to finish his book before that of his competitors, and it shows. The first half of Lacey's book is quite sound; the second half far less so. The book also sensationalizes, emphasizes sex, and gossips in an effort to enhance its sales value. Too bad; Lacey, if not pressed could and would have done better.

Ford Omitted

Ford's brand name remains one of the world's best-known. But it did not make the cut in a 1994 *Fortune* article which noted that "Matsushita's Panasonic and National brands [are] almost as well known around the world as Nestlé, IBM, Coca-Cola, and Kodak."

Brought Down to Earth

Two articles downplay Ford's importance on the world stage.

One is a *Parade* item based on a survey by Landor Associates, and image-management firm which tested 2,140 brand names on 3,000 consumers in the U.S., Japan, and Western Europe. Was Ford one of the best recognized brand names, as a Ford enthusiast might presume? No, the three brand names that most impressed consumers were Coca-Cola, IBM and Sony, followed by Porsche, McDonald's, Disney, Honda, Toyota, Seiko, and BMW.

One presumes that Ford has better brand recognition in the U.S. and Europe than in Japan, where the company is not a major presence. Conversely, Coca-Cola is Japan's best-selling soft drink, IBM is one of Japan's leading computer firms, and each of the other enterprises cited above has good brand recognition in the Land of the Rising Sun.

The second article concerns the Ford Trimotor airplane, which was omitted from a listing of the "25 most important aircraft in the history of manned flight" by La Federation Aeronautique Internationale, of Paris, the one international agency which sets up, defines, and verifies all aviation world records. Most of the honored planes are either military aircraft or "one-flight" planes such as the Wright Flyer, *Spirit of St. Louis*, and Rutan Voyager. But the Douglas DC-3, Boeing 747, and Concorde, all passenger craft, are cited, and it comes as a surprise that the Trimotor isn't.

Charcoal Briquets

Charcoal briquets, which Henry Ford started making in 1920, today provide the economic underpinnings of Parsons, W.Va.

Parsons, population 1,900, "is to barbecues what Detroit is to cars," reports the Associated Press. The town, set amid the oaks and elms of the Allegheny Mountains, is home to the 40-acre Kingsford Charcoal plant, the Northeast's largest producer of charcoal briquets, a staple for backyard barbecues.

Ford began producing pillow-shaped charcoal lumps in 1920 to dispose of sawdust and wooden scraps from his Iron Mountain/Kingsford, Mich. plant. Initially the product was used for tobacco curing and cooking on ships and trains. Today, briquets add up to a half-billion dollar industry, and are used by an estimated 62 million households for barbecuing.

Kingsford Products Company is named for E.G. Kingsford, Ford's relative by marriage, and early head of the enterprise. The company's Parsons plant runs 24 hours a day year-round except for Christmas, Easter, and the first day of deer hunting season. "I could probably field a crew for Christmas," says plant manager Harold McCloud, "but you can forget about the opening of deer season."

Before Ford opened his first briquet factory, cooking with charcoal was risky. Each piece had different burn characteristics. "You'd have a fire that cooked at 600 degrees at one time and another time you'd have a fire that cooked at 400 degrees," states McCloud. "Ours burn so that a cooking temperature of between 380 and 400 degrees is maintained."

The manufacturing process begins when sawdust and wood scraps are sucked into a 1,900-degree furnace and reduced to black ash, from which the carbon has been cooked out. The ash then goes to a mixer where sawdust and coal are added, along with nitrates, lime, and borax to make the mixture stick together and provide for an even burn. After the mixture is steamed, it is formed into briquets by presses. "We want a good red glow, without a flame, that will cook food without charring it," said a Kingsford quality control supervisor. "And we don't want any smoke, mesquite briquets excepted."

Ford sold Kingsford in 1950 to Clorox Company, the present owner. Kingsford now markets charcoal to 16 Eastern states, ranging as far west as Michigan. "We make a billion briquets a year here," says McCloud.

The Parsons plant and its 150 employees are vital to economically-depressed Parsons. "God help us if Kingsford left," says Marilyn Smith, editor of the *Parsons Advocate* and chairwoman of the Parsons Chamber of Commerce.

Dual Dealerships

"In the early years of the auto industry," reader Al Wiggins, of Aurora, Colo., asks, "did Ford make its dealers stick to selling Fords only?"

The answer is no, and the above photo (circa 1904-05) of the Atlas Automobile Company, located in Western Pennsylvania, makes the point. Ford's Model A, center, is flanked by four cars of other makes.

Atlas' sign also is revealing, noting that the firm stores or sells on commission or consignment, and also exchanges or buys "2nd hand automobiles," indicating a used-car market at that early juncture.

Ford is the only make which furnished and/or rated signs on the dealership's front. At right a non-Ford script sign says, "The Celebrated Ford Automobiles." Above the Model A, the sign reads "World's Record Mile 39 2/5 seconds, Jan. 12/04 The Ford We Have It Runabouts Tonneaus An Automobile of Beauty A Joy Forever (two illegible words) for Western Pennsylvania." Also on the sign are the words "High Power Simple Low in Price Easy to Operate" and "The Best Ever Silent High Grade Accessible."

The stores' premises could stand some sprucing up – note the trash cans at right. A Mail Pouch tobacco sign appears above the car at extreme left.

As Ford grew more powerful, the company could and did insist that its dealers sell Fords only. Ford still prefers that its dealers handle only Ford brands, but many of its stores also sell competing makes.

Old Dealership

They don't build 'em like that anymore – "that" being the old Ford dealership in the center of this photo. The well-maintained building, now occupied by Locascio's Hardware, stands in Hammond, La. Ford Script is enclosed in the rectangular areas above the garage door and the right-hand show window. Thanks to reader D. Briggs, of Arcadia, Calif., for forwarding the picture.

A "1918-19" Model T bought by C.D. "Red" Murray, of Colby, Kan., at age 14 in 1927. When bought, the car was a "touring" with the back half missing. Murray bought the speedster body for $5.

Boy Dealer

"In March 1934, I was told by Ford's Kansas City branch manager that I was the youngest Ford dealer in his branch, maybe in the U.S.," writes reader C.D. "Red" Murray, of Colby, Kan. At the time Murray was 22 and half-owner of Colby's Ford dealership.

Murray kept his interest in the agency until August 1937, then acquired the town's Plymouth-De Soto franchise. Subsequently, Murray farmed, sold real estate, and developed a "ritzy subdivision," according to the *Colby Free Press*, which recently ran a story on Murray's salad days.

Murray acquired his first car, a "1918-19" Model T at age 14 in exchange for a city lot his father had given him for Christmas. Murray wasted no time in defining his priorities, exchanging the lot for the car on New Year's Day.

The car, recalls Murray, was a "touring" with the back half missing. He soon spent $5 to buy and have mounted a speedster body, then sold advertising space on the body. Among the painted messages was one for Pratt & Golden Hardware: "Hardware that will stand hardware." In addition to advertisements, the car sported such snappy lines as, "Give me liberty or give me breath," "Exit, in case of fire" (with arrow pointing toward the open top), and "Sick cylinders" (on the front).

Murray sold his T to a member of a traveling harvest team in 1928. "I never saw it after it left Colby," says Red. "The harvesters traveled north."

Asked by his father what he

intended to do with the money obtained from the sale of his Model T, Murray replied, in the best car nut tradition, "buy another car."

Murray has subscribed to *Cars & Parts* since it was published in Memphis in the 1960s.

Dealership Memories

Ford dealers at times were an independent lot, as attested by J.F. Sledge of Richmond, Va., who worked for his uncle's agency between 1934-39.

"When I finished high school in 1933," Sledge recalls, "I was unable to go to college due to financial reasons, and couldn't find a job. A year later my uncle, who was a Ford dealer, offered me a job as a 'gofer' at $50 per month. He had been a medical doctor, but became fascinated with the Model T after buying one in 1916 for use in his medical practice. He gave up his medical career for a Ford dealership.

"My uncle was rather wealthy for the times, and one day, about 1935, a new Ford representative came in – they were known in those days as road men. The representative says, 'Dr. Reese, we do not have a financial statement for you in our files.' Apparently this man was unaware that Henry Ford had never given out a financial statement himself.

"Reply from Dr. Reese, 'Do I owe Ford Motor Co. anything?' Answer: 'No sir.' Reply: 'Then I will make a deal with you. When Henry Ford gives me a copy of his statement, then I will give him a copy of mine.' Of all the looks on a man's face – he appeared to be stone-faced. His reply was that he would discuss the matter with his superior. End of story."

In an earlier day, recalls Sledge, "a Ford dealer often was coerced into taking some Fordson tractors regardless of whether he had ordered them or wanted them. One day Dr. Reese was notified by the local freight agent that there were six tractors on a siding that were addressed to him, and were C.O.D. He called Ford and stated that he didn't order the tractors, and that they should come and get them. The tractors sat on the siding for about a month until Ford moved them to another destination."

Sledge also recalls the ordering procedure during his dealership days. "For instance," he recalls, "a dealer would sell a car in the morning, order it from the assembly plant in the afternoon, and pick it up at the assembly plant the next day in time to deliver it that afternoon.

"I stayed with my uncle for five years, and left in 1939 to go with another Ford dealer," concludes Sledge. "My uncle was rather bitter, stating to everyone who would listen that he gave me a job when I needed one, and now that he needed me, I was leaving. He didn't speak to me for some time until he got the message that I was doing well. Then he began stating that I was his favorite nephew, and that he had taught me all I knew. He passed away in 1959, at which time he and I were the best of friends. The old saying that time heals all wounds certainly applied to the two of us."

Bowen Motor Company

"One of my eccentricities is being what I call an 'urban archaeologist'; that is, someone always searching for automotive-related buildings," writes reader Tom Link, of Kernersville, N.C.

"Several years ago," Link adds, "while driving through Sanford, N.C., a town of about 12,000 population, I spotted a magnificent old building once belonging to the Bowen Motor Co. and selling Lincolns, Fords, and Fordsons. From the size of the building (three full stories), I assume that Bowen was a distributor, as well as a dealer. Certainly a town of Sanford's size could not have supported a plant of this size by itself. In the early '20s, auto demand was largely seasonal and distributors absorbed off-season production and held it for seasonal sale to their

The abandoned Bowen Motor Co. building in Sanford, N.C. The white area at upper right contains the words "Bowen Motor Co. Lincoln Ford Fordson." The white space at left center advertises "Ford Service Bowen Motor Co." The building must have served owners of Ford products for miles around, and likely Ford dealers, as well.

Ford Mechanics

Seven mechanics of a Detroit Ford dealership, Hall-Dobbs, take a break from work in the late 1930s. "I heard a rumor that Joe Hall, second from right, was a tail gunner during World War II, and was killed," says John C. Jackson, San Jose, Calif., who furnished this photo. "Vince Williams, second from left, had a bad limp back in the 1930s. He said it was a result of his broken leg, making it shorter. I saw him again in Cheboygan, Mich. around 1955, and the limp had disappeared. He said his leg had been broken again, and they did a better job of setting it the second time." Jackson, not pictured, served the dealership as a self-described "all around gopher on parts rebuild, office, tow truck, motorcycle, and floor man."

assigned dealers. I imagine the full basement of this large building once held a lot of Model Ts.

"The building is now standing vacant," continues Link. "Some modifications have been made and there is some occupancy of the front part of the building. However, a look through the cathedral-type windows in the old shop area reveals only some rusty junk and a deteriorating wood plank floor. I fear the building won't last long."

Photos forwarded by Link show that the building is located on the Business Route of U.S. 1 and U.S. 421. The structure had to have been built after Ford's 1922 acquisition of Lincoln and during the Fordson's heyday in the early/mid-1920s. As Link suggests, Bowen probably was both a distributor and retailer of Model Ts, and may have assembled Tin Lizzies, as well.

Detroit Iron

If there was an award for miles traveled to buy a car, it likely would go to the Betshcart family of Switzerland. For four consecutive years, during the mid-'80s, family members Wendel, Mary, and Ed, flew into Detroit to buy vehicles from Jack Demer Ford, a Wayne, Mich., dealership.

The relationship began when the Betscharts jetted into the Motor City in expectation of buying a car from the Ford factory. "They just sort of showed up at the airport and called Ford," said Tom Cameron, new-car sales manager at the dealership. "Then somebody at the airport told them that buying a car from the factory was impossible."

Eventually, they were directed to the Demer dealership by an anonymous tipster at the airport. They bought new LTDs for three successive years. When the LTD was replaced by the Taurus, the Betscharts asked for a car similar to the LTD. Cameron tried to sell them a Taurus, but they didn't want that European look. "They wanted the American look. A Mercury Marquis station wagon with 23,000 miles on it hit the mark," Cameron related.

"How do they get the cars back to Switzerland," a *Detroit Free Press* reporter asked Cameron. "Beats me," he replied. "I think by boat."

Sidney Weinberg

Henry Ford II's most trusted outside board member was Wall Streeter Sidney Weinberg, a director from 1956 until his death in 1969.

In 1987 I asked William T. Gossett, Ford's general counsel from 1947-62 and a fellow director, about the Weinberg-Ford relationship. He replied as follows:

[Weinberg] "was very influential with Henry, who tended to follow his suggestions more than any other outside member of the board. Weinberg dominated the board for several years. Unless you could get something approved by him, in addition to Henry or [Chairman Ernest R.] Breech, you wouldn't have a chance. Weinberg admired Breech, whereas Breech didn't trust Weinberg and regarded him as a self-seeker and a 'brown-noser,' to use an old expression.

"But he had Mr. Ford's confidence," I noted. "Why?"

"Weinberg," he answered, "had glib and quick ways. He had a sense of humor, but a warped sense of humor .... He never went to college, never went through high school. He just picked up what he'd learned. He once went into a pawn shop and bought a Phi Beta Kappa key and wore it. He had no right to, but he did ....

"When Sidney was 70 years old, he was told that he had to get off the board because of the retirement age rule ... Henry came to me and said, 'I want to make an exception. I want to keep Sidney Weinberg on the board after 70.' I said, 'Well, Henry, I'm certainly not going to oppose that, but have you thought it through? If he's given preferential treatment, you'll never get him off. You'll extend it one year, ad infinitum. If you do that for Sidney Weinberg, what about Don David, who preceded Sidney on the board. What about Paul Cabot?' He said, 'I don't give a damn. I'm going to change the rule to the extent necessary to keep Sidney on the board. I'll tell these other guys that it doesn't apply to them.' "

"I didn't think he'd do it," Gossett concluded, "but he did."

Paul Cabot

In 1989 I interviewed 90-year-old Boston Brahmin Paul C. Cabot in his capacity as a former Ford Motor Company director.

"I've long heard the rhyme about the Lowells speaking only to Cabots and the Cabots speaking only to God," I ventured.

"I had a very close friend named Arnold Lowell," he replied, "who always put it the other way – that the Cabots only speak to Lowells and the Lowells speak only to God."

"Do you speak to many people other than God?" I asked. "Oh, yes," he laughed. But I've been kidded about that ditty since I was in school. My mother never liked any part of it. At one time a Jewish family changed its name to Cabot. Some wit said, 'Here's to Boston, home of the bean and the cod, where the Lowells speak only to Cabots, and the Cabots speak Yiddish, by God!' I've always liked that."

Female Directors

"How many women have served on Ford's board of directors?" asks reader Carl Tappan of Mt. Vernon, N.Y.

Three. Eleanor Clay Ford, widow of Edsel Ford; Marian S. Heiskell, of the family which publishes the *New York Times*; and Ellen R. Marram, president and chief executive officer of Nabisco.

Heiskell retired from Ford's board in 1989, the same year Marram, 43, became a director. At Nabisco, Marram, a Wellesly College graduate, administers an organization with 17,000 employees and $2.5 billion in sales. Often asked about succeeding in a "man's world," Marram says flatly: "I don't spend time focusing on the woman issue. I know that there have been people I've encountered who have treated me differently because I'm a woman. But, that's their issue. I just focus on being an effective executive."

Philco's Fade

Two of the best known brand names in U.S. industry were joined with the acquisition of Philco by Ford in 1960. But, the acquisition was a "disastrous failure," states the book, *Made in America: Regaining the Productive Edge*, prepared by the MIT (Massachusetts Institute of Technology) Commission on Industrial Productivity.

"Philco made television sets and appliances, had just entered the computer business, and had started a semiconductor operation, all in the Philadelphia area," the book states. "A nearby R&D laboratory was developing new technology, including innovative semiconductor devices, large-scale computers, and optical readers for the postal system ...

"Ford concentrated much of the decision making for these businesses at its Detroit headquarters, however, where its emphasis was on strong financial controls. Under Ford's stewardship, all of the businesses rapidly declined and were eventually sold off or abandoned. Ford shifted its high-technology efforts to the steadier, more lucrative military and aerospace sector." The name Philco eventually was consigned to the dustbin of U.S. industrial history.

Downsizing

What a difference a few years make!

A Ford news release dated September, 1989, notes that the company "is the second largest car and truck producer in the world; second largest finance company in the world; third largest tractor producer in the world; second largest glass company in the United States; second largest U.S. Savings and Loan institution; and the eighth largest U.S. steel company." The release also noted that Ford was prominent in space technology.

Within 18 months, however, the company sold its tractor, steel, and space technology operations. Ford entered the tractor business in 1917, the steel industry in 1920, and aerospace in 1956.

Which Way To Go?

"Ford has gotten out of steel, shipping, tractor and aerospace," writes reader Paul Jamison, of Long Beach, Calif., "and would have gotten out of its glass business if it could have sold it. I've read that Toyota plans to buy into the housing, telecommunications, and other businesses. Who's got the right approach?"

Who can say? What we do know is that Ford abandoned several fields because they (a) were losing money (b) were believed to have limited potential (c) were distracting the company from its core business.

As for Toyota, its president, Hiroshi Okuda, was quoted in January 1997 as follows: "If you look back in history, there hasn't been a single industry that continued to be profitable for more than 40 to 60 years. We aren't bold enough to think the auto industry is immortal."

Of the two approaches, I like Toyota's best. It's quite possible that Ford, during the next cyclical turndown in the auto business, will wish that it had its eggs in several baskets.

Dress Code

Ford, along with many other companies, has relaxed its dress code in recent years. On Fridays Ford employees may wear slacks and sweaters, but not blue jeans, sneakers, or tank tops.

British-born Chairman Alexander Trotman first liberalized office wear when head of the company's North American Automotive Operations, and then at World Headquarters. His predecessor, Harold A. (Red) Poling, was against the idea.

Trotman himself continues to wear daily a double-breasted suit, starched shirt, and suspenders, a wardrobe he describes as "informal, but disciplined."

Henry Ford, despite his humble origins, always wore a suit and tie when in a business setting and, like most men of his day, a hat as well. He frequently wore three-piece suits, and most often they were gray. The auto king wore both bow and conventional ties. When driving a tractor, camping out, or chopping wood, he took off his coat, but not his tie.

The industrialist's executive associates and friends were similarly garbed with the exception of Thomas A. Edison, who when camping with Ford, Harvey Firestone, and others, put aside his tie.

When a member of Ford's Public Relations Staff in the early/mid-1950s, your commentator and his fellow workers invariably wore a suit, white shirt, and tie. Usually the suit was gray or charcoal gray. This dress code prevailed for decades, although other-than-white shirts finally were allowed.

In the 1950s Fordists were not required to wear hats, which had been passé among young men since World War II. General Motors men, however, were supposed to wear hats at all times as I learned when several of them and I visited a saloon associated with Jack London, in Oakland, Calif. in 1955.

In the 1970s a university professor turned Ford economist, wore a sports coat and slacks to his World Headquarters office on a Friday. Pointedly, his boss asked him if he was getting an early start for the weekend. Getting the message, the newcomer wore only suits thereafter.

Trotman thinks that freedom from formal office war is a morale booster, but he is not sure whether it improves productivity. Henry Ford, were he around, probably would not take any chances; formal attire would remain in force. Henry Ford II, I have the feeling, would be more inclined to bend on this issue. It was he, after all, who having grown sideburns, made it all right for others to do the same.

Editor's note: Ford employees now can dress casually every day.

Ford Executives

In 1990 I spent many hours viewing films prepared by Ford for its management and dealers between 1947-87. Cataloged for the company in 1989 by Jonathan Twyman, of Ann Arbor, Mich., the films show numerous executives and subjects. While watching the footage, my impressions were recorded on tape and later transcribed onto 47 typed pages. Here are a few comments about certain executives, plus random thoughts expressed at the time.

"Henry Ford II is speaking to employees at the company's 75th anniversary celebration in front of World Headquarters. He has a good voice, somewhat on the high side, although not as high (or whiny) as that of GM's Roger Smith. He mentions that he's pleased to see in attendance representatives of so many third- and even fourth-generation Ford families, just as his family is. There is a colorful ceremony in which flags are raised in tribute to the countries in which Ford has plants. The song 'It's a Small, Small World,' is played. Some Ford employees are garbed in the clothing of the nations from which their ancestors came and in which Ford has factories. A white fellow wears a sash labeled 'South Africa.' "

"Lee Iacocca, in a 1976 film aimed at dealers, is promoting the Dingell Clean Air Amendment, as opposed to the administration's Brodhead or Waxman proposals, which he deplores. He is most articulate. I am impressed by his earnestness and the force, if not always the logic, of his arguments. Although he speaks convincingly, his hard, shifty eyes give him away. He has a surprising large nose and small mouth."

Handsome and urbane Alexander Trotman, Ford's chairman and CEO, as he looks today. He is one of the executives who appears in management/dealer films recently reviewed by your commentator.

"In a 1975 film on the company's Diversified Products Operations, Executive Vice President Don Petersen (a future chairman), is ill at ease as he speaks. He introduces likable, capable, colorless Tom Page, vice president-electrical, electronics, and climate control operations. Seeing the latter on this film makes it easier to understand why some Ford executives believe that Page's lack of charisma hurt his chances of becoming the company's president or chairman."

"Harold A. (Red) Poling, executive vice president, North American Automotive Operations (later chairman), is speaking to dealers at the time of the Escort/Lynx introduction. A straight talker, Poling comes through as being friendly, open, and engaging, also very businesslike. One feels comfortable and reassured while listening to him."

"John Dykstra, president from 1961-63, speaks on quality. Staring into the camera and obviously making use of whatever passed for a teleprompter in those days, he is as wooden as a schoolboy giving his first oration. Only his mouth and eyes move, the latter ever so slightly. He says that Ford has been the industry's styling leader for a long time and that it now also is its quality leader, its cars having the 'look, sound, and feel' of quality. They may have had the 'look, sound, and feel' of quality, but they did not have honest-to-God quality in Dykstra's day."

"Alexander Trotman, chief car planner (now chairman), is singing the praises of the forthcoming 1977 Thunderbird. Bright-looking young fellow. Black hair; wears the same kind of moustache he wears today. Reading from a script, he's stiff and walks like a robot. As he lauds the T-Bird's fuel economy, I am reminded that my '77 Bird got 11 mpg in the city and 16 mpg on the road. My next Ford, a '78 Fairmont, although it got 16 mpg in town and 21 mpg in the country, was the world's worst car on ice and snow."

"Harold Sperlich, vice president-car operations, also speaking in support of the '77 model lineup. In appearance, sharp as a tack; speaks well; pretty good voice, very much at ease."

"Louis Lataif, vice president-sales operations, later president of Ford of Europe (now dean of Boston University's business school), participates in a filmed teleconference at the Chicago Auto Show in 1986. Gives an excellent presentation."

"Charles H. Patterson, executive vice president-manufacturing, speaks with a very strong Scottish accent, seemingly having lost none of the burr brought from his native country. Indeed, in this mid-1960s film he almost sounds like a caricature of a Scotsman. Right hand planted on a table, he sits motionless as he speaks."

"Here's Henry Ford II again, appearing on a film preview of events scheduled for the company's forthcoming 50th anniversary. Leans on a platform about elbow height, one hand in his pocket. His face is full moon. What a big waist! At 35, he's a youthful Perry Mason/Raymond Burr."

"Henry II once more, this time at the company's Cologne, Germany plant in 1954. He is selling capitalism, telling the Germans to emulate Americans if they wish to succeed mightily. The audience listens attentively, befitting citizens of a

Ford in California

Henry Ford, front and slightly to the right of center, poses with several aides and unidentified men in Los Angeles. Ford's secretary and chief of staff, Ernest G. Liebold, stands front and slightly to the left of center, and Ford spokesman William J. Cameron appears between Ford and Liebold. Publicist Fred L. Black is shown above and to the right of Ford.

We do not know the occasion, nor the date the picture was taken, but each of Ford's aides was involved with the magnate's national newspaper, the Dearborn Independent, *and it is possible that the picture was shot in March 1919, when Ford was vacationing in Los Angeles. The picture was taken by Keystone Photo Service, then located in L.A.'s Chamber of Commerce Building, and was forwarded by reader Mike Skinner of Dearborn, Mich.*

defeated and still have-not nation. On the Rhine River waterfront – and the flat-banked, fast-flowing river has an evil look from this vantage point – he signs his name to a monument, actually a column, next to a plaque showing profiles of his grandfather, his father, and himself. Chancellor Erhard also affixes his signature to the column, which I photographed when visiting Cologne to interview Ford of Germany executives in 1988."

"As one views these films, it is abundantly clear that they have much to tell us about executives' appearances and mannerisms and perhaps something of their personalities and character as well. A very instructive exercise."

Product- and plant-oriented films will be discussed in a future column, and my thanks to Twyman for making the films and catalogues available to me.

Chairman Henry Ford II, second from right, flanked by the men he named "presidents" after firing Semon E. "Bunkie" Knudsen in 1968. From left to right, Robert J. Hampson, Lee A. Iacocca, Ford, and Robert Stevenson.

Surfeit of Presidents

"Was there a time in the 1960s when Ford had a chairman and three presidents?" asks reader Juan Hernandez of San Antonio, Tex.

Sort of. After firing Semon E. "Bunkie" Knudsen as president in 1968, Henry Ford II was undecided as to his replacement. Rather than name a president, he gave presidential titles to the heads of three major groups: Lee A. Iacocca, president, Ford North American Automotive Operations; Robert Stevenson, president, Ford International Automotive Operations; and Robert J. Hampson, president, Ford Nonautomotive Operations. Iacocca and Stevenson also were executive vice presidents and members of the Ford board. The group presidential titles were discarded when Iacocca was named company president in 1970.

Avery on Ford

Rummaging through my files, I found the text of a speech delivered by Clarence W. Avery, chairman of Murray Corporation, at a dinner for 35-year Ford employees at the Dearborn Inn on December 19, 1944. The event was one of the last official functions attended by Henry Ford, then 81 years of age. Henry's wife, Clara, and grandson Henry II also were present.

Avery, who had more to do with the details of introducing the moving assembly line than anyone else, recalled that he had been a manual training teacher at Detroit University School before joining Ford as a part-time employee in November 1911 and a full-time employee in June 1912. One of his students was Henry's son, Edsel, who died in 1943.

Avery recounted several of Ford's practical jokes, including a time when Ford, while sailing from Dearborn to Escanaba, asked the company's treasurer, Frank Klingensmith, if he could examine the latter's new, expensive watch. After looking at the watch, Ford said, "Nothing but a cheap imitation – no good at all!" With that he hurled the watch on the ship's deck, breaking it into many pieces. Mortified, Klingensmith picked up as many pieces as he could find, carefully wrapped them in a piece of paper, and put them into his pocket.

From time to time, Klingensmith confided his feelings to others, asking "Why do you suppose he did it? Do you suppose Mr. Ford will buy me a new watch?" Several days later, at breakfast, the original watch turned up, a cheap imitation having been deftly substituted for destruction.

On the same trip Ford, weary of talk regarding the merits of various cigar brands, bought the best cigars he could find, secretly inserted into their ends a couple of rubber bands, and passed them out to his executives. None of the smokers commented about the cigars, although production boss William Knudsen cleared the lobby of an Iron Mountain hotel with one of them.

Avery credited Ford with outlining the future of mass production, "how the cars should move, rather than the men and stock," then added, "It was my privilege, at a later date, to put into operation many of the ideas he so carefully outlined."

Avery also commented on the difficulty of manufacturing Model T windshields on a conveyor. "Mr. Ford approved the development of a continuous method of making plate glass. This proved to be ... a heartbreaking task. At one time, when we had spent a million and a half dollars and not yet produced glass on a commercial scale, I remember approaching Mr. Ford with the feeling that he would be disgusted, and throw out the whole experiment. I recall saying to him, 'If this experiment works, Mr. Ford, we will save many times the money we have spent.' His reply was 'What do you mean, if it works? It must work. Forget the money you have spent, and go back and make it work.' We succeeded in producing uniform thickness glass at a cost of one-fifth of what we had been paying to the glass manufacturers. Such determined executive support can and does produce miracles."

Avery worked for Ford until 1925 when he resigned as chief development engineer to join Murray, a leading bodybuilder, as chief engineering and manufacturing manager. In 1928 Avery was named Murray's president, in 1930 its chairman, which post he occupied until his death in 1949. He was elected to the Automotive Hall of Fame in Midland, Mich., in 1990; your commentator was among those who nominated him.

Edsel and Roy

"My father and Edsel Ford had a nice relationship with respect and genuine liking for the other," writes Florence Barbier Diamond, who lives in Georgetown, Ky., of A.R. (Roy) Barbier, a Ford advertising executive from 1920-42.

"Edsel and I danced together at one of the Ford dances several months after Daddy had been unceremoniously fired," Diamond continues, "and I can still see his face and hear his words as if it had happened only yesterday. There was a look of concern – almost pain – in his face when he asked how my father was doing, and then asked to be remembered to him. It was sad then and still is today.

"I think the picture that best reflects the easy relationship between the two is one that was taken in the Ford Rotunda with them seated with a third person (probably an ad man from one of the agencies). It's the only picture I can remember seeing of Edsel in outright laughter (although there probably are some others), and it doubtless was generated by one of my father's witty remarks. On the back of that picture is written, 'Entertaining the Boss.'

"Looking back on the Ford years. I'm almost certain that Daddy, knowing Henry Ford's personality and low regard for advertising, deliberately kept a low profile and was truly fortunate to have Edsel to work under. Who knows, maybe without Edsel there might not have been an advertising department."

An "Edsel man," the capable Barbier was fired by Henry Ford's henchman, Harry Bennett, in 1941. He rounded out his distinguished advertising career with MacManus, John & Adams, the agency for Pontiac and Cadillac.

Light Moment

Ford Advertising Manager A.R. Barbier, center, Edsel Ford, right, and Office Services Manager A.G. Coulton, left, share a light moment in the Ford Rotunda. (Photo from the Henry Ford Museum and Greenfield Village).

No Excuses

Charlie Beacham, a Ford marketing executive during the 1950s/1960s, had a reputation for succinctly getting to the heart of matters. William P. Benton, a fellow marketing executive, whom I taped in 1989, illustrates as follows:

"Once Mr. Beacham was asking district managers why their sales were so low. The guys made all kinds of excuses, saying 'if only so-and-so had happened, or if this or that had happened.' Finally, Mr. Beacham said, 'Yes, and if a bullfrog had wings, he wouldn't bump his ass all the time.' "

Remembering Leo

Henry Ford II could be a soft touch for an old friend, a case in point being an appearance at New Jersey's Glassboro State College in October, 1973. Ford spoke at Glassboro solely because his invitation came from Leo Beebe, head of the Business Studies Department, who worked closely with HFII 1945-72.

"I am here basically at the invitation of Leo Beebe," Ford's speech began. "He and I have been friends for some 30-odd years. It started during the war and Leo and I have been associated in various kinds of undertakings since Day One.

"Seeing that some of you who are here this morning are students in his class I might just tell you one story about Leo because I am a tremendous admirer of his. It always amazes me how he can adapt himself to various kinds of situations and do such an outstanding job. This story I'm about to tell took place many years ago, sometime in the middle '50s.

"We were called at Ford Motor Company, and asked if we could supply somebody who could run a Hungarian refugee camp. This was at the time of the problems with Hungary, and there were lots of refugees leaving Hungary and coming to the United States. There had to be a staging area set up somewhere here in the State of New Jersey to accept all of these people who were leaving Hungary and wanting to come to this great country of ours.

"I asked Leo whether he'd consider going down and operating this refugee camp where these people could come and then be dispersed around the country. He said yes he would. And he came down and did a magnificent job as he always has done.

"But there was one story he told me that I think is amusing and really bears repeating. This was basically an Army camp and the chief fellow in the camp was a general. I'm not criticizing generals in this story, but I think it's rather amusing.

"Leo went to the general one day, and he said 'General, you know we've got all these Hungarians coming in here.' The general said yes he understood that. He'd seen them, although he just ran the camp as sort of a housekeeper.

"Leo said to him, 'There are women involved in this group, and there's absolutely no hairdressing parlor for the women in this camp.' The general said, 'What do they need a hairdressing parlor for? They're refugees from Hungary. They can get all that done after they leave here.'

"Leo said, 'They're human beings, and it seems to me that the women who are coming here from overseas from this problem in Europe certainly deserve the same kind of treatment that all the rest of us would expect here in the United States.'

"I think that little story gives you a kind of an insight into the kind of a guy Leo Beebe is. It's always been a pleasure for me to be associated with him; I've been a friend of his over these many, many years. Now, I'm going to get to my notes" ...

The statement is vintage off-the-cuff Henry Ford II, who was always at his best when speaking from his heart about a friend and/or business associate in front of the latter's friends.

Leo returns the sentiment, stating in a letter written in 1988, the year after Ford's death, "I had great affection and respect for Henry Ford II for 45 years, and in many ways I feel as close to him now as ever."

Leo Beebe

An assessment of Henry Ford II is provided by Leo Beebe, HFII's naval instructor during World War II. Beebe joined the company at Henry II's invitation in 1945, and served the firm in many important capacities before retiring in 1972.

"Henry Ford ... is a friend of mine – was and is," Beebe told Jim Aberts of *Super Ford* magazine. "I don't claim to have ever been an intimate friend. I never really worked directly for Henry Ford except in the Navy. At Ford I was always two or three steps removed, although I had significant responsibilities and would see Mr. Ford from time to time and did projects for him."

Henry II never cared much for personal publicity, according to Beebe, and wouldn't even look at press clippings. He recalled how Henry II took over the company after World War II: "He literally saved it. I watched that operation go on and he damn near did it single-handedly. He had a lot of guts and good instincts, and he brought Ford Motor Company around. I'll tell you something – he made a lot of people rich, or helped them to be rich, including Lee Iacocca. I'm sure Henry Ford isn't a saint, but then, who is?

"I liked Iacocca," Beebe adds. "I'm

not 100 percent sympathetic with some of the things he said about Henry Ford. I understand his problem [being] fired by Ford, but Henry's not as bad in my view as Iacocca has portrayed him in his book. I'm a little bothered about that."

Beebe was a public relations executive, and my boss's boss when I worked for Ford in the 1950s. When I offered my resignation to complete work on a doctorate in 1955, he called me in, and said, "Dave, I hate to see you give up your job and seniority. The company doesn't have half-time jobs, but if you'll give us 20 hours a week, we'll pay you full-time, and you can continue with your career."

It was a generous offer, as I told my doctoral adviser at the University of Michigan. His response was realistic. "A 20-hour week, with the best of intentions, can become a 25-hour or 30-hour or 40-hour week when there's an extra need for your services, and there will be. You've said you want to pursue a Ph.D. Put your job behind you, and do so." Good advice, and I've passed it on to a number of doctoral candidates who've been tempted not to put first things first.

I never forgot Beebe's kindness. In 1982, after having been out of touch with Leo for many years, I received a phone call from him in his capacity as dean of the Administrative Studies Department of Glassboro State College, Glassboro, N.J.

"Can you participate in our college's Distinguished Lecture Series?" he asked. "But first let me tell you we don't have much money for your fee."

"Leo," I replied, "in 1982 nobody has much money. When do you want me?"

"We really, really don't have much money," he repeated.

"Forget the money," I said. "If you can spring for a plane ticket, I'll be there. I owe you anyway for offering me full pay for a half-time job when I left the company in '55." Leo remembered, and chuckled.

I worked hard on that address, and it went well. I was glad because if there ever was a program chairman I wanted to look good, it was Leo Beebe, a man who anytime can promote a speech from me for plane fare, or lunch alone, if he really, really doesn't have much money.

Harry Bennett

Revealing information about Henry Ford's chief aide, Harry Bennett, is presented in a privately published book, *The Personal History of Douglas Roby*. Roby's firm, American Metal Products, was a seat supplier to Ford Motor Company during the Bennett era. The biography, prepared by Roby's daughter, Hermine Roby Klinger, was published in 1987.

Bennett's castle, designed by Henry Ford and Bennett, was located near the homes of Roby and Harry Kipke, University of Michigan football coach during the 1930s. Kipke was Roby's college roommate and football teammate, and he, like Roby, was a Bennett intimate. "It got to the point that Bennett was sitting on the Michigan bench during games," Roby recalled. "Their closeness didn't last; they ended up as enemies."

"Bennett," Roby reminisced, "had horses, Palominos, and a track on his property. He and Kipke used to ride together .... They got into some monkeyshine activities with the horses. Mrs. Kipke got thrown from her horse and hurt her back badly. She never rode again ....

"Harry was divorced from his first wife, Margaret Steele. She had been a teacher at the school in Greenfield Village. Harry always had a boat that was docked on the Detroit River. I remember once that Harry dumped a bucket of ice water from the top deck onto his wife's head after a disagreement they had had. Harry later married a nurse named Esther. She had worked in the hospital at the Ford Motor plant ....

"Harry Bennett was a courageous man," Roby continues. "He would wade right into physical battles when he was head of plant protection at Ford Motor .... Our company, American Metal Products, was organized by the union at the same time as the Ford Motor Company. We ... couldn't have the union before the auto manufacturer, or we would lose the Ford business .... Bennett was communicating with the union for years before, trying to buy people off, and prevent union movements in the plants."

Roby drove Fords. "One day," he recalled, "I was invited to lunch at the Ford Administration Building. Bennett told me to drive into the parking garage for the big shots and come through the basement to his office. While I was at lunch Harry had my car taken over to the plant and had the four-cylinder engine replaced with a V-8!"

After being fired by Henry Ford II, Bennett sold his estate, which, in addition to 40 acres along Geddes Road east of Ann Arbor, included an island in the Huron River. The estate now is owned by one of my University of Michigan Business School colleagues, Prof. Aneel G. Karnani, a native of India.

Thanks to former student Jody Glancy, of Ann Arbor, for lending me a copy of her grandfather's autobiography.

Long Reach

Henry Ford's top aide, Harry Bennett, assisted by Paul Marcus, coauthored a paperback book, *We Never Called Him Henry*, in 1951. The book was highly critical of Ford.

Surprisingly, the book's manuscript was read by Ford Motor Company's Legal Staff before publication. It happened this way, according to the company's New York public relations representative, the late John Sattler, who told me the story in 1988:

"The manuscript was shown to prospective publishers in New York," Sattler recalled, "most of whom turned it down. It was considered 'too hot.' Fawcett Books elected to bring it out – perhaps largely for its controversial value. I was tipped to this by a friend at Fawcett who was departing for another job, and felt no reason to keep the information confidential.

"I alerted the Newsom organization (the company's public relations consultant) and Ford Dearborn. Bill Gossett (Ford's general counsel) and the legal staff got into this matter immediately, with a particular concern about any references to Henry Ford II which might be either inaccurate, detrimental, and/or libelous. Our people had an opportunity to see the manuscript, make some adjustments and the book was subsequently published."

Bennett never knew that Ford had reviewed the manuscript before publication, and Marcus – unless he was "playing ball" with the publisher – did not either. We can only speculate as to what changes were made. In any event the book is uncritical of Henry II, in contrast to the sharp criticism of his grandfather, and now we know why.

As for Bennett's honest opinion of Henry II, he said the following to me in 1973:

"I didn't trust Henry. We got along face-to-face, but he was two-faced. He couldn't tell the same story twice. The older he got, the more stuck he got on himself. You couldn't tell him anything. He also went to Mommy with everything."

Never Called Him Henry

"I have just finished reading Harry Bennett's book, *We Never Called Him Henry*, writes reader Bob Cawley, of Kenthurst, New South Wales, Australia. "I enjoyed it very much."

"My book supplier," Cawley remarks "claims that this book is rare – says that the Ford family is said to have tried to buy all available copies after its release. Is this so?"

Neither the Ford family nor the Ford Motor Co. seems to have tried to buy up

Harry Bennett, 81, and David L. Lewis, 46, on the porch of Bennett's Las Vegas home in 1973, when Bennett submitted to two days of interviewing.

Harry Bennett and feline friend pose for your commentator's camera on Bennett's Las Vegas front porch in 1973. Bennett liked cats, whether lions, tigers, or pussycats, and made pets of them all.

copies of Bennett's book (as they did in 1922 with Dean Samuel S. Marquis' *Henry Ford: An Interpretation*). But in the early 1950s Detroit area librarians believed that Ford was asking card holders to borrow the book and not return it. Consequently, many libraries, including the Detroit Public Library, withdrew lending privileges and permitted the paperback to be read only on their premises.

This book, printed on newsprint, has always been difficult, but never impossible, to find in the Detroit area. I have bought copies for as little as 10 cents and seen them advertised for as much as $30.

In 1973, when interviewing the 81-year-old Bennett in Las Vegas, I had a copy with me for Ford's ex-aide to autograph. Before removing it from my briefcase, Bennett expressed regret that he had written the book, adding that he had done so – with the collaboration of Paul Marcus – when angry with Henry Ford. Having cooled off, he told Marcus to tell the publisher, Fawcett Publications, to cancel publication plans. But Fawcett, armed with a contract, proceeded.

My copy of *We Never Called Him Henry* stayed in my briefcase until my return to Ann Arbor.

No Bennett Tapes

"I've heard that the taped recollections of many of Henry Ford's associates are on deposit in the Henry Ford Museum's Archives," writes reader William Klauss, of Middletown, Ohio. "Is Henry Ford's strongman, Harry Bennett, one of those who was taped?"

No. Ford Archivist Henry E. Edmunds tried to interview Bennett in his home in Desert Hot Springs, Calif., in the early 1950s, his visit having been arranged by Bennett's friends. But Bennett, according to Edmunds, "would brush off questions with comments such as, 'That was so long ago I don't even want to talk about it.' I must admit the interview was not very fruitful. At that stage, I guess he just didn't give a damn."

Bennett gave your commentator his first interview in many years – and his last as well – in 1973 in his home in Las Vegas. At age 81, he was ready to talk, and did so at length on a great variety of subjects. The interviews appeared later in two *Detroit Free Press* Sunday magazine articles.

Harry Bennett's "log" cabin as it looked in 1973. The "logs" actually were made of concrete. The winding staircase leads to a patio which overlooks Lost Lake and was used for barbecuing in Bennett's day.

Bennett's Retreat

Robert Rowley, 65, the overseer of a large, ersatz log cabin in which Henry Ford's henchman, Harry Bennett, and his cronies alternately relaxed and caroused, recently retired.

Rowley, 21 years in the job, thinks there may have been a good side to Bennett. "Most people thought he was mean," he told the *Detroit Free Press* ... The people up here (Farwell, in central Michigan) "thought Bennett and his men were running around in the woods with machine guns, but that's an exaggeration. They came up here to get away from the city." Still, Rowley showed a reporter a hidden space under a hinged table "where they kept their guns."

The cabin, built between 1941 and 1943, is on Lost Lake, 10 miles northwest of Farwell off Highway 115. Surrounded by 2,300 acres of woods, lakes, and swampland, the 8,000-square-foot building from the distance looks like a log cabin. But up close it is seen to be made of concrete, molded and painted brown to represent logs, complete with slashes for bark and indentations for fake knotholes.

The cabin was bought in 1965 by the Boy Scouts of Oakland and Macomb counties for $350,000, the money being raised in a drive led by John De Lorean, then a General Motors executive. Each summer 2,000 Scouts camp on the premises.

Rowley was hired by the Scouts to manage the property, and lived in the cabin for seven years before moving into a more modern house nearby. "Some things had been stolen," he observed, "but a lot of Bennett's stuff was still here, clothes and papers, things like that. It was as if he walked off and never thought about it again. I guess he was like that."

Rumors of gun turrets in the cabin were proved false. But Rowley did discover a secret basement passageway behind a bookcase that swings out from the wall. The passageway leads to an outside swimming pool. Rowley bricked up a window in the tunnel that looked into the depths of the pool. "The window was there so they could watch the girls swim," he said.

Furniture in the four-bedroom cabin was built by Ford craftsmen from Dearborn. Chairs and tables were made from cedar and oak covered with leather that has become cracked and stained. Bennett's painting of a mounted Indian still hangs in the cabin's main room.

Guards were posted around the property when Bennett visited, according to Rowley. "At one point they started building an eight-foot-high chain link fence around the place," he added, "but the Department of Natural Resources made them stop. It's 11 miles around the property."

When Rowley was living in the cabin, he wrote Bennett, telling him about the current status of his retreat. "People said he didn't care, that I'd never hear from him," said the overseer. "But I wrote him anyway. He never answered."

Bennett lived near Desert Hot Springs, Calif., then Las Vegas until shortly before his death on January 4, 1980 in a Los Gatos, Calif. nursing home.

Bennett Aide Dies

Stanley Fay, who worked for Harry Bennett, Henry Ford's chief aide, died at age 77 in Birmingham, Mich.

Fay was one of many University of Michigan athletes given jobs by Bennett during the Great Depression. He was captain and quarterback of Michigan's 1933 national championship football team; and in 1932 took snaps from center Gerald Ford, who became the country's 38th President.

Fay served as Bennett's personnel assistant for 14 years. In 1973 he told me, "I love the guy [Bennett]. He was wonderful to me, like a second father .... He loved life, and he had a hell of a good time. He could play the saxophone and clarinet real good, and loved music. He was one of a kind."

Bennett, fired by Henry Ford II in the fall of 1945, had only one post-Ford business connection – a partnership with Fay and attorney Byron Geller in the B-F-G Manufacturers' Representatives Co. with offices in downtown Detroit. The partnership lapsed in February, 1946.

Some of those who've recently authored Ford books requested interviews with Fay, but were turned down. Fay evidently thought they would knock Bennett. Said Fay's son, William, "My father was very loyal to Mr. Bennett, and thought he took a terrible rap."

Friendly Persuasion

It took both Henry Ford II and Lee Iacocca to persuade Vice President and General Manager, Ford Division William P. Benton to transfer to Europe in 1977. The story, told me by Benton in 1990, presents a compassionate side of Henry Ford II.

"Iacocca called me in October of 1977, and said that he wanted me to move to Ford of Europe. I said I didn't want to go. He said, 'But we've already talked about it with Mr. Ford and everybody else, and it's been approved. You've got to go.' I said, 'No, I don't have to go; I can quit.' Iacocca responded, 'You can't do that.' I said, 'I can; I'll just quit.' He said, 'You go home and think about it.'

"The next day, he buzzed me, and I said again, 'I don't want to go.' He said, 'Mr. Ford wants to see you.' I said, 'Fine, I also want to see Mr. Ford.' I really was upset for a lot of reasons. It wasn't right to just call me in and say, 'Bingo, you're off to Europe.'

"So I went to see Mr. Ford. We had a long talk, and ... he said, 'Bill, this is Lee's idea. I don't know what he's trying to do, but let me tell you why I'm willing to go along with him. First of all, we need you over there. We need a man of your ability, your background. You would be good for Ford of Europe. And Ford of Europe will be good for you.'

"Then he said, 'I understand that you have just moved into a new house, and that all of this comes as a little shock to you.' 'You're right,' I said. 'We just moved into a new house we just bought. My wife is in an absolute state of shock.' He answered, 'Don't sell your house. Keep it. You won't be in Europe that long. Besides, take my word for it, investment in real estate is the best investment anyway.' He also said, although not in these exact words, I've lost my tail in the stock market, but I've made a lot of money in real estate.'

"We talked about an hour. Again, he said, 'I'd like for you to go.' Finally, I said, 'Okay, I'll go.' Then he said a very nice thing that I'll never forget. 'Bill,' he said, 'if you have any trouble financially holding onto that house of yours while you're in Europe, you call me personally, and I'll see that you get taken care of.' I'll never forget that comment from him.

"So I went over there ... I was miserable as hell the first six months [as vice president-sales], and after that I settled down and really fell in love with the place."

Later, at Iacocca's invitation, Benton was a member of Chrysler's "Gang of Ford," and rose to the firm's presidency.

Bourke's Departure

Why did William O. Bourke, once regarded by many as a future Ford president and perhaps chairman as well, abruptly leave Ford Motor Co. in 1980? Neither Bourke nor others publicly commented on the matter – until Bourke recently did so in a videotape court deposition.

Bourke's videotape was shown as evidence in a $110 million lawsuit against Ford officials by a fired vice president, Thomas Feaheny. Bourke wasn't a party to the lawsuit, but his testimony was sought by both sides. (Feaheny lost the suit.)

Summoned by Ford executive Philip Caldwell on March 12, 1980, Bourke, according to a *Detroit News* report on his deposition, was informed that Caldwell would succeed the retiring Henry Ford II as company chairman. He also was told that Donald E. Petersen, then executive vice president for international operations, would be named president.

"There was a silence," said Bourke, who then quoted himself as saying, "I'm finished. I quit." At the time Bourke, 52, was executive vice president in charge of the company's money-losing North American Automotive Operations. His departure was labeled a retirement.

Bourke now is president of Reynolds Metals Co., Richmond, Va.

Breech Assessment

In 1985 I asked William T. Gossett, Ford's general counsel from 1947-62, to assess Ernest R. Breech, Ford executive vice president (1946-55) and chairman (1955-61).

"He was one of the brightest executives I've ever seen," he began.

"As brilliant as Robert McNamara?" I asked.

"McNamara," Gossett observed, "was a serious-minded professorial type. He could talk, he was bright and decisive, he was loyal, and he had fine character. But Breech was a man of spectacular intellectual brilliance. He took the CPA exam with 1,500 people in Chicago, and passed with flying colors. Not only was he No. 1, but he got a gold medal for his achievement ....

"I never heard McNamara tell a story, whereas Breech could mimic anybody and tell great stories. Breech could stand up before a group, without a note, present a speech, and receive a standing ovation. To employ the language of the *New York Times*, Breech was as 'smart as a whip' ....

"We were in Wall Street .... going over papers, and came across a proposition expressed in an algebraic equation. The bankers said to him, 'We've got a mathematician in an office in the back of the building. Let's show it to him, and he'll work it out.' Breech said, 'I'll work it out.' He then went through that algebraic equation just like a hot knife through butter .... They were all immensely impressed.

"Breech did a splendid job for Ford, and is on my top-10 list of the company's most able executives."

Norton Brotherton

"I have a Ford book presented to my grandfather in 1921 by a Norton T. Brotherton," writes reader Kyle Johnson, Brookline, Mass. "He seems to have had a Ford connection. Do you know anything about him?"

Brotherton grew up next door to the Fords in Detroit, and was a boyhood friend of Henry Ford's son, Edsel. He started working for Ford Motor Company while attending the University of Michigan. He wished to quit school, but was encouraged by the senior Ford to remain, and received an engineering degree in 1907.

Beginning in 1919 Brotherton's Detroit advertising agency began placing Fordson tractor advertising and publishing *Fordson Farmer*, and in 1922-23 handled Lincoln advertising and published *Lincoln*, a motoring magazine. In August 1923, when Ford reestablished its Advertising Department, Brotherton was named advertising manager and his firm, Brotherton Company, was awarded the lucrative Model T account. Brotherton also handled Ford publicity in 1923-24.

Brotherton's advertising was praised by the trade press, but disliked by dealers, who objected to the elimination of individual agents' names in favor of the line, "See the Nearest Authorized Ford Dealer."

Brotherton and his agency were dismissed in January 1924, after the adman, a heavy drinker, encountered Harvey Firestone aboard a train. Firestone told Henry Ford that the intoxicated Brotherton had made an ass of himself, shouting to anyone who would listen that he handled Ford's advertising.

Brotherton had charge of advertising, personnel, and sales promotion for Argus, Inc., an Ann Arbor, Mich. camera manufacturer from 1940 until his retirement in 1950. He died in Ann Arbor on January 9, 1971.

Caldwell Retires

Philip Caldwell, 78, Ford's chairman from 1979-86, retired in January as a managing director at Lehman Brothers, a New York global investment banking firm. The first non-Ford family member since 1906 to head the Ford Company, Caldwell deserves more credit than anyone else for the firm's sparkling early 1980s turnabout.

In late 1982 and early 1983 the press speculated that retiree Henry Ford II, still the board's dominant force, might sack Caldwell. The rumors were quashed only when strongly denied by HFII and the company began making profits in the first quarter of 1983.

Caldwell's great product legacy is the 1986 Taurus/Sable duo, which he backed at a time when the company's finances were precarious and many others questioned the cars' "jellybean" styling.

Thanks to reader Mike Skinner, St. Clair Shores, Mich., for forwarding an *Automotive News* article on Caldwell's retirement.

Ford Chairman Philip Caldwell in a light-hearted moment in 1983. Most Ford executives remember a more serious Caldwell, who squeezed out of them every ounce of talent they possessed. Caldwell has what once were called "Franklin teeth" – they're air-cooled.

James Couzens, second from left, aboard a Great Lakes boat during the early years of Ford Motor Co.; Henry Ford, far left, faces Couzens. The remainder of the men, including the gent third from left with the sizable stomach, are unknown. (Photo from the Henry Ford Museum and Greenfield Village)

Nothing to Brag About

James Couzens, Ford Motor Co.'s first secretary and business manager, was noted for his honesty and bluntness, both admirably illustrated in a copy of an Oct. 24, 1903 letter which Couzens sent to H.J. Koehler, then owner of H.J. Koehler Sporting Goods Co., of Newark, N.J. Koehler, also a Rambler dealer, later built the Koehler truck.

"Your postal card of the 21st received," replied Couzens. "We have no pictures of our factory. We have not a very pretensions (sic) one and do not believe after you have see it that you would care to have one. Regretting that we have nothing that will answer your purpose."

"Mr. Koehler maybe thought of selling Fords," observes Hayden R. Shepley, of Toughkenamon, Pa., forwarder of the copy of Couzens' letter, which was in a scrapbook which Koehler's widow loaned to a friend of Shepley's years ago.

John Dykstra

"Ford's least-known president seems to be a man named John Dykstra," writes reader John Frampton, of Rochester, N.Y. "What can you tell us about him?"

Dykstra, shown here with Henry Ford II in the early 1960s, was a "hands-on" manufacturing man who had done, or could do, almost anything that anybody else could do on the floor of a Ford plant. He ranked high in the Ford hierarchy when Robert McNamara unexpectedly left Ford's presidency to become Secretary of Defense in early 1961. Henry Ford II needed a quick replacement; also time to choose a long-term president. Dykstra, only 27 months away from the retirement age of 65, filled the gap.

Dykstra's election to the presidency cheered Ford's Manufacturing Staff, which long had felt neglected; and Dykstra, true to his heritage, placed major emphasis on manufacturing and product quality during his brief tenure.

Dykstra was head of Ford's Highland Park, Mich. plant on the one occasion I talked with him. As a member of the News Department, in 1953 or 1954 I took a press release to him for clearance. He displayed a forceful personality, notwithstanding a tremor in one hand, and quickly approved my news release. (Photo from the Collections of the Henry Ford Museum and Greenfield Village.)

Joseph Galamb. (Photo courtesy of Henry Ford Museum and Greenfield Village, Dearborn, Mich.)

Joseph Galamb, Model T Designer

Hungarian-born Joseph Galamb, who contributed importantly to the design of the Model T, was eulogized at a June 1995 meeting between Michigan Gov. John Engler and Hungarian Prime Minister Gyula Horn. The officials met at Dearborn's Greenfield Village, where they were given a ride in a Tin Lizzie.

"Joseph Galamb," the governor told the press, "is the one most responsible for the Model T. He had only nine dollars in his pocket when he came to the U.S. He had great training in Budapest. Henry Ford saw the talent Galamb had and gave him a job. Henry Ford would spend many nights in his rocking chair talking to his Hungarian employee. They would talk for hours about cars and possible concepts. They finally came up with the idea for the Model T."

Ford hired the Hungarian engineer in 1905. Galamb had received a good technical education in Hungary, had worked in automobile plants in Germany, and after coming to the U.S. in 1903, had been employed by Westinghouse about a year, and by the Stearns Automobile Company for another. Short, dark-haired, with a small mustache, he looked like a figure from a Ferenc Molnar drama.

Galamb was one of many Ford associates who heard the founder repeatedly say that they must build a car that "anybody can buy." When it came time to develop the Model T, Galamb, considered a particularly important contributor, was put to work in a separate cubicle adjoining the general experimental room.

A brilliant tool designer and draftsman, Galamb turned Henry Ford's ideas into blueprints and graphic sketches, and throughout his life credited the founder with the flivver's basic concepts.

Presiding over the Ford Company's Engineering Department, Galamb contributed importantly to Fordson tractor development and the firm's World War I tank program. In 1919 he was given responsibility – but limited authority – for experimental engineering. Although discontented with the outmoded Model T in the mid-'20s, Galamb, like almost all Ford executives, remained discreetly silent on the subject in the presence of Henry Ford.

After Ford finally abandoned the Model T in favor of the Model A, Galamb was assigned to design and engineer the new car's body and frame. He continued to develop body designs until retirement.

In 1982, Hungary's exhibit at the Knoxville World's Fair showed pictures of Galamb and a brass-radiator Model T and described the engineer as the "designer of T Model Ford."

Although one does not wish to foment an international incident, Galamb was not the T's sole designer. He was, however, one of its principal designers.

Ford Executive Vice President Del Harder, right, shakes hands with William Clay Ford at the groundbreaking for a new Ford plant in Dearborn in the 1950s. To the left are Bill's older brothers, Benson, left, and Henry II. Given Bill's prominence in the photo, the ceremony appears to have been tied to the breaking of ground for the new Continental plant at I-94 and Oakwood Boulevard. (Photo from the Archives and Library of the Henry Ford Museum and Greenfield Village.)

To Save Or Not To Save

Through the years, as widows of Ford executives have shown me the "personal" files of their husbands, I've come to think that, just as a man's grave marker reveals something about him, so do the files removed from his office upon retirement.

What is learned? Something about the person's sense of the importance of history and his place in it. Something about his sense of privacy – and reluctance to share with his successors the details of his business dealings. And perhaps something about one's ego.

I've seen files that fill half a basement or garage, but more often only a box or a few boxes. The smallest of the packets came from the family of Del Harder, Ford's top manufacturing man from 1946 until 1962.

Harder, often referred to as the "father of automation," died at 81 in 1973. Shortly thereafter, his family informed a mutual friend, Dr. Dewey F. Barich, president of the Detroit Institute of Technology, that it wished to commission a Harder biography. Your commentator was invited to prepare it.

I met with the family, and was given Harder's "files." They consisted of a dozen or so documents in an 11 x 14-inch manila envelope. Included were a few Ford organizational charts, vintage 1962; reports on Harder's trips to Europe and South America in 1957; the script of a Ford of Britain presentation given the same year; a photo of Harder and others visiting a Monroe, Mich., nuclear power plant; the basic specifications of the 1961-62 Fairlane; and a floor plan of the 12th (executive) floor of the World Headquarters Building.

Not much to go on, as I told the luncheon group, and plans for a Harder biography subsequently were dropped. But modest Del Harder has not been forgotten. Every book on the history of automation and the general history of manufacturing discusses his significant role in the development and growth of automation, and every Ford history book notes that he was a key figure in the Ford Co.'s post-World War rebirth.

Gossett Dies

William T. Gossett, 93, once one of Henry Ford II's top advisers, died July 23, 1998 in Bloomfield Hills, Mich.

Gossett joined Ford in 1947 as a vice president, general counsel, and board member at the invitation of newly-appointed Executive Vice President Ernest R. Breech. Gossett had worked for Breech at Bendix Aviation Corporation, a GM subsidiary.

For a time Gossett was one of HFII's most trusted aides, as evidenced by their adjacent offices. But the relationship soured, and in 1982 Ford evaluated Gossett for me as follows:

"I never understood him, and never liked him personally. Breech chose him.

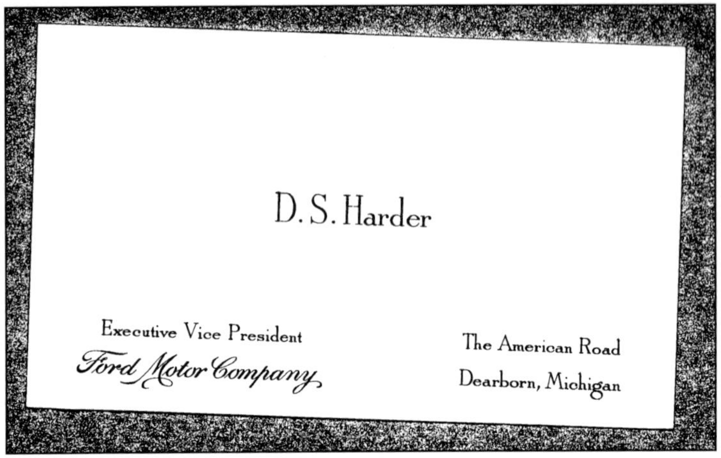

Harder's Business Card

Del Harder's simplicity – and the simplicity of his times – is suggested in his unadorned business card, which merely lists his name, title, and address, the latter without a zip code of even five, much less nine numbers. One thing hasn't changed – the company's name is printed in Ford Script.

He came out of a Hughes firm [Hughes, Shurman and Dwight] in New York. He had a personality problem. His wife was Chief Justice [Charles Evans] Hughes' daughter. I think he always wanted to be on the Supreme Court, and everything he did was aimed at how it would affect him getting on the Supreme Court. This didn't impress me a goddamned bit. I didn't care who was on the Supreme Court. I had to run a motor company. I never had any respect for him. Everything he did was done for his own reasons. Ernie Breech will tell you something different."

"He thought better of him?" I ventured.

"Oh sure .... He stayed until 1961 [actually 1962]. At that time I had put Arjay [Miller] up as executive vice president and given him most of the staffs [including Office of the General Counsel]. So [Gossett] said, 'well, I quit.' I said, 'OK.' He said, 'I think I'm going to get a job in Washington.'

"Well, he came back and said, 'I don't want to quit.' I said, 'Well, you quit, sorry.' I never, never felt that he was sincere about anything to do with me. I'd say he was a fair to a middling lawyer. I don't have great respect for lawyers in general because I think they are basically parasites."

After leaving Ford, Gossett was named a U.S. ambassador and served as a deputy special representative for trade negotiations with the European Common Market. Upon completion of that assignment he joined the Detroit law firm of Dykema, Gossett, Spencer, Goodnow and Trigg. He was elected president of the American Bar Association in 1968.

After Gossett left Ford, HFII converted the attorney's office space into a second sitting room and a private bedroom.

Iacocca Admired

Lee Iacocca has been ranked by Americans surveyed by the Gallup poll as the second most admired person in the world. The ex-Ford president is the only businessman ever named to Gallup's top 10 list. In 1946, in Gallup's first "most admired" poll, Henry Ford was cited, although not accorded top 10 status.

Others who made Gallup's recent ranking, in addition to No. 1 President Reagan and Iacocca, were Pope John Paul II, Jesse Jackson, Billy Graham, President Jimmy Carter, Archbishop Desmond Tutu, Terry Waite, Sen. Edward Kennedy, and Vice President George Bush.

Iacocca has been bumped from *Industry Week*'s ranking as "the most-respected chief executive officer in the country." This last time around, the magazine, which surveys leading executive search firms, placed Citicorp chairman John S. Reed on top, while Iacocca slipped to seventh. Ford's chairman, Donald E. Petersen, was rated 10th.

Big Deal

Henry Ford II's firing of Lee Iacocca on July 13, 1978 recently was cited by the *Detroit Free Press* as one of "150 moments that made Michigan." The "moments" were designated by the newspaper in commemoration of the state's sesquicentennial.

" 'Well, sometimes you just don't like somebody.' With that explanation," says the *Free Press*, "or so the story goes, Henry Ford II fired Lee Iacocca .... Observers said the falling out was the inevitable result of a clash of titanic egos.

"Ford partisans said, as president, Iacocca acted as if he already were chairman," continued the *Free Press*. "Iacocca said ... that Ford's treatment of him took the form of irrational persecution."

Interesting that Iacocca's sacking is regarded by the *Free Press* as a monumental moment. It did have certain repercussions, for it ensured that Ford Motor Co. would not be headed by Iacocca and that Chrysler Corp. could be. One could speculate, at length, on what all this has meant.

One thing's for sure – Lee's autobiography would not have become an all-time bestseller had he not been canned.

HFII Criticizes Iacocca

Henry Ford II, thanks partly to Lee Iacocca's autobiography, has a reputation as a big-car man and for being largely responsible for the Ford Company's lackluster products of the 1970s/early 1980s.

In March 1982, however, HFII told me, "I am not a big-car man. I like small cars better. Harold Sperlich [product development chief] and Lee Iacocca were fill-out-the-cube guys. That's how we got cars that aren't selling today. I was fighting like hell to get the Lincoln a lot smaller, but, hell, nobody would buy the idea. We just didn't have people paying attention to the proper things. We got behind, and that's just the way it was.

[Iacocca] "thought he was playing proper attention to product development. But he got thoroughly confused in his later years by what the hell to do, and he had a new program every two or three months. The organization was totally discombobulated .... There is just one hell of a lot of things that got let go that shouldn't have been let go. It was sloppy."

Iacocca and People

"I've always said that Lee Iacocca was the best salesman I ever saw and the worst handler of people," Robert W. Hefty, an ex-Ford public relations executive, told me in 1988.

"Iacocca," Hefty observed, "would sit in a Product or Design committee meeting and just chew people out right and left, rather than take them into his office afterwards and chew them out in private. He seemed to delight in embarrassing his underlings. I've seen people like Tom Feaheny [vice president-vehicle research] get apoplectic when Lee chewed them up one side and down the other. He used to do the same thing with Hal Sperlich [vice president – car operations, Ford North American Automotive Operations and later creator of Chrysler's minivan] and a lot of others. It just seemed to me that it was a terrible reflection on the man that he couldn't reserve that for the privacy of his office.

"This may be petty – but he always called you by your last name. 'Hey, Hefty, come on in here,' or 'Frey, come on in here.' It wasn't just the PR people either. It was his top aides. That always connoted to me a lack of respect for the individual. Not only did these people have first names, but they were all on a first-name basis. I always overlooked these little peccadilloes of his, because he probably didn't intentionally mean to demean anybody. It was just his way of doing things."

Iacocca Supporter

In 1989 I sought to tape Chrysler Chairman Lee Iacocca with respect to his Ford career. Word came back that Iacocca figured that he had said all that could be said about his Ford years in his book, *Iacocca: An Autobiography*.

On the contrary, I reasoned, there's much more he could say, and I had just the questions for him.

I asked several former Ford board members for assistance in getting to Iacocca, among them ex-Ford President and Stanford Business School Dean Arjay Miller, ex-TWA Chairman Carter Burgess, and State Street Investment Corporation Chairman George F. Bennett, each of whom I had taped. None could help, but Bennett's letter clearly revealed where he stood on Lee Iacocca, 11 years after Lee's sacking by Henry Ford II.

"The treatment which [Lee] received from the company," Bennett stated, "was, in my judgment, not only unfair, but bordered on being cruel .... He was a towering figure in the company's history and was, and is, a master marketer and manager."

Lee and Henry II

While flying from San Francisco to Detroit in 1989, my seatmate was an intelligent, articulate professional woman, Pamela M. Rider, of Bloomfield Hills, Mich., home to many of autodom's elite. She works for a television network in Detroit, and has more business contact with Chrysler than Ford or General Motors people.

Making conversation, I asked her what she thought of Lee Iacocca's 1984 autobiography. Her views about Iacocca, which I recorded, perhaps are representative of a good many of the book's readers.

"I was left with the feeling, after reading that book" she responded, "that this guy was such an incredible businessman, such a patriotic person, and had such a love for business and a love for his country. He had God-like proportions. After reading that book you wanted to go out and vote for him for president. One of the things that I liked was that he came out and said what he wanted. He said what he believed. Henry Ford really sounded like a terrible human being in that book, a seriously terrible human being."

"Did you believe everything you read in Mr. Iacocca's book?" I asked.

"Well," she replied, "I had heard other 'terrible things' about Henry Ford."

"What had you heard?"

"That he was a tyrant and that it was his way or no way at all ... [and] that he was a very difficult man, that he was privileged, and was not especially a benevolent person."

"And so you found it relatively easy to believe Lee Iacocca's book?"

"Yes. Also, at the time I read the book it was when Iacocca had just saved Chrysler. And not only was it important for me as a Detroiter that he saved Chrysler, but, he helped our economy when things were bad, and the Japanese were taking over. This guy gets canned by Henry because he was good, too smart, and too capable. Henry was so jealous, and it must have been true because Iacocca went over and saved Chrysler and look what he did, right? So it must have been true.

"At the time the book came out, the mood of the country was, 'This guy is great. This guy saved Chrysler.' So it was very believable that this guy was telling the truth about what an ogre Henry was. Plus, Henry had left his wife. I'm not saying that from a morals point of view, but the guy was less than admirable in the way he was conducting himself. There were all these ugly rumors about how terrible he was to his wife and how he deprived her and how he drank. The mood of the country was anti-Henry Ford. Right?"

"Have you retained or revised your opinions?"

"I think that Henry probably picked some good people to run the company after he left. But I think he probably got more credit than he likely deserved."

Iacocca's book obviously did an excellent selling job, one worthy of a salesman of the caliber of Andrew Carnegie, Richard Sears, Harley Procter, and Billy Durant, to name a few of America's "crackerjack" salesmen. First and foremost, Iacocca sold Iacocca. He also unsold Henry Ford II. The truth, as is so often the case, lies somewhere in between. Iacocca, even with his "God-like proportions," has as many warts as the Wicked Witch of the East. Ford, if also flawed, was a decent man and good businessman in many ways.

Book in Chinese

Lee Iacocca's book, *Iacocca: An Autobiography*, written with William Novak, is to be published in an "authorized" Chinese edition in The People's Republic of China.

Iacocca's American publisher, Bantam Books, says that the translated work will be "a first for a nonreference book written by an American." That may be, but reprints of Iacocca's autobiography have circulated for months in China, thanks to editions published in Taiwan and Hong Kong. I know, having been given one in October 1987 by a student of foreign trade following my lectures at the Wuhan Institute of Technology, in Wuhan, Hubei Province. The paperback was listed at five yuan ($1.88), but my copy was acquired for about half that price, having been displayed in a sidewalk bookstall for some time and being in less than mint condition.

By Chinese standards, Iacocca's autobiography was a bestseller, and its readers, like those in America, tended to believe everything Lee had to say. In fact, one reader, knowing that I had access to Henry Ford II, asked me to ask HFII to apologize to Iacocca "for all of the mean things," he had done to Lee. I agreed to do so, figuring that HFII would have been amused by the request. Alas, Henry II died while I was in China.

Iacocca Mellows

Can this be Lee Iacocca having a kind word for the late Henry Ford II?

"My difficulty with Henry Ford was over long before he died last year," Iacocca wrote in a 1988 issue of *Fortune*. "Most people were remembering the last years of his life, when Henry was sick with a bad heart, realizing that he was mortal and worrying about his health day and night. I tried to remember the years beginning in 1960, when we were buddies.

"A lot of people told me Henry Ford II did me a favor 10 years ago by firing me," Iacocca noted in the five-page *Fortune* article. "They said that if I had stayed at Ford, I would have been in a comfortable ivory tower. The company would have given me a gold watch when I retired, and that would have been the end of my life ... By getting canned in 1978 I got thrown into a situation where I became a leader."

Iacocca, who had few, if any, kind words for Ford in his first book, *Iacocca: An Autobiography*, and few words of any kind about HFII in his second book, *Talking Straight*, in his *Fortune* article recalled how he and Ford "hunted together, we went to parties together, we caroused Europe together. I remember the 16 good years, and not the two bad ones in 1977 and 1978."

Blame It On HFII

Since Leaving Chrysler in 1992, Lee Iacocca has been described as a hypocrite and a traitor, and criticized for his egotism and greed. In a *Fortune* article "How I Flunked Retirement," Iacocca partially blames Henry Ford II for his mistakes and reputation.

Lee Iacocca, cigar in hand, motor running, as he appeared during his Ford years.

"I wasn't ready for (retirement)," Iacocca explains. "When you're a CEO, you never rub shoulders with the people who make your cars, or buy them, or service them. When I flew corporate, I was alone most of the time ... If a limo picked me up, I got to know the back of the driver's head. It was worse at Ford (than at Chrysler). They really treated you like a king, because Henry Ford II wanted it that way."

Although Henry II was treated like a king, he did not always insist on, or desire, such treatment, while Lee did. Take the case of the Ford Co.'s expensive Boeing 727 jet. HFII came to regard the plane as an unnecessary expense, while Iacocca, who personally supervised its refurbishment, flew it constantly and came to regard it as an essential perk. When Henry II sold the plane to the Shah of Iran, Lee was greatly upset.

In retirement, Iacocca largely devoted himself to moneymaking schemes. His involvement with Kirk Kirkorian's attempted takeover of Chrysler netted him millions, but cost him much in reputation. Also, he fought to gain state approval to help organize a gambling casino in the Detroit area. His best bet, wags said, was to make a Native American woman his fourth wife.

Iacocca's admission that he never rubbed shoulders with the people who made, bought, or serviced his cars helps explain why he failed in retirement, and also why Ford and Chrysler cars suffered in quality during his regimes.

S.S. Marquis

Samuel S. Marquis was an important figure in early Ford history. He headed Ford Motor Co.'s Sociological Department from 1916-21, and also wrote one of the most perceptive biographies of Henry Ford, *Henry Ford: An Interpretation*, in 1923.

Before joining Ford, Marquis had been rector of St. Paul's Church in Detroit and dean of the Motor City's St. Paul's Cathedral, whose construction he spearheaded in 1911. He is thus mentioned prominently in a 1924 book on St. Paul's, recently forwarded by reader Mike Skinner, of Dearborn.

The book contains a chapter in which the dean discusses fund-raising for the edifice. The text notes that Henry Ford, once a member of the parish, did not contribute to cathedral construction. He did, however, provide "generous financial assistance" for the remodeling of Cathedral House, an adjacent youth recreational facility. Years later, in 1947, the cathedral itself was to be the scene of Ford's funeral service.

A chapter by Marquis' successor describes the dean as a man "with a magnetic personality that drew conflicting elements into a unity, with the prophet's gift of preaching, with zeal and energy unbounded and with vision of more than unusual power ... The beautiful cathedral building will ever remain the visible monument of his ministry. He needs no greater, and few men there are who have achieved so great."

Marquis is described by Ford biographers Allan Nevins and Frank Ernest Hill as a man of cheery temper, vigorous personality, and abounding energy, keenly interested in economic conditions and the lot of the working man. His labors for St. Paul's Cathedral having exhausted him, the authors add, "his doctor early in 1916 ordered a year's leave of absence. He said, 'A change of work would be more beneficial to me than being idle,' and accepted Henry Ford's offer of the directorship of the Sociological Department ... Marquis had been an advisor in the early activities of the department. As the pastor of Henry and Clara Ford, he knew them both intimately – Henry calling him 'Mark.' "

The clergyman performed admirably at Ford, but was impelled to

Henry and Mark

Henry Ford, left, and Dean Samuel S. Marquis, as they looked during the teens when Marquis administered Ford Motor Co.'s Sociological Department. The Episcopalian priest later wrote one of the most revealing of Ford biographies, Henry Ford: An Interpretation.

resign in 1921, by which time it was clear that the sun was setting on the Sociological Department and that harsher and more capricious, irrational labor relations policies were being adopted by the company.

A biography of Dean Marquis has yet to be written; assuredly he is worthy of one.

Miller Arboretum

The Arjay Miller Arboretum, named for Ford's president between 1963-68, has been dedicated on the grounds of the Ford Co.'s World Headquarters in Dearborn, Mich.

Miller, a native Nebraskan who placed a high value on trees and other greenery, founded the arboretum when a company vice president in 1960. Since that time the arboretum's collection of trees and shrubs has grown from 230 to more than 1,000 varieties of trees and shrubs, all native to Michigan. The arboretum is the largest in the world devoted to trees and bushes of a single state. There are 10 varieties of oak, seven of ash and maple, and six of hickory. Other varieties include the pawpaw, Kentucky coffee, tulip, and shagbark hickory trees, and such flowering trees as crab apple, redbud, wild plum, and Juneberry. In all, there are more varieties of trees and bushes in the arboretum than on the entire continent of Europe.

The 30-acre L-shaped arboretum is open to the public from dawn to dusk, seven days a week. For easy identification, trees are marked with plaques giving information folder can be obtained by writing Ford horticulturist Dave Wood at Building Service Department, Room B56, Ford Motor Co., Dearborn, MI 48121.

Ford board members turned out almost en masse for the arboretum's dedication ceremony, and Miller, Ford Chairman Donald E. Petersen and Henry Ford II gave talks. Henry II, to the delight of the audience, ignored a prepared speech, and began his remarks by saying, "I don't know the difference between a coffee tree and a tulip tree, or, for that matter, a damn thing about trees and bushes – I'm just here to tell you what a good guy Arjay Miller is." He then proceeded to do so. Every speech should be so spontaneous, so honest, and come so much from the heart.

Unceremonious Sacking

Walt Murphy, who served two decades as Lee Iacocca's public relations man, has commented on his dismissal by Henry Ford II. His remarks were made before the Senior Men's Club of Birmingham (Michigan).

"My 20 years or so as Lee's press agent began to unravel when Henry Ford called Lee Iacocca into his office at three o'clock the afternoon of July 13, 1978, and fired him.

"Shortly after, I met with Lee in his office to talk about a statement for the press. I spent the rest of that day with two associates ... trying to write a news release on what happened between Henry and Lee. We never did get an acceptable draft.

"At midnight, I headed home. By one o'clock, I was dead asleep. At two o'clock, my bedside phone rang.

"The voice on the phone said, 'This is Henry.' 'Henry? Henry who?' 'Henry Ford.' 'Yes, Mr. Ford.' 'Do you still love Lee Iacocca?' 'Do I what?' 'Do you still love Iacocca?' 'I like him very much, of course.' 'Then you're fired too. Starting tomorrow.' I gladly took early retirement five months later.

"I was not demoralized, outraged, or driven to despair by Henry Ford's action. I didn't like it. Probably because of the resiliency that comes from drinking Irish Bushmills whiskey and the balanced perspective of a loving wife, life went on."

Whatta Way to Go

When resigning from Ford in 1980, Marvin Runyon, vice president-Body and Assembly Operations, was displeased with his departure arrangements, as he informed me in 1989.

Vice presidents, upon leaving the company, routinely were given a car and a silver tray inscribed with other vice presidents' signatures. At his farewell party Runyon received neither.

Also, Runyon was asked to sign a statement stipulating that he would not work for a competitor. No one else having been asked to so stipulate, Runyon refused. He blamed the request on a *Wall Street Journal* article indicating that he might be a good person to head newly-formed Nissan of America.

Upon relinquishing his company car, Runyon leased Lincolns for himself and his wife through Budget Rent-a-Car. His wife, however, spitefully arranged for him to be picked up by a Cadillac limousine on his last day of work.

That last day, Runyon discussed his treatment with his boss, Harold "Red" Poling, then executive vice president, North American Automotive Operations, later company chairman. Poling explained that the board had given "everybody hell because Lee Iacocca had been given a car, then joined Chrysler." Declining Poling's belated car offer, Runyon said, "If I go to work for a competitor, I don't want you to get chewed out. You're too nice a guy to have that happen to you."

Runyon later received a tray, Poling explaining that the company was "out-of-stock on trays" at the time of the going-away party. The shortage, Runyon reasoned, should have been mentioned at the party. "That whole episode was funny," he concluded.

Shortly after leaving Ford, Runyon became chairman of Nissan of America, then chairman of the Tennessee Valley Authority. He now is Postmaster General of the U.S. Wish I had asked him what he was driving when I taped him at TVA's headquarters in Knoxville, and also wonder what he's driving now.

Hal Sperlich

In 1989 I asked Edsel Ford II to identify "unsung heroes" at Ford. He named Harold Sperlich, vice president-car operations, North American Automotive Operations, for whom he had worked in the mid-1970s.

After being fired by Henry Ford II in 1977, Sperlich took his minivan concept to Chrysler, where his brainchild became an enormous success.

"Sperlich," Edsel said, "is one of the greatest product people ever to grace our industry. [Hal's] ability to envision what consumers want was phenomenal." In addition to the minivan, Edsel recalled, Sperlich also plumped for a Ford-built front-wheel-drive, fuel-efficient car of Escort proportions. "I wonder," Edsel mused, "what would have happened ... if the company had decided to build the Escort instead of the Pinto."

"I had some long and difficult conversations with my father about Hal Sperlich," Edsel added. But Henry II, fed up with Sperlich's argumentative ways, decided that the executive must go. Later, at Chrysler, he sold Lee Iacocca on the minivan.

Shinoda Talks

Larry Shinoda, who was responsible for designing the Mustang's Boss 302 and Boss 429 editions, spoke to *Detroit Free Press* columnist Paul Lienert about his 16-month career at Ford Motor Co.

Shinoda's tenure was brief because he was a "Knudsen man"; he was hired after Semon "Bunkie" Knudsen was named president in 1968, and released after Bunkie's dismissal in 1969.

"Gene Bordinat (Ford's design chief) thought I was a spy for Knudsen," says Shinoda. "I went to Italy on assignment to Ghia [Ford's design house in Turin] and ... a guy watched me 24 hours a day for two weeks." Shinoda remembers one Ford associate more fondly – William Clay Ford, Henry Ford II's youngest brother: "He'd stop by the studio at night, have a cup of coffee, and just chat with some of the guys there. He knows a lot about design .... He's a class guy."

Shinoda, 56, has been president of Shinoda Design Associates, of Livonia, Mich. for the past 10 years. Among his clients are Penske Racing, Hendrick Motorsports, and Miller Brewing. Since 1955, in addition to working for Ford and himself, he has served Studebaker-Packard, GM, and White Motor, where he rejoined Knudsen.

Shinoda says he's been talking to "a couple of people" about writing a book on his career.

Admits Mistake

Ford executives seldom admit to company mistakes, but Chairman Alex Trotman, at the '96 Taurus press introduction, confessed that the firm erred by failing to launch a minivan in the 1970s.

"I helped develop the minivan idea that [product developer] Hal Sperlich took to Chrysler when he became an executive there," Trotman remarked. "We've made mistakes at Ford," he shrugged, adding that "that one got away."

Trotman could not foresee that the '96 Taurus redesign would qualify as another mistake in that it has been less competitive against the Toyota Camry and Honda Accord than its predecessor.

Bought a Ford, Lately?

An admission by Ford Chairman-elect Alexander Trotman that he does not own a Ford car prompted headlines throughout the country.

The executive, the *New York Times* reported, cannot remember the last time he bought a car. The last vehicle he bought was a Japanese motorcycle. Although he purchased cars while on overseas assignments, he has, the *Times* adds, "never had the experience of buying from an American dealer, haggling over price and trade-ins, or fussing with matters like auto insurance or registration. Nor has he had to endure the charms of service managers or the fear that strikes in the heart of almost everybody who confronts the cashier who says the repairs cost far more than expected.

All this may seem odd, at least to someone who does not work in or around the Motor City," the *Times* adds ... "and it highlights a traditional facet of Detroit car culture: car borrowing programs for white-collar workers. For these managers, cars are always new, gassed up, and ready to go."

Ford and other automakers say the programs familiarize executives with their cars and trucks and those of their competitors. But critics say the practice perpetuates the insulated nature of Detroit, in which the people who spend billions trying to get Americans to buy cars do not take the simplest steps toward understanding the travails of ownership.

Trotman informed reporters that he didn't "see why I should [buy a car]. I know a lot of dealers, and I don't see why I have to buy a car to get in touch with the dealer-customer relationship.

"It surprises me," David E. Davis, editor-in-chief of *Automobile* magazine, who added that the familiarity of executives with their products has faded since the era of Henry Ford. "They've gradually distanced themselves," he said. Still, he added, "If I were in Mr. Trotman's position, I would own a car, and if I didn't, I wouldn't tell anyone about it."

At the time of his press conference, Trotman said he was driving a Mark VIII and a Taurus station wagon as part of the company's evaluation program. He also drives many competitors' cars for comparison purposes.

The article failed to add that Big Three chairmen and presidents traditionally have been furnished drivers as well as cars. Henry Ford drove minimally after driving a Model A off the road in 1927. Henry Ford II usually was chauffeured, although I recall him driving a Mercury Monarch to his brother Benson's funeral service in 1978. It is doubtful that HFII owned any of the cars he used.

Trotman's immediate predecessor, Harold A. Poling, acknowledged that he had not purchased a Ford vehicle since 1968.

Rank obviously has its privileges.

George Walker

"He gave the world the Thunderbird – and the Edsel," the *Arizona Daily Star* reports. "Also troop carriers, toasters, and the Eureka vacuum cleaner. *Time* put him on its cover. Charles de Gaulle kissed him." Who was he?

"George Walker, of Tucson," the newspaper proclaims. "At 91 Walker's walk is measured, the voice sometimes tremulous. But he wears a Givenchy tie around the house. And he can still pick up pad and pencil and within seconds sketch a willowy female form draped in front of an automobile.

"More than 60 years' worth of products have flowed onto the sketch pad – and into the showrooms, the department stores, and the kitchens of America," the *Star* continues. "All of it with that unmistakable George Walker look. Style, they call it. Streamlined curves, flowing lines, grace and elegance – that's the way Walker designed tomorrow's products. Today.

" 'It gives me such a kick to walk into someone's home and still see something I designed years ago,' says Walker.

"Always he lived the image implied beyond the sketch," the *Star* adds. 'A stylist,' Walker told *Time* in 1957, 'has got to show style in his cars, in his home, his clothes and his person.' He did his best: 40 pairs of shoes, 70 suits, and a $50,000 office.

"Walker was riding high in those days, flush with success from the Ford Thunderbird – and still hopeful about the Edsel. 'The Cellini of Chrome,' *Time* dubbed the man."

Walker, according to the newspaper, designed the 1949 Ford, turning "a boxy frame into sleek smoothness, integrating the car's fenders into the body, and giving Ford its first really new design in years. The car was a smash in the showroom. Six years later, Walker struck gold again with the 1955 Thunderbird. Henry Ford II rewarded him with a vice presidency.

"Nine hundred people labored under his fabled pencil in the land of the chrome bumper and the tail fin," the *Star* adds. "Walker yelled and screamed to take off the fin. 'But management liked the fin,' " he said.

"Walker takes sole credit neither for his successes nor his failures. 'It took 900 people to design a car,' Walker says, which may help to ease the sting of the Edsel. 'People just did not like that radiator,' is about all he will say on the matter ....

"Walker speaks kindly of Henry Ford II, but dismisses former Ford President Lee Iacocca with what may be the most damning words he knows: 'The man had no style.' "

HFII On The Whiz Kids

Numerous writers have commented on Henry Ford II's hiring of the Whiz Kids. In 1982 I asked HFII to tell me the story in his own words, and he did so as follows:

"I hired them personally. I got a telegram (in the fall of 1945) from Tex Thornton – who just died by the way – saying that he and nine buddies wanted to go to work together for one company. They said they had been in something called Stat-control, which had been set up in the Air Force by Bob Lovett and General 'Hap' Arnold. Before the war Lovett had been with Brown Brothers Harriman (an investment banking firm) and during the war was wartime assistant secretary of war for air. I knew him since he was a friend of my family's and I also had met 'Hap' Arnold ...

"I didn't know who the hell Thornton was, nor any of the people in the telegram he was associated with. I gave the telegram to our so-called office manager and told him these fellows sounded interesting and to have Thornton come here to talk with him. The office manager came to my office one day and said that Thornton was too hot for him to handle and that I had to talk with him. I said OK.

"I did talk with Thornton, and he said that his group wanted to work together in one company and that it was looking at the C & O Railroad, of which Bob Young was the chairman ... We talked things over and they decided to come. They came before Ernie Breech (HFII's right-hand man starting in mid-1946).

"Bugas (industrial relations manager) laid out a training program ... We were short of all kinds of people. I thought that these fellows must have had pretty good experience during the war and they no doubt could bring to the Ford Motor Company a lot of things that we didn't know anything about. This company was pretty antiquated. Accounts payable was figured by weighing paper. They piled it all together and weighed it. If it weighed one pound they figured it was x dollars .... I happened to know that because I worked in that department for about three months, on purpose. I wanted to find out what went on.

"In the beginning there was a certain standoffishness between Ernie Breech and the Thornton guys. Ernie didn't quite know what the hell they were doing. They were sort of jealous that I'd brought him in to be the top man and upset over having to work for him. So they were looking at each other and trying to decide how to behave. It eventually worked out, and the guys got good jobs of one kind or another."

Thornton was not destined to remain long at Ford, however. Frustrated in his desire to report directly to HFII, he became a vice president in the Howard Hughes' organization in 1948. Later, he served as chairman of Litton Industries.

Two other Whiz Kids, Robert S. McNamara and Arjay R. Miller, became Ford presidents; another, J. Edward Lundy, an executive vice president; and two others, James O. Wright and Ben D. Mills, vice presidents.

Whiz Kids

A 1993 book, *Ford's Whiz Kids: The Founding Fathers of American Business – and the Legacy They Left Us*, by John A. Byrne, chronicles the lives and careers of the 10 ex-Air Force officers hired by Henry Ford II in 1945.

Among the Whiz Kids, Robert S. McNamara and Arjay Miller later became Ford presidents, and four others, J. Edward Lundy, James O. Wright, Ben D. Mills, and Francis C. Reith, became vice presidents. Their leader, Charles "Tex" Thornton, after leaving Ford in 1948, became chairman of Litton Industries.

The author erroneously credits the Whiz Kids with Ford's post-World War II "rescue." In actuality, a seller's market and Ernest R. Breech and his mature team played a much greater role in reviving Fords fortunes – and "in a coup worthy of a conquering Caesar, reshaping American business and its approach to power." Such heady claims bring to mind some good advice an editor once gave me, "Don't exaggerate. The truth is big enough."

Remarkably, Byrne quotes verbatim conversations among the Whiz Kids to the point that I wonder if he or the Kids tape recorded all of their conversations over the years. In the "Notes and Sources" section, however, the author informs us of the origin of these direct quotations.

Acknowledging that he "constructed a novelistic rendering" of the Whiz Kids' story, Byrne states that he "took some fictional license to recreate a few scenes, but only when supported by interviews with direct participants. Sometimes, for example, a Whiz Kid could not recall the dialogue in a meeting, but could remember the tone or substance of the discussion. I created a few lines that would reflect the tone of the session as recalled by a key participant."

Actually, Byrne created more than a few lines in this fashion, and to such an extent I question where documentation leaves off and imagination begins.

The 581-page book concludes with a discussion of the Whiz Kids' post-Ford activities and the present whereabouts of the six survivors, McNamara, Miller, Lundy, Wright, Mills, and Charles E. Bosworth.

The author is a senior writer for *Business Week*.

The American Road

Details concerning the filming of *The American Road*, Ford's 50th anniversary film, are provided in a letter from James B. Stoney of Whitestone, N.Y., son of George C. Stoney, the film's producer and director.

"Much of the 'period' footage," recalls Stoney, "was recreated by my father and his crew at the Henry Ford Museum in Dearborn or on the back lots of various Hollywood studios. My father attended a Labor Film Festival several years ago, and saw several sequences that were said to be 'stock' footage from Ford Motor in the teens and twenties. Actually, the footage was from the shots my father did in the fifties. He gets quite a kick out of talking about it.

"The sequences in the film that I know were recreated are: 1. The shots detailing the original assembly line (with men pulling the Model T frames by ropes); 2. The shots of the salesman showing the farmer the Model T and the shots of the family getting into a Model T and going out for a ride (the fat woman with the hat is my mother, and she was pregnant with my sister Louise at the time); 3. The opening sequence of the doctor traveling by horse-and-buggy to make a house call, then using a Model T; 4. The sequence of the young couple getting directions from a farmer; and 5. The entire Ford workshop sequence of Henry Ford building the Quadricycle and breaking out the doors so he could take a test drive (notice that the actor playing Henry Ford is breathing fog because they shot the scene at the Henry Ford Museum in December; the actual event took place in June or July).

"A great many of the shots of the teeming city were taken from various feature films of the 1910s and 1920s," adds Stoney. "A lot of the stunt shots of the Model T – being driven on top of large culverts and going up and down steps, for example – were staged by Ford and inserted into newsreels and feature films as subtle advertising for Ford. (This kind of thing makes the modern practice of product placement in a feature film look like weak copy.)"

The senior Stoney, now 75, teaches at New York University. He was coproducer of the '89 Emmy Award winner in the News and Documentary category for a PBS Special, "We Shall Overcome." The Stoneys presently are working on a film about the 1934 textile mill strike in the South.

"The only thing that my father didn't like about Ford," concludes Stoney, "was that they wouldn't let him drive his International Harvester Travelall onto the plant grounds in Michigan. But, they did give him a great bargain on the two Ford Econoline vans he later purchased (in one of which I had my first driving lesson).

The American Road continues to be one of the best, if not *the* best, films the Ford Company has made on its founder's life, its history, and the history of the automobile in general. The film contains many memorable scenes, the most moving of which shows Henry and Edsel Ford slowly strolling through the Dearborn Engineering Laboratory to the accompaniment of a poignant melody and Raymond Massey's narration. If you get a chance to see this film, do so.

Take This Job, And ...

Early Ford hourly workers resigned from the company for a variety of reasons, as revealed in a paper, "Uneasy Partners: Workers and the New Technology Highland Park Plant Ford Motor Company 1910-1916," by Kathleen Anderson Kraus of the University of Hartford.

Assembler Wallace Doherty, for example, in 1916 told his foreman he wanted an afternoon off. His foreman insisted that he stay on the job. Doherty quit, saying he had "plenty of money anyway." Enameler Ray Daniels, hired in 1916, quit in 1917, rather than accept transfer from the radiator repair department. Daniels was being demoted after having "borrowed" tools for personal use without permission.

Other workers quit, according to their supervisors' reports, for such reasons as "work too hard," "can't stand fumes in test," "wages too small," "denied transfer," "unwilling to work nights," "went back to school," "leaving to get married," "moved," "went into business for himself," and just plain "dissatisfied."

Workers were discharged for reasons listed as "lazy," "unsteady," "dishonest," "destructive of property," "drunk," "laying off work," and "refusal to obey orders."

Painter Charles Hassen, for instance, was fired for being "absent too often and fighting with coworkers." Hassen also had complained that "working hard makes him tired." Earl Michael was hired in 1916, and hung on until 1923, when fired because his supervisor had spent all day looking for him. When found, Michael confessed his absence, while claiming that it was "too hot to do crating." Leon Ostrowski, a bench hand, was sacked when caught stealing a hammer. An inspection of his home turned up another Ford hammer, four towels, a commutator cover, and a soldering iron head.

Many employees were reasonably content with their employment, and spent their working careers with Ford. Others expressed pride in being Ford men, as indicated by a letter to a company publication by a man named Taliaferro:

"Wear your (Ford) badge in plain sight," Taliaferro told his coworkers. "One employee was kidded for saying, 'Our factory.' Certainly (it is) ours, and don't ever get the idea it is not, for if you don't look at these things in the right light and stick up for the company that is doing so much for you then you are not a Ford man. You just work here."

Professor Krause's research is based on employment jackets of the Highland Park Plant's hourly work force between 1910-13. About 13,000 of the jackets are on file in the archives and research library of the Edison Institute (Greenfield Village and Henry Ford Museum).

Fords Out Front

Employers and their workers have expressed their distaste for foreign-built cars in various ways. Imports have been banned from employee parking lots or been permitted to park only in remote areas, and some vehicles have been smashed, ceremonially and otherwise.

But discrimination against "alien cars" isn't new, says reader John C. Jackson, a former Detroiter now living in San Jose, Calif. "At one time," he writes, "if a Ford worker drove something other than a Ford product to work, he was required to park his car at the center of the parking lots. Only Ford products were allowed to face the fences."

"He Stays Fired"

"Once I make up my mind about something," Henry Ford once told the Mexican artist, Diego Rivera, "nothing will reverse my mind."

Ford made the statement to Rivera when the artist beseeched the industrialist to rehire a Ford photographer the magnate had fired because he'd smoked in the darkroom of the Rouge Plant. Rivera had used the photographer as a model for his huge fresco painting on Detroit in the Motor City's Institute of Arts.

The artist's appeal fell on deaf ears. "He stays fired," declared Ford, and that was that.

The anecdote appears in Stephen Pope Dimitroff's *Apprentice to Diego Rivera in Detroit*, forwarded by Mike Skinner, Detroit, Mich.

Ford's Department Store, Bay City, Mich., is unabashed in its use of Ford Script in its signage. The store has no connection with Ford Motor Company. (Photo by Michael Skinner, St. Clair Shores, Mich.)

Ford Logo Best

The Ford oval is Detroit's "best corporate logo," according to the *Detroit Metro Times*. In fact, says the paper, "that free-flowing, scripted, better idea from Ford Motor Company is one of the most widely recognized in the world."

Ford's logo had gone through changes, notes the publication. "Highly-stylized tails on the letters "F" and "d" were dropped in favor of the more modern script seen today. The oval was added to the script as early as 1912, and the corporate blue color became a standard part of the logo around 1928."

Since 1928, the logo has undergone only slight modification. A number of new logo options was considered in the mid-1960s, the paper was informed by Tom Foote, manager of the company's Corporate News Department. But it was decided that "Old Henry really did have a better idea with his scripted, oval trademark, and it was retained."

Although it may seem as if the present logo has always been used by Ford (the script dates to 1903), the company used a "winged pyramid" trademark from 1912 to 1916, and block letters for the Ford Script for more than two decades after World War II.

The winged pyramid trademark was designed by Ford's advertising manager, Glen Buck, who described it as "a happy combination of two of the oldest Egyptian symbols – the pyramid symbolizing strength and stability – the scarab wings symbolizing lightness and grace. Here is the new sun of the Ford advertising system," rhapsodized Buck in one of many articles extolling the trademark. "It shall be the 'blazing flag' around which the Ford forces shall rally."

More than half the space of some Ford ads were devoted to reproductions of the trademark. Dealers were ordered to have it painted on their sales windows and were strongly urged to use trademarked letterheads. After Oct. 1, 1912, the number plates on all Model Ts bore the emblem. Within a year of its introduction, the winged pyramid trademark was widely established all over the world.

In 1916 the company's Operating Committee questioned whether the winged pyramid trademark should be continued. This body referred the question to Henry Ford, who abolished the logo after being told that "scarab" is another name for "dung beetle."

What's In A Name?

Ford had a problem during the 1920s, as revealed in the company's April, 1924 Ford Service Bulletin, reprinted in the *Model T Times*, publication of the Model T Ford Club International.

The problem, noted the publication, stemmed from Ford's great prestige, and involved a "struggle to prevent the dissipation and appropriation of our trade name and trademark by promiscuous use.

"What does the average person think of when he hears the word 'Ford' mentioned," rhetorically inquires the magazine, ... "the Ford automobile or its designer and manufacturer, Henry Ford? And what has brought about this situation? The answer is obvious – the greatest automobile value on the market and continued satisfaction of millions of owners.

"No wonder then that the name 'Ford' assumed the proportions of a magical term – a universal term, and one to conjure with in the advertising field. When we consider these facts it becomes only too obvious why the Ford Motor Company is so zealous in protecting this invaluable work – the principal part of its corporate name, as well as its common law and registered trademark ...

"There are thousands of reputable individuals, partnerships, corporations, etc., not connected with the Ford Motor Company who are inadvertently making use of the word in connection with their various enterprises, and who, because they are reputable and consider fair dealing and clean competition paramount, readily discontinue the use of the name 'Ford' when our rights and their corresponding obligations have been called to their attention.

"On the other hand," continues the publication, "we find an appreciable number of individuals, partnerships, corporations, etc., whose motives are not, we regret to state, as clean and as fair as those referred to. It is this latter class that cause trouble.

They see at a glance great advertising value in the word 'Ford' and invariably allow their own selfish interests to assume control of their conscience and with what results – a multitude of cases of unfair competition and infringements, which if allowed to continue unabated would lead to the inevitable – complete dissipation of our trademark rights and irreparable damage to our business.

"This latter class of infringers are a real menace to good wholesome business and should be removed. Frequently we are forced to adopt rather strong measures against some of these individuals and even though this is an expense in some cases, we are more than compensated by the results obtained as we have yet to lose a lawsuit involving our trademark or trade name rights."

Your commentator still occasionally sees the Ford logo used by non-Ford Motor Co. business firms. One such instance involves a Newton, Miss. ice cream manufacturer, which features Ford Script in its advertising on I-59 at Exit 165 near Toomsuba and also in front of a Stuckey's Restaurant in nearby Kewanee.

Oldest Old-timer

The oldest old-timer listed in the Ford Old Timers Club's 1998 membership roster is George E. Bates, St. Louis, who joined the company in 1922.

The name interests me all the more in that I worked for "Mr. Bates" in 1950-51 when he was assistant manager of the St. Louis Lincoln-Mercury Assembly Plant and I was editor of employee publications.

A "hands-on" guy of the old school, Bates was always in the thick of things, especially production bottlenecks. My only direct contact with him was taking his picture on ceremonial occasions. Just as well, for Bates was as "rough as a cob," and I wasn't.

Showing The Way

"I was busily cutting a steel rod with a hacksaw when someone tapped on my back," 82-year-old ex-Rouge Plant worker Gido Valli told a *Tokyo Shinbun* reporter. "It was Henry Ford. I felt I must have done something wrong."

But Ford quietly said, "Let me see that. You are supposed to pull a hacksaw like this. It does not work right if you pull it too fast because the blade gets hot and won't move the way you want it to. Work it slowly." After demonstrating several times, Ford told Valli, "Now you try it."

That simple gesture changed young Valli's opinion of Ford. Before that time he had regarded the magnate as "an insidious person who treated his workers like slaves." After meeting Ford, he liked him.

Valli got a $30-a-week Ford job in 1936 by paying a $50 bribe. Describing working conditions in the Press Plant, he recalled, "You couldn't even go to the toilet. Unable to hold it in, some workers even relieved themselves in their pants." Conditions improved after the UAW gained recognition in 1941. "We had 15-minutes recesses in the morning and afternoon. All of a sudden, they treated us like humans. It was like we were in heaven."

Valli's father, an Italian immigrant, joined Ford in 1929. Four generations and 10 members of the family have worked for the company for a total of 269 years. "I doubt if you can find any example like ours," said Valli, who retired 23 years ago. Recalling his humble origins, he concluded, "I have been able to realize the American Dream."

The article was published in Japan's leading newspaper, *Tokyo Shinbun*, on April 12, 1998. The article also quoted your commentator as to Henry Ford's three most important contributions: the Model T, mass production, and his wage-price practices.

Henry's Engine Man

"My father was the machine shop foreman in the engineering laboratory of the Ford Motor Co. for 27 years," writes Winifred Andersen Goeboro, "and that is the reason for this letter.

"Father was an immigrant tool and die maker from Denmark, and had spent some time in the Danish merchant marine before World War I," Mrs. Goeboro adds. "During that time, he became the engineer on steamships, and so he was quite an expert on the repair and maintenance of steam engines. Steam engines were one of the greatest interests of Henry Ford. Many times over the dinner table, the story was told of Henry Ford coming to my father and saying, 'There is an old machine that we just got; see if you can get it running.' The literal interpretation of this to my father was 'get it working like new.'

"I would venture to guess that the majority of the steam engines in Greenfield Village and the Henry Ford Museum were renovated by my father. He sometimes had to build new parts that were damaged or missing, as there was no source to buy parts. The many small plants that Henry Ford had out in Dundee, Clarkston, Northville, etc., all had steam engines. Many Sundays, the family would go on a ride and invariably we would end up touring these plant sites so that Father could point out the governors on the steam engines and proudly announce that he had made them .... "Henry Ford often brought his grandsons, Henry II and Benson, to see the machines demonstrated, and their visits also were a topic of conversation over the dinner table on many occasions.

"Henry Ford researched the use of soybeans, and my father was part of that research. Machinists and tool and die makers (my father's trade) always have dirty hands, but while the work on soybeans was going on, my father was able to clean his hands with the by-product of the squeezed soybeans and his hands were lily-white.

"During the Depression and even before the twenties, our lifestyle was one of practiced frugality. Father wore the typical shop apron used at the time, and the strings would wear holes in the shoulders of his shirts. Incidentally, white shirts were worn by everyone even though machine work tended to be dirty. Mother spent many an evening patching the shirts and reinforcing the shoulders as well as turning the collars to get added mileage out of the white shirts. Such patching drew the attention of Henry Ford when he commented on the handiwork and precise sewing on father's shirts. He also noticed that Father always had rough, brown bread for his lunch sandwiches and approved of such a good dietary item. It fitted his own philosophy of eating healthy.

"Father was called on to work at the Fair Lane powerhouse when there was a breakdown or problem. He told of one such time when he was on the catwalk out over the water and lost his footing. Luckily, he only got a good drenching and was able to save himself. He announced at dinner, 'You almost lost me today.'

"On one occasion, he was sent to the Fair Lane mansion because there was a problem with the upstairs plumbing. With no one to direct him, he wandered into Mrs. Ford's dressing room and politely excused himself. Mrs. Ford was most gracious and told him the problem was in her bathtub. However, when Father saw that all the fixtures were gold plated, he returned to the engineering lab and told others that he couldn't handle the job and to send someone else ....

"During the twenties and especially during the thirties, many people contacted Henry Ford with sad stories of great need, usually expecting a handout. Father observed this many times when he was at work. He also observed Henry Ford making efforts to avoid such persons by hiding behind the large posts in the lab or by hiding in the toilets. For this reason, even though Mother chided him for not asking Mr. Ford if my sister and I could attend the Greenfield Village schools, Father refused to ask for any favors. He enjoyed the camaraderie of Henry Ford and their nearly daily discussions of steam engines (also diesels), and he would not do anything to jeopardize that relationship.

"When Father died, about three and a half years after Henry Ford, he was honored by a five-minute shutdown of all the laboratory's machines on the day of his funeral. He died at the age of 57 on Nov. 1, 1950. It is for this reason that his story was never entered into the Ford Archives [set up the following year]."

Knew Henry Ford

William F. Duggan, who joined Ford in 1922 and had personal contact with Henry Ford and Thomas A. Edison, died on March 27, 1995 at age 95.

A first-generation Irish-American, Duggan worked in a variety of jobs that brought him in contact with Ford. "One time," his daughter, Frances Murphy recalled, "Mr. Ford was going up the steps and tripped over a piece of carpet. Dad happened to be there and helped pick him up. Mr. Ford said, 'Get this fixed.' Dad had that carpet fixed within an hour."

From Russia With Love

The year was 1913. Eighteen-year-old Mark Tuban, recently arrived from Russia, asked for a job at Ford's new Los Angeles Assembly Plant. He was told there wasn't a vacancy. But, unable to understand English fully, he showed up for work the next morning, grabbed a broom, and began sweeping the floors. Three weeks later he was on the payroll. Three-quarters of a century later, he remains associated with Ford Motor Co. – as a Ford Power Products distributor in Mountain View and Fresno, Calif.

Tuban's story is told in a recent edition of *Power Times*, published by

Ford Power Products Operations. Tuban was born Sept. 5, 1895 in the Ukraine, according to the article. "As a 20-year-old, he served as a corporal in a U.S. field artillery unit in France during World War I. He returned home a naturalized American citizen ....

"Early on in his career with Ford, Tuban was introduced to the company's founder. Henry Ford took a liking to the hardworking youngster and sent him to Dearborn to study the Fordson tractor. Soon, Tuban was coordinating the domestic and international sales of Ford trucks and tractors.

"In 1926, Tuban was named manager of the Ford Tractor Road Show – a traveling educational show of 40 Ford trucks and tractors – and was sent to Russia as part of a five-man team to determine the feasibility of a Ford tractor plant in Russia. The group recommended against building a plant. Upon his return from Russia, Tuban was called on to brief President Herbert H. Hoover on the results of the trip. Tuban's report today is filed in the Hoover Library at Stanford University.

"The following year ... Tuban joined International Parts and Services. For the next eight years, he resided in Panama .... After a decade of serving Ford internationally, Tuban became interested in retail sales. He bought his first Ford dealership in Mountain View, Calif. ....

"At the age of 44, Tuban served as a Marine first lieutenant in the South Pacific. Commissioned as a motor transport officer, he coordinated vehicle landings on Saipan, Tinian, Guam, and Iwo Jima. His heroic efforts earned him the Bronze Star and praise by General Howland Smith, who said, 'Mark was trying to repay the U.S.A. for the opportunity it had given him to live in America.'

"Tuban returned to Mountain View after the war and built a new, ultramodern dealership – Mark Tuban, Inc. In 1961, a year after receiving a degree in journalism from Stanford at age 61, Tuban acquired an industrial engine distributorship. In 1968, he became an Autolite (now Motorcraft) parts distributor. In 1973, he built a new facility in Mountain View to house his parts and engine businesses. Since 1975, he has been concentrating on his parts business, which now has combined sales of about $9.3 million.

"Today, Tuban looks back with pride, yet remains modest. 'I was in the right place at the right time,' he says. 'I owe my success to Mr. Ford's genius in starting this industry. He had a mind that was absolutely unique.' "

Cash Boy

Henry B. Tonnies was 29 in 1914 when he joined the cashier's office at Ford's Cincinnati Assembly Plant. "But he was still called a 'cash boy,' his son, reader Robert A. Tonnies, Cincinnati, recalls.

Almost all cars made at the plant were paid for in cash and driven away by purchasing dealers. Several times daily Henry deposited the money in a downtown Cincinnati bank, sometimes returning with stacks of $1 and $5 bills for employees' Saturday noon pay envelopes. "No one thought it unusual for him to be running around town with several thousands dollars in a canvas bag," Robert observes. "He was never robbed."

Henry bought his first car, a 1915 Model T, in 1917, and drove it for eight years. When promoted to head cashier in 1925, he purchased his first new car, a moss green Model T touring car.

That same year a Ford "inspector," on a routine visit to the Cincinnati plant, asked to see the home Henry and his wife had bought in suburban St. Bernard in 1917. "It is nice," the inspector said, "but not up to the standard expected of a Ford executive." The family, increased by three since 1917, willingly moved into a much larger house nearby. "This entailed taking on a rather large mortgage which the family would later regret when the Great Depression hit," Robert recalls.

Production/quality problems associated with the Model A forced the Cincinnati's plant closure in the summer of 1929. All salaried employees and most hourly workers were offered jobs in Detroit. "A number accepted the offer," Robert remarks, "but my father, not knowing that the Great Depression was just around the corner, declined. It was almost two years before he finally found another job as manager of a ladies dress factory."

Survivor

A young Ford worker, Lloyd Edward Paupst, who called Henry Ford "old man" and pushed him aside, is the subject of a *Detroit Free Press* "Michigan Memories" article.

A native of Ontario, Paupst, states his daughter, Lois A. Dyer, Ann Arbor, Mich., joined Ford's Highland Park Plant as a toolmaker after military service in World War I. He worked the midnight shift.

One night, a machine broke down and spewed oil on the floor. As Paupst repaired the equipment, a man watched him work. "Old man," the toolmaker said, "I have to clean up this mess now. You can get hurt here. Get out of my way." Shoving the man aside, he finished his work.

After the man left, the shift boss told Paupst that the "old man" was Henry Ford. Paupst was worried about his job, but reasoned he had done what should have been done. Ford must have thought so too, because nothing came of the incident.

Paupst, his daughter added, served several weeks as a plant guide to deposed Kaiser Wilhelm's grandson, Prince Louis Ferdinand, when the latter began working for the company in the late 1920s. Years later, when the prince toured the Willow Run Bomber Plant, to which Paupst had been transferred, the workman was enthusiastically greeted as "Lloydie" and embraced. Paupst's fellow workers were considerably impressed by his friendship with royalty.

Paupst served Ford for 42 years, ending his career in the Purchasing Department of Henry Ford Museum and Greenfield Village.

One Laugh Too Many

"My relations with Ford executives were generally good," recalls Ford old-timer Carl J. Wurdock, Avon Park, Fla., "except for Harry Bennett [Henry Ford's chief aide]. Not that he and I clashed, but it happened this way:

"My office was on the first floor [of the old Administration Building], and Bennett's was just below mine. Sometimes we used the same toilet. One day four or five of Bennett's henchmen burst into my office and asked me if I had been downstairs to the toilet. It appears that someone reached over and whacked Harry in the head with a hot towel. I thought that was funny and laughed. But Bennett's men did not think it was funny.

"From that day on my fate [as By-Products Sales Manager] was sealed. Programs were canceled, and I finally reached the conclusion that I was all through at Ford. I thought it over for a long time. Then I walked down the lane to the employment supervisor and resigned, lock, stock, and barrel from the Ford Motor Co. I gave up pensions, etc. I was 51 at the time. I am 85 years old now, but I am still glad I worked for Mr. Ford. He was real. I still associate with my old Ford buddies. That means more to me than anything."

A Pixie Revealed

"I have come face-to-face with the elder Mr. Ford three times," recalls Ford retiree Robert L. Bodor of Birmingham, Mich., who joined Ford in 1943.

"One of the times was in Mr. Charles Sorensen's office. I said something in explaining some blueprints – probably having to do with some wartime project – and he winked at me."

Henry Ford had many sides. Bodor saw the pixie in him.

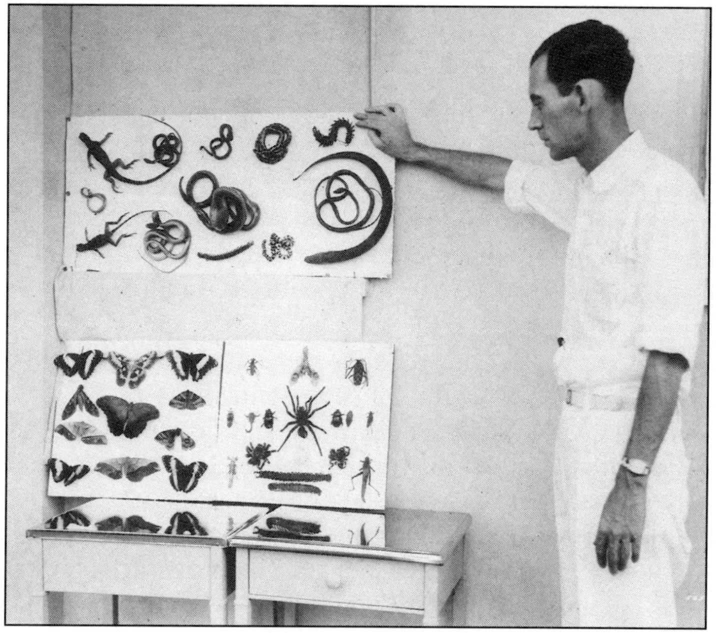

Reptiles, butterflies, and insects found on Henry Ford's Amazon rubber plantation. (Photo from the Collections of the Henry Ford Museum and Greenfield Village.)

Ford Honored In Brazil

After dark in São Paulo, Brazil, your commentator posed with a large sculpted head of the first Henry Ford. The artwork was placed in front of Ford of Brazil's headquarters in September 1988 during a ceremony attended by Ford officials and São Paulo municipal leaders.

Ford in the Amazon

"They are typically American villages ... it's just like visiting a live museum," says an official of Brazil's Agriculture Ministry of Henry Ford's former Amazon rubber-producing communities, Fordlandia and Belterra.

"The houses are well preserved and equipped with crockery, home appliances, books, and all sorts of

A group of nude, painted Indian girls visit Henry Ford's Amazon rubber plantation. (Photo from the Collections of the Henry Ford Museum and Greenfield Village.)

objects imported from the U.S.," adds the official. "Even the old record players still work."

Between 1928 and 1945, Ford invested $25 million in the upper valley of the Tapajos River in the state of Para. It was in this same valley that the English scientist, Henry Wickman, removed 70,000 rubber tree seeds to England and the Far East. Afterwards, the Amazon lost its place as the world's leading rubber producer.

Fordlandia, a 15-hour boat ride from the city of Santarem, had 5,000 employees. Its village had 225 houses, telephones, a power station, a saw mill, an ice plant, Para's best hospital, and a week's cold-storage capacity.

Ford planted 1.9 million rubber trees on Fordlandia. Unfortunately, the trees were attacked by a fast-spreading fungus, the dothidella ulci, which makes leaves fall. Unable to check the fungus, Ford abandoned Fordlandia in favor of Belterra, which had a different soil and less humidity.

At Belterra, located below the Tapajos River, 60 kilometers from Santarem, Ford replicated Fordlandia. Some 3.2 million rubber trees were planted, but they, too, were attacked by fungus. Technicians finally contained the plague through grafting, but Ford, spinning off its founder's pet projects worldwide, abandoned the Amazon after World War II. Meantime, the company had shipped its Rouge Plant tire factory to the Soviet Union and rubber again was flowing to tire makers from the Far East. In leaving Brazil, Ford accepted a symbolic fee of 5,000 cruzeiros for its land and improvements made upon it.

Fordlandia and Belterra were placed under the control of Brazil's Northern Agronomical Institute. In 1975 the government set up an inter-ministerial commission to study the plantations' options. Today, even though the projects' one million hectares have a population of almost 20,000, the government has yet to decide what to do with them.

Oldest Canadian Plant

"You occasionally write about Ford's oldest U.S. plants," writes reader Jacques Chalfont, of Montreal. "What's Ford's oldest Canadian plant still in operation?"

Perhaps the Windsor Engine Plant, built in 1922 for vehicle assembly, engines, and stampings. Ten years later it was producing V-8 engines, which makes it a pioneer of V-8 production.

The factory was closed in 1990, then reopened in 1995 after management and the Canadian Auto Workers negotiated an agreement calling for a reduction in job classifications and the use of teams. The rebuilt facility now makes some of the world's most advanced V-8 engines for the F-150 truck.

Ford of Canada

A 1904 patent from Henry Ford, granting Ford of Canada "all my rights, title and interest in and to my invention," recently was found in a grease-covered cardboard box in a dingy storage room at Windsor Engine Plant No. 1. The document was found by Ford of Canada accountant Brian Mutterback as he was cleaning out the storage room to make way for new records.

Henry Ford's signature appears on the patent, found in a package wrapped in a brown paper bag. It is the only Henry Ford signature ever found by Ford of Canada, according to historical consultant Sandra Notarianni.

Other boxes contained handwritten ledgers from pre-Model T days showing shipments of Models N, R, and S to Port Elizabeth, South Africa and Auckland, New Zealand, as well as to such Canadian destinations as Saskatchewan Auto and Gas Co., Sarnia (Ont.) Auto and Bus. Co., and Don Auto in Winnipeg. Each car, recorded with its serial number and destination, seems to have been tested inasmuch as the ledgers record such remarks as "Noisy time gear" and "reverse noisy" signed by test drivers.

The boxes also contained copies of lawsuits by companies claiming that Ford stole their designs. In 1928, for example, Wedgrite Piston Co. sued Ford over a patent for the magneto, which produced the spark to start the engine. Losing, Wedgrite had to pay $1,300 in costs.

The records are described by Ford of Canada personnel as being a company equivalent of the "Dead Sea Scrolls."

Thanks to reader Leandro Apolloni, of Windsor, for forwarding the *Star*'s article on the find.

Yank Heads Ford Canada

An American, Jim O'Connor, has assumed Ford of Canada's presidency for the first time since Henry Ford's son, Edsel, resigned the office in 1929.

New Yorker O'Connor, previously sales and marketing manager of Ford's Parts and Service Division in Dearborn, was given the Canadian job with a mandate to improve dealers' service and customers' satisfaction. Having served as Ford of Canada's vice president of sales from 1984-86, he's already familiar with the dealer body. Canadian dealers, it may be added, generally handle only one make of car, because of Canadian restrictions against dual franchises.

Ford in China

"Ford's Reputation in China" is the subject of a recent essay forwarded to your correspondent by a young Chinese engineer, Zhang Lichao, an employee of the Wuhan Internal Combustion Engine Factory, located in the big industrial city of Wuhan, Hubei Province.

"In many Chinese minds," states Zhang, "Ford stands for the luxury American car and high quality and performance. Chinese city dwellers over 40 remember Ford as an auto giant; many young Chinese also have learned of Ford in recent years.

"From 1930 to 1949, the Chinese president, top government officials, and leaders preferred to be driven in Fords. The Lincoln was the car of choice of China's ruling elite. The streets of Shanghai ... teemed with shiny new Fords. Most of the prominent businessmen had Ford luxury cars, each worth 20 gold bars at that time. A businessman with his own Ford was a proud man indeed, because his Ford represented power, social position, and the treasure he had amassed.

"Today Toyota advertises in China, 'Wherever there is a road, there is a Toyota.' A driver, 67, who drove for businessmen for 20 years, told me that 'before 1949 it was a fact that wherever there was a road there was a Ford.' Of course, at that time there were roads only in the cities.

"Now the Japanese car has replaced the American car. The Chinese of the People's Republic know Toyota, Nissan, and Honda as household words. Many of them know of Ford's name, but they have never seen a Ford car or truck with their own eyes.

"A repairman, 70, who repaired trucks in the temporary Chong Qing [Chungking] during the war against Japan, recalls that most of the cars and trucks that he saw were American, and the quality of Ford's cars and trucks was excellent. Of the few Japanese trucks that he repaired, he often saw that many of their parts had been replaced with American-made parts.

"A senior repairman in his sixties has worked on automobiles of over a dozen manufacturers from all over the world. When asked to name his favorite, the response immediately was 'Ford's cars. My favorite was the Lincoln.'

"This same repairman worked in Guam during 1946-48. He saw a documentary film about the history of Ford Motor Co. and remembers that Henry's wife, Clara, was warm to her husband in the film. She helped him to check some information. Later she married him, and took care of him well. Henry Ford, he felt, got strength from his close family. The repairman was stirred by the woman, and thought that behind every successful man there is a woman. He thought that if Henry Ford had not met Clara in his life, there probably would not be a Ford Motor Co.

"A chief engineer at one of central China's auto plants, when asked to name the most influential man in auto history, answered without hesitation. 'Henry Ford.'

"Many Chinese youth today recognize Lee Iacocca's name as well as that of Henry Ford II. Iacocca's autobiography has been a recent bestseller in China. Seven Chinese publishing houses have issued Iacocca's book. Iacocca's book was the first to introduce the American auto circle to the Chinese public, so many young people accept Iacocca's words as gospel.

"But older Chinese are more skeptical about Iacocca's comments on Henry Ford II. An old auto engineer says, 'I know the American auto industry well. Today, Iacocca is an American hero, but Henry Ford II also was a giant in the auto industry, and he used his power wisely to save his company in its dark days after World War II.' ... Says an editor of an auto magazine. 'In my opinion, it was natural for Henry Ford II to fire Iacocca.' As an old Chinese proverb says, 'It is impossible for two tigers to share a mountain.' "

Hemming and Hawing

Many U.S. business executives are frustrated by dealings with the Chinese. They could have been forewarned if they had had access to the following hitherto unpublished report by a Ford delegation which visited China in 1976.

Background: Ford and other Western companies had no contact with China from 1949, the year of the Communist takeover, until the mid-1970s. In 1974-75 Ford had two brushes with the Chinese. Maurice Sury, a Ford of Europe marketing executive, was a member of a British trade delegation that visited Cathay in 1974; and Joe Auton, managing director of Ford of Singapore, spoke briefly with members of a Chinese trade delegation visiting Singapore in 1975.

In September 1975 the first Chinese trade delegation to visit the U.S. stopped in Dearborn. Although Ford Chairman Henry Ford II was out-of-town at the time, in December he received a much-valued invitation to visit China with a group of company executives. Heart trouble forced HFII's withdrawal from the Ford delegation, headed by Vice Chairman Philip Caldwell. The mission: "to evaluate the potential of Ford doing business in China."

In addition to Caldwell, members of the Ford party were Frank Erdman, president, Ford Asia-Pacific; Wayne Fredericks, executive director, International Government Affairs; and HFII's "man," Walter Hayes, vice president, public affairs, Ford of Europe. The group visited Canton, Beijing, and Shanghai between Feb. 19-27, 1976.

During their visit the Fordmen heard two comments about their company's founder and ran across only one Ford product. (1) Chen Chi-hsien, deputy managing director of China National Machinery Import and Export Corporation (Machimpex), who had visited Dearborn in 1975, remarked that he "had long known about Ford as a company and recalled seeing Ford cars in China during the pre-Revolutionary period. (2) Hao Shao-hsien, another Machimpex official, noted that "Your name as a manufacturer is very famous in our country." (3) A Ford Cortina with Chinese registration was parked outside the entrance to the building occupied by the China Council for the Promotion of International Trade.

The Ford delegation hoped their Beijing hosts – trade and machinery ministers and plant officials – would make some specific business proposals. They made none, regarding the visit as nothing more than an opportunity to get acquainted and exchange views. Repeatedly, the Chinese plumped for most favored nation trading status, release of frozen Chinese assets in the

U.S., and U.S. cooperation in bringing Taiwan into the Chinese fold. Until such matters were resolved, it was explained, China was unlikely to do business with Ford and other U.S. firms. Ford, Caldwell noted, had non-U.S. subsidiaries which could supply China. Even so, the Chinese insisted, Ford was an American company.

The Ford delegation brought along Chinese-language brochures showing their products, and sought permission to exhibit at the Canton trade fair. The fair, they were informed, was for Chinese products only.

During long discussions with chain-smoking Chinese over interminable cups of green tea surrounded by walls decorated with Chairman Mao's quotations, the Fordists tried in vain to learn of a grand design for the Chinese vehicle industry. Officials knew what their ministry or plant did, but little of what others in their industry did. It proved almost impossible to determine chains of command and who was responsible for what, other than "somebody up there."

Repeatedly, in the straightforward manner of American businessmen, the Fordmen tried to interest the Chinese in Ford products and future business contacts. Invariably the Chinese were vague and evasive. Other units usually were said to be responsible for whatever was being discussed. Direct questions frequently were ignored in favor of monologues and hemming and hawing on unrelated topics.

The Ford delegation had come to wheel and deal, but the Chinese wished only to talk. Not until the 1990s would Ford begin to do business in China.

China Copies

Somewhere in China there are 250 very special copies of Lorin Sorensen's *The Ford Road*, reports book dealer Art Spindler of Grosse Pointe Farms, Mich.

The special copies, Sorensen informed Spindler, were bound with maroon leather covers, gilt edges, and taffeta paper end-boards, the design on the cover being identical to that of the brown leatherette covers of the regular book. The copies were taken to China by Henry Ford II in 1978 and presented as gifts to HFII's hosts.

Sorensen put aside four of the China copies, and is "saving them for his kids." He says about 20 China copies are floating around the U.S.

Don't Hold Your Breath

The world's top 20 auto firms are bidding to win China's approval to build a "family car." The Chinese, the UK's *Car Magazine* reports, "want to put their people on wheels, and are looking for a latter-day Henry Ford or Ferdinand Porsche, creator of the Volkswagen, to help them."

In presenting its proposal to the Chinese, Ford – which for decades sought to disassociate itself from the Model T – invoked the memory of the flivver and its role in developing the U.S.'s auto culture. The company recommended that China replicate its European-built Fiesta, a fine car but surely not to the 1990s what the "universal car" was to the post-1908 era.

As for anticipating another Henry Ford, not only China, but also the U.S. and many other countries are looking for one. He'll be along, too, just as soon as someone designs a car that is as much of a breakthrough as the Model T, develops a manufacturing process that improves living standards as quickly and as much as the moving assembly line, and overnight doubles the wages of his workers while reducing the workday.

Don't hold your breath.

Ford and China

Henry Ford's ghost was trotted out at a Shanghai press conference held by V.A. Koshkarian, president of Ford Motor (China) Co. Ltd.

Koshkarian, the *China Youth Daily*

reported, announced that the Henry Ford Museum's Archives had recently found a letter from Sun Yat-sen inviting the industrialist to develop China's auto industry. "You can achieve the same career in China on a larger scale," the letter stated. "In China, you will have opportunities to express and realize your thoughts and ideals in the form of a new industrial system."

Actually, the letter, dated June 12, 1924, has been known to Ford historians for decades. It invited Ford to become China's economic adviser, not to develop a Chinese auto industry, of which there wasn't a semblance in 1924.

Sun was sent a "nothing" reply by one of Ford's secretaries, who seemingly was unfamiliar with Sun; and it is likely that Ford never even saw the letter. Sun likely learned about Ford through the latter's 1922 autobiography, *My Life and Work*, which in translation circulated around the world.

During the same era Germany's finance minister said his country would welcome Ford as an "economic dictator"; a group of German businessmen suggested that he should become their nation's Kaiser; and one wing of Polish monarchists wanted him to assume their country's throne. Ford never considered any of these offers, and would have failed miserably had he accepted any of them.

Ford In Egypt

"Didn't Ford once build cars in Egypt?" inquires Robert Sutton, of Oakville, Ont. "A dollar bet is riding on your answer."

You win. Ford assembled cars in Alexandria, Egypt, for decades – until the Arab League's boycott of Ford products in the mid-1960s. The company, in fact, still owns the plant; it remains idle even though the League's boycott ended in 1986.

As noted in the above advertisement, Alexandria's buildings in the mid-1930s covered a ground area of about 42,000 square feet, comprising "spacious showrooms and modern offices, depots and stores, together with a group of workshops that form the largest automotive service station in the Near East."

The ad further states that visitors were welcome to visit the "headquarters of the Ford organization for the Near East – the Ford Motor Company (Egypt) S.A.E., – situated at Rue Soter, Mazarita, in a building which has become a familiar landmark in this great Mediterranean seaport."

Room with a View

A Finnish member of the Volunteer Chapter of the Early Ford V-8 Club of America recently wrote the editor of the chapter's *Volunteer V-8 Ford Voice*.

The member, Jussi Ponkamo, owner of a '36 Ford cabriolet, noted that the club's Finnish chapter "opened the V-8 season traditionally on the first day of May and drove some 30 miles to a small coastal town named Parainen where we enjoyed our Labour Day lunch in a cozy restaurant. We ate in the same place last year, too. The headwaiter recognized us (or our cars) immediately and said, 'I have your table ready for you – with a view of the parking lot as usual.' "

Fordson Estates Ltd.

Documents and photographs relating to Fordson Estates, Ltd., a farming venture started by Henry Ford in England in 1931, are for sale.

Owner of the records is Anthony Rosen, of Headley, Hampshire, England, who for the past 15 years has kept the company alive by paying its annual registration fees.

In a December 20, 1994 letter, Rosen stated that, in the hope of perpetuating the company, he recently offered it to "someone/anyone at Ford's, or the Ford Museum. Much to my surprise," he added, "they are not interested in what I would have thought were unique artifacts."

Henry Ford conceived the plan which grew into the Fordson Estate and its Henry Ford Institute of Agricultural Engineering while visiting England in 1930. His object was to show how agriculture could be improved and made more profitable; to stop migration from rural land to the city; and to increase the farm laborer's return. Created by the purchase of about 10,000 acres at Boreham, Essex, the institute was supported by Ford until his death. Details on the estate's history may be found in Sir Percival Perry's *Ten Years' Romance: An Agricultural Experiment*, published in London in 1934.

Anyone interested in acquiring Rosen's documents may write him at Rosehill, Arford, Headley, Hampshire GU35 8DF or telephone or FAX Headley (01428) 717540.

Ford Rejects Rolls-Royce

"I've heard that Henry Ford had a chance to buy Rolls-Royce," writes reader Alan Whitby, of Toronto. "Did he make a mistake in not doing so?"

Ford was offered a chance to buy near-defunct Rolls-Royce of America, Inc., in 1927, and so were General Motors, Studebaker, and the Dodge Brothers. All took the view, in the words of Rolls' president, H.J. Fuller, that "the Rolls-Royce car is not worth the price, and that in the way it is designed and constructed, it could not be built, even in quantities, at a price ... which would enable it to become a profitable thing."

In the early 1930s, Ford and Rolls were briefly linked through Rolls of America's Brewster subsidiary, which bought 135 Ford V-8 chassis and fitted them with Brewster bodies. The resultant Brewsters, priced at from $2,800 to $3,000, sold well, and amused Henry Ford, who welcomed the gratuitous boost to his firm's reputation from this strange alliance between the makers of the world's most common and uncommon cars.

Dirt Pays Off

A cigarette box containing earth taken from the groundbreaking of Ford's Dagenham, England, plant in 1929 recently was auctioned for $11,780. The boxful of earth was presented to Henry Ford's son, Edsel, by Dagenham workers, and eventually came into the hands of Edsel's son, Henry Ford II.

The box was among items auctioned at HFII's English estate, Turville Grange. An Arabian rug received the highest bid – $44,174. The auction netted more than $1.5 million.

Eleven-year-old Henry Ford II, clad in knickerbockers, attended Dagenham's groundbreaking ceremony, at which his father turned the first spadeful of earth.

First Overseas Car

"Which Ford car is the first to have been designed specifically for a foreign market?" asks Wilson Samuelson, Oak Park, Mich.

It was Model Y, Ford of Britain's four-cylinder "baby" car, introduced in 1932 and sold alongside the Model A. The Y's motor was rated at only 8 hp – important for lower taxation – although it actually produced almost 22 hp. Priced at 120 pounds, lower than cars offered by major rivals Morris and Austin, the Y gave Ford of Britain a new lease on life, and also assisted Ford of Germany and Ford of France.

The Model Y was designed in Dearborn by American engineers. Its progress was closely monitored by Henry Ford, even after prototypes had been shipped to England. In January 1932 both he and Dagenham Plant General Manager A.R. Smith (later Sir Rowland) were found beneath the new model adjusting the brakes.

The View from Ireland

Henry Ford II's fondness for Ireland, home of a paternal great-grandfather, William Ford, who emigrated to America, was recalled after the industrialist's death by *Ireland News*.

"Ford's commitment to his company's Irish operations was sharply underlined in recent years," reported the *News*'s Gerry Mulligan, "when the parent company had to inject over £75 million into the devastated balance sheet .... Despite the depressed state of the Irish car market, where crippling State taxes have stifled car sales, Ford's have been determined to hang in. Henry Ford II would not sanction a total pull-out of Ireland.

"A major rationalisation plan including the sell-off of the Cork assembly site for £1.75 million this month [September, 1987] has continued to steer Ford back into the black in Ireland. The giant Ford plant, idle since the car assembly operation pulled out three years ago with a loss of 800 jobs, is now to become an industrial park.

"Henry Ford II," concluded Mulligan, "was said to have been personally very saddened by the need to cut back the Cork operation." Indeed he was, as were Ford's other top executives. But the plug had to be pulled, and it was.

Gwaith Ford

A sign in both English and Welsh points your commentator's way to Ford's Swansea, Wales, plant. The factory makes rear axles for cars and trucks and gearboxes for trucks.

Honda's Ford Connection

"What brings my memory to Ford the most is something that happened when I was six years old, even before I went to elementary school," reminisces Soichiro Honda, 83, founder of Honda Motor Co.

"At that time," he recalls, "a Model T Ford happened to come to my village. That was the first time I had ever seen an automobile, and I chased that automobile down the road. Every time that Ford car stopped, it left a little bit of oil slick underneath. And I smelled that oil slick, and I enjoyed it thoroughly."

It was a smell that would remain with Honda throughout his active career, which ended in 1973. Honda's remarks were made at Dearborn's Henry Ford Museum, which displays the first U.S.-built Honda, a 1983 Accord.

Penetrates Iron Curtain

"Is it true that Ford shipped some cars to the U.S.S.R. during the height of the Cold War?" asks reader Frederick Hunsinger of Poughkeepsie, N.Y.

Yes. In 1956 the company sold eight 1957 Fords to the U.S. Embassy in Moscow for $1 each. One of the cars appeared on the streets of Moscow two days before being unveiled in New York, as reported by the *New York Herald Tribune* on October 2, 1956. The idea cooked up by the embassy and Ford, was to awe the car-starved Soviets with a typical American car.

Getting the advance car to Moscow took some doing, and the shipment was shrouded in secrecy for fear that the Russians, if they knew what the capitalists were up to, might keep the car on a rail siding indefinitely.

In Dearborn, the car was put into a closed van, which raced to New York's Idlewild Airport. The van carried loading experts and mechanics, who quickly disassembled the car's front end and loaded the 3,700-pound vehicle into a plane.

After being flown to Helsinki, the car was reassembled by Finnish mechanics, boxed, and placed on a Soviet rail car. Nothing was heard of it for 14 days, when a coded message announced its arrival. Moscovites crowded around to gaze at the Fairlane 500 four-door sedan's low lines (56 inches) and length, at 17 feet longer than most of Europe's most expensive luxury vehicles.

The car's optional equipment included an automatic transmission, radio, heater, and whitewall tires.

A Return to the U.S.S.R.?

News stories on Ford's participation in a consortium of U.S. companies exploring business opportunities with the U.S.S.R. have prompted a number of articles on Ford's historical involvement with the Soviet Union.

Model Ts were sold throughout Czarist Russia, and large numbers of Fordson tractors were exported to the U.S.S.R. during the 1920s. So many Ford tractors and trucks were in operation that contemporary observers claimed that Henry Ford's name was as well known as that of any Russian.

Ford took a benevolent view of the Soviet Union's efforts to build its economy. In 1929, his company and the U.S.S.R.'s Amtorg Trading Corporation signed an agreement calling for construction of two assembly plants, one of which later became known as the Gorky Automobile Works and remains in operation today.

"Ford agreed to help set up the plants, which were to assemble the Model A (dubbed the Gaz A by the Russians) and various derivative vehicles," recalls *Ward's Auto World*. "As the factories neared completion, Ford advisers went to Russia and some 150 Soviet workers were sent to Dearborn for training. The exchange was an interesting forerunner of the training methods used today by Japanese transplant operations in the U.S.

"The 1929 agreement forecast production of 100,000 cars and trucks a year with the Russian government contracting to buy 72,000 units over a four-year period," adds *Ward's*. "Exact figures are unavailable, but by the time Amtorg ended its contract with Ford in 1934 actual vehicle production was believed to be considerably lower than the original targets.

"From Ford's point of view, this first 'joint venture' with the Soviets was not a financial success; the final balance sheet showed a $578,000 deficit.

"With an auto industry – of sorts – in operation, the Soviets tried to go it alone. But Ford was not completely rejected; in 1932 Amtorg ordered 104 Lincolns (including 10 with V-12 engines), ostensibly for use in transporting capitalist visitors around Moscow.

"Since the 1930s, Ford has had few significant dealings with the Soviet Union, except for a much-publicized visit to Russia in 1970 by Henry Ford II. His talks with the Soviets over the construction of a heavy truck plant were fruitless [mainly because of U.S. government objections].

"The future, however, looks more promising for Ford," opines *Ward's*. Assuming that all goes well in the current trade negotiations between U.S. and Soviet consortia, it's possible to foresee the day when the Ford Scorpio, or its successor, might be produced at the same Russian plant that once turned out the Model A."

Ford, concludes *Ward's*, is considering plans to help the Soviets modernize the aging Gorky auto plant and to replace the U.S.S.R.'s aging Volga car with a mid-size Ford, possibly the European-built Scorpio.

"Marble" Ford

Many Ford vehicles are museum pieces, but none in the manner of a "marble" Mondeo at St. Peterburg's Russian Museum.

Originally called the Marble Palace, the museum, an 18th century confection of luminous pink marble where czars once danced, was renamed the Lenin Museum after the Communists came to power. The Soviets placed Lenin's armored truck on a granite pedestal in the courtyard and emblazoned it with the legend, "The Enemy of Capital."

In June 1994 Ford's world car, the Mondeo (Contour in the U.S.) was painted to look like marble and set on the pedestal formerly occupied by Lenin's vehicle. Some consider the Mondeo as art, others as a cheap commercial stunt. To the museum, which received a $50,000-plus Ford donation in return for enshrining the car, the Mondeo is more than art; it also is a statement.

"For generations we've had this image of the armored car imprinted in our memory – a metal car used to kill people," said Museum Director Vladimir Gusev. "The most important thing is to distance ourselves from this gloomy image." In keeping with this view, Gusev exiled Lenin's truck, on which he gave speeches, to the city's artillery museum.

The Mondeo exhibit is the brainchild of German artist H.A. Schult, who made his name in his native country by freezing, crunching, gilding, and otherwise transforming Fords. Schult gets cars free from the company in return for what amounts to free advertising. In Cologne, Ford of Germany's headquarters, a Schult-created car with wings of gold, perched on a tower above the city museum, has been part of the city's skyline since 1989.

Some critics have skewered Schult for what they consider the transparent commercialism of his work. His response: "People like to see this kind of freedom. This kind of art is part of freedom."

But even among Russian Museum employees, the Mondeo's artistic merits are dubious. Curator Ludmilla Lisetskaya dismissed it "as an advertisement that we hope will not be there for long." Another curator, Olesya Turkina, observed that the museum is "describing the ultimate victory of capital. This isn't art; it's a pure economic and political gesture."

To appease such critics, Gusev said that the "marble" Ford will be a temporary exhibit. One has the feeling that it can be had for the right price.

Swiss Model Ts

A fleet of six Model T trucks launched Switzerland's largest private company, Migros, according to *European Magazine*.

The 1925 Ts, used by founder Gottlieb Duttweiler to bridge the gap between producer and consumer, sold coffee, rice, pasta, sugar, coconut fat, and soap on Zurich's streets at prices up to 40 percent lower than at retail.

Today Migros is Switzerland's largest supermarket chain, and also owns many other businesses.

Henry Ford of Turkey

Vehbi Koc is the "Henry Ford of Turkey," having launched his country's auto industry and become its leading industrialist and one of its richest citizens. Also like Ford, he sprang from humble origins, and worked his way up.

Koc began selling Model A Fords in Ankara, his nation's capital, in 1928. At the time, Ford dealers in Turkey reported to the Ford office in Alexandria, Egypt.

During his first visit to the U.S. in 1946, Koc hoped to meet the senior Henry Ford. But, as noted in the magnate's 1977 book, *The Autobiography of a Turkish Businessman: My Life Story*, Koc learned that the Dearbornite's mental and physical state made it "not possible to see Ford or even to shake hands and say hello."

Koc next visited the U.S. in 1948. Having followed Henry Ford II's rise within the company, he wanted to meet the Ford scion. A director of General Electric, with which Koc did business in Turkey, was asked to furnish a letter of introduction. On the strength of the letter, Koc journeyed from New York to Detroit.

"We gave the letter of introduction to Ford's secretary. The secretary, either upon her own initiative or because it was the truth, said that Mr. Ford was heavily engaged and could not see us. Disappointed, we left Detroit. Upon returning to Turkey, a letter was waiting for me in my office, signed by Henry Ford. It said that he regretted having been unable to meet me and would see me the next time I visited the United States.

Koc began negotiating with Ford in 1954 to set up a joint venture in Turkey. In 1956, he again visited the U.S., this time as the winner of a competition among 34 Near East Ford distributors. Before setting out, he obtained a letter to Henry II from Turkey's Prime Minister Adnan Menderes. At the same time, Koc informed HFII about his Dearborn visit, and requested an appointment. Ten days later, he received a personal invitation from HFII.

Ford suggested that Koc visit his office on Nov. 6, shortly before the presidential election. The Turk asked that the meeting be postponed to Nov. 9. "My reasons for putting off our meeting were two-fold," he explained. "I thought that such an eminent businessman would be deeply interested in the elections and so his mind would be preoccupied when he talked with me, and also I wanted to know which party Mr. Ford favored.

"Ford met as at the door of his office," recalls Koc .... "I had carefully written down the points for discussion on board the *Queen Mary*, and had sent a copy to Mr. Ford, so he would also be prepared. He had read my report and asked numerous questions.

"We were to have our photographs taken. An embossed world map hung on the wall of Mr. Ford's office and we took our places in front of this map, under Turkey. The necktie of a person from Ankara does not always stand straight, and mine was crooked. Mr. Ford straightened my tie and told me to smile while our photographs were taken. After that, the formal part of the meeting was over and it was time for lunch. We left Ford's office to go up to his private dining room in his private elevator. He wanted to operate the elevator himself; instead of going up we went to the basement. He joked, 'They have entrusted this organization to a man unable to operate an elevator.'

"We went up again and walked into the dining room. Since the building was newly completed, this was the first time he had eaten in this room, he said. The Ford head office building had 12 stories. It was a magnificent building that had cost $38 million to build.

"There was informal conversation during lunch. Ford was 38 years old then. He was six feet tall and portly. He drank two large bottles of Coca-Cola. After this intimate lunch he turned us over to his executives for discussions ....

"We understood from the talks that Mr. Ford still remembered the bitter experience of the assembly plant his company had set up in Tophane, Istanbul in 1928, and therefore was reluctant to give the company name or to have stock in an assembly plant in Turkey, but he seemed willing to support such a venture by loans."

Ford also sent a letter, dated Nov. 28 1956, to Prime Minister Menderes, stating that his company would provide assistance to Koc with the object of "providing a facility in Turkey for the assembly of Ford trucks." The company subsequently offered Koc a $250,000 loan, but with such stiff terms that the Turk rejected it in favor of a Turkish government loan.

In the 1960s Koc went on to build Turkey's first assembly plant and his country's first car, the Anadol. He also concluded an agreement with Ford for technical assistance. Koc's firm and Ford have had cooperative arrangements ever since.

Plant Rundown

"How many of Ford's present U.S. plants were built during Henry Ford's lifetime?" inquires Joseph Carrigan of Forest Hills, N.Y.

Nine, with the oldest of them, Dearborn Assembly, having been built within the Rouge complex in 1918. Next-oldest Ford plants are Chicago Assembly and Norfolk Assembly, 1924; and Twin Cities Assembly, 1925. Other facilities built during Ford's lifetime include Dearborn Stamping, 1938; Dearborn Tool & Die, 1939; Dearborn Engine, 1941; Dearborn Frame, 1946; and Atlanta Assembly, 1947.

Ford's oldest Canadian factory is Windsor (Ont.) Engine 1 & 2, built in 1923.

The largest of Ford's U.S. plants are Kansas City Assembly, and Lorain (Ohio) Assembly, both 3.5 million square feet, followed by Wixom (Mich.) Assembly, 3.25 million square feet. Lorain is the largest employer, with 5,613 on the payroll, followed by Kansas City Assembly's 4,219. St. Thomas (Ont.) Assembly is the largest of Canada's Ford plants: 3,801 employees.

The smallest of the company's plants is Ford Motor Co. Caribbean, built in Puerto Rico in 1964 and a producer of bearings, pumps, and shafts; it has 110 employees. Wixom, which assembles Ford's largest cars, is generally believed to be the world's most profitable factory.

Ford's westernmost U.S. plant is Kansas City Assembly, although its North American Automotive Operations has engine and stamping/assembly facilities in Chihuahua and Hermosillo, Mexico, respectively.

Ford Factories

Excellent brief commentaries on Ford's Piquette, Highland Park, and Rouge factories are provided in a paper, "Fordism and the Rational Factory," by Lindy Biggs of Massachusetts Institute of Technology.

"Piquette Avenue was built in the style of textile mills," states Biggs, (being) a long narrow building measuring 402 feet by 56 feet with three floors." Auto production in 1904, she adds, "differed little from the way any other heavy goods such as carriages, wagons, or machinery were built."

Ford sales soon outgrew Piquette's capacity, even though the company, like all other pioneer auto firms, bought almost all of its parts from small manufacturers. Ford, says Biggs, was the first to establish a major production operation, starting engine and rear axle production in its Beaubien Avenue plant in 1905. The parts were transported by horsecart between the Beaubien and Piquette factories. Ford also bought buildings next to the Piquette Plant in order to move engine production closer to assembly operations. But, even with the expansion, the company was constrained. The solution: the Highland Park Plant, placed into operation at the start of 1910.

Highland Park created a stir in architectural circles because of the unusual amount of glass used to enclose the building, notes Biggs. The 'window walls' inspired observers to affectionately call the building the Crystal Palace, in reference to London's famous glass hall built for the Great Exhibition in 1851. Highland Park, notes Biggs, "is almost universally praised by American architectural and industrial historians as the first 'daylight' factory."

Highland Park's major buildings, like some of the buildings at the previously built Packard Plant, were constructed with reinforced concrete. The technique greatly reduced floor vibration from machines, making multiple stories more feasible for heavy manufacturing; required fewer interior columns that the older mill construction, opening up space on the shop floor; and provided the strength needed for window walls to be used in multistory factories.

Why multistory? Because, says Biggs, early in the century it was easier to move parts and materials vertically by elevator and crane than horizontally across factory floors.

Biggs also describes Highland Park in terms of the "old shop" – buildings put up before 1914 – and the "new shop" – buildings designed to accommodate mass production techniques.

Highland Park, although one of the world's largest factories, could not satisfy Ford's plans for expansion. The answer lay in the Rouge Plant, covering an area so great and with so many diverse operations that it looked more like an industrial city than a factory – not least because it ultimately would have an 80-mile internal set of roads and more than 100 miles of railroad track.

The low-rise, highly integrated Rouge represented a new generation in factory design and permitted Ford to process raw materials as well as to expand its manufacturing base. For decades, the Rouge, the world's largest plant, was regarded by many as being one of the most efficient of factories. It inspired many other manufacturers, including Toyota.

Henry Ford, Biggs concludes, consistently was more willing than others to spend money on expansion and new manufacturing techniques. Perhaps it was this aspect of the Ford factory system that led David Hounsell, in his book, *From the American System to Mass Production*, to observe that "it seemed that the Ford Motor Co. did not want to make money as much as it wanted to build cars." And, build them it did, almost 10,000 a day in the Model T's heyday.

Sets Record Straight

Conventional wisdom has it that Ford's first factory, the Mack Avenue Plant, was earlier a wagon or a carpenter's shop, rather than a new Ford building.

Not so, reports Lindy Biggs, of Massachusetts Institute of Technology, in her paper, "Fordism and the Rational Factory." Biggs reports that the "small, inconspicuous building," built to Henry Ford's specifications, was constructed in 1903 by Albert Strelow, owner of the property, a contractor, and one of Ford's 12 charter shareholders.

How did the conventional wisdom arise? One fount is Henry Ford's autobiographical *My Life and Work* (1922), ghostwritten by Samuel Crowther, who simply made a mistake. Another was Allan Nevins' *Ford: the Times, the Man, the Company*. Nevins may have been influenced by *My Life and Work* and also may have misread a letter written on June 4, 1903, by John

Anderson, another shareholder. Anderson's letter describes the plant as "a dandy. I went all through it today. It is large, light, and airy, about 250 feet long by 50 feet wide, fitted up with machinery necessary to assemble the parts, and all ready for business."

Biggs bases her belief that Ford built the Mack Plant on her examination of Detroit street directories of 1902 and 1903. The 1902 directory shows the Mack Avenue lots 673-691 were vacant; the 1903 publication states that lots 688-691 were occupied by Ford Motor Co.

The Mack Avenue Plant at first employed "ten or a dozen boys and a foreman," notes Biggs. Labor was performed by skilled craftsmen. Management was minimal, with the principal owner/operator (Ford) and the foreman also being skilled craftsmen, creating more of a collegial relationship than a hierarchy.

Ford production soon outgrew the Mack Plant, which was abandoned in 1904 in favor of the new Piquette Avenue Plant. Nothing remains of the Mack Avenue building, formerly located at the crossing of the Belt Line Railroad. The Piquette Plant still stands at Piquette and Beaubien avenues.

Mack Avenue Site

The approximate site of Ford's first factory, Detroit's Mack Avenue Plant, as it looks today. The location is in a depressed area on the Motor City's near east side.

Ford's First Factory

Ford's first factory on Detroit's Mack Avenue. Curiously, a carriage, not a car, stands at the side of the building. A Detroit Auto Painting Co. sign indicates that Ford was not the structure's sole occupant. (Photo from the Collections of the Henry Ford Museum and Greenfield Village.)

Mack Plant in Later Years

This photo of Ford's first plant, on Detroit's Mack Avenue at the Belt Line Railroad, was taken of the abandoned building in 1941. The railroad watchtower and signal were added after Ford vacated the plant early in the century. (Photo from the Collections of the Henry Ford Museum and Greenfield Village.)

Birthplace of T

Ford's 94-year-old Piquette Plant, one of the world's oldest auto factories, as it looked in April 1998 with members of the Henry Ford Heritage Association gathered alongside. This building saw the production of Models B, C, F, K, R, and S, plus design, development and initial assembly of the Model T. Part of the three-story brick building, 402 feet long, 56 feet wide, is now used for medical-record storage and by a linen/uniform service. Although structurally sound, the plant is endangered by urban renewal. The Heritage Association hopes to arrange for fuller plant utilization and preservation. (Photo by Michael Skinner, St. Clair Shores, Mich.)

T Design Room

Henry Ford and his assistants developed the Model T in this very space, the northeast corner, third floor, of the Ford Company's Piquette Plant in Detroit. While the work progressed, Ford sat in his mother's rocking chair, similar to that occupied by your commentator, holding a model flivver. (The photo was taken by Michael Skinner, St. Clair Shores, Mich., at a plant open house, Sept. 27, 1998.)

Ford's Highland Park (Mich.) Plant during its heyday. The powerhouse, center, and Administration Building, to its right, were razed in 1959. The office building to the left of the powerhouse still stands in dilapidated condition, as does a considerable portion of the remainder of the old factory. The Henry Ford Trade School, to the left of the surviving office building, is not among the survivors, nor is the former test track, left center. (Photo from the Collections of the Henry Ford Museum and Greenfield Village.)

On Being a Ford Guide

The subject of guiding visitors through Ford's big Highland Park, Mich. factory is discussed in a *San Francisco Chronicle* article of October 12, 1913 forwarded by reader Ken Kaufmann, Arcadia, Calif.

"We have amusing experiences," said a guide named James. "People have no idea of the extent of the plant before they take a trip through it, and many of them have but little idea of what they have seen after they have gone through. And the comparisons they make are a big laugh. They are always trying to size up something by the size of something they are familiar with. A big farmer was going through one day, and when he passed the gear-cutting machines with the streams of soft soap playing on the metal to cool it, he said: 'Gee! Them things look like a bunch of cream separators.'

"Then they get funny ideas of what they are going to see. I was taking a party of women through one day and one asked me where the slaughterhouse was. That was a new one, and I guess I stuttered in asking her what she meant. 'Why,' says she, 'I read a piece in the paper about the thousands of cows that are killed every year to furnish the leather for the upholstery, and I wanted to see the slaughterhouse.'

"One of the funniest was a bunch of Englishmen that was here. I was telling all about the enormous quantities of material used and that the screws used in all the 185,000 cars made this year, if put end to end, would stretch from here to Cleveland and stick out away over Ohio.

" 'But you cawn't do it, y'know,' said one of the Britishers.

" 'Can't do what?' says I.

" 'Stretch those blooming screws from Detroit to Cleveland,' he answered, 'because you couldn't attach them together and (even if you could) they would interfere with navigation [on Lake Erie].'

" 'Can you beat that? Well, those are only samples of what we get everyday.'"

Highland Park Plant

"There are many postcards which show Ford's Highland Park (Mich.) Plant," writes automotive card collector Wade E. Leonard, of Mt. Clemens, Mich. "But, I think this one is among the best."

Leonard's card, above, pictures the plant in full flower. Undated, the card appears to have been printed during the teens, judging from the appearance of the cars on Woodward Ave., which fronts the factory.

Some of the historic plant still stands, including the office building at left center and the "high-rise" buildings at right center. The powerhouse and administration building, front center, were razed in 1959. The old office building is vacant and in a very poor state of repair; part of one high-rise building is used for Ford records retention.

Caught In The Act

Reader Andy LaBorde recently had an experience known to many a curious Fordophile, and we'll let him tell about it in his own words.

"I have always had a passing interest in Henry and his company .... In the last year my Ford interest has increased, mainly because my wife has become an assistant professor at Wayne State University [in Detroit]. Being 'DINKS,' we have maintained our home in Milwaukee and an apartment in Belleville, Mich. With frequent long weekends in Detroit, thanks to your excellent book [*The Public Image of Henry Ford*], I have had time to poke around in 'Ford Country.'

"We have done the usual things; touring Edsel's home and Fair Lane and buying yearly passes to the Ford Museum. I sought out Henry's gravesite on a cold, clear winter afternoon and was surprised by its location. It seems to be out of place, until you think back on his earlier life style, then perhaps it is the proper resting spot.

"Anyway, the reason for this overdue fan letter came about after reading about the Highland Park Plant in the September issue of 'Ford Country.' Earlier, I had 'discovered it' while roaming up Woodward Avenue one Friday while my wife was at work.

"I saw the Michigan historical plaque in front of the administration building and put two and two together from portions of your book I had remembered reading. Being mindful of the surrounding neighborhood, I decided to take some pictures of the plant from my car. After driving around the outside, I noticed cars coming and going through an open gate. Since it was open, and the place looked like it was not really being used for any type of industry, I drove in. BIG MISTAKE!

As I was about to take a picture of the Ford logo on the water tower from my Sable wagon, a private rent-a-cop drove up and asked what I was doing. I explained my historical interest in this property, etc. With a dumb/bored look on his face he stated that pictures were not permitted. I explained that I had not had enough time to take any, thanked him, and headed for the gate.

"I was almost at the entrance when

he roared up in front of me, blocking my way. He said I had to go inside and talk to his boss. My first thought was great, now I can see what's inside. My second thought was to lock my camera in my car before I went in. After telling my story to the 'boss,' a 5-foot tall black woman with a Jamaican accent, she informed me that she would have to have the film from my camera. (That's why I left it in my car.) I politely told her to go jump in the lake. After I insisted she summon a Detroit cop to settle the matter, I was on my way. As I left I noticed the gate was now kept in a down position.

"By the way, what I did see inside wasn't much. Huge, empty corridors painted that ugly industrial green color. If only the walls could talk ....

"I have enjoyed your 'Ford Country' column off and on over the years," concludes LaBorde. "It was one of the reasons I finally resubscribed to *Cars & Parts*. I wish I had saved some of the old issues, but you can't save everything."

Like Andy, I've had a few encounters with security guards. I once was ordered out of Ford's Ypsilanti, Mich. Plant, while taking pictures of the complex's original powerhouse/hydroplant, now nestled inside the much larger factory. Later, I arranged to visit the plant legitimately – in fact, had first done so in 1953 as a member of Ford's News Department.

Another time, while photographing Ford's former Big Bay, Mich. sawmill, I was apprehended by a security officer, who, thinking I might be a surveyor, asked for my film. He was mollified when a University of Michigan identification card strongly suggested that I was a mere professor with an interest in Ford historical sites. Lots of times, it may be added, I was not accosted while roaming company property and blending in with the work force.

One can understand why a security guard, given his orders, would ask an interloper to leave Ford's former Highland Park Plant property which, incidentally, Ford no longer owns. But why demand LaBorde's film? Having toured most of Highland Park's buildings in recent years, thanks to my research interests and also serving as a moderator for a documentary film made there, I cannot imagine how pictures taken in the venerable, ghostly factory could be harmful to anyone.

Highland Park

Ford had deep roots in Highland Park, Mich., now an economically-depressed Detroit enclave. In 1910, Henry Ford opened the world's largest auto plant in the city; in 1913 the plant was the first in the industry to build cars on a moving assembly line; and in 1914 the company announced the $5-dollar daily wage from there. In 1927 Henry and Edsel Ford drove the 15-millionth Model T off Highland Park's line; from 1945-73 the company built tractors at the plant; and in 1981 Ford's real estate subsidiary, Ford Land Development Corp., sold the factory to a private real estate group which has done little with it.

In 1989 the eighth-grade class in Highland Park's Barber Elementary School wrote to Ford family members, including Edsel Ford II. In addition to recalling Ford's history in Highland Park, the students asked for help for the school.

Family members gave the letters to Ford Land Chairman Wayne Doran, and Ford Land adopted the school. During the last several years the company has donated computers and clothing to the institution and set up workplace mentoring programs.

The relationship has led to a much more important Ford-Highland Park connection, Ford Land having agreed to head a group of suburban developers to advise the city on how to find new uses for the 600-acre site Chrysler will leave behind when it moves its headquarters to suburban Auburn Hills, Mich. in 1995. Chrysler is expected to offer the city millions of dollars worth of economic aid when it departs, and this money is expected to implement the plan devised by the advisers, who are donating their services.

As for Ford's old Highland Park plant, some space has been leased for the storage of documents and machines, but most of the buildings are vacant and are slowly deteriorating. The buildings will not fall, however. Indeed, they were built so strongly by Ford and his great architect, Albert Kahn, that structurally they have every chance of standing as long as Rome's Coliseum and Athens' Parthenon.

"Dining" In The Rouge

"The 'lunch wagon' was a very memorable phenomenon of the Rouge Plant," recalls Ford Richardson Bryan, the eminent Ford historian, who worked in the plant between 1941-51.

"Shortly before the middle of each shift," Bryan recalls, "long trains of metal-covered wagons were drawn by Fordson tractors into the Rouge by a private concessionaire. (This profitable concession was rumored to be owned by the 'mob' in payment for there being no harm done to the Ford grandchildren.)

"The wagons were each dropped off at strategic locations, where the tops were opened to display the day's offerings of soup or chili, a choice of sandwiches, fruits, desserts, milk, and coffee. The food was actually not bad, although many liked to ridicule it with remarks much more distasteful than the food. Prices were reasonable –sandwiches 10-15 cents, 1/2-pint milk 10 cents, pie 10 cents, two cupcakes 10 cents, soup 10 cents, chili 14 cents, etc.

"Most production workers brought their lunches from home, gulping them down in the 20 minutes of allotted paid time. A long lineup at the wagon could leave them without enough time to eat what they had purchased. Non-production salaried workers had more flexibility with 30 minutes allowed without pay. Both hourly and salaried workers ate at their work site – sitting on the floor or wherever. Lunchtime also was the chance for the few workers who dared to look for a secluded niche between buildings to sneak a cigarette. However, they risked being fired if a service man (security guard) caught them in the act of smoking. Many addicted to tobacco were inclined to chew tobacco or use snuff, both of which were allowed on the job.

" ... (During the immediate post-World War II period) the old food wagons were largely replaced by large, clean lunchrooms and cafeterias serving hot dishes at very reasonable prices," continues Bryan. "In 1948, a full, hot meal including drink and dessert could be purchased for 65 cents plus 3 cents tax. These facilities were now operated by the company on a nonprofit basis.

"The private dining rooms for management personnel offered luxurious service, a wide selection of expensive foods for a fixed $1.50 per meal – charged to one's private account. The lunch bucket and brown bag still prevail in production areas because of the extra time required to utilize cafeteria facilities."

Bryan has served as a volunteer at the archives and research library of the Henry Ford Museum and Greenfield Village since his retirement from Ford's Scientific Research Laboratory in 1974.

Rouge Art

"You've occasionally written about Diego Rivera," writes Alexander Hagorian, of New York City. "How about Charles Sheeler, another artist of some importance in Ford history?"

Sheeler's photographs and paintings of Ford's Rouge Plant, along with Rivera's Detroit Institute of Arts' murals, summarize the development of automotive iconography in the late 1920s and 1930s.

In 1927 Ford commissioned Sheeler – and no doubt Henry Ford's son, Edsel, helped make the decision – to do a series of documentary photographs of the Rouge. The artist, in an effort to portray America's industrial might, focused on building exteriors.

In February 1928 one of Sheeler's Rouge photographs, "Criss-Crossed Conveyors," was reproduced in *Vanity Fair*, a magazine noted for its chic snob appeal. Under the title, "By Their Works Ye Shall Know Them," the caption stated that "The Ford automobile factories ... lay claim to being the most significant public monument in America ... an American Mecca." Sheeler later used the photo at the center of three shots called "Industry," arranged like a religious triptych.

Sheeler's best-known Rouge-related paintings are "Classic Landscape" and "American Landscape." These paintings have been highly esteemed in the art world. Sheeler's works have contributed to a widespread notion that the Rouge was an artistic, as well as industrial, triumph. Of few other factories has the same been said.

Navy Service School

The U.S. Navy Service School at Ford's Rouge Plant in Dearborn is discussed in the Winter 1994 issue of the *Dearborn Historian*, quarterly publication of the Dearborn Historical Commission.

The article, by Ford R. Bryan, notes that the school, largest of Ford's World War II instructional programs, was started on December 6, 1940, a year before Pearl Harbor. Located on the southwestern edge of the 1,200-acre Rouge complex, the installation housed 2,000 Navy men. Ford financed the station, leasing it to the Navy for one dollar a year.

On January 15, Bryan notes, the initial contingent of 150 men arrived and Henry and Edsel Ford, speaking over two radio networks, turned over the school to the Navy, represented by Rear Admiral Chester W. Nimitz, chief of the Navy Department's Bureau of Navigation. Nimitz was commander of the Pacific Fleet during World War II.

Naval students received 90 days of instruction, spending eight hours a week attending lectures by Fordmen on mechanical theory, blueprints, the use of tool sand instruments. Classroom, library, and laboratory space were provided in the Ford Apprentice School, located in the Aircraft Building (now the Dearborn Engine Plant) and the "B" Building (which now builds Mustangs). Thirty-two hours per week were devoted to machine work in various factory buildings under the supervision of Fordmen. The men were trained to become machinist mates, metalsmiths, shipfitters, and basic engineers.

In December 1944, the school was converted to a Radio Technicians School and Ford instructors were replaced by Navy trainers. During the four years the school was taught by Fordmen, January 1941-December 1945, 22,303 Navy men received training.

Although Bryan's article does not mention it, Henry Ford's chief aide, Harry Bennett, was, in Nimitz' words, "tireless in his efforts to perfect plans for the school." An enlisted sailor in his youth, Bennett was commissioned a lieutenant commander in the U.S. Naval Reserve in February 1941. Lt. Henry Ford II was stationed at the school early in World War II.

Emperor Akihito

Japanese Emperor Akihito's 1990 and 1993 visits to the U.S. recalls his visit to Ford's Rouge Plant in Dearborn in November 1953. Your commentator, then a member of Ford's News Department, was among those who accompanied the 19-year-old prince along the tour route.

The prince's visit was regarded as fairly routine by Fordists and the press. After all, many important people visited the Rouge in those days. Furthermore, Japan, emerging from occupation by U.S. troops and weak economically, commanded minimal respect, and the diminutive prince, dressed in an ordinary suit, looked much like the college student he was.

Now Emperor Akihito is the symbolic ruler of one of the world's richest and most powerful nations. Participants in his Rouge tour of yore took for granted that some day he would assume the Chrysanthemum throne. But no one talked about Japan becoming an automotive power.

Rouge Steel Sold

Rouge Steel Co., which traces its origins to 1920 and occupies about 500 acres of Ford's Rouge complex, has been acquired by Marico Acquisitions Co.

A wholly owned subsidiary of Ford, Rouge Steel is the eighth largest steel producer in the U.S. Its 3,300 hourly and 750 salaried employees produced about 2.5 million tons of sheet metal in 1988.

Marico, established expressly to acquire Rouge Steel, is headed by Carl L. Valdiseri, retired chief operating officer of Weirton Steel and a lifelong steel man. Ford, an equity participant in Marico, is expected to buy 40 percent of its U.S. and Canadian steel requirements from Rouge Steel for the next 10 years.

Rouge Steel has undergone major modernization programs during the past five years, and turned a modest profit in 1988 following eight years of losses. Ford wanted to sell the property for many years, but had difficulty finding a buyer. One obstacle is the plant's location – in the center of the Rouge.

Rouge's Remaining Plants

"The old Rouge Plant used to have 34 integrated factories," writes reader Cal Norton, of Morristown, N.J. "What's left now?"

Skyline of the Rouge Plant at dawn – and at a time when companies were proud of their factories' smoke and made no effort to disguise it. (Photo from the Collections of the Henry Ford Museum and Greenfield Village.)

The 1,200-acre Rouge manufacturing complex today includes Dearborn Assembly Plant, which produces Mustangs; Dearborn Engine Plant, which makes 1.9 liter Escort engines; a frame plant which makes chassis frames for Ford's larger cars and trucks; a tool and die plant; and an electricity-generating plant. Rouge Steel, which the company set up as a subsidiary in 1981, then sold to Marico Acquisition Corp. in 1989, includes blast, basic oxygen, and electric furnaces, a continuous casting facility, slabbing mill, hot strip mill, cold mills, and a half-interest with USX in an electrogalvanizing plant.

The UAW would like the Rouge to be returned to its glory days, when it usually had 60,000-80,000 workers, and more than 100,000 in 1929 and during World War II. In making this recommendation, the union points to the success of Toyota City and its just-in-time production techniques. But the Ford Co., while acknowledging that the Rouge taught Toyota much of what it knows about just-in-time production, has no desire to rebuild the old plant. The complex, it notes, "includes our oldest manufacturing facilities, some of which could not be modernized without extraordinarily heavy investments."

Bring Rouge Back

Ford's aging Rouge complex should be transformed into a "complete modern manufacturing center to rival GM's Saturn and Buick City plants and Mazda's new Flat Rock Plant," says UAW's top Ford bargainer.

"We have at the Rouge what General Motors and Mazda and Saturn and all the rest of them are trying to build – a complete complex," UAW Vice President Stephen Yokich, director of the union's Ford Department, said recently.

"It just bewilders ... me how a company that already has it in place and could build from it just hasn't made that decision yet. Our goal as a union is to save the Rouge complex. I don't know if we can, but we've been trying."

Oldest Ford Plant

Ford's oldest surviving plant, Dearborn Assembly, as it looked upon completion of the company's first Eagle boat (submarine chaser) in July 1918. The exterior of the plant, the first building constructed within the giant Rouge complex, looks much the same today, except for the accumulation of seven decades of smoke, fly ash, dust, and grime. The interior of the plant, now used for the assembly of Mustangs, has been repeatedly renovated. (Photo from the Collections of the Henry Ford Museum and Greenfield Village).

Rouge Investment

Ford is set to spend $2 billion to improve its historic Rouge Plant, once the world's largest factory.

Planning to assemble a new Mustang in the Rouge in 2001, the company will invest $1.25 billion in the factory's body and paint shops, another $500 million in its engine plant, plus $88 million each in its frame and tool & die units, and $71 million in its stamping plant, according to a UAW document.

Rouge plants now employ 8,000 people including 6,500 Local 600 members. The complex remains Ford's largest concentration of employees and plants.

Rouge Air Healthy?

Can the environment at Ford's Rouge Plant actually be good for your health? Maybe. In any event, three current members of the Ford Old Timers Club are centenarians, 35 are in their nineties, and 200-plus are in their eighties. These figures top the national average, says George Hall, secretary-treasurer of the organization.

One of Ford's centenarians, Robert Coulter, 106, came from Ireland on the *Lusitania*. Coulter, who spent 30 years on the company's assembly lines, credits his parents for his longevity. "If you plant a strong plant," he says, "it grows."

Fordists with at least 25 years of employment are eligible for membership in the club, which in 1992 is observing its 40th anniversary.

The Rouge Plant, for those not personally acquainted with it, for decades was one of North America's lustiest smoke-belchers. Its emissions drove to distraction Canadians living to the east across the Detroit River, and its fly ash covered nearby cars as surely as the dew covers Dixie. The Rouge Plant now has better breath – thanks to air-pollution control efforts and downsizing of the old factory.

Factory Square Apartments

Part of Ford's old Atlanta Assembly Plant has been made over into 123 apartments, all of which open into the structure's natural atrium. The remainder of the edifice is devoted to small stores and garage space for occupants.

The upscale one- and two-bedroom apartments, four stories in height, rent for $670 to $800. Security is tight, admission to the apartment area requiring a key or the assistance of the building's manager.

The plant, built in 1914, assembled Model Ts, Model As, and V-8s before becoming a tank factory in World War II. Later it was used as an armed forces induction center, and was known as the War Assets Building. The building is within walking distance of famed Peachtree Street and downtown Atlanta. The structure is recognizable at first glance by its familiar Ford factory architecture including such trappings as generous window space, inlaid tile in the brick exterior, front entrance canopy, and water tower.

Buffalo Assembly Plant

"You've written about many of Ford's old assembly plants," writes reader Alexander R. Ross, of Buffalo, N.Y. "How about writing about the old Ford plant in my hometown?"

Permit me to quote from an excellent 1985 story on the plant by Richard Huntington, of the *Buffalo News*. As Huntington states, the ex-Ford factory, located at Main and Rodney avenues, was occupied in 1985 by Trico Products Corp., and was known as Plant No. 2.

"The building, as big as it is," observes Huntington, "and even with larger, ungainly additions to the rear, always seems happily graceful. The most obvious reason for this grace is the series of low terra-cotta arches that march quietly across the top of the brick structure, plus the other delightful terra-cotta decorations .... There also are handsome horizontal and vertical arrangements of the bricks, which make well-proportioned geometric patterns across the facade ....

"A plaque on the northeastern wall identifies the building as the place where the Bell Aircraft Corp. in 1941-42 designed and built America's first jet aircraft, the XP-59A ....

"Buffalo is well-known for its many distinguished factory buildings, from its grain elevators to the famous Pierce-Arrow building on Elmwood Avenue," continues Huntington. "Trico Plant 2 has to be counted among them. The building is not revolutionary in design, and from the viewpoint of modern architecture, it cheats a bit by gaining much of its handsomeness through decorative additions.

"It's also worth noting that the 1913 building isn't totally an original design. Architect Albert Kahn, who designed it with Ernest Wilby, based the Buffalo facade on another Ford plant in Cambridge, Mass., by architect John Graham ....

"There is a silver water tower and brick smokestack. Affixed to the water tower is a Trico logo. The word 'FORD' can faintly be seen running vertically up the stack ...

"The whole building is pretty delicate – for a rough-and-tumble factory building, that is. The building definitely is no brusque emblem of the industrial revolution. It doesn't wear is machine-age heart on its facade. It doesn't bear down on you like a gigantic steam engine from the past.

"Plant 2 has a gentler spirit. Designed to serve the industrial age, it offers nostalgic echoes of a distant, more elegant time before the machine took over. It radiates an old-style humanism which is always an enjoyment – and maybe a necessity – amid the blandness of many of our newer buildings."

High praise indeed. One might add that Ford's former Buffalo Assembly Plant not only is based on the Cambridge Plant, but also strongly resembles most other Ford assembly facilities of the 1909-16 era. Nearly all of the World Wars-era plants remain in use, as this column has noted through the years.

Cambridge Assembly Plant

Ford's former Cambridge (Mass.) Assembly Plant is being renovated for use as a manufacturing and office building.

The owner, Massachusetts Institute of Technology, is spending $13 million on the five-story, block-long building, which stands at 640 Memorial Drive at Brookline Street, opposite the Boston University Bridge. The Charles River site affords a fine view of Boston's Beacon Hill and tall buildings.

The old plant was occupied by Ford from 1913-33; then by R.H. White, a department store, and Polaroid, the camera maker, from 1956-87, although the latter ceased manufacturing in the building in 1984.

The inside of the building has been gutted, windows removed and reglazed, and white-glazed terra-cotta trim repaired and/or replaced. Two automobile-size freight elevators and one small, four-person passenger elevator are being removed in favor of six-passenger elevators.

A near-duplicate of a large clock that once topped the west facade is being readied for installation. Out back, a towering, five-story high "train shed," which once accommodated freight cars filled with Ford stock, is being reshaped to become the main entrance for the new tenants.

The first tenant will be Lifeline Systems, Inc., of Watertown, which makes and services personal emergency response systems. Lifeline, which as 275 employees, has singed a 10-year lease to occupy the ground floor and half of each of the upper four floors – a total of 100,000 square feet.

The building, when renovated, will look much as it did in Henry Ford's day, except for the windows. The original windows were composed of a grid of small panes, whereas the new ones will have wide panes deemed more appropriate for office use. Some sense of the old grid will remain, however, with three rows of smaller panes preserved in the upper section of each window opening. In addition, MIT may display a Model T in the building's lobby.

Thanks to readers Fred Roe, of Holliston, Mass., and Phil Dumka, of Carlisle, Mass., for forwarding news clippings on the old plant's renovation.

Charlotte Plant

Ford's former Charlotte (N.C.) Assembly Plant is shown as it stands today at 1820 Statesville Avenue. Now a drug company warehouse, the building looks much as it did in Ford's day except that its windows have been bricked.

The 300 x 800-foot plant, designed by Detroit's E.C. Ball, could assemble 400 Model Ts daily. Opened in 1924 in Charlotte's then outskirts, the facility now is close to downtown.

The factory, closed in June 1926 because of a decline in Model T sales, was reopened in 1929 to produce model As. It was shuttered again in March 1933, never again to assemble cars. Reopening in 1934 as a sales and service operation, the plant was sold to the U.S. Army in May 1941 for the manufacture of ammunition. The building housed a Ford sales office until December 1941.

Ford established a branch plant in Charlotte in 1914 at 222 North Tryon Street, where bodies were installed on built-up chassis. In 1916 the branch was moved to a four-story structure at 210 East Sixth Street, this facility being superseded in 1924.

After World War II, Ford opened a parts depot and the Charlotte District Sales Office were joined at a new facility at Wilkenson Boulevard and Dixon Road. Sixteen years later the sales office was moved to 309 Sharon Amity. The parts depot and sales office were moved to Atlanta in the early 1990s, and the service office was closed in 1996.

Thanks to reader Nick Wilkens, Charlotte, for forwarding photos and information about Ford's Charlotte activities.

Cincinnati Quality

There was big trouble at the Cincinnati Assembly Plant in 1928-29, recalls reader Robert Tonnies, Cincinnati, whose father, Henry, was the plant's head cashier.

"When workers attempted to assemble the first Model A on the new assembly line ... nothing fit right," Tonnies writes. "A lot of parts had to be returned to Detroit to be reworked, and a team was sent in to teach the workers how to build the more complicated A. The first "A" was due off the line about May 1928, but I think it was October before the first car rolled out."

"Problems persisted," Tonnies adds. "Production was not meeting its goals and quality was poor. Ford decided in the summer of 1929 to close the plant as soon as the on-hand inventory was used up."

The plant remained empty until the mid-1930s when remodeled by Sears, Roebuck into a retail farm and garden store. It was abandoned again in the mid-1970s, and now is vacant.

Cleveland Plant

"I have driven by the Cleveland Institute of Art a number of times and know that it was once a Ford factory," writes reader Ken Humphries, Euclid, Ohio. "Can you tell me about the history of the building?"

The plant was built in 1913 as part of a big expansion program prompted by increasing Model T sales and the introduction of moving assembly lines in Ford's Highland Park, Mich. factory. Designed by Albert Kahn, the factory incorporated the architect's trademarks – reinforced concrete and vast window space. The building was remodeled in 1923 and remained in Ford production until 1932.

After changing ownership several times, the structure was bought by the Cleveland Institute of Art in 1981 for $250,000. Renovated with the aid of $4 million in state bonds, the facility was renamed the Cleveland Institute of Art Factory. The building was entered in the U.S. Department of Interior's National Register of Historic Places in 1976 and added to the Register of Cleveland Landmarks in 1984.

Columbus Plant

The history of Ford's ex-Columbus, Ohio Assembly Plant is told in a 26-page brochure forwarded by reader Rick Lindner, Columbus.

Ford's Columbus, Ohio Assembly Plant when photographed by the author in 1979. The building looks much the same today.

The illustrated desktop publication includes reprints of articles, drawings, invoices, and other documents, including a 1926 federal government permit for the plant's hospital to dispense opium.

Plans for the four-story plant, located on the former J.J. Knox Lumber Co. site at Cleveland Avenue and Buckingham Street, were announced in an Oct. 23, 1913 *Columbus Dispatch* story. The 207-by-106-foot building was to be constructed of reinforced concrete with a red pressed brick exterior, finished with white oak. The exterior was to be ornamented with terra cotta and cut stone, and there was to be a combination quarry stone and composition roof. The first-floor showroom and offices were to have tile floors and marble bases, and the main stairway was to be in marble. The "strictly fireproof" Albert Kahn-designed structure was to cost about $100,000.

When opened in 1914, the new plant was "out in the country." A contemporary photo shows a horse in the front yard of a house across the street from the factory and Sells Circus's winter home toward its rear.

The Columbus Branch, as it initially was called, assembled Model Ts, and distributed cars and tractors to southern Ohio, West Virginia, Kentucky, and Indiana. Dealers usually picked up vehicles at the plant, and drove them to their hometowns. "How they took tractors home is a mystery to me," Lindner remarks.

Because of increased demand, the Columbus Plant was expanded in 1916 along Cleveland Avenue, giving the building the "L" shape which it has today, and in the 1920s the showroom displayed Lincolns as well as the Model T and Model A. Reduced sales during the Great Depression forced the plant's closure in 1936, then its sale to the Electric Power Equipment Co., after which Ford rented the roof and top floor for storage of cars.

Bought by the State of Ohio for $400,000 in 1943, the building was used for record storage by the Ohio Bureau of Employment Services until 1976 when acquired by Kroger. Kroger, having previously built a bakery on the former Sells Circus property, expanded its bakery into the Ford structure.

Lindner recently arranged for members of the Columbus-area Model T and Model A clubs to tour the building. While there, they saw a video which depicted the structure as it appeared during its Ford years.

Dallas Plant

When Ford opened its Dallas plant at Canton and Williams streets on July 4, 1914, it was the city's largest employer with more than 90 workers. Today developers are seeking tenants to fill the same number of loft-style apartments in the four-story brick building.

"We're already about 50 percent preleased," Joe Beard, president of Westdale Asset Management Co., of Dallas, told the *Dallas Morning News*. Occupancy began in December 1996.

The first automobile factory in the Southwest, the plant cost $175,000. It assembled 5,000 Model Ts annually from 1914 through 1924. An auto sales room occupied the west half of the ground floor, and the upper floors were used for parts storage, auto assembly, and vehicle repairs. Although Ford opened a larger assembly plant near Fair Park in 1925, it continued to use the older building for a showroom and warehouse.

After World War II, Adam Hat Co. acquired the structure and occupied it until 1986. The following year a developer announced plans to convert the edifice into a home for clubs, offices, and residences. But his plans and those of others were thwarted by Dallas' economic downturn in the late 1980s and early 1990s.

Organized by Canadian investors, Westdale has gutted the building's interior, replaced the small-pane windows, and created an atrium from the ground floor to the roof. The basement has been turned into secured parking.

The development delights Libby Willis of the National Trust for Historic Preservation. "It's great that redevelopment finally is coming to fruition," she says. "This building has a lot of history that goes with it. Westdale will seek to have the structure designated an historic landmark."

Thanks to reader Glen Whitt, Plano, Texas, for forwarding the *News*' story on the plant.

Denver Assembly Plant

"I read 'Ford Country' all the time and have your book," writes reader Loren Jacobson, of Littleton, Colo. "In the last issue of *Cars & Parts*, you wrote about Ford's old Milwaukee factory.

"I wonder if you have any information about what I think was a Ford factory in Denver – at 900 S.

Broadway, currently the headquarters of Gates Rubber Company. I've gone past this place uncounted thousands of times since I was a little kid in the mid-30s. I understand this was built as a Ford assembly plant, but I cannot remember it being anything except part of the Gates complex. And I've never seen anything about it in the local papers. If you have the story on this place, it might also be of interest to readers other than me."

The four-story building, constructed in two sections, was indeed a Ford assembly plant. The first section, designed by Seattle's John Graham, was built in 1913. The second south half, designed by Detroit's Albert Kahn, who followed Graham's design, went up in 1916. The structure has its original facade and atmosphere, except for the second and third floor, whose reflecting Solarban windows look very out of place.

Ford owned the building under the name of a wholly-owned investment firm, Neosho Investment Company. In July 1943 Neosho leased the structure to the federal government which used it for offices and storage. A wartime Red Cross station also was located therein.

In June 1944 the lease was terminated, and in March 1945 Charles Gates, founder of Gates Rubber, bought the building and land and added it to his expanding complex across the

Ex-Denver Assembly

Ford's former Denver Assembly Plant as it looks today.

street. The edifice's name was changed to Unit 31.

Each floor of the building, except the basement, is 312.3 by 128.9 feet, providing a total floor area of 41,157 square feet. Basically of column and slab construction, the structure's reinforced concrete strut columns are on a 28-foot grid system and vary from 31-inch cores on the first floor to 17-inch cores on the fourth. On the first floor, the column tops fan out to six feet and are decorated with large capital F's. The reinforced concrete floors are nine and one-half inches thick and are somewhat uneven due to settling of the foundation. The walls are also nine and one-half inch concrete covered by brick on the north, west, and south sides.

The very solidly built structure already has outlasted most of the Model Ts, Model As, and V-8s assembled therein, and it seems likely that it will remain in use long after most of today's Tauruses and Explorers have gone to the Great Junkyard in the Sky.

Duluth Plant

How sweet it would have been – an assembly plant for Duluth, Minn. – had it been built.

On May 3, 1916, the *Virginia* (Minn.) *Daily Enterprise* was aglow with the news: "The Ford Motor Co. will erect an automobile assembling plant at Duluth costing from $500,000 to $1,000,000, according to an announcement made yesterday by C.D. Hildebrand, special representative of the Ford Motor Co., who arrived in Duluth yesterday to select a site for the Detroit concern.

"Low freight rates on Ford parts and accessories which the Great Lakes traffic affords is the lodestone which draws the factory to Duluth," gushed the *Daily Enterprise*. "It is planned to make this point the distribution center of this section of the country. There is a big probability that other factory branches will be supplied from Duluth after the establishment of the branch here.

"An assembling plant here would receive parts not in carload lots, but by the shipload," noted Hildebrand. "A large crew of men would be employed here to assemble the cars ready for shipment to agents. By operating these assembling plants, much is saved in freight charges. The factory will give employment to scores of skilled mechanics, and will be a big addition to the industrial life of Duluth."

There was only one problem – the plant was never built, and Ford never offered a precise reason as to why. But we do know that the company already had an assembly plant in the Twin Cities. A second plant was unneeded to serve the Upper Midwest.

Thanks to Minnesotan Michael Bukovac for forwarding the *Daily Enterprise*'s article.

Fargo Assembly Plant

Ford's Fargo (N.D.) Assembly Plant, built in 1914, has housed Kaye's Printing for many years. As the company states in a promotional brochure, "it's unusual for a building this old and this big – 80,000 square feet – to be made of poured concrete. Which is great because it's literally rock solid when a dozen presses are running!" Thanks to reader Kenneth R. Belland, of Fargo, for taking and forwarding the photo.

Jacksonville Plant

Ford's former Jacksonville (Fla.) Assembly Plant is now used as a warehouse.

When opened in March 1925, the plant – 207 feet wide, 802 feet long, and three stories high – was one of the largest factories in the southeast. In operation until 1932, the facility first assembled Model Ts, then Model As. At its peak the plant turned out 150 cars per eight-hour shift, assembled 45,000 cars annually, and employed 600 persons.

The plant is located on the St. Johns River, just north of Mathews Bridge. In its heyday, the factory was frequented by ocean-going ships which brought parts in and took Ts and As out. Assembly operations were phased out in the throes of the Great Depression, but the plant was used as a parts distribution depot until the late 1970s when it was replaced by a new depot on Commonwealth Avenue.

Since its closing, the plant, located at the foot of Wambolt Street, has been successively used by World Cars (a Toyota importer), a van conversion firm, a boat builder, an importer of European cars and Wood-Hopkins Contracting Co.

The plant and surrounding property are for sale, according to J. Harold Saniford, equipment division manager for Wood-Hopkins. But the leaking facility must be extensively renovated before it can be fully utilized again.

Although Henry Ford couldn't foresee the Great Depression, he was right in this choice of a port of entry/exit for Ford parts and cars. Proof: Jacksonville today is the nation's leading port of entry for foreign-made cars and trucks, annually bringing in more than 600,000 vehicles.

Thanks to my daughter, Lani, of Jacksonville, Fla., for acquainting us with the plant's fate.

The Henry Ford Avenue Bridge, Long Beach, Calif., in a half-open position. The bridge, adjacent to Ford's former Long Beach Assembly Plant, has a 220-foot center span with 110-foot movable leaves between 50-foot towers on each end. Behind the Ford Bridge is the Heim Bridge, one of five land links to Terminal Island, home of the Long Beach Naval Shipyard and the Long Beach Navy Base. (Photo courtesy David L. Higgins, San Pedro, Calif.)

Henry Ford Bridge

Want to buy a bridge? You don't have to, for the 71-year-old Henry Ford Avenue drawbridge in the Port of Los Angeles is yours for the asking, if you are willing to move it.

The 70-foot-wide bascule-style bridge, complete with train tracks and control room, is being offered to any taker to make way for construction of a new double-track lift bridge over the Cerritos Channel in Wilmington. The old structure, one of only two surviving bridges of its kind in North America, is the only rail link between Wilmington and Terminal Island, home of the Long Beach Naval Shipyard and the Long Beach Navy Base.

If there are no successful bidders, the Los Angeles Harbor Department, which owns the bridge, will have it torn down in 1996. "We've had about six applications come in so far," reports Shaun Shahrestani, the port's project manager. "The interested parties are from all over the country – from New York to Los Angeles, but we're not sure yet how many of those are actually interested in the bridge or just want to get in on the construction project."

One reason for the bridge's razing stems from a report prepared by the port in conjunction with the U.S. Coast Guard. The report concludes that the bridge doesn't meet seismic safety codes and that it would cost more to rehabilitate it than to build a new span.

When built in 1924, the structure was named the Badger Avenue Bridge for the street it traversed. When Henry Ford opened his Long Beach Assembly Plant in 1929, both the street and the bridge were renamed in his honor. However, the railroad which used the bridge has never called it anything except the Badger Bridge (or BAB), and its logs still list it that way. Railroad employee and reader David L. Higgins, San Pedro, Calif., who supplied the above information, is unsure whether the replacement bridge will be named Badger or Henry Ford.

At the time of its construction, the bridge was the only land link to Terminal Island. Subsequently, four additional spans were built to the island. Only the Ford bridge serves a railroad.

"I've worked here as a bridge tender for six years," Higgins says, "and have gotten quite attached to this working antique. It is still operated by the controls installed in 1924."

The Long Beach Assembly Plant, in operation until the late 1950s, was razed several years ago.

Site of Ford's former Long Beach (Calif.) Assembly Plant, once below sea level, now filled in with gravel and sand. To the right of the fill is Henry Ford Avenue and the twin-towered Henry Ford Avenue Drawbridge. (Photo by Robert C. Drew, Ontario, Calif.)

Long Beach Plant

The following commentary on Ford's former Long Beach (Calif.) Assembly Plant was forwarded by reader Robert C. Drew, Ontario, Calif.

"Adjacent to the Cerritos Channel, located in the oceanside city of Long Beach," Drew writes, "there is a vast, empty field. This is the former site of Henry Ford's Long Beach Assembly Plant.

"Thousands of wild sunflowers grow where thousands of Ford cars were once assembled. Huge trucks are busily dumping hundreds of tons of gravel and sand, trying to raise the plant site above sea level." The site sank, Drew points out, because underground oil was pumped out by rigs located immediately east of the property. A 17-foot sea wall was built to keep the Pacific Ocean at bay, but the three-decade-old factory was abandoned in the late 1950s in favor of a new assembly plant 30 miles inland at Pico Rivera.

The plant site, Drew adds, is now owned by the City of Long Beach. A valuable parcel, it has immediate access to Long Beach and Los Angeles harbors via the Cerritos Channel and to the L.A. freeway system via the new Terminal Island freeway.

Plans for the site may include construction of a large off-loading dock for ships carrying imported vehicles. The 50-foot channel permits deep-draft vessels to tie up at the very foot of the property.

Henry Ford insisted that all of his plants be at water's edge. One of his better ideas – except when also at the edge of an oil field.

Los Angeles Plant

Craig Edmonds, Saugus, Calif., while restoring a Model A, sought to learn where his car had been built and became "interested in Ford factories in general." His research led him to L.A.'s downtown plant which now houses Imperial Toy, an importing company. The building previously had also served as the main merchandising distribution center for Bullock's Department Stores, now Macy's.

The pre-World War I plant is located at 2060 East Seventh Street at Santa Fe Avenue. (Photo courtesy Craig Edmonds.)

Mahwah Plant

Few auto factories the size of Ford's sprawling Mahwah (N.J.) Assembly Plant have been obliterated within 35 years of opening. But the Mahwah facility, like Hannibal's Carthage, has been razed to the ground except for a small, soon-to-be-destroyed ex-paint shed.

There is a difference between Carthage and Mahwah, however. The former's site was sown with salt by the conquering Romans, so that nothing could grow there in the future. Mahwah's plant site now is occupied by a Sheraton hotel and a Japanese-owned Sharp factory.

Mahwah deserved to be razed. Of all of Ford's domestic assembly facilities, the Jersey plant was the poorest in terms of labor/management relations and vehicle quality.

San Antonio Site

"Enclosed is a picture of the building that occupies the address of the old San Antonio Ford Plant," writes reader Craig Edmonds, Los Angeles, Calif.

"My sister knew of a coworker who would be going to San Antonio on a business trip," Edmonds continues, "and she asked him to take a picture of whatever was on the Ford plant site. I have no idea if this is the original building since I don't have an era picture, but this is the right address (really doesn't look like any of the other plants). According to the man who took the picture, this is not in the greatest of areas, much like the area around the old Los Angeles Plant."

Craig is right. The building with the Aztec Theater sign is not Ford's former 221 W. Commerce Street, San Antonio wholesale branch, nor does it look like any of the company's other teens-built assembly branch plants.

Faced with factory overcapacity in 1980, Ford weighed the closing of Mahwah and the 56-year-old Norfolk, Va. assembly plant, the latter having a reputation for high quality work. The newer plant went down, sending a strong signal throughout the Ford organization that quality and harmony counted in closure decisions.

Omaha Plant for Sale

Ford's former Omaha Assembly Plant is vacant and for sale.

Ford produced Model Ts, Model As, and V-8s in the building from 1916 until 1933, then used the structure as a parts depot until the mid-1950s. The building was first sold to Western Electric, then, in 1959, to Faberges Tip Top Division, a maker of hair care accessories. Tip Top abandoned the plant in 1986.

The building, at 16th and Cummings streets, remains in good condition, and reader Jeff Caplan, of Omaha, is among the preservationists hoping to save it.

Wayne Tours

After a lapse of a decade, Ford once again is offering a plant tour – of its Wayne (Mich.) Assembly Plant.

But don't expect to walk in unannounced, or to tour the plant any day of the week. Visitors must have advanced reservations, and can come only on Thursdays.

Ford discontinued plant tours in 1980 because of cost-cutting requirements. Prior to that year, more than 200,000 visitors annually toured Dearborn's massive Rouge Plant. Today, the downsized Rouge is scarcely visitable. Steel operations, once the heart of the complex, have been sold to Marico Acquisitions Co. The 74-year-old Dearborn Assembly Plant, which continues to build Mustangs, is hardly a company showplace.

Ford is resuming tours because of the "tremendous pent-up public demand to see our plants," according to spokesman Dave Caplan. "We get a lot of calls from Detroiters with out-of-town guests who want to see an auto plant."

The Wayne Plant, which assembles 73 Escorts hourly, is one of Ford's most modern facilities. Tours start at the factory's new stamping plant, then move into the assembly facility. Guides are plant retirees, who explain the generalities of stamping, engine installation, painting, trim work, and final assembly. Visitors even walk past the rework area, where employees repair the assembly line mistakes that aren't supposed to occur. At the end of the line, they sometimes see competitors' cars draped with a sign, "let's take a look at our competitors."

Those who wish to tour Wayne Assembly can call 734-467-0452 from 8 a.m. to 4 p.m. Visitors must be at least 10 years old.

Tours also are offered by Cadillac's Detroit-Hamtramck Plant (313-972-6000) and by Flint's Buick City (810-236-4494). Cadillac tours take place Tuesdays, Wednesdays, and Thursdays, and Buick tours are offered on Tuesdays and Thursdays. Advance reservations are required by both plants.

Green Island Closes

Green Island, one of Ford's oldest plants, ceased production in November 1988. The factory began making Model T radiators in 1923, and continued to build copper/brass radiators and heater cores until the end. Ford's switch to aluminum radiators and cores contributed to the factory's demise.

"I have to relate the closing to a person who has cancer," said James Roti, president of UAW Local 930. "You have that hope that you're going to be cured, and finally you realize there's not hope. It's all gone."

Ford told workers in early 1986 that it planned to close the plant, and offered transfers to Plymouth, Mich. Union members fought hard to keep the plant open, even going so far as to distribute leaflets to shareholders at the company's annual meeting in Detroit in 1986. They hoped for a new Ford product, for a new owner, or an employee-owned factory, then set their minds on protecting as best they could those who inevitably would be left jobless. Still, said Dennis Bourdeau, 46, a 22-year plant veteran, "everybody was hoping until the last minute."

Henry Ford laid the plant's cornerstone in August, 1919, in the presence of his camping friends,

A postcard view of Ford's former radiator plant at Green Island on the Hudson River. The only clue as to the year of card's issuance is that its reverse side calls for a one-cent stamp.

Thomas A. Edison, Harvey Firestone, and naturalist John Burroughs. The factory was an exemplar of Ford's belief in hydropower, having generated part of its electricity needs from the flow of the Hudson River.

Green Island Site

Ford's former Green Island, N.Y. plant, which made radiators from 1923-89, may become a tire recycling facility.

Still owned by Ford, the factory was put on the market in October 1996. A local developer is negotiating with Ford to purchase the 44-acre property, according to Sean Ward, executive assistant to Mayor John J. McNulty.

The hydroelectric facility, at 75 Tibbits Avenue, at its peak in the 1970s employed 1,500 persons. Since abandonment, the building has been well maintained.

Ford visited the Hudson River site, adjacent to a government-built dam, while on a camping trip with Thomas Edison, Harvey Firestone, and John Burroughs in 1919.

Thanks to reader William Borntraeger, Scotia, N.Y., for forwarding a *Schenectady Gazette* story on the plant.

Ford in Hamilton

"You've shown pictures of a number of Ford street signs in your column," writes reader Neil Raeder, of Parkersburg, W.Va. "I saw another one when visiting Hamilton, Ohio. It's near an old plant. Was it originally a Ford plant?"

Yes. Henry Ford bought a Miami River hydropower site for the Hamilton Plant in 1919, and in the 1920s it employed a work force of 1,500 and made 14,000 steering wheels daily. After producing parts for Ford-built aircraft engines and B-24 bombers during world War II, the plant was sold to Bendix Corporation in 1951, and has had a number of owners since. When last I visited the factory in 1979, the City of Hamilton owned and operated the plant's hydroelectric facility, and it was producing power for the municipal power gird.

Ford Tire Plant

In 1942 Ford shipped its Rouge Tire Plant to the Soviet Union under World War II lend-lease provisions. This column's report that "No American ever saw the equipment after it was unloaded" prompted the following response from reader Mel Chase, Newark, Del.:

"A gentleman who worked for the Farrel Company (makers of Banbury mixers which compounded natural rubber and other ingredients into useable stock) told me that he had seen tire plants in Russia during the 1970s which looked markedly similar to the Ford design! He also reported that there are records which indicate that some of the plant equipment was lost in the North Sea when a ship was torpedoed by the Germans."

The plant produced almost 8 million tires bearing the Ford label between January 1938 and its dismantlement between September 1942 and June 1943.

Village Industry Tour

After touring Henry Ford's Southeastern Michigan rural hydroelectric plants on Oct. 29, 1994, reader Andy LaBorde, Milwaukee, Wis., forwarded the following comments on the mills:

"My first observation," he noted, "is why aren't there more historical plaques, or at least small ID signs, at most of these sites? I know the State of Michigan has printed a brochure that is very helpful, but 'This is it' signs sure would help."

"Our first stop," LaBorde continues, "found one of the generators at the Rawsonville Plant undergoing repairs, but the other one was humming along. The Saline Plant was overrun with a large wedding reception, and its Raisin River Café was not open, but I did notice that it has a 'Henry Ford Room.'

"The Manchester Plant is owned by a Milwaukee company, Johnson Controls. A look through the smoked glass windows revealed a fancy reception area complete with shiny turbine heads among the potted plants. The Sharon Hollow Plant is now a winery. Its generator is on display and in use during winter months.

"After a little wine tasting at Sharon Hollow, we still managed to find the Brooklyn Plant. The state brochure mentions something about it being made into a 'museum of power.' If that's the case, they have a long way to go! There were various electrical generating do-dads scattered about inside, but nothing that resembled a museum. It is also currently being used as a food pantry. (The Brooklyn Plant, owned by Lee Koepke since 1989, houses Model Ts and antique engines awaiting restoration. As part of his projected "museum of power" Koepke hopes to restore the mill's hydroelectric equipment.)

"As advertised," LaBorde adds, "the Tecumseh and Dundee plants are recycled community centers. Unfortunately both were closed on the day of our visit. It's nice to see that Milan has done a first-class job of converting the old Ford mill into its city hall.

"We had our most rewarding experience in Macon. At first we were going to skip the village because it was getting late. I'm glad we didn't. After first getting instructions to the Dynamic Kernels Mill at the Macon General Store, we had no trouble locating it. What a great location!

"The door to the glassed-in engine room was open, but no one was around. We soon met Joe O'Neil, co-owner of this treasure. He gave us the 50-cent tour, as well as some history on the mill. Your name came up almost immediately by the way. O'Neil seems committed to restoring the mill single-handedly. I got a quick look inside his nearby house (built by Henry Ford). It looks like it has been expertly restored. He referred to it as his 'cottage.'

"O'Neil has purchased an almost exact copy of Dynamic Kernels' original steam engine from Tom Monaghan, owner of Domino's Pizza. The engine once was on display at the Henry Ford

Museum. Inside the mill, the workmanship appears to be first-class including the shiny woodwork in the milling and grinding areas.

"The best part was when he spun the wheel for us. Squeaking was followed by the sound of rushing water bubbling into the holding chamber. Mr. O'Neil has added two small spotlights below the wheel for added effect after dark."

Noting that most of the mills have smokestacks, LaBorde wondered if they once made use of auxiliary steam engines similar to that at the Dynamic Kernels mill. The answer is "yes," and so did the powerhouse at Henry Ford's Dearborn estate, Fair Lane. In fact, Henry Ford ran a running battle with mill managers, the magnate insisting on relying exclusively on water power, the managers remonstrating that droughts hampered production. Through the years the bulky boilers and other steam equipment have disappeared from most of the mills.

Village Industries

Henry Ford's "village industries" – small hydropower plants built in Southeastern Michigan and elsewhere – have fascinated people for decades. They are summed as follows in Prof. Howard P. Segal's scholarly essay, " 'Little Plants in the Country': Henry Ford's Village Industries and the Beginning of Decentralized Technology in Modern America," appearing in *Prospects: The Annual of American Culture Studies*, edited by Jack Salzman.

"The village industries are not simply historic relics ... Nor are they merely futile efforts to 'freeze' history, flights from reality having no relevance to Ford's time, much less to ours.

"On the contrary, these nineteen experiments ought properly be seen and appreciated as 20th-Century versions of the 'machine in the garden' seeking new but still necessary balances between the all too common anti- and protechnological extremes. Certainly Ford's repeated emphasis on uniting agriculture and industry through this and related schemes suggests that same search for a balance in modern America.

"Moreover, along with other projects of his later life – from his educational programs to his agricultural experiments to his industrial and world's fair exhibits to his Dearborn collections and institutions – they provided a vision of a new social order in America. Far from just looking backward, as is usually assumed, Ford was also looking ahead – and with less guilt over what the automobile and mass production had done to agrarian values than is usually assumed.

"As Ford often remarked, the farther people could look back, the farther they could then look ahead. Technology had admittedly created problems, but it had also solved many problems and, Ford believed, would continue to do so. And as Ford ... had put it in [his book] *Today and Tomorrow*, "We have both lost and gained in the movement of modern industry. Our gains are many times greater than our losses; we can keep all of the gains and repair some of the losses.

" ... Ford's orientation thus gradually shifted from that of a mechanical engineer to that of a social engineer. His concern was no longer the automobile or even mass production, but the whole of American society – and its future as much as its past – in regard to decentralized technology, as he conceived and implemented it in his village industries. It is surely tempting to conclude that Henry Ford indeed had a better idea."

Brooklyn Plant

Henry Ford's small Brooklyn, Mich., hydropower plant has been abandoned, and is for sale.

Ford opened the plant in 1939, and it made horns, starters, switches, and other auto parts until 1967. Jackson Gear Co. had been the facility's most

Down by the Old Millstream

Ford's Brooklyn (Mich.) Plant as it looked when new a half-century ago. The dam is at right, the powerhouse beneath the stack, the tailrace at lower center. Ford provided picture windows for his powerhouses so that visitors could look into them. (Photo from the Collections of the Henry Ford Museum and Greenfield Village.)

recent occupant. But, Jackson's business fell upon hard times in the early 1980s, and the plant limped along a few years, then closed.

Water continues to flow over the Ford-built dam, and the plant remains in a sylvan setting alongside an attractive, compact millpond. But, the window in the plant's front door was broken the last time reader John Harrison of Brooklyn drove by, and there as evidence of picnicking in the entrance hall. Eight of the plant's picturesque lampposts still stand, although only two still have lamps and one leans badly. One can only hope that a buyer can soon be found, and will satisfactorily maintain the plant and premises.

Dundee Hydro Plant

"I used to live near Dundee, Mich.," writes reader Clyde Haase, of Davis, Calif. "Whatever has happened to the water power plant Henry Ford had there?"

The 19th century Greek Revival mill, which Ford restored in 1935-36, made copper welding points for the Ford Company until 1954, when it was sold to Wolverine Fabricating and Manufacturing Co. Wolverine operated the plant until 1970, then gave it to the village of Dundee for $1. Since then the River Raisin structure has housed village offices, a community center, and a museum which focuses on Dundee history.

Cherry Hill Plant

The last, most unique, and least publicized of Henry Ford's village industries – a small plant at Cherry Hill in Canton Township of Michigan's Wayne County (which also includes Detroit) – sits empty as it awaits new tenants in an idyllic rural setting.

Prospective buyers occasionally look at the 6,293-square-foot cinder block

Ford's former Dundee, Mich. River Raisin Plant and dam. A tree trunk rested atop the dam when this photo was taken in the 1950s. (Photo from Henry Ford Museum and Greenfield Village.)

plant and an adjacent 3,100-square-foot building, but back away upon learning that the site lacks water and sewer lines.

Forty years ago the scene was quite different, as noted in an article in the *Canton Township Sesquicentennial Time Capsule Edition*. The article, by township resident and Eastern Michigan University student John Tobin, is the first we've seen on the facility.

In 1944-45, writes Tobin, Ford's freshly-scrubbed Cherry Hill Plant was producing door locks, machined brass radiator petcocks, and ignition components. Most of its approximately 30 employees, were disabled veterans of World War II.

Most of the vets were recruited from Veterans Administration hospitals, especially one in Battle Creek, Mich. Some had empty sleeves pinned to shoulders, others peered through heavy lenses at their machines; still others, some former prisoners of war, battled mental problems.

Henry Ford, who repeatedly demonstrated an affection for veterans, bought the plant in 1943 from Wilson Dairy, along with 175 acres of adjacent farmland. The plant occupied 14-1/2 acres. Ford's total investment, as of 1946, was $266,522, of which $111,187 was in buildings, $27,432 in land, $62,405 in land improvements, and $30,418 in power equipment.

Ford, who usually publicized his activities to the hilt, downplayed his Cherry Hill operations. The vets were to be rehabilitated sans limelight. Consequently, even Cherry Hill residents knew little about the automaker's experiment.

Ford took special pride in the facility, occasionally visiting it with his grandsons and company officials. The automaker and his entourage ate with employees from six large picnic tables in the dorm's Spartan dining room.

The plant was closed about October 1945, following Henry Ford's retirement. Other village industries were abandoned shortly thereafter as young Henry Ford II began to spin-off his grandfather's money-losing ventures.

Over the years, the Cherry Hill facility changed hands several times, being owned successively by Extruded Hinge, Young Spring and Wire, Lus-Trus, and since 1969 by the William E. Hennels Co. Hennels made air and hydraulic equipment in the factory until 1980. Although the property's fate is uncertain, Canton Township and the Canton Historical Society hope to

The last of Henry Ford's village industries, Cherry Hill, awaiting new tenants.

incorporate it into a historic district.

Ford characteristically concerned himself with Cherry Hill's school as well as manufacturing. As the story goes, the automaker, in 1943, while driving through Cherry Hill, came upon a woman and her 10 children by the side of a road. Stopping to see if he could be of assistance, he learned that the woman's husband was out of work and the family was homeless. Taking charge, Ford gave the husband a job in his factory and housed the family on his newly-acquired nearby farm. While seeking to enroll the children in Cherry Hill's one-room schoolhouse, he learned that his farm was not within the school district.

Undissuaded, Ford told the school board he'd renovate and expand its 68-year-old schoolhouse and pay the salary of a second teacher if the board would allow the 10 children to enroll. The offer was accepted, and Ford paid for a $22,000 addition, hired another teacher, and arranged for his Greenfield Village art, dance, music, and carpentry teachers to tutor Cherry Hill students. He also donated looms and sewing machines to the Cherry Hill School, and saw to it that students were given free medical and dental treatment at Detroit's Henry Ford Hospital. The school, like the factory, was cast adrift by the Ford Company after the founder's death. Its building still stands, however, and serves as a storage area for the Plymouth School District, to which it was annexed in 1955.

Flat Rock Plant

Architect Albert Kahn's original drawing for Henry Ford's Flat Rock (Mich.) Plant was found last year by the present owner, Flat Rock Metal, Inc., and now hangs in the firm's conference room.

"It's nice to display a little part of our company's history," says Michael Shields, a company executive and a student in my evening class, "The Global Automotive Industry."

Built in 1923, the plant for years made most of the Ford Company's horn buttons and head, rear, deck, and dome lamps. It was sold in 1950 to Flat Rock's Moynahan Bronze Co.

Henry Ford's Flat Rock, Mich. Plant initially was served by his Detroit, Toledo & Ironton Railroad and owned by the Grand Trunk when this photo was taken by the author in August 1979. On the other side of the hydropowered factory runs the Huron River.

Macon Buildings

"I have read that Henry Ford operated a high school in the village of Macon, Mich.," writes reader Carleton Philips, of Howe, Ind. "Is the school still there? If so, I'd like to see it on my next visit to Michigan."

The high school's two buildings still stand. Owned since the 1950s by the Archdiocese of Detroit, they have been used as dormitories by the brothers assigned to operate a juvenile rehabilitation program on the premises. Other buildings dating to Ford's day include Ford's former sawmill and powerhouse. The high school once served Lenawee County students for miles around. Many new buildings have been erected since the archdiocese began receiving state money to operate its rehabilitation program.

Macon High School

Manchester Plant

A small ex-hydroelectric plant built and operated by Henry Ford in Manchester, Mich., recently changed hands. The home of the Marketing and Technical Services Center of Hoover Universal Plastics Machinery Division after 1982, the building now provides quarters for Johnson Controls Plastic Technology Group.

While one of Henry Ford's "village industries" between 1941-57, the plant made instrument clusters. It now makes plastic soft drink bottles and injection and blow-molding components and assemblies.

The factory remains in an attractive setting on the east side of Manchester. A Ford-built dam and pond are nearby, and the River Raisin's tailrace romps alongside.

Manchester Plant

Old Plant, New Use

The owners of Henry Ford's former hydropowered Saline, Mich., soybean processing plant, Carl and Micki Weller, and their daughter, Wendy. The Wellers live on the Saline plant's top floor and operate an antique store on the first and second floors. Wendy manages a ground-floor café. This photo was taken on the terrace of the Henry Ford Estate-Fair Lane in Dearborn, Mich., where the Wellers were attending a meeting of the Henry Ford Heritage Assn.

Ford's Waterford Plant as it appeared in the mid-1930s. This photo shows the rear of the plant and the tailrace. (Photo from the Collections of the Henry Ford Museum and Greenfield Village.)

Waterford Plant

Waterford Pond, created by a Michigan dam bought by Henry Ford in 1924, recently was drained overnight, leaving approximately 300 fish stranded and dead in a nearby picnic area. Workers found a hole at the base of the dam, for which repairs had been planned for some time.

Ford's Waterford Plant, located near Northville, was one of six company-owned hydropowered factories on the River Rouge. Waterford's 82 employees built gauges for Ford vehicles until the 1950s.

The property now is owned by Jonna Companies, of Farmington Hills, Mich., a commercial construction and property management group.

Ford Rotunda

"I continue to enjoy your 'Ford Country' column," writes Jim Edison, of Indianapolis, "and also continue to marvel at your endless knowledge about Henry Ford, the Ford family, and the Ford Motor Company (I continue to marvel at how much I don't know). I sincerely hope that *Cars & Parts* will publish another collection of 'Ford Country' articles so that we 'Ford nuts' can have it all handy in one volume."

Edison enclosed a nostalgic article published in the November/December 1994 issue of *Reminisce* by Ed Kerr, of Dearborn Heights, Mich., entitled "I Grew Up with the Ford Rotunda."

Kerr was reared a quarter-mile from the Rotunda, built in 1934 for

The Ford Rotunda as it looked in its post-World War II heyday. (Photo courtesy Henry Ford Museum and Greenfield Village, Dearborn, Mich.)

Chicago's A Century of Progress Exposition, then removed to Dearborn to serve as the "Gateway to the Rouge."

"Every summer day in 1935," the author recalls, "I took a bike ride to the construction site. The structure rose 110 feet and looked like a giant birthday cake. The center was originally open to the elements but was later enclosed with a dome. The landscaping was breathtaking for a kid raised on a 40-foot lot in Dearborn. Expansive lawns, huge trees, flowering shrubs, and fern-edged waterfalls made the site exquisite.

"Behind the building were 21 'Roads of the World,' duplicates of roads in other countries. Visitors were driven over these roads and through the lush gardens in the latest model cars. After sunset, the three rings on top of the Rotunda were floodlighted, each with a different color. Every eight seconds, the color on each ring changed. From my front porch, this was a beautiful sight year-round.

"The Rotunda was air-conditioned, a luxury in those days, Inside the building were mural-lined walls and, of course, the latest Fords, Lincolns, and Mercurys. In the center stood a 45-foot diameter rotating globe of the world.

"One wing contained ... a comfortable modern movie theater and stage ... During the day films were shown continuously - industrial newsreels, cartoons, and fabulous travel adventures. As a frequent visitor, I learned more about industry, geography, and current events than I did in grade school.

"The Rotunda was open to all at no cost, even to kids like me in shorts and dirty tennis shoes ... as long as we behaved. The only time I was reprimanded was when I hooked up the battery cable on a Lincoln so I could sit inside and listen to the radio.

"Tours of the nearby Rouge Plant, the biggest industrial complex in the world at that time, left from the Rotunda every hour. The tour included the steel mill, glass plant, and engine building, always ending at the final

The Rotunda being consumed by fire in 1962. Only the north wing (bottom center), housing the Ford Archives, was spared from the flames. (Photo courtesy Henry Ford Museum and Greenfield Village, Dearborn, Mich.)

assembly line, which to me was the most interesting.

"The Rotunda closed during World War II and was used as an office for Ford war production. But after the war, the Rotunda reopened in all its glory, and the popular annual Christmas show was held once again. By the '50s I was married and introduced my own children to the wonders I'd known as a child. They still talk about it.

"But it was the Christmas decorations and the added roof that led to the Rotunda's demise. On November 9, 1962, roofers were repairing the roofing deck when somehow their hot tar kettles ignited the cork insulation. The flames spread to the combustible Christmas decorations being unpacked for the approaching holiday season. In only 45 minutes, the historic showplace was reduced to a heap of ashes (the north wing, housing the Ford Archives, was spared thanks to a firewall).

"The next day I walked through the rubble in disbelief, overwhelmed by the memories of my happy childhood hours there, and of my wife's and children's visits to Santa. The Rotunda was never rebuilt, but to us it will always be the most beautiful building in the world."

I share Kerr's fond memories of the Rotunda, having worked in it as a member of Ford's News Department in 1952-53 and having researched my doctoral dissertation in the archives in 1957-58. Among many memories associated with the Rotunda are the rededication of the building on June 16, 1943 (the company's fiftieth anniversary), at which newscaster Lowell Thomas spoke; press conferences were conducted in the theater by Henry Ford II and Executive Vice President Ernest R. Breech; and the 1955 Thunderbird was unveiled by HFII's brother, William Clay Ford.

Today, the Rotunda site is covered by grass, and only a small opening into the tunnel (now closed) that runs beneath Schaefer Road between the site and the Administration Building hints that an exceedingly handsome edifice once stood there.

The Model A, not the Fairmont, gets your commentator's vote as first-year sales champion. Posing with this 1928 model are Hollywood's reigning couple, Douglas Fairbanks and Mary Pickford, among the A's early purchasers.

A copy of the Ford Motor Co. stock certificate issued to Henry Ford on June 26, 1903. The 39-year-old Ford was awarded 155 shares – amounting to 25.5 percent of the total – in return for his engine and engineering know-how.

First Year Sales Champs

Remarkably, five of the six cars which have set U.S. first-year sales records are Fords.

The all-time first-year sales record goes to the '78 Ford Fairmont, with 422,690 deliveries. Runner-up is the '65 Mustang with 418,812 unit sales; followed by the '60 Falcon, 417,174; '80 Citation (including some Novas), 398,000; '70 Maverick, 340,809; and '62 Fairlane, 335,441. These figures are provided by the Motor Vehicle Manufacturers Assn.

Personally, I'd rate the 1928 Ford Model A as the first-year sales champion. It went on sale in December, 1927, and although only 125-140 units were being produced daily by year's end, 778,572 vehicles were manufactured (and close to that number sold) in 1928. Assuredly, first-year sales of the Model A far exceeded those of the Fairmont, Mustang, etc.

Overseas Sales

"Has there been a year in which Ford has sold fewer cars in the U.S. than overseas?" inquires reader Leo Ross, Wichita, Kan.

Yes, in 1981, when the company sold 1.54 million cars domestically, 1.71 million in foreign countries. That year U.S. sales were depressed, while Ford of Europe was flying high.

Something Funny Here

"I am an 87-year-old widow. I've had 280 shares of Ford Motor Co. stock since 1917." Helen Greenwood, Riva, Md., recently wrote *USA Today*. "I've heard the Ford family is selling their shares. Should I sell my shares or hold onto them and wait for a big dividend?"

The owner of Ford stock since 1917? Not likely, as reader Gary Custer, Harrisonburg, Va., points out. At that time the Ford Co. had only a handful of shareholders – Henry Ford with 58.5 percent, plus James Couzens and his sister, Rosetta Hauss, John and Horace Dodge, Horace H. Rackham, John W. Anderson, and the heirs to the John S. Gray estate. "Either this story has a typographical error," says Custer, "or this lady was flimflammed."

III

FORD PRODUCTS

Ford has produced more than a quarter-billion vehicles. Its most notable product remains the Model T, regarded by many as the Car of the Century. The Tin Lizzie, along with the Beetle, is the most fondly remembered old car, and, with the Bug, Jeep, and Edsel, the most publicized.

For decades it was thought that the Model T would be the best-selling car of all time. But its record has been eclipsed by the Beetle, VW's Golf, Toyota's Corolla, and Ford's F-Series pickup. Ford would add the Escort to this list, but I do not inasmuch as its European and American versions have nothing in common except their names and size.

The Model T should long retain its place in Ford's sales lineup inasmuch as its sibling rivals are either out of production or fall far short of the flivver's output. The fourth-ranked nameplate is the Galaxie, followed by the Fiesta, Mustang, Fairlane, Econoline, Model A, and Thunderbird.

The Model A perhaps is Ford's second most distinguished nameplate, if only because it outsold all of GM's cars combined in 1929 and 1930, the last years the company was No. 1. The Model A still holds the record for first-year Ford sales, although Ford in turn has so credited Falcon, Mustang, and Fairmont.

Ford's most important vehicles include the V-8, Thunderbird, Mustang, F-Series, Explorer, and Taurus, although they has been less profitable than many think, while Lincoln Town Car and Expedition/Navigator have been huge moneymakers. The company's most notorious vehicle is the Edsel, although the Italian-made Pantera is the worst car it has ever sold.

Winners or losers, old Ford products are cherished by their owners. Many of the following stories suggest why.

Redesigned Fords

I asked Ford how many "completely redesigned" cars have been produced by the company.

My interest in the subject was piqued by a *Newsweek* story stating that the Taurus/Sable represented "only the third complete redesign of the standard North American sedan in Ford's history." A response came from C.M. Gumushian, assistant manager, Advanced Product and Technology Department.

"What's needed here," Gumushian says, "is a clear definition of what is meant by a 'complete redesign' of a vehicle. The Model T was all new in its time; the 1928 Model A also was all-new. In addition to the first Ford V-8 (221 cubic inches), the new 1932 model also offered the four-cylinder engine carried over from the Model T and A. Does this, then, make the Model A and '32 model all-new cars if they shared a powerplant with another vehicle?

"On the other hand, the 1949 Ford was truly an all-new car because there was no interchangeability of components with other vehicles that preceded it (except for some fasteners). The same is true for Taurus and Sable – these are all-new vehicles from the tires on up. There is nothing in these cars that is shared with any other passenger car Ford presently builds. In fact, the fasteners are all unique – they are all metric. The entire vehicle is metric.

"The 1932 V-8 was the first V-8 engine in Ford's history. The displacement of that engine was 221 cubic inches. Are you aware that 30 years later when we introduced the 1962 Fairlane, the vehicle was offered with an optional V-8 engine whose displacement also was 221 cubic inches? That's 30 years of progress for you. Of course, it was a more sophisticated powerplant. Even though the displacement was the same, power output and torque were appreciably higher.

" ... As I see it, there have been at least four all-new vehicles from Ford – in the North American scheme of things. I'm certain there will be those who will argue that the 1965 Ford was all-new. Here again, the definition is important. I maintain that the 289-cubic-inch V-8 engine was carried over from a previous year, along with chassis and suspension systems from earlier cars."

Detroit Museum's Wish List

In 1989, the Detroit Historical Department, which operates the Detroit Historical Museum, and the Detroit Section of the SAE compiled a wish list of "the 100 cars, trucks, and military and other vehicles most significant to the history of the Detroit area." The list includes 22 Ford-built vehicles and offered the following comments about each:

1909 Model T. Detroit Historical Department (DHD) owns a fine 1911. To emphasize changes, a later model, preferably closed (the first closed T was built in 1919) is desirable. DHD has a 1923 Touring. One of the Model T's forerunners, the S or the N, is also a good comparative vehicle.

1917 Fordson Model N Tractor. Ford's first successful mass-produced tractor.

1928 Model A. The highly successful successor to the Model T. Car should be closed and feature one of the colorful paint schemes available. Alternative: A station wagon would also be desirable, since Ford produced the first auto-manufacturer-built wagons.

1932 Ford V-8. Henry Ford's personal mechanical triumph, the low-cost V-8.

1932 Lincoln KB. Actually a pre-1932 Lincoln would also be nice, such as the 1928 that inspired the Model A, or a 1934 convertible sedan.

1936 Lincoln-Zephyr. A less expensive Depression-era Lincoln, the Zephyr was exquisitely styled and pioneered body construction.

1939 Mercury. Ford's successful midprice market debut. A club coupe would be most desirable.

1940 Lincoln Continental. What began as a custom model for Edsel Ford went into production on the basis of its beauty of design.

1949 Ford. The first really new body for Ford in years, and its first postwar design – highly successful if rather sloppily built. A six-cylinder would be a nice departure from the V-8 synonymous with Henry Ford.

1955 Continental Mark II. A beautiful would-have-been killed for economy reasons, the European-influenced design resisted the crass spread of chrome which was to culminate in the ugly cars of 1958.

1955 Thunderbird. The first Ford "sports car"; a timeless design.

1957 Ford Ranchero. The pickup evolved from the sedan into a different vehicle entirely. In 1957, Ford revived the truck-as-car idea. Others followed.

1957 Ford C-Series Truck. This cab-over engine design was Ford's first entry into the heavy-load/large-capacity market formerly left to specialty-truck companies.

1958 Edsel. The basic idea – broadening Ford's line to cover more of the midpriced market – blossomed with the wrong car at the wrong time with the wrong name. A legendary failure.

1960 Ford Falcon. The Big Three responded to the import threat with their first deviation from standard-sized cars. The Falcon was the first of the compacts, and was highly successful.

1961 Lincoln Continental. The '61 convertible brought back both the four-door convertible and a restraint to luxury car styling; it defined the marque's "look" for years. DHD has a 1964 sedan.

1961 Ford Econoline Van Truck. Ford's Falcon drivetrain successfully integrated into a design based on the Volkswagen microbus.

1964 Ford Mustang. The first sporty personal car was a success with virtually all market segments. The collection should have one with 289 V-8 and standard shift. Ads are important with this car, with their emphasis on a youthful market. DHD has the original 1963 styling prototype.

1966 Ford Bronco Truck. Ford's successful entry into the four-wheel-drive market resulted from its failure to secure a military contract for this vehicle. The Bronco marks the Big Three's invasion of this preserve of Jeep and International Harvester. An alternative would be a Ford pickup from this era. The "domestication" of the pickup made it the most popular vehicle style in the country by the early '80s. And, it remains so well into the '90s.

1971 Ford Pinto. This was the compact Ford should have introduced in 1960 – a true compact, although it was dubbed a subcompact. Introduced with European engine and transmission.

1986 Ford Taurus. A totally new car symbolizing the "Europeanization" of the American auto industry and the rise of the aero look. This front-wheel-drive sedan allowed Ford to outearn GM for the first time since 1924. DHD has a production prototype sedan, also ads in billboard and video format. A Mercury Sable station wagon would be desirable as well. The Sable design was the prototype, and the wagon is more distinctive than the sedan.

1988 Ford Probe. A car symbolizing the growing interconnections between Detroit and foreign companies: Incorporates a Mazda chassis, with a Ford-designed body, built at the Mazda plant in Flat Rock, Mich.

T, Lincoln Top-Rated

Two Ford-built cars, the Model T and 1932 Lincoln KB, are named among the 10 "Greatest American Cars" by Brock Yates in the February-March, 1986 issue of *American Heritage*.

Yates, author of *The Decline and Fall of the American Automobile Industry*, acknowledges that there "is often little relationship between quality and commercial appeal, although no 'best' list of American cars ... could possibly omit the Ford Model T. Its artistry lay in the rudiments of its purpose, in its stark functionalism and its extraordinary social impact ... it is honored as the most popular American Model of all time."

"The legendary Tin Lizzie," continues Yates, "had only three significant modifications: the alteration of the radiator shell form brass to black-painted steel and the additions of electric lights and a self-starter. A few months before its demise ... Henry Ford permitted his pristine flivver to be decorated with wire wheels, balloon tires, and a few paint colors besides the legendary basic black.

"The Model T was more than an automobile," adds Yates, "it was an engine of social change, and its impact on the twentieth century far transcends its role as a simple device of four-wheel transportation. As the first major product of the moving assembly line and as the machine that triggered the mobility that still infuses this society, its place in history is assured ... Because of the convulsions this elemental little automobile worked on every stratum of society here and abroad, it can justifiably be argued that Henry Ford influenced the course of recent history as much as Lenin, Churchill, Roosevelt, Einstein, or Adolf Hitler.

"To be sure, Ford was in many ways a home-brew scientist, and as is often the case, he followed up a few good ideas with dozens of bad, silly, and downright outrageous ones. But his crowning achievement remains untouched. In trying to articulate the range and depth of his gawky, tinpot jalopy had on civilization, one is reminded of the words of the fine automotive writer and historian, the late Ken Purdy:

" 'The Ford Model T was as close to the expression of genius as any automobile has been, indeed one might say as close as any mechanical device has been. It expressed, with almost absolute purity, Ford's idea that the automobile should be a universal tool.' This it was, not only the narrow sense of its marvelous utility on the road but also in the broader context of levering an entire population off the farms and into a more complex, mobile, and urban way of life."

Lincoln's K series, Brock notes, was introduced in 1932, and its high point "was reached in 1932 with the KB, a giant V-12 built very much in the spirit of the multi-cylinder, smooth-running, exquisitely crafted behemoths of the day ... each Lincoln as shipped from the factory in a giant dust-free paper bag in railroad cars that had been swept and cleaned. As was the case with all the great cars of its ilk, the Depression hammered mercilessly at Lincoln sales, and as Cadillac did with its La Salle, the company was forced to take refuge in its cheaper Zephyr in order to survive. But survive it did, to carry on what has become the second-oldest luxury car make to prevail in the American market."

Yates also assesses engines, stating that the 1955 Chevrolet's 265-cubic-inch V-8 [and] the flathead Ford V-8, the Model T four-cylinder, the Volkswagen air-cooled four, the Ferrari V-12, and the Duesenberg eight [are] "the greatest – if not the very greatest – passenger-car powerplants ever built."

The non-Ford cars on Yates' list: the 1932 Model SJ Duesenberg, 1932 Stutz DV-32, 1933 Model 1247 Pierce-Arrow, 1930 Cadillac V-16, 1931 Marmon V-16, 1932 Packard 906 Twin Six V-12, 1937 Cord 812 and 1955 Chevrolet Bel Air.

World's Worst Cars

Three Ford-built products are among the 54 cars cited in the book, *Lemons: The World's Worst Cars*, by Timothy Jacobs.

In addition to the Edsel (1958-60), the Pinto (1970-76) and the Torino (1971-77) make the list. Somehow the 1971-74 Pantera escapes listing. General Motors has three entries – the early Corvair (1961-65), Vega, and its 1978-83 diesels; Chrysler also has three – the 1934-37 Airflow, the 1963

Ford had high hopes for the Pinto, comparing it at the time of its introduction to both the Model A and Model T. But the Pinto fell far short of its older brethren, and recently was cited as a lemon in a book on the world's worst cars.

Turbine, and 1977-80 Dodge Aspen. A couple of Japanese cars are listed: the pre-1971 Subaru and the 1973-75 Honda Civic.

Jacobs states that the Edsel had a "yawning beak of a grille that made the casual observer think of a nesting bird gaping wide for a worm ... also an eagle with its mouth open as it pursues its prey, or Basil Rathbone, as Sherlock Holmes, making a pronouncement between puffs on his pipe.

"Set far to either side of this grille were quad headlights in pairs that bulged upward and outward like the eyes of an infuriated corporate director, 'lording it' over the second, muted horizontal grillwork that ran under them in subservient complement to the gaping maw at the center. The fenders were incongruously squared off: this squareness was emulated by the bright chrome bumper, which underscored the design's stunning failure to mate the curve and the angle."

Jacobs goes on for several pages to enumerate the Edsel's other exterior and interior failures, mechanical ailments, troublesome gadgetry, and so on.

The Pinto is criticized for its "astonishingly puny automatic transmission, which produced a car that seemed to have the motive power of a wet sponge." The Pinto's "most dismal aspect," says Jacobs, "was its propensity to explode in a ball of flame when hit from behind. That even a moderate 'fender-bender' could result in death by fire is a numbing fact that hangs over the 1970-76 Pinto like the shadow of the Grim Reaper."

Jacobs criticizes "the Torino's body design which contributed to the pooling of water on surfaces, encouraging a pervasive rust problem. In fact, it had a reputation as a 'biodegradable car,' due to its tendency to rust rapidly and over large body areas – a tendency that was exacerbated by a paint job that was prone to peeling."

Other Torino woes, says the author, involved the brakes, transmission, carburetor, fuel line, power steering, suspension system, and the tendency of wheel bearings to wear out rapidly. Ironically adds Jacobs, Ford finally got the Torino right by 1977, then discontinued it.

Three Fords

Three Ford-built cars are among the 47 autos treated in Jeff Daniels's book, *The Anatomy of the Car*, which traces 100 years of automotive development from the Benz Tricycle to the 1988 Porsche.

The Fords are the Model T, the 1962 British Cortina, and the 1980 British Escort.

After enumerating the T's well-known technical advances, Daniels states that the Tin Lizzie, by remaining in production for 19 years, may "well have held back purely technical progress. In some of its aspects, such as its transmission, it was almost a technical blind alley. Its real significance in the wider world of motor car design was that it made other designers think more carefully about the needs of large-scale production; the need, above all, to avoid undue complexity and to ensure the interchangeability of parts."

The Consul Cortina, as the Cortina was first called, is said to have found "its place in any study of vehicle evolution because it introduced two concepts which have become increasingly important to all designers in the last 20 years ... it was finely tuned to the needs and desires of its target market; and it had a light and efficient structure."

The Cortina, according to Daniels, is "arguably the first car anywhere to be designed under the influence of market-research techniques ... In essence, the Ford research found that despite the fashionable trend towards front-drive and adventurous engineering, there remained a large potential market among buyers who preferred a conventional simple, easily understood and serviced car."

The British Escort, says the author, was Ford's second front-wheel-drive car, the first being the Fiesta, introduced in 1976. The Escort was an immediate success, becoming the company's bestseller in Britain and other European markets ... (and) it showed how the advantages of front-wheel-drive for smaller cars were too great to be ignored, and with its introduction only two of the world's car manufacturers, General Motors and Toyota, seemed still to need convincing of that."

Most of the cars cited in the book were designed in Europe, perhaps because Daniels, an Englishman and former Datsun (UK) and Citroën (UK) public relations officer, is more familiar with European cars than American- and Japanese-built vehicles.

Oldest Nameplates

Two Ford cars, the Thunderbird and the Lincoln Continental, are among the oldest nameplates in the U.S. auto industry, according to *Automotive News*.

The oldest nameplate – not make – is the Chrysler New Yorker, introduced in the 1938 model year. Second and third are the Oldsmobile 98 and Oldsmobile 88, launched for the 1941 and 1949 model years, respectively. Rounding out a list of the 10 oldest nameplates are Cadillac DeVille, 1949; Chevrolet Corvette, 1953, Cadillac Eldorado, 1953, Thunderbird, 1955; Continental, 1956; Pontiac Bonneville, 1958; and Buick LeSabre, 1959.

Four other Ford products also go back a quarter-century or more – Mustang, 1964; LTD, 1966; and Cougar and Marquis (now Grand Marquis), 1967.

Two of the oldest nameplates in the U.S. auto industry, the pre-World War II Lincoln Continental, at left, and the 1955 Thunderbird. (Photos from the Henry Ford Museum and Greenfield Village)

If anyone disagrees with this list, write John K. Teahen, senior editor of *Automotive News*, who seemingly researched the topic most thoroughly.

Quadricycle Success

Reacting to a *Modern Maturity* article which states that Henry Ford's first car, his 1896 quadricycle, was "not a success," reader Jack Kissling, Waretown, N.J., writes, "You really have to wonder where this guy [author T.C. Browne] researched his material when he states that the quadricycle was 'not a success.'

"To me," Kissling adds, "a car that gave several years of good service, survives 100 years, and served as the launch pad for one of the largest companies in the world is nothing short of a remarkable success."

Ford sold his quadricycle to Charles Ainsley, Detroit, in 1896. "I had built the car not to sell but to experiment with," he said later. "I wanted to start another car. Ainsley wanted to buy. I could use the money and we had no trouble in agreeing on a price."

The car, according to Allan Nevins' *Ford: The Times, the Man, the Company*, "gave extraordinarily good service to its third owner, A.W. Hall, a Detroit bicycle dealer, who wrote as follows to Henry Ford in April 1899.

" 'You will be surprised,' Hall reported, 'when I tell you that the little carriage is still doing its usual duty. I disposed of it this spring and the little rig was still in fair shape after all the banging around that it has had and I guess you know that was considerable; I ran it almost two years as you know and about the only trouble I had was that one tire and the spring on the sparkers working loose.' "

Hall added that he would like to be a repeat Ford customer. Henry was so pleased with the letter that he preserved it; and it was uncovered by archivists a half-century later.

Ford's Drive Historic

"It was 96 years ago this very week that Henry Ford made the first safe nighttime drive through the streets of Detroit, "Tonight Show" host Jay Leno recently told his audience.

"Actually," added Leno, "that was also the last safe nighttime drive through Detroit."

Ford Jokes

We've been favored with several Ford jokes passed on by nonagenarian Tom Stock, of Grosse Pointe Farms, Mich., who found them in a box in which he had saved letters and other papers ranging from 1912-1920. The jokes appeared in *Detroit Saturday Night*, a popular journal of the day, and here are a few of them.

"Every rose has its thorn. Henry Ford, with all his wealth, still feels impelled to ride in a car of his own make."

"The Rector: 'What would be your idea of the best way to spread the gospel to the uttermost part of the earth?' Fair and frivolous parishioner: 'How would it do to put a Bible in every Ford car?' "

"A man in a big Rolls-Royce saw a fellow motorist standing by the roadside looking helplessly into the branches of a tree. 'My car is up in the tree,' explained the helpless one. 'Up in the tree?' repeated the other, aghast. 'How the deuce did that happen?' 'Well,' was the reply, 'it is a Ford, and I was just winding it up when it sprang out of my hand.' "

Any Make So Long As ...

Edward Newson, of Hove, East Sussex, England, says he "bought a Model T in 1916 for 100 pounds and liked it so much I couldn't bear to change [makes]."

In July 1994 Newsom celebrated his 104th birthday by driving his Escort Ghia. In 79 years behind the wheel, he has been without accident.

Now What To Do?

Tom Maliskey didn't mean to build a 1925 Model T pickup in his New Baltimore, Mich. barbershop, but he did, and now he's wondering how to get it out.

Maliskey, who has operated his shop for 28 years, three years ago paid $75 for a pile of T parts, intending to assemble a pickup in the back of his place of business. But on a cold winter weekend he brought the front axle, and, inspired by customer interest in the project, kept adding to the vehicle until he got it built. Now he's not sure how he'll get the car out of his shop, as none of the building's doors or windows are big enough for an escape.

Maliskey's pickup assembly recently was described by local historian Walter Schwanbeck as the most spectacular feat in the history of the town, population 5,000. I've another candidate for that distinction, for it was on the cinder-covered ice of Lake St. Clair's Anchor Bay, which washes New Baltimore, that Henry Ford set a world's speed record for the mile (91.37 miles per hour) on January 12, 1904. After setting the record, Ford and his assistants ate a muskrat dinner at New Baltimore's Chesterfield Hotel.

Housemates

A 1920 Model T racer is one of four cars kept inside the house of Hugh Hawthorne, of Richmond, Va. Hawthorne's house is built on a hill so that cars can be driven in on two levels.

Hawthorne has a 1907 Ford Model N, eight Model Ts, several Edsels, and a Ford Skyliner. His first love is the Model T. "We're poor folks coming from the country," he says, "so I've always had a soft spot for the Model T. The first car I can remember was my father's T."

Thanks to reader Charles D. Edmonson, Hampton, Va., for forwarding a *Richmond Times-Dispatch* article on Hawthorne.

Model T Tale

"I am an avid reader of your 'Ford Country' column, and would like to share with your other readers memories of the Model T I owned as a

20-year-old in 1937," writes Leo L. Matthews, West Hartford, Conn.

"It was a 1927 model I bought for $15," Matthews recalls. "The seller filled the gas tank! This was a part of the last run of the T. It had battery ignition and wire wheels. To check out the battery I traced its cable to its hiding place under the backseat. To check the oil one still had to half crawl under the car to check the two spigots instead of a dipstick. Lubrication points were oil cups.

"Not being mechanically minded I didn't know what to check out for possible danger. Coming home from a date late at night suddenly the whole front end seemed to collapse. The wishbone went from the front axle to just under the transmission to a ball joint where it became detached and unsprung the front leaf spring. Getting out of the car I managed to twist the wheels enough to steer the car into an adjoining lot. I left the car there intending to return on Saturday in daylight to see what I could do.

"A couple of days later two men appeared at my door asking if I owned a Model T parked on their property. 'Yes' I replied, 'but I don't know how to fix it.' The upshot was they offered two dollars for it as is. I took them up on it as I was in a spot, signed the registration over to them, and pocketed the two dollars.

"This little tale ... has made a good one to tell over the years."

Nice Try, But ...

"At 14, I was driving a hand-me-down Model T three miles to school and to handle chores on the farm," writes reader Murvin H. Perry, Johnson City, Tenn. "The car had started life as a three-door touring car in 1925. It had worn a succession of bodies, being a tudor coach until the wood in the door frames rotted away, then a fordor sedan before being cut down for my use.

"The cutting down involved chopping off the windshield posts at the level of the lower half of the glass, and removing the top, doors, and backseat. The backseat was replaced by a wood bed, built in the fashion of a wagon box, which rested neatly between the rear fenders to make a pickup truck.

"On a bright spring day on the way to or from school, I don't remember which, I spotted a girl I wanted to impress. I pulled down the gas and accelerated for a maneuver I had seen daredevil drivers perform at the county fair – a high speed sliding corner.

"Yanking the wheel sharply to the left, I threw the car into a slide and poured on the throttle while correcting to maintain direction. I relished the way the old Ford responded. Gravel sprayed and dust flew. Relished it that is until I heard a strange flapping and saw several spectators laughing and pointing to a tire rolling down the road alongside me.

"My first thought was that one of the watchers had sent the tire rolling, but I wondered, who could roll a tire that fast. Then I realized the flapping sound was the inner tube on the right rear wheel. Held to the rim by its valve stem, it was flailing the fender as the wheel revolved.

"Air pressure in the old clincher tire had simply been insufficient to hold the casing on the rim. The slide had torn it from the wheel and let it roll to overtake me as the unprotected tube, punctured by gravel, flapped uselessly alongside the naked rim.

"The tire itself escaped damage, but it was a long way home on the rim. And I was a long time saving $3.25 to replace the ruined inner tube. As for the young lady, she took up with another guy who didn't even have a car."

Curator's Favorite

Of all the cars displayed in the Henry Ford Museum, which of them is the "curator's choice" – the curator being Leslie R. Henry, a retired head of the museum's Transportation Department.

"Without hesitation," Henry wrote in a recent edition of *Model T Times*, "I choose the bright red 1909 Model T Ford Touring as my favorite. More wistful than impressive in appearance and more prosaic than flashy in performance, it is still delightful to drive and easy to handle. Once started, its 20-hp engine will speed it along all day at 45 mph and will pull it up any paved hill in high gear.

"Of course, starting the car is always unpredictable," adds Henry. "Sometimes the engine will start on compression, as if magically, at the turn of the ignition switch. Other times, nothing short of backbreaking cranking will do the job – and then often only after the transmission is engaged and one rear wheel jacked up to eliminate the drag of cold oil in its multiple-disc clutch!"

Looking Backward

"As youngsters back in 1926," writes reader Whitman C. Daly, 83, Berkley, Mich., "my fiancée and I thought it would be cute to be married in Canada. So I drove my 1925 Model T Ford coupe on the Detroit River ferry on that cold Tuesday, and we were married in Windsor's Central United Church manse. We renewed our vows, 60 years later, at the church."

Daly recalls that the ferry ride cost 35 cents, 25 cents for the car, and a nickel per passenger. "Detroit was a beautiful and interesting city in the 1920s," he adds, "and so clean. All the automotive and industrial plants were within the city limits and most could be reached by streetcar, the fare being a nickel, plus one penny for a transfer to two additional car lines.

"One also could ride jitneys .... In the spring of 1923, Lincolns began appearing amongst the jitneys. Also, the Police Department began using Lincoln touring cars which were called cruisers and were driven by a policeman in uniform accompanied by two or three detectives in plain clothes. These Lincolns could outrun just about any automobile and during Prohibition they were the favorite cars of rumrunners, all of them being painted black."

A "Ford Man" Writes

"Ford Country" items have prompted readers to share recollections and Ford-related news since the column's inception in 1974. Representative of many such letters is one from Robert G. Heinfeld, of Ada, Ohio, as follows:

"I have always read with great interest your 'Ford Country' articles. I am a Ford man from my early days, having ridden in my father's Model Ts. We had two – one for work (he was a water well driller) and the other a Sunday driving car.

"When I read your article about Geeting Ford, of West Manchester, Ohio [founded in 1914; went out of business in 1992], the name just came right off-the-page to me, because I remember this agency. On one occasion, while traveling through West Manchester, our Model T broke down almost right in front of Geeting's. Memory eludes me as to what happened next, but at any rate we were able to go on to our home in New Bremen, Ohio.

"By a coincidence, just recently, while stopping by Benkin's auto memorabilia store in Tipp City, Ohio, I saw on the counter a sales pad from Geeting Ford. So I bought it immediately.

"I also have something to add to your information pertaining to one of the oldest Ford agencies. It concerns a Ford dealership which was opened here in Ada by Charles Cole in 1904. It is still a Ford agency. But what is more important it is still in the same building in which it started out in 1904. Years back, an addition was added to the building, but the original building still contains the Service Department.

"Another thing: While traveling through the Detroit area a few years back, I saw a restaurant sign with the blue Ford Script, but with the word "Food" inside. You had written about the restaurant [Henry's Place, now defunct] earlier in your column. Keep on writing the great articles on Ford folklore and the interesting tidbits. I enjoy them immensely."

Okay, Bob, I'll keep on writing, and, if readers like you keep supplying material, we'll all live happily ever after.

Fuel Efficient

Model Ts were capable of good mileage, as noted in a 1925 issue of *Ford Dealer and Owner*.

A Ford foreman, reports the publication, made 33 miles to the gallon when driving his family from Detroit to Indianapolis and return. An El Paso, Tex., Ford dealer racked up 29 mpg in a Texas endurance run which crossed the Continental Divide twice at an altitude of 8,400 feet.

In a 48-mile San Diego endurance run, 15 closed Fords averaged 30 mpg, the least economical getting 20 mpg, the most economical 47 mpg. In the open Ford class, the 46 T contestants averaged 29 mpg, the best of the lot getting 48 mpg. All of the cars were fitted with standard Ford gear ratios and stock equipment.

Thanks to reader C. Bud Wilson for forwarding the article.

Aspirin/Model T

Many products have been compared to or equated with the Model T. Among them is aspirin.

In a recent *Orlando Sentinel* article comparing aspirin with much higher-priced medicines, aspirin is said to be "a Model T that without any tinkering or modifications is still running with the Corvettes and Ferraris."

Model T Freshener

A "Model T Car Freshener" is being sold by Avon Products. About 3 inches long and a half-inch wide, the yellow freshener depicts the front and back of a Model T. The word "Avon" appears on the back, just below the spare tire.

The fragranced car pomander, as Avon calls the freshener, is made of "synthetic wax, paraffin, fragrance, ethylene/vinyl acetate, copolymer, color, benzophenone-12, and UV absorbers." It comes with a green cord, plus advice neither to hang the freshener over the rearview mirror nor to leave it in the car when the outside temperature exceeds 100 degrees.

The freshener smells good, as fresheners should. But in addition to a sweet-smelling fragrance, Avon perhaps should offer a black freshener with the genuine fragrance of a Model T. It wouldn't appeal to everyone, but Tin Lizzie owners should find it to their liking.

Model T's Peers

The Model T has long been acknowledged to have had "character," and a recent *New York Times* article on the Kodak Brownie camera offers confirmation. "Like Mickey Mouse, Charlie Chaplin, and the Tin Lizzie," reports the *Times*, "the Brownie became world famous, a kind of character."

The Model T and Brownie shared several characteristics, among them cheapness of price and ease of use. They also were contemporaries and long-lasting, the T having been produced from 1908-27, the Brownie from 1900 into the 1960s. The two products undoubtedly had many owners in common, the inexpensive Brownie and Tin Lizzie being a perfect match for budget-minded, picture-taking motorists of the era.

Model T of Computing

IBM's most successful and innovative product – the IBM Personal Computer – is referred to as "the Model T of computing" in Paul Carroll's book, *Big Blue: The Unmaking of IBM*.

Ironically, the PC put IBM on the path to ruin. The company had become rich by selling huge mainframe computers with profit margins of up to 70 percent. IBMers regarded PCs, with their much smaller margins, as mere accessories to their "big iron." Too few realized that desktops were making mainframes obsolete. In 1992 IBM announced a $4.97 billion loss, third worst in corporate history, trailing only GM and Ford.

In contrast, Henry Ford's great fortune was founded on the low-price Model T. The luxurious Lincoln, acquired in 1922, was profitless for many years.

Tall "T" Tale

"A recent *Motor Trend* article says 'more than one million Ts are in existence and operable today,' " reports reader George Brock, of Evansville, Ind. "Isn't that number on the high side?"

Yes. In 1953 Ford Motor Company estimated the number of extant Tin Lizzies at 100,000; in 1971 automotive historian Leslie R. Henry, taking into account subsequent large-scale T restoration, put the number of survivors at 300,000. It hardly seems credible that 700,000 flivvers could have been restored during the past quarter-century.

Motor Trend, adds Brock, also reported that Sears, until closure of its catalog sales department in1993, still sold all of the T's " 'vitals' such as tires, timers, band lining, and even bearings and axle sleeves." This assertion is also surprising inasmuch as Sears' catalog in 1975 advertised only one of the T's 4,830 parts – engine gaskets – and seemed to sell them more for sentimental than business reasons. During the T's heyday, the Sears' catalog devoted more space to flivver parts and gadgets than to men's clothing.

Oldest Model T

One might think that the oldest known Model T would be in the Henry Ford Museum or Smithsonian Institution. Not so, according to Don Emmons, writing in *Collector Car Illustrated*; it belongs to Ken Keesee, Anaheim, Calif., a T collector for many years.

Keesee's two-pedal car, No. 131, was manufactured in Dec., 1908 in a plant still standing on Detroit's Piquette and Beaubien avenues. The month's manufacturing run began with No. 102, and finished with No. 309, a total of 207 cars.

Keesee has owned No. 131 since 1980; it had been a part of the late Bill Harrah's Reno collection prior to that time. The car, according to a 1936 edition of a Ford magazine, was first sold in Syracuse, N.Y., and was still in that city in 1936.

Keesee owns another distinctive T, No. 4888, built in June, 1909. The car is like any other standard '09 touring car – except that it has an aluminum body attached to the conventional wood framework. The Ford Co., notes Emmons, built a few experimental aluminum bodied Ts to check weight differences. The bodies were fashioned by Pontiac Aluminum Co. Keesee has owned the aluminum-bodied car since 1978.

Keesee's rare Ts have been winners at every show entered except for the Pebble Beach Concours d'Elegance, where the oldest car was a runner-up. "But for a Model T even to be invited to Pebble Beach is a major feat in itself," observes Emmons. "Only 100 cars are so honored each year."

Thanks to Detroit's Mike Skinner for forwarding the story.

Tito's T

Marshall Tito, Yugoslavia's World War II partisan leader, was a Model T owner, according to Basil Davidson's book, *Special Operations Europe*.

In April 1941, shortly after Germany's invasion of Yugoslavia, Tito

Mexican T

This tapestry depicting a Model T graces the lobby of Ford of Mexico's headquarters building in Mexico City. Although the car's design is that of a Model T, and the license plate sports the letter "T," the plate also cites the year "1903" – which predates the Tin Lizzie launch by five years. Ford of Mexico's posh headquarters is housed in the Edificio Bolivia, named by builder/owner Simon Patino, the Bolivian tin king.

Welsh Model T

A lounge and public bar named The Model T is located near Ford's Bridgend, Wales, plant. The establishment serves evening meals and afternoon carvey, complete with Hofmeister beer and traditional ales. That's all I know about the place, since it was closed when I drove by after having visited the plant.

hid in Zagreb, capital of the state of Croatia. All cars were requisitioned by the police, but Tito bricked up his Tin Lizzie in his garage to avoid turning it in and having to reveal his identity.

After one of Tito's helpmates told the police about the car, Tito escaped on an overnight train to Belgrade.

Thanks to David Hayward, of Hounslow, Middlesex, U.K., for passing on this yarn.

Eastern Europe's Model T

The Model T continues to invite comparison, as evidenced by Suzuki's declaration that it wants its subcompact Swift "to be cheap enough to become Eastern Europe's Model T – a car that puts ordinary people on the road." The car will be built in Hungary.

There have been numerous attempts to out-Model T the Model T, the most successful of which is Volkswagen's Beetle. Ford's Pinto was a mixed success, its Asian-built Fiera and Yugoslavia's Yugo were failures.

Fords in Russia

Model T photos taken in Russia in 1912 and published in *Life* in 1937 recently were forwarded by reader Nathan Pickles, of Asheville, N.C.

One of the pictures shows a gentleman seated in the backseat of a chauffeur-driven flivver, a muddy street in the foreground. The other depicts a Tin Lizzie mired in mud up to its axles, its well-heeled passengers apparently wondering what to do next.

The photos were sent to *Life* by Donald Friede, West Hollywood, Calif., who wrote the magazine that his "father, M. Sergey Friede was the Ford representative in Russia from 1907 until the 1917 Revolution. During that time," continues Friede, "it is safe to say that nine out of ten cars in Russia were Fords. The reason is not hard to see when you look at these photographs, taken in 1912, showing roads which from my own experience I know to have been typical of those to be found in any part of Russia at the time."

This photo, appearing in the December, 1912 Ford Times, *shows Ford's dealer in Russia, M.S. Friede, at left, with the Model T touring car which won a 1,954-mile endurance run held in May, 1912 under the auspices of the Imperial Russian War Department. Also pictured is Emperor Nicholas II, the central figure among the three leading officers who are inspecting competing cars in the Palace Grounds at Peterhof. As a result of its victory, the Tin Lizzie was recommended by the War Department "as the most serviceable car for use in the Russian Army." Forty-five European cars, including the Mercedes, Benz, Charron, and Napier, and two U.S.-built vehicles, the White and Ford, were entered in the trial. The T was the only machine to complete the journey without a single penalty. (Photo from the Collections of the Henry Ford Museum and Greenfield Village.)*

Model T's Heyday

The Model T's relative importance on the mid-1920s auto scene is underscored in a 1924 Montgomery Ward tire/auto supplies catalog bought recently at a flea market by reader Vernon Hales of Kearney, Mo.

Of the catalog's 51 pages, 15 are devoted to tires and accessories for Fords. "Prices for Ford parts were quite a bit less than those for other cars," reports Hales. "A Ford carburetor was $4.25, while a Chevrolet carburetor sold for $11.45. A new Ford radiator, with shell, sold for $11.45, a front spring $1.40, a rear spring $4.50, crankshaft $7.25, a pair of headlamps $3.90, and Rajo OHV kit for $54.95."

Hales inquired as to the wages of Ford workers in 1924 so that he could "put Model T prices in perspective." Ford plant workers earned $6 a day in 1924, same as in 1919, and kept all of it inasmuch as people in that wage bracket paid no income taxes, nor were they docked for Social Security. They thus could buy the cars they made, although they had to ante up cash for them. In 1924, a T touring sold for $295, the cheapest flivver, a runabout, for $265.

School Daze

The following poem, "Ode to a Ford," was written on the inside cover of a 1917 high school textbook, *Early European Civilization*, by Walter Wallin, father of reader John Wallin, of Manteca, Calif.:

Little car, little car
How I wonder what you are
Climbing all the hills on high
Passing all the others by.

The first one passed just lightly fussed
The second growled and loudly cussed
The third one swore and finally roared
You cannot stop it, it's a Ford.

Other scribblings, common to many adolescent musings, include:

If this book should chance to roam,
Kick its tail and send it home.
If there should be another flood

For refuge hither fly,
If all the world should be submerged
This book would still be dry.

The page carried an address: "Corner Tin Can Street and Barbed Wire Ave., Blackhawk, S.Dak., U.S.A."

John, in forwarding a copy of the page, observed, "This goes to show that bored students are nothing new." Makes me wonder what my own students are writing when supposedly taking notes on my lectures.

Ts Or Bikes For Cops

Model Ts were widely used by police departments in the teens and twenties, but Indian Motorcycle Co. was doing its best to discredit and replace them, as indicated by articles in the company's dealer newsletter, *Contact Points*.

Under the headline, "Another City Finds Fords Not Suited for Police Service," the March 3, 1924 issue of the publication flails the flivver.

"During the past few months we have furnished you with a quantity of data to prove the fallacy of Fords for police service," declares the newsletter, "but when city after city supplies us with ammunition for another shot on the same subject we are going to pass it on to you so that you can load your guns and go hunting for police business.

"We have [already] shown you the experience of Springfield, Mass., where it cost $1,737 more to operate seven Fords than it did seven Indian Scouts, with 1,500 more miles to the motorcycles' credit.

"We have also shown that Columbus, Ohio spent an average of $462.56 each for their 12 Fords in oil, gasoline, and repair charges for a period of one year, or $82.56 more in one year on each car than it originally cost.

"Now, from Omaha, Nebraska comes word from Police Commissioner Henry W. Dunn to the effect that their experiment with Fords in patrol service was not at all satisfactory, and after a few months' trial they are to be abandoned, while the number of motorcycle officers will be increased.

"The Commissioner in doing away with the Fords states: 'The day of the old foot patrolman in residential districts is practically a thing of the past, and future police work will be handled by men on fast moving vehicles (motorcycles), as a large majority of thieves of all kinds now operating in the residential districts are using machines to make their get-away. If officers do not have a machine to move as quickly as the thieves, the officer has very little chance of pursuing or catching them.' "

A few years earlier, *Contact Points* quoted Henry Ford in an effort to sell its machines. Excerpting from an *American Review of Reviews* article, the Dec. 15, 1921 issue of the cycle publication cited Ford's reply to a critic of the magnate's advocacy of lightweight railroad locomotives.

" 'Were you ever arrested for speeding?' asked Mr. Ford.

" 'Yes, why?'

" 'Who arrested you?'

" 'A motorcycle cop.'

" 'Exactly,' rejoined Mr. Ford; 'a motorcycle cop on a machine perhaps one-tenth as heavy as the one you were driving came up behind and went right past you. We'll also find out how to do it with light construction on the railroads.' "

There was, of course, a place for motorcycles in police work, just as there was a place for cars, and even horses, bicycles and shank's mare (feet). In fact officers on foot patrol are making a comeback in some cities these days. But to Indian, the motorcycle and its low cost of operation overrode all other considerations. Well, maybe it would concede that a paddywagon or two would be helpful – unless arrestees could be expected to ride behind the cop, or on the handlebars.

Thanks to Don Doody, Vancouver, B.C., for favoring us with Indian's newsletters.

T for Tow

A Ford postcard recently arrived in the mail from Peter Winnewisser, of Cazenovia, N.Y., a leading collector of the genre. This one, like so many of its brethren, shows the Model T towing a much larger car, and carries the caption, "The Big Car's burning up the road. Why sure! Just see by whom it's towed."

Such postcards both derived from and contributed to the T's vaunted reputation for reliability. The Tin Lizzie might spray the roadside with loose nuts and bolts (leading some critics to suggest that each flivver be equipped with a squirrel for retrieval purposes), but it did "get you there and get you back," which was the bottom line in the early days of automobility.

Comic Postcards

A listing of Ford comic postcards has been compiled by Tim O'Callaghan, Northville, Mich., working with a fellow collector, Peter Winnewisser, Cazenovia, N.Y. Most of the cards were issued between 1915-20, the height of the Ford joke craze. Some of the cards remained in circulation for as long as the Model T was produced, 1927.

Thirty-eight of the cards were published by Cobb-Shinn/Commercial Colortype Co., which produced cards with such titles as "War is H--- and so is riding in a Ford," "A Ford don't need gasoline, it can run on its reputation," "All I have to say is that a Ford is a rattling good car," and "Are you going to raise your Ford to be a jitney?"

Twelve of the Cobb-Shinn cards have a Dutch flavor with such tag lines as "My droubles vas all schmall vones – I own a Ford," "Der only ding vot a Ford efer dies from vas oldt age," "It vas no disgrace to own a Ford budt idt might vell be already yet," and "Ven I die I vandt mine Ford buriet mit me vur idt has alvays got me outdt of efery place I hafe been yet in."

Thirty cards were published in three series by Witt with such titles as "A Ford is like a bathtub – you don't like to

As depicted in this Cobb-Shinn postcard, "Even the birds (as they sing 'Cheap, Cheap') know a Ford when they see one." The card was mailed with a one-cent stamp to Mrs. C.H. Krauser, 934 Pear St., Reading, Pa. (place of mailing and date unintelligible), and its message reads as follows: "Sister: Will look for you Sat. 1st don't forget and bring my umbrella along. I need it: and if you can get me such a screen like you have for your bedroom you can get them at Hoffman you can get them in my styles get the big one. Armic." (Card from Peter Winnewisser, Cazenovia, N.Y.)

be seen in one," "Fords don't always rattle like this – only when they're going," "When the big car says 'No use to try,'/the little Ford goes up in high," and "The big car eats up barrels of gas/But the little Ford ain't in that class."

Sixteen cards were published by J. Raymond Co., Chicago, the only firm to number its offerings. Among its tag lines are "John! How many times must I tell you not to wash your Ford in the bathtub" and "The passengers are the only shock absorbers on our Ford."

More cards keep turning up, notes O'Callaghan, who will share his list with readers in exchange for a SASE and is willing to coordinate a master compilation for fellow collectors. O'Callaghan, a Ford aviation authority, may be reached at P.O. Box 512, Northville, MI 48167, phone 248-449-2652.

Record Price For T

A record Model T price – $21,500 for a 1912 Torpedo – was paid at a recent Tulsa auction, according to the July-August, 1992 edition of the *Model T Times.*

The Torpedo Runabout was bought by a Japanese, and will be displayed in a Tokyo auto museum. The car is right-hand-drive, suggesting that it was assembled for export. The vehicle was restored in 1971, after having been found on a farm north of Council Bluffs, Iowa.

Owner of the car between 1972-92 was H.H. Wilson, of Colorado Springs, Colo., noted in Model T circles for solo trips through Alaska, the Yukon, Northwest Territories, Labrador, and Newfoundland in a 1915 T roadster. Wilson says his favorite cars are Tin Lizzies and Jaguars – "the T for total dependability, Jags for style; the '12 Torpedo had both."

Remarkable Pricing

We all know that Henry Ford's Model T price-cutting was remarkable. How remarkable? A 1997 book, *Creating Modern Capitalism*, edited by Harvard professor Thomas K. McCraw, provides an answer:

"Perhaps the most spectacular price reduction in American business history up to that time came in the most expensive of all consumer goods, the automobile .... Henry Ford's Model T, which in its first year of production (1908) sold for the comparatively low price of $850, could be purchased in 1916 for only $360. By 1924 Ford rode the experience curve to remarkably low costs. In 1924 the Model T was selling for only $290, and the 1924 Ford was a much better car than that of 1908 or 1916."

Elsewhere, the book notes that System/360, IBM's flagship product from the late 1960s through the 1970s, "was the most successful big-ticket product introduction in American business since the Model T Ford."

Golf Outproduces T

The Volkswagen Golf has overtaken the Model T as the world's third most produced vehicle, giving VW two of the top three sellers.

The Beetle, launched in 1938 and still being built in Mexico and Brazil, is the all-time bestseller with more than 22 million units. The Toyota Corolla, launched in 1966, is second with about 20 million units. The Golf moved into third place when producing 15 million-plus units in June 1994.

Thanks to reader Bob Cawley, Kenthurst, New South Wales, Australia, for forwarding a newspaper article on the Golf's achievement.

Model T Publicity

The Model T year in and year out gets more press play than any other defunct car including the Edsel (the Jeep and the original Beetle, still in production, also are frequently publicized). A sampling of recent references:

Noting that the Secretary of the Treasury has approved a plan to issue five new quarters each year starting in 1999 and that each quarter will feature a design honoring each state, the *Detroit News* wonders whether Michigan's quarter, to be issued in 2004, should feature the Model T, the Mackinac Bridge, or a wolverine.

Chiming in, the *Detroit Free Press* regards as quarter-design possibilities the Model T, the Mackinac Bridge, a lake freighter, Detroit's Renaissance Center, the Round Island Lighthouse, and the state's distinctive double-peninsula profile.

Discussing the retrieval of travel bags at airports, the *Free Press* states, "So you're standing at the carousel. You can't tell your bag from anyone else's. It has wheels and a handle. And just like the original Model T, every one is black." (As readers of this column are well aware, not every Tin Lizzie was painted black.)

A contributor to Ann Landers' advice column insists that nursing homes have improved greatly in recent years, and that "your readers who wrote to complain [about them] are in the Model T era."

"These Model Ts of the Digital Age will help wire the world," says *Business Week*'s March 23, 1998 issue of the Compaq Rosario and other personal computers priced below $1,000.

Fiat, the *New York Times* notes in its July 19, 1996 edition, introduced the Palio, "a European Model-T for the '90s," in its bid to build a car with worldwide appeal.

As the Vespa celebrated its 50th year of production in 1996, the Paris-based *International Herald Tribune*'s Sept. 21-22, 1996 issue observed that the motor scooter did for transportation in postwar Italy what the Model T did for the United States earlier in the century."

Model T Races

Roaring Lizzies: Model T Ford Racing in Alberta, 1941 to 1951, is the descriptive title of a 1992 illustrated paperback written by Kelly Buziak and published by the Friends of the Reynolds-Alberta Museum Society.

One of the most popular of Alberta's sporting events during the 1940s, Model T racing, was introduced by Calgary's Lions Club as a way to raise funds for the Waifs and Strays Society of Britain.

The first race was a 100-miler at the half-mile Victoria Park horse track. Rules stipulated removal of roofs and glass windshields and that vehicles use standard Model T mechanical parts.

Backseats, running boards, engine aprons, fenders, and lights also were removed, making some of the cars little more than a chassis, steering wheel, and a gas tank. Underslung springs could be used, permitting lowering of the chassis. There were neither roll bars or seat belts. Drivers wore leather helmets and goggles reminiscent of World War I pilots.

All of the drivers were amateurs, and remained so throughout the racing era.

Approximately 12,000 people attended the first race, which required almost four hours for completion, the winner averaging 33 mph. There were 15 "crack-ups," but no serious injuries. More than $5,000 was raised for British children impacted by World War II, prompting other cities to sponsor shortened races in support of wartime causes.

Contests were held in Edmonton, Red Deer, Vegreville, Olds, Lethbridge, Innisfail, Hanna and Grande Prairie, in addition to Calgary. Most of the events were organized by Lions Clubs, usually in connection with a holiday, local fair, or sports day. More than 18,000 fans attended Calgary's 1944 race, more than 13,000 Edmonton's 1943 event. Wartime drivers resorted to their gasoline rationing coupons for fuel. One death occurred, in Calgary, in 1943.

After 1945 Model T racing experienced a slow, steady decline. The Calgary race drew 15,000 in 1946, 13,000 in 1948, 10,000, in 1950, and only 2,000 in 1951. The Edmonton race, which usually drew approximately 10,000, was discontinued after 1948 with the razing of the racing site's grandstand.

Public interest in flivver races waned as the novelty wore off and people were less inclined to support charitable events after war's end. In addition, some of the winning drivers turned to other kinds of dirt track racing.

Thanks to reader Don Radbruch, Sagle, Idaho, for forwarding the book.

Survivor

A tale of the sole six-cylinder Model T is told by columnist Jack Perkis in the March 1977 issue of the *Oneida Lake Gazette*, publication of the Oneida Lake Region of the Antique Automobile Club of America.

Visiting Sarasota's now defunct Horne's Transportation Museum some years ago, Perkis spotted a chassis with running gear and a flathead six-cylinder engine. The museum's director told him that the vehicle was the only surviving prototypes among ten built in the mid-1920s by Ford's son, Edsel.

Upon learning of the prototypes, the elder Ford, who had a passionate dislike for six-cylinder engines, smashed nine of them with a sledgehammer on a Sunday afternoon, according to the director. Because it was at a vendor's shop, the 10th vehicle escaped destruction, and eventually came into Horne's possession.

In 1997 Perkis learned that the chassis is displayed at Sarasota's Bellm Car & Music Museum. "Perhaps," he concludes, "some day I'll renew the acquaintance."

Thanks to reader and *Gazette* editor Bob Zenter, Baldwinsville, N.Y., for forwarding the column.

Model T Snowbird

Memories of a 1927 Model T "Snowbird" are recalled by Roy Newcomb, of Anoka, Minn., in a recent edition of *Reminisce Extra*.

"My Dad was a rural mail carrier in northern Minnesota," Newcomb reminisces, "and his motto was 'The mail must go through!' But in those days, the roads were awfully hard to get through – especially in winter, when they were not passable with an ordinary car. So Dad bought a 'Snowbird' kit for his 1927 Model T.

"These kits were made by a firm in Wisconsin and came completely unassembled. I remember as a boy helping Dad put together literally hundreds of parts, especially the tracks. The front wheels were replaced with metal skis, and the rear driving wheels had special tires with bars that fit into matching depressions in the tracks.

"Because the Model T was a rather light car, the extra strain of driving the tracks resulted in occasional breakdowns. Sometimes, Dad worked late into the night to prepare the 'Snowbird' for his route the next day. Later on, Dad got another kit for a Model A. This car was better able to take the strain and had fewer breakdowns."

Snowmobiles

Many Model T-based snowmobiles were produced in Michigan's Upper Peninsula during the late teens and early 1920s, states C. Fred Rydholm's 1989 book, *Superior Heartland: A Backwoods History*.

The first of the snowmobiles was fashioned from a T truck by "some inventive fellow" in 1918, Rydholm recalls. The front wheels of the vehicle were removed, and wide wooden or metal skis were attached to the front axles. The front wheels then were mounted behind the rear wheels and two endless tracks were mounted on each side of the back sets of tandem wheels, over the tires.

The snowmobiles performed satisfactorily on packed snow or in sleigh ruts, or even in new snow if not too deep. But they were useless in new, deep snow or big drifts, and were abandoned in the mid-1920s as main roads came to be plowed.

None of the flivver snowmobiles was patented.

Thanks to reader Mike Skinner, St. Clair Shores, Mich., for forwarding Rydholm's book.

They All Laughed

I recently listened to one of George Gershwin's 1930s songs, "They All Laughed." The lyrics note that "they" always have laughed at innovators and dreamers. "They" also laughed at two struggling romantics who, by getting and staying together, have silenced their critics and "have the last laugh now."

The bouncy song thus declares that they all laughed at Columbus for saying the world was round, Edison for recording sound, the Rockefellers for building Rockefeller Center, the Wright brothers for thinking that man could fly, Marconi and his wireless, Whitney and his cotton gin, Fulton and his steamboat, and Hershey and his chocolate bar. Surely, I thought, Henry Ford and his Model T will pop up in the lyrics, and of course they did in the immortal lines "Ford and his Tin Lizzie/Kept the Laughers Busy." Made my day.

Fascinatin' Rhythm

While listening to George Gershwin's 1920s song, "Fascinatin' Rhythm," I was surprised to hear that the lyrics refer to the Model T. After all, the song's thrust is that a fascinating rhythm is agitating its singer.

But along came these lyrics:

"Fascinatin' rhythm, I'm all
aquiver,
What a mess you're making,
The neighbors want to know why
I'm shaking,
Just like a flivver."

The Tin Lizzie reference perhaps is less surprising when one reasons that lyricists generally write of familiar things, and nothing was more familiar than a flivver in the 1920s.

Now if we can find lyrics in which a T twosome spark in the dark on a lark in the park or spoon or croon a tune in June 'neath the moon.

Eastward Ho!

A 1933 trip in a 1920 Model T from Spokane, Wash. To the Chicago World's Fair and back via Pikes Peak recently was chronicled in the *Detroit Free Press* by Tom Downs, a Lansing lawyer.

Downs bought the T for $20, then purchased a bodyless parts car for $5. He and two buddies drove to Chicago in about a week, and the entire trip took about a month. "Being 17," he recalled, "we traveled economically and slept on the side of the road with blankets, not even a sleeping bag.

"A fairly common experience for us was to be awakened in the morning by a teenager saying, 'Ma wants to know if you'd like a cup of coffee.' We would follow him to the farmhouse and Ma would start us off with homemade apple pie and then treat us to a full breakfast of bacon and eggs. After we visited for a while, she would pack us a lunch to help us on our way."

To feed their "oil-guzzling" T, the trio obtained used heavy airplane oil from airport mechanics, then cut it with kerosene. Gasoline was 20 cents per gallon; sometimes a dime bought a "large half-gallon" from a friendly mechanic.

The car was hand cranked. "If it was being temperamental," Downs remembered, "all we usually had to do was jack up the rear wheels and crank away with them spinning freely. It usually would start right up. There was no battery or generator either. The light ran off the magneto. The faster the car went, the brighter the lights. Thus, if at night a person slowed down at a stop sign, the engine had to be put in neutral and revved up in order to get any light.

"I gave up the car in 1924 when I left for college," Downs concluded. "But that old Ford was very well built, very simple, and we did have a lot of fun with it."

Yosemite or Bust

A 1914 Model T, which first traveled from Lankershim, Calif. (now North Hollywood), to Yosemite National Park back in 1924 repeated the journey in August 1989. The car is owned by reader Fred Fox who, with his son, made the latter-day journey.

The original Yosemite run was made by Fred's father, Walter, who had bought the car from his brother Charles in 1924. Charles had purchased the flivver from its original owners in 1920.

Walter Fox stopped using the T in 1928, and from about 1930-56 it sat outdoors, and the body fell into disrepair. Fred restored the car and, with his mother and father, drove it to Yosemite in 1964. He plans to drive "Old Lissie," as he calls his vehicle, to Yosemite in 1999, 75 years after the original journey.

"I suspect," says Fox, "that few, if any, families still own a car that was driven by a family member to Yosemite 65 years ago."

Still Chuggin'

Model Ts still get their owners there and back, as attested by a recent *Vintage Ford* article on six Tin Lizzies driven from Prince Albert, Sask., to Dearborn and back in the summer of 1988.

The travelers ranged in age from 9 to 82. Their 22-day trip covered 3,600 miles, and they had to contend with flat tires, engine, transmission, radiator, rear end, magneto, and other troubles. But everyone completed the trip.

While in Dearborn, the participants visited the Henry Ford Museum and Greenfield Village. But they missed a bet by not driving to their cars' spawning ground, the Highland Park Plant, which made Lizzie's major parts, even though most flivvers were assembled elsewhere. The picture they didn't take could have arrayed the Ts in front of a fading Michigan Historical Commission sign entitled, "Home of the Model T," and an abandoned, decaying office building.

The trip's chronicler, Brendy Kedves, summed up, "These cars are truly amazing machines. Actually, when in their prime, they had to push a lot harder on the gravel ruts they called roads than they did on our trip." Kedves was reminded of a poem:

There was a little man,
His name was Henry Ford.
He got a piece of wire,
And a two-inch board.
A little bit of gas,
And an old tin can.
He put it all together,
And the darn thing ran.

Ford Railster

Model T railsters once transported New Zealanders, according to an *Auckland Star* February 6, 1926 article forwarded by reader Kevin M. Crowe, of Takapuna, N.Z.

Traffic was so light on many lines of the government's Railway Department that steam trains could not operate profitably on them. One solution, it was thought, was to convert one-ton Ford chassis into rail coaches driven and serviced by one man.

The first of two experimental T railsters was used on a small branch in Wairarapa, from Woodside to Greytown. It carried 11 passengers, and its backseats were made to drop on hinges to provide space for luggage, milk cans, and other goods. Although an emergency door was provided at the back, passengers entered from either side of the front of the vehicle, enabling the driver to collect fares. Axles of the chassis were strengthened and reduced to the railway gauge, and disc wheels with light section flanged tires were added. No steering wheel was required.

At 30 mph, the coaches got 16 to 18 miles mpg with a full load, including a turntable. The car could be turned at any point by ascertaining the coach's balance point, placing a plate beneath the body to mark the spot, placing a jack between the balance point, clamping the springs with clips fixed to the vehicle, making a few turns on the jack, and balancing the coach on a small ball-bearing turntable attached to the jack. "It is easy," the *Star* states, "for one man to turn the coach in two minutes." If necessary the chassis could be reconverted to road use.

"The Ford railster," the publication adds, "if it stands up to the traffic requirements of small branch lines, should save many of them from being closed." We are left to wonder whether the experimental Ts proved their worth.

Crowe found the "cutting" when cleaning out an estate. "The method of turning the 'Ford railster' is certainly ingenious," he remarks. "Always enjoy your 'Ford Country,' " he adds, "although I drive a '70 Eldorado!"

T to the Rescue

Two Model Ts donated to the American Red Cross by Henry Ford helped fight a 1917 typhoid epidemic, according to an article, "Helping the Army at Home," in the January, 1918 edition of *Public Health Nurse Quarterly*.

The Tin Lizzies were furnished to a Red Cross unit assigned to care for workers newly moved into areas surrounding Army cantonments. One of the cars went to inspectors, the other to nurses.

"The town (designated only by the initial 'L') is widely scattered and streetcar service inadequate," reported the article, "and unless one has worked the same territory without a car, one could not appreciate the difference in the amount of work with a car. One nurse doing the outside work now makes from 90 to 130 calls a week, many of them actual nursing calls and often to rural districts."

Moreover, states the article, the cars enabled medical personnel to observe and report on people breaking quarantine rules. A dairyman so observed by a motorized nurse was "arrested, tried, and fined."

A photo of one of the Ts in a winter setting appears in the article. Top up, sans side curtains, the touring's hood is covered by a padded horse blanket. A doctor is at the wheel, and a nurse is seated in the rear seat, while another nurse stands alongside.

Thanks to reader Cheryl Easley, Berrien Springs, Mich., herself a nurse, for forwarding the article.

Model T Tractor-Trailer

"In going through my late father's effects," writes reader Dale Johnson, of Owatonna, Minn., "I found a picture of my father's tractor-trailer which I am enclosing. I think there are probably very few older such combinations. My uncle tells me this one probably had a 1917-18-19 Model T engine and transmission, as the whole family couldn't have raised $20 at that time.

"The picture," continues Johnson, "is of my father, Paul Johnson, then of Carthage, S.D., and was taken in 1924. The truck was used to haul corn to Mitchell, a distance of about 42 miles (probably an all-day trip).

"My uncle helped build the tractor and thought it probably had 18 or 20 horsepower, the kind of power a good lawnmower has nowadays. It died a premature death when someone poured cold water in it while it was hot and cracked the block.

"I've been a reader of *Cars & Parts* and your column for more years than I care to think about, and have enjoyed both immensely."

Half-T-Half-Hansom

The first metered taxicab was half Model T-half hansom cab, according to an article in the Fall 1992 edition of *American Heritage of Invention and Technology*.

The taxi, part of a 75-cab fleet operated by New York's B&W, was a Model T from the radiator to the back of the front seat. The passenger compartment was taken off a vehicle that the taxi had made obsolete, the horse-drawn hansom cab. At the time, 1919, according to author Bobby Lowich, a cab built from scratch would have cost $2,500 to $3,000; a Model T sold for about $700; and old hansom carriages cost next to nothing. The owner could buy a Ford, shear off the section behind the front seat, extend the chassis, widen the frame, adapt and stick on the hansom cab, weld, sand,

Model T Tractor

A converted Model T dubbed "The Grasshopper" pulls homemade gang lawnmowers at Wentworth Estate, Wells, Maine, in 1935. Aboard the tractor is its creator, Reginald Jones, uncle of reader David M. Scott, of Wells, who forwarded the photo.

paint, and add a roof covering, and have a taxi for $1,500 to $1,700.

The finished product, adds Lowich, also "may be considered the first customized stretch car."

Thanks to Mike Skinner, Dearborn, Mich., for forwarding the article on the invention and first application of the taxi meter.

Tin Lizzie Preachers

A recent *New York Times* article refers to "itinerant horse-and-buggy and Tin Lizzie preachers" who used theatrical techniques to importune the faithless and entertain the faithful.

During the teens and twenties, more evangelists drove Model Ts than any other car. But the most popular female preacher on the American scene of these years, Aimee Semple McPherson (1890-1944), traveled in a 1912 Packard.

Preaching in tents, concert halls, boxing rings, and speakeasies, she delighted in posing in front of her "Gospel Car" while dressed in an ethereal-looking long white gown.

Bones

Did Henry Ford trade a Model T for a full set of Mongolian dinosaur bones? That's the question posed by Dr. Marcia Woolf, of Providence, R.I., who was informed in January 1995 by an Italian filmmaker that such an exchange occurred during the teens. Allegedly, the flivver was traded to a Mongolian Buddhist leader.

I replied that I am unfamiliar with such a trade and know of no dinosaur bones having been exhibited by the Henry Ford Museum/Greenfield Village.

Dr. Woolf then asked if Ford could have given the bones to an institution specializing in dinosaurs. Again possible, but most doubtful inasmuch as Ford tended to collect only for his own museums. Also, I've seen no news stories connecting Ford and dinosaurs, and it's difficult to believe that the auto king, had he participated in such a novel deal, would not have publicized it. Still, insofar as Henry Ford is concerned, anything is possible.

President Dwight D. Eisenhower at the wheel of South Dakota State's "Bummobile" in 1956.

A Ford Goes to College

The following story about a Model T mascot was submitted by Murvin H. Perry, Johnson City, Tenn., under the above title. Rather than rework the yarn, let's simply let Perry's words speak for themselves:

"A 1912 Model T Ford is the prized possession of the student association at South Dakota State University at Brookings. Although school officials have recently spent more than $1,250 refurbishing the ancient automobile, it continues to be displayed in a manner that car aficionados would consider sacrilegious.

"With great glory, but little dignity, the Ford assumes a central role in the celebration of 'Hobo Day', the annual college homecoming. Dressed in the most outlandish rags they can improvise, the students at this agricultural college each fall stage one of the most colorful spectacles of the Northwest. The old T, affectionately christened 'the Bummobile,' serves as regal transportation for the king and queen of homecoming. Each year it conveys its cargo of ragged royalty through a three-mile parade in the morning, and to the stadium for the football game and coronation ceremonies at half-time.

"The T is equipped as it came from the factory with acetylene headlights, polished brass radiator and windshield braces. The only modifications have been to move the coil box under the hood and to install a battery and switch to allow running on either battery or magneto.

"Its most recent refurbishing was financed by a gift from graduates who raised the money by selling souvenir photographs of couples posed in the old Ford during the Fabulous Fifties Reunion in the summer of 1987.

"The car was presented to the student association in 1939 by Frank Weigel, a Flandreau, S.D., farmer who had admired the Hobo Day celebration.

"It required a major overhaul and repainting in 1949 after an incident that nearly ended the saga of the famous old Ford.

"On Thursday morning, Oct. 28, 1948, members of the student body at State discovered that the garage that held the Bummobile had been raided by fraternity men from the rival University of South Dakota at Vermillion. The venerable vehicle had been stolen.

"A week of frantic bargaining followed during which the president of State appealed to the student body of the Vermillionites to make a sportsmanlike offer for ransom and return of the car.

"Newspapers seized the story and the columns were filled with the statements from USD supporters to the effect that they would paint the car bright red, their school's colors, drive it in their own homecoming parade, then dismantle it, and present each University student with a nut, bolt, or bearing as a souvenir of their complete humiliation of State.

"Search parties from State combed Vermillion for the hiding place of the prize. The National Guard was alerted to quell violence in case State students attempted a reprisal raid. (There was good reason. The previous fall, Sioux Falls police had returned to headquarters in cruisers painted yellow and blue when they tried to halt a raiding party from State that was painting a dormitory at Augustana College in the blue and gold colors of State.)

"Finally a settlement was reached which allowed USD students to drive the car in their homecoming parade. State students cast and presented a trophy attesting to the car coup and further agreed to return the crest of the fraternity house which they had 'captured' the year before in exchange for the Ford's safe return.

"The rough usage experienced in the theft necessitated a complete overhaul and repainting for the Bummobile. Its front wheels had been lashed to the rear bumper of a modern car, and it had been towed the 90 miles from Brookings to Vermillion at many times the speed at which it was designed to travel. New parts were not available, so the old connecting rods were rebabbited and the body was sanded and painted a new shiny black.

"For many summers the old car has been filled with beard-growing members of the State band and sent to fairs and local celebrations as an animated advertisement for the State homecoming.

"Visitors to the campus during preparations for the celebration, including governors and presidents, are apt to be met at the airport by six bearded students in the Bummobile and treated to a ride in the ancient Ford. President Dwight Eisenhower, on a visit to the campus in the early 1950s, took the wheel himself and followed directions to the campus as he drove the old T through the streets of Brookings."

Obviously, the Bummobile is an old Ford that has neither died nor faded away.

Fords Make Guinness Book

A Model T and a Model A are among the cars recognized by the *Guinness Book of World Records*.

A T was involved in "the longest tow on record," states *Guinness*, "one of 4,759 miles from Halifax, Nova Scotia, to Canada's Pacific Coast .... Frank J. Elliott and George A. Scott of Amherst, Nova Scotia, persuaded 168 passing motorists in 89 days to tow their Model T Ford (in fact, engineless) to win a $1,000 bet on Oct. 15, 1927.

"A 1929 A was driven in reverse from New York City to Los Angeles (3,340 miles) July 26-Aug. 13, 1930, without stopping the engine once," continues *Guinness*. The drivers, Charles Creighton and James Hargis of Maplewood, Mo., "arrived back in New York on Sept. 5, again in reverse, completing 7,180 miles in 42 days.

"Creighton was a mechanic and Hargis an interior decorator. Their motto was 'Seeing America Backward.' ... They attached the headlights to the rear of the car and drove at speeds varying from 8 to 10 mph. On the open road, they locked the gearshift in reverse so it would not pop out."

World War II Model T

Historically, the U.S. Army long has been accused of preparing to fight the next war with the last war's weapons. A case in point involves the Model T and World Wars I and II.

During World War I the Model T was cited for "gallantry in action" in a number of battlefield dispatches. Ten machine-gun-laden Ts were used to drive Germans from an entrenched position on the Marne River, and the sturdy little car was the only vehicle that could get through to wounded men during the first five days of fighting in the Argonne Forest.

By providing motive power for flat boats, the T saved a detachment of British soldiers from starvation in Africa. British General Edmund Allenby attributed the success of his Palestine campaign to "Egyptian laborers, camels, and Ford cars." According to Lowell Thomas, lecturing during the war on the Middle Eastern campaign, Allenby rode in a Rolls-Royce, but always had a Ford on hand as a kind of insurance.

In 1940, a year before the U.S. entered World War I, the Army had need of a tough, nimble, cross-country vehicle. Given the T's contributions to the First World War, the Army, according to *American Heritage*, considered the possibility of procuring a stripped-down Tin Lizzie fitted with airplane tires.

Such a machine might have proved useful during the Second World War. But can anyone doubt that the vehicle chosen, the four-wheel-drive Jeep, was much more useful; indeed, was tougher, more nimble, peppier, faster, and a better hill climber than a flivver with or without airplane tires.

Moon Machine

A painting featuring a Model T on the moon was on sale at a recent car meet at Berry College, Rome, Ga. The idea may seem farfetched – until one thinks about it. A Tin Lizzie, even on a lunar surface, would get one there and back. Moreover, a used T costs less than a custom-built "moonrover." (Photo courtesy of reader Mike Skinner of Dearborn, Mich.)

Treats From a "T"

A custom-built 1925 Model T truck has been serving popcorn, peanuts, and other treats to passersby in Eastern New York for more than 40 years, according to a recent Associated Press article.

The flag-bedecked truck was operated by Albert Rich, of Cambridge, N.Y., for a score of years, and has earned a living for his daughter, Dottie Madison, for the past 22 years.

Model T Cranking

A picture that demonstrates the incorrect way to crank a Model T is featured in "A New Use of the Herbert Bone Screw System: Treatment of a Displaced Radial Styloid Fracture," an article appearing in the January 1993 issue of the *Othopaedic Review*.

"Various automobiles, including the Model T, often appear in advertisements in orthopaedic journals," reader Peter C. Weber, M.D., writes from Olney, Illinois, "but rarely feature an automobile in the body of an article." As Dr. Weber notes, sudden reversal and kickback, if one pushes rather than pulls on the crank almost surely will cause a radial styloid fracture. This injury was common during the Model T era.

A GM Model T

"I once read about GM having unearthed a 'Model T Chevrolet,' " writes reader Francis Harrington, of Buffalo. "Have you ever heard of it?"

Yes. The vehicle, a 1920 truck, was found in a Bay Port, Mich. junkyard in 1965 and had, according to the *Detroit News*, an identification plate reading as follows:

"Chevrolet Model T. Reg. U.S. Pat. Office. Carrying capacity 2,000 lbs. Do not overload. Fill storage battery every two weeks with distilled water. See instruction book for information on operation and care of various units. Chevrolet Motor Co. When writing mention Model 'T', car No. 2871."

After its discovery, GM removed the truck to one of its Detroit shops and restored it at a cost several times its original 1920 price of $1,325 without body or cab. A spare engine was found and front fenders were replaced. A Flint, Mich. wheelwright made new front wheels, and various other components also were handmade. The vehicle was freshly painted and polished.

After restoration, GM hauled the truck from town to town in a huge trailer towed by the corporation's biggest truck, a 280-horsepower Turbine Titan III. After being set down, the Chevy T scampered around its giant brethren to illustrate GM's progress in truck building.

The *News* made much out of Chevrolet's "malice aforethought" in displaying the Chevrolet Model T, asking readers to imagine how Leonardo da Vinci would have felt if some other artist had stepped forward and claimed to have painted the Mona Lisa.

"After all," the *News* observed, "the Model T is to the Ford Motor Co. what

Temporarily Pastured?

Breathes there a car with soul so dead that of it truly can be said that it can't be revived, especially if it's a Model T complete with engine and body? Don't let the condition of this relic deceive you. Many of its sisters, no less dilapidated, have been restored to mint condition, and are treasured by their owners. Your commentator knows, having a 1921 touring which went through such a metamorphosis. (Photo courtesy of the Motor Vehicle Manufacturers Assn.)

Wallace the Bruce is to Scotland, George Washington is to America, and Winston Churchill is to England. It was the Magna Carta of motordom, the Emancipation Proclamation of the stableman, at once both the high adventure and the necessity of a nation .... Until now, William Shakespeare's claim on Hamlet was less secure than Ford's title to the legend of the Model T."

Actually, if Ford said one word about Chevrolet's Model T, that word was not recorded by the Detroit press. The *News*' story does indicate, however, that the name "Model T" still generated publicity – and that the newspaper's reporter, Will Muller, was equally well versed in Model T, British, and American history.

"Henry Ford Heaven"

"It was 'Henry Ford heaven' at the second annual Model A festival in downtown Sharon, Wis.," rhapsodized the June 21, 1998 issue of the *Rhinelander* (Wis.) *Daily News*.

Those approaching Sharon, population 1,250, from the east were greeted with the signs, "We know you've come a long, long way. We know you'll love our Model A Day. Burma Shave." More than 180 Model As lined the community's main drag, the architecture of which evokes the early years of the century. Residents, as well as Model A owners, dressed in 1930-era clothing. Festivities included a film on Henry Ford's life presented by the Sharon Historical Society.

The event is reminiscent of the Ford Days staged in hundreds of small communities throughout the country from 1921 to 1931. Local merchants, at the instigation of the local Ford dealer, would invite every owner or driver of a Ford in the surrounding area to come into town on a certain day. Special bargains were offered by all places of business, and a carnival atmosphere prevailed as Main Street was taken over for parades, band concerts, vaudeville performances, dancing, queen crownings, and Model T and other athletic contests.

Prizes were liberally awarded to contest winners and to owners of the cars carrying the biggest load of farm produce, the most eggs, the most children, the five prettiest girls, and so on. Model T owners turned up by the thousands, and virtually took over some towns inasmuch as drivers of other cars were usually fined if they appeared on the streets with their vehicles. Nearly all of the 1,300 Fords in Appanoose County, Iowa, invaded Centerville in 1922; more than 15,000 Ford owners and members of their families spent the day in Opelousas, La., the same year; and 20,000 persons brought more than $200,000 worth of goods on Ford Day in 1931 at Chickasha, Oklahoma.

Although Ford Days were still going strong in 1931, as attested by items in the *Ford News* and the company's detailed exhortations to branch managers to spread the idea to all communities within their jurisdiction, they seem to have died out quite suddenly thereafter. Perhaps depressed business conditions dampened the enthusiasm of many Ford dealers and their fellow merchants. Even more important, as the proportion of Ford owners shrank during the late 1920s and early 1930s, there undoubtedly was less justification for a Ford Day for Ford owners within the various communities.

Thanks to reader Joseph E. Jankovic, Three Lakes, Wis., for forwarding the *Daily News*' story.

The Noble Lincoln

The Lincoln car recently was cited by the *Detroit Free Press* as one of 15 cars making up America's automotive "nobility." Among Lincolns, the Model Ks produced in the early 1930s received the warmest praise.

When Ford bought Lincoln in 1922, the luxury car already had engineering excellence, but was somewhat homely. Within three years, Edsel Ford and outside bodybuilders had transformed it into one of the most handsome vehicles of its day. Under Edsel's guidance, Lincolns, especially the Zephyr and Continental, retained that distinction through the pre-World War II era.

Not a Better Idea

Henry Ford originally tested all of his cars' engines, then tested only a fraction of them, as reported in many articles and books. But, he should have tested all of them, says reader W. Boissevain of Los Altos, Calif.

"My parents' 1930 Lincoln, a lady's car used locally only for the first four years of its life, used a lot of oil. Any complaints about oil usage always met with the same responses: "Wait for it to break in"; "you don't drive it enough, etc.

"In the early spring of 1934, my parents drove to Denver from Missoula, Mont. Four quarts of oil later they had the Denver dealer pull the engine apart – customer's cost, of course. The findings: the oil rings were missing; the engine was never assembled properly.

"Lincolns surely could have had better quality control than Fords. A test run on the block would have uncovered the rings flaw. This car, after repairs, ran until World War II, when it died of a frozen, burst block. Not testing that Lincoln's engine was not one of Ford's better ideas!"

Fit For a Prince

This Lincoln limousine was used by Prince Higashi-Fushimi of the Japanese Imperial Family. The photo, forwarded by David Hayward, Southhampton, England, initially was published in the British *Ford Times*.

Raw Deal?

Did Henry M. and Wilfred C. Leland of Lincoln Motor Car Co., get a raw deal when Henry Ford acquired their firm in 1922? Reader Loren Jacobson, Littleton, Colo., is inclined to think so, as did the Lelands themselves.

"Several years ago," writes Jacobson, "I read a biography of the Lelands and other automotive history heroes which indicated that Ford did not 'save' Lincoln, but instead essentially stole Lincoln from the Lelands with some very underhanded tactics. Ford did not do what he told the Lelands he would, and the whole story reflected no real credit on the Fords. I don't know if any of us would like to be 'rescued' in the fashion this was done."

Jacobson has a point; the Lelands had legitimate complaints. The most definitive analysis of the Lincoln story may be found in Allan Nevins' and Frank Ernest Hill's *Ford: Expansion and Challenge 1915-1933*, published in 1957.

Lincoln Statue

A life-size 300-pound bronze statue of Abraham Lincoln that once stood in front of Lincoln's Detroit headquarters was stolen from its downtown Detroit Public Library pedestal in late September 1997, then recovered three days later.

Three persons were seen loading the statue into the back of a Ford Escort hatchback. "I don't know if it's going to be melted down, or had something to do with fraternity hazing," library spokeswoman Pat McClary said. "We're just glad it's back."

Found face down on the ground near an elementary school on Detroit's east side, the statue had a damaged left foot, split head, and numerous abrasions. After repairs, the library plans to restore the statue to its pedestal.

The 82-year-old statue, after being presented to the City of Detroit by Ford in 1958, was remounted on a grassy triangle at Farmer and Library streets. Torn from its pedestal by vandals in 1985, and also ravaged by Michigan winters, the effigy was restored in 1986 at a cost of $9,000. The money was contributed by almost 2,000 Michiganians, much of it in pennies donated by schoolchildren.

Abraham Lincoln's statue as it appeared in front of Lincoln's headquarters building from the teens to the late 1950s. One of a batch of six, the statue was designed in1898 by a German immigrant, Alfonso Pelzer, Salem, Ohio. The statue's right hand is relaxed, it is open, extended forward in a gesture of friendship. The left hand bears a scroll bearing the words "Proclamation of Emancipation" on its unfurled edge. Etched on the pedestal is the inscription, "Let Man Be Free." (Photo courtesy National Automotive History Collection, Detroit, Mich.)

Lady Out Of Lizzie

"Do you have the lyrics to 'Henry's Made a Lady Out of Lizzie'?" asks reader Gene Barclay, of Akron, Ohio.

The song, composed in 1927 by Walter O'Keefe, pays tribute to the Model A, successor to the Model T. The melody is perky and pleasing, and the lyrics do well by it, although like most lyrics, they don't read as well as they are sung.

Here are the first two stanzas of the song:

Have you seen her, ain't she great?
She's something you'll appreciate.
I'm sure you understand just what I mean.
Everybody, everywhere's falling for her now.
I'm talking 'bout the new Ford, and boy, it's a wow!
Lay off people, lay off folks,
None of your sarcastic jokes.
Henry's made a lady out of Lizzie.
No more bruises, no more aches
Now she's got those four wheel brakes.
Henry's made a lady out of Lizzie.
She's even got a rumble seat,
And lots of style and class;
The horn just seems to holler out,
"Toot – toot they shall not pass!"
The Lincoln cars just yell out loud,
That they are mighty, mighty proud,
Henry's made a lady out of Lizzie.

Recalls Model A Intro

The Model A's introduction in 1927 is recalled by reader Charles Hulse, of Flint, Mich.

"Dad I went down to the Port Huron, Michigan, Ford dealer, Al Parfett, the biggest dealer in Michigan's Thumb Area," Hulse writes. "The crowd that day was very large. Even though we were Chevrolet people, since my Dad was a district sales manager for Chevrolet, I thought the new Fords were really great."

Hulse also recalls having seen car-haulers heading toward Detroit loaded with many older cars that he did not recognize. His father told him that Ford was getting them off dealers' lots and feeding them into the Rouge Plant's blast furnaces. Some of these vehicles, he added, were said to have been saved by Henry Ford Museum personnel and stored in the Highland Park Plant.

Generic Design

The make of the four cars shown on the back of a $10 bill has been a controversial subject for years. Dennis David adds to the discussion in an article, "What's on the Back of a Ten-Dollar Bill?" in the January-February 1998 issue of the *SAH Journal*, newsletter of the Society of Automotive Historians.

Designer of the engraved die for the bill was Louis S. Schofield of the Department of the Treasury's Bureau of Engraving and Printing. In 1927 Schofield designed four cars for the vignette, all patterned after a model sketched expressly for the bill. The car is represented as being "generic," although it is said to resemble a Model A or a Hupmobile. If one looks closely, David says, the four cars shown on the bill (three in the distant background) are slightly different.

Actually, the car has to be generic inasmuch as the federal government is not allowed to endorse a commercial firm or product.

The Model A's design was not revealed until December 1927, presumably after Schofield had completed his work.

Model A Makes List

"Over the years," writes auto historian Ralph Dunwoodie, of Sun Valley, Nev., "auto-related clubs and magazines have asked me to participate in top 10 polls, etc. I've declined every time but once, and that was on the most economical, dependable cars. I put in the Model A Ford and the Valiant/Dart Slant 6s, and both made the list."

High praise for the Valiant/Dart to be listed with the Model A, which has been referred to as the best car ever built, pound for pound, dollar for dollar.

Model A Confiscated

A mint-condition 1931 Model A recently was confiscated in a Detroit drug-running bust. The owner, a 58-year-old Dearborn man, was apprehended at a gasoline station on a charge of possession with intent to deliver more than 650 grams of cocaine.

The car's fate? "Everything we confiscate gets auctioned," said Wayne County Sheriff Robert Ficano. "Some way, we'll get something for it."

One can only speculate as to why the drug runner was making deliveries in a 1931 Model A, inasmuch as it's been nigh on 60 years since Model As have blended into roadside scenery. An Escort would have been a more logical choice for such work.

Model A Wheel

In 1932 Leo Oberst, New York, and his son, Lee, while driving their Model A down a small hill, saw a spoked wheel and tire roll past them. To their surprise, it was a rear wheel of their car. Even so, the car remained steady. At the bottom of the hill a wheel nut was taken from each of the other wheels, put on the errant wheel, and the Obersts proceeded.

For years Lee's son, Bob, thought the story embellished – until a friend recalled a similar experience. Bob now regularly tightens wheel nuts on his '29 A.

The story appears in the April 1998 issue of *Oneida Lake Gazette*, publication of the Oneida Lake Region of the Antique Automobile Club of America, Bob Zenter, editor.

Model A Town Car

"Are there any 1930 Model A Town Cars out here," mused Roger Arcara, editor of *Exhaust Whistle*, newsletter of the Westchester, N.Y. Region of the Antique Automobile Club of America.

A reply came from Carle L. Garrett of Cincinnati:

"I have a 1930 Model A Town Car ... I understand that Ford U.S. made 63 Town Cars in 1930; Murray 27, and Briggs 27. I think that only two of these cars exist. I have a Murray, and there is a Briggs in New England ... In 1929, Ford U.S. built 913 Town Cars, and I understand that only 22 or 23 are still around."

Arcara also received a letter from Bob Swanson of Ridgefield: "I've seen a 1930 Ford Town Car. About 10 years ago one was trailered into the flea market in Rhinebeck, N.Y. It was one of the roughest cars I've ever seen. Some idiot had tried to braze patch panels into the doors and lower body panels. The same car was featured in an antique-car auction in upstate New York two or three years ago. There were photos of it in magazine ads."

"The 1930 Town Car qualifies as a really rare American automobile," Arcara concludes.

Grandpa of the Road

The adage, "They don't make 'em like they used to," perhaps should be used once more, then laid to rest, as one contemplates Frank Hartmaier's 1929 Model A Ford. The roadster has been driven approximately a half-million miles, remains in regular service, and has never broken down.

The car has been owned for all of its 63 years by the 78-year-old Hartmaier of Schwenksville, Pa., who claims that his vehicle runs "as smoothly as a sewing machine." It "isn't a museum piece," he adds. "It's a working, day-in-day-out car I drive all the time." The half-million miles is an estimate. The odometer broke in 1944 at 416,000 miles.

Hartmaier has repainted the car four times, had the engine overhauled three times, and the upholstery replaced twice. He gets replacement parts from firms that specialize in old-car parts. He does oil changes and tune-ups himself.

Hartmaier has been offered $12,000 for his Model A, but he refuses to sell – too many memories are linked to it.

Ford expressed surprise upon hearing of Hartmaier's long-term relationship with his car. "This is a record," declared spokesman Bill Carroll.

Model A First Car

A *Detroit News* series, "My First Car," prompted Detroiter Joe Trowern to write about his first car, a 1930 Model A. Perhaps others will see something of themselves in his story.

"On my 16th birthday in 1941," Trowern recalls, "my father took me to a used car lot to buy my first car. Because World War II was closing in on the U.S., certain products, including tires, were becoming hard to get. So when the salesman showed us a Model A with five decent tires, including the rear mounted spare, my Pop and I were interested.

" 'I'll make you a deal,' " offered the salesman. 'Give me 10 bucks for each tire, and I'll throw in the car.' Pop snapped up the offer.

"Driving home that day, I felt all the exhilaration of owning my own car. It not only drove well, but was economical. The engine was so simple I could work on it myself.

"After repainting it by hand, I decided to add some patriotic slogans. The radiator grille carried a large 'V' for victory. On the spare I boasted 'Berlin or Bust!' and the left rear tire warned 'Nazi Beware.'

"For more than a year, my Model A took me everywhere I wanted to go. I had enlisted in the Army while still in high school, and was summoned for infantry duty while only 17. Pop helped me put my cherished Ford up on blocks in one corner of our garage.

"I was assigned to one of General George Patton's Third Army infantry divisions ... and by the time I was 19 I'd been shot a couple of times and had been awarded a Battlefield Commission. At 20 I was sent home as a disabled veteran. On the day I returned, Pop asked, 'Do you want to take your car off the blocks?'

"More than three years had passed since my Model A's engine had run. On the first push-start attempt, it began to run as smoothly as ever! I was truly home again."

Matter of Definition

"One man's junk is another man's treasure" is a line familiar to every old-car enthusiast. Unhappily for Rawley Patton, of Columbia, S.C., the reverse of that statement can apply as well – at least in the eyes of a judge.

Patton was fined $168 for cluttering his yard with eight Model As. "Some people call my Model As junk," he said, "but I probably have $25,000 worth of junk here." He added that he's cannibalizing the eight As to produce four or five working cars. Patton will appeal his fine.

Model A Goes 190 MPH

The world's speed record for a Model A probably is held by a 58-year-old woman, Roberta J. Nichols, manager of Ford Motor Co.'s alternative fuels program.

Nichols once hit 190 mph on the Bonneville (Utah) Salt Flats in a stripped 1929 A powered by a Chrysler V-8 engine. In addition to overseeing the testing of cars powered by methanol, ethanol, natural gas, and other sources, Nichols spends many weekends under the hood or behind the wheel of her 1954 Mercedes 300SL.

Automotive Art

Model A headlamps were used to illuminate the stairs of architect Richard Neutra's "masterful Lovell House" in Los Angeles, according to a *Smithsonian* article on art and 20th century industry.

Neutra, an Austrian who settled in California, was obsessed with the variety of building materials available to American architects. One of his students joked that "for Neutra, Sweet's Catalog (for building products) was the Holy Bible and Henry Ford the Holy Virgin."

The article also notes that Ford hired industrial photographer Charles Sheeler to photograph the Rouge plant for an advertisement, and that some of Sheeler's pictures of the Rouge remain among the most highly regarded of industrial photos.

Thanks to reader Gary Custer of Harrisonburg, Va., for forwarding the article.

Model A Analogy

The Model A is cited in an old-fashioned sense in Vice President Al Gore's 1992 book, *Earth and the Balance: Ecology and the Human Spirit.*

Warning of the adverse effect of automobiles on the global environment, the vice president laments, "We are content to see hundreds of millions of automobiles using an old technological approach not radically different from the one first used decades ago in the Model A Ford."

Model B Jitney

"In your 1987 book, *Ford Country,*" reader Jil McIntosh, of Oshawa, Ont. writes, "you show a 1930 sedan with a caption saying that it may be the only Model A jitney in the country."

In response, Jil has forwarded a 1993 photo, taken in Juneau, Alaska, of "what may be the country's only Model B jitney." The vehicle is owned by Dockside Jewellers' Jack Tripp, who puts a student at the wheel each summer to cruise the streets and provide free rides to anyone anywhere in the city, "The car looks original," Jil adds, "but under the hood it has a 283 and the dual exhausts give it away."

Why More Fords?

Why are more 1930-era Fords around than Chevrolets? Dick Larrowe, of Corbett, Ore., writing in the *Society of Automotive Historians Journal*, offers a clue:

"I once had a conversation with the man who had charge of replacement parts for the Chevrolet Div. of GM for the state of Oregon and southern Washington," states Larrowe. He said that from 1928 to 1932, Chevrolet did not use mechanical parts that were easily interchanged from year to year. "On the other hand, Ford Model A parts could be interchanged for the entire production run of 1927 through 1931.

"This was of significance later when both makes had little or no value as used cars. In Oregon, this period ran from about 1945 to 1965. During these years, cars were kept running by their owners' use of junkyard parts. It was possible to keep Chevrolets running on used parts ... but more thought was required, more mechanical skill, and a knowledge of interchange manuals. If a Ford was required, chances were that a part from a '28 could be bolted right onto a '31."

V-8 Engine Top Rated

Ford's 1932 V-8 engine is rated by Alex Mair, vice president in charge of GM's technical staffs, as one of the "six car engines so innovative for their time that they changed the course of engine design."

"Henry Ford wanted to beat Chevrolet," Mair recently told the *Detroit News*. "So he told his engineers to develop a V-8 with a single-piece block. They said it couldn't be done. He said he'd get someone else to do it if they couldn't. This engine really made the V-8 accessible to every man."

Mair's other engine choices include the 1930 Cadillac V-16, the 1937 Chevrolet "Blue Flame," 1949 Cadillac Kettering, 1949 Olds Rocket, and 1955 Chevrolet small-block V-8. The list strikes one as being top heavy with GM power plants, but Mair is entitled to his opinion same as everyone else.

Showing Off

A V-8 Deluxe Three-Window Coupe's transverse suspension impressed visitors at the Ford Exposition of Progress at Detroit's Convention Hall in 1933. The exposition celebrated the company's 30th anniversary.

Ease Off Mates

The placard describing a 1937 Ford V-8 utility vehicle in England's National Motor Museum in Beaulieu, Hants., caught my eye, and made me wonder if one of its claims is, as the English say, "a bit much."

"The famous Ford V-8 engine, introduced in 1932," says the sign, "became the workhorse of the world; some say the Second World War would have been lost without it."

If "some" say that, it could be that "some" are stretching things somewhat, for with all due respect to this excellent engine, it hardly seems that the war's outcome hinged upon it. If the Ford V-8 weren't available, another engine would have been used in its stead. Although the substitute might not have performed as well, one assumes that it would have sufficed.

The reference to the engine reminds me of an exaggerated statement I've seen to the effect that the Fordson tractor was crucial to Great Britain's survival in World War I.

Cars & Cows

"Is it true that Henry Ford once criticized eight-cylinder cars?" writes Charles Uhles, of Sedalia, Mo. "After all, he introduced a V-8 in 1932."

Ford was enamored of four-cylinder cars from the time he built his famous racing cars – Arrow and 999 in 1902 – through the Model T and Model A eras. In fact, he once said, "I've no use for a car that has more spark plugs than a cow has teats."

Obviously, he changed his mind.

Bonnie and Clyde Car

One of the most infamous of V-8s – the "git car" Bonnie and Clyde were using when shot to death in 1934 – toured the southern part of the country as part of the fifth annual Interstate Batteries Great American Race.

The car, riddled with 167 bullet holes, was gawked at by thousands. One of the onlookers was Raymond Woods of Meridian, Miss., who said he first saw the car as a 6-year-old in 1937. The car was also on tour at that time. Woods confessed that he's still "scared to touch" the vehicle.

Bonnie and Clyde didn't hold the title to the car; just stole it from a Topeka, Kan. couple. It took them to Arcadia, La., where they were ambushed by lawmen after stopping to assist the "stranded" father of an accomplice. Fortunately for the car's promoters, law officers leadsprayed the car, as well as Bonnie and Clyde, who were 20 feet from the vehicle. After all, one or two bullet holes would scarcely have the visual impact of 167 perforations.

Car Buff Tour Book

There are two 1934 "Bonnie and Clyde" Ford V-8s, plus a movie version, according to *Tour Book for Antique Car Buffs*, by Richard E. Osborne.

One of the cars in which B and C allegedly were gunned down is in the Tragedy in U.S. History Museum in St. Augustine, Fla., alongside the vehicle in which actress Jayne Mansfield was killed. The other claimant is in Whiskey Pete's Hotel-Casino off I-15 at the Nevada-California border. The movie car is in Herbie's Antique Car Museum, Charleston, S.C. As to which of the B and C cars is the real McCoy, you, gentle reader, may take your pick.

'32 Stocker in Smithsonian

The prestige of '32 Ford stock racing cars recently was raised a notch when a coupe was accepted by and displayed in Washington's Smithsonian Institution. Donor is Lee Hurd, who raced the vehicle to more than 130 heat, semi, and feature victories in New England stock car competition during the early 1950s.

After being displayed in the Smithsonian, the car was loaned to the Eastern Museum of Motor Racing in Latimore Valley, Pa.

Thanks to reader Tom Konop, of Terrace Park, Ohio, for forwarding an article on the display for *Pit Chatter*, a bimonthly publication of the Atlantic Coast Old Timers Auto Racing Club, 55 Hilliard Rd., Old Bridge, N.J. 08857.

Hollow Triumph

Ford V-8s won the first three places in the stock car class of the 1934 Pikes Peak Hill Climb. After the victory, Ford's advertising agency, N.W. Ayer & Son, blanketed the press with news releases and also sent film clips to dealers, suggesting that they pay local theaters to show them. Many did.

Ford's triumph was hollow, however,

as reader Dan Radbruch, Sagle, Idaho, recently pointed out. The year 1934, he notes, was the first year stock cars ran as an experimental class at Pikes Peak, and only three Fords were entered! "Oh well," he adds, "facts never stopped an advertising agency."

Rumble Seat Romancing

We've always suspected a certain amount of tumbling went on in rumble seats, and now comes acknowledgement of same from California.

Two elderly ladies, according to a San Francisco newspaper columnist, were looking at a restored V-8 coupe with a rumble seat. One exclaimed to the owner, "My husband bought a brand new V-8 from Hughson Ford (Ford Motor Co.'s first dealership) in 1932 for our honeymoon. I believe my first son was conceived in the rumble seat."

With such goings-on, little wonder that a popular song of the era was titled, "Tumble in a Rumble Seat."

V-8 Railcar

"I've read about the Model T and Model A being used as railroad inspectors' cars," states reader Clarence Deming, of Phoenix, Ariz. "As a V-8 owner, I'd like to know if the V-8 was ever used for this purpose."

The Great Northern Railroad (now part of the Burlington), which runs from the Midwest to the Pacific Northwest, assigned 1933 V-8 standard sedan railcars to each of its largest divisions, according to a 1983 *V-8 Times* article.

The vehicles, which checked for track irregularities, were equipped with demountable rims, horns, marker lights, and headlight lenses. Caboose lamps were mounted high on the rear of the car, and flange wheels were mounted inside the tires. The V-8s were supposed to precede any train carrying the President of the U.S., and may have done so on occasion, although the publication did not report on any such assignments.

Getting the V-8 Right

Light is shed on the V-8's well-known brake and oil problems, and solutions to them, by Donald Pickles, Southfield, Mich., a Ford manufacturing engineer between 1921-68.

"Mr. Edsel Ford and Ford Chief Engineer, Mr. Laurence Sheldrick wanted to put hydraulic brakes on the new 1937 model," recalls Pickles. "They proceeded with the engineering until Mr. Henry Ford found out about it. Mr. Ford fired Mr. Sheldrick, and had the engineering changed back to mechanical brakes operated by steel cables. This hurt Ford sales because the cables stretched and caused periodic adjustments necessary to maintain brake efficiency. Mr. Ford did not want to pay royalty fees to the Wagner Electric Corp., which made hydraulic brakes. However, starting with the 1939 Ford they had to change to hydraulic brakes. This was the beginning of the use of hydraulic brakes on Fords. Meanwhile, Mr. Sheldrick got a job with General Motors."

Addressing the oil problem, Pickles notes that "Mr. Henry Ford, with the help of Mr. Charles Sorensen, pushed the design and development of the 1932 Ford V-8 engine. Ford was the first to produce a high-production V-8 cylinder block assembly, casting it in one piece. Mr. Charles Sorensen personally helped develop the patterns and molds and the cores for this engine. The only problem they had with this engine casting was controlling the walls of the cylinder diameters and the location of the cylinder cores. There were some variations in cylinder wall thickness, which caused some engines to use excessive oil (and give Fords a reputation as "oil burners").

"Mr. Ford and Mr. Sorensen and the engineers decided to install cylinder sleeves made from fender sheet metal, which at that time was 16 gauge. I was given the responsibility for processing the operation lineup and designing the dies for these operations, also specifying the mechanical punch presses for producing the cylinder sleeves. This addition to the engine was very successful, resulting in the elimination of the engine's excessive use of oil."

Pickles retired from Ford at age 62 in 1968.

The '34 V-8

Reminiscing comes easily, if one was 18 years old in 1937, out of high school for a year, and had just acquired a 1934 Ford V-8 three-window rumble-seat coupe. Here's how reader John C. Jackson of San Jose, Calif., recalls his prize possession.

"Admittedly the car is secondhand," writes Jackson in the second person. "But, it's in very good condition, with a black paint job and cream wire wheels. You bought it for $265 and a Model A. The tire size is 5:50 x 17, and the engine is a mighty 85 hp.

"You've added an oil pressure gauge and a hydrostatic water temperature gauge – both styled for the '34 dash. An ammeter, gas gauge, and speedometer with trip odometer are original equipment. There's a cigar lighter with a little green 'eye' that glows when the lighter is hot. (Mr. Ford would never allow a 'cigarette lighter' in his cars. They were always 'cigar lighters.') Under this lighter is a small but adequate pullout ashtray.

"The glove compartment lid has a wood grain finish, as does the rest of the dash. It also has a clock the size of the speedometer. The clock doesn't work. A Ford radio can be installed instead of this compartment. A door with a radio dial is substituted for the one with the clock.

"The rumble lid is opened by turning a handle to the right of the rear window. This causes the lid to pop open. The rear window can be opened by turning a small T-handle on the same panel as the lid release.

"You find you sit rather low in this coupe – at least by today's standards. The steering wheel is of the plain black three-spoke type, and the light switch and horn button are mounted in the hub. This switch was modified in 1932 from the Model A's to avoid having one's coat sleeve accidentally turn on the parking lights. The ignition switch and steering lock are located at the juncture of the steering column and the dash. The starter switch is next to and above the brake pedal by the firewall. The light switch (remember it's on the steering wheel hub) is OFF when centered. Turning clockwise one notch activates the cowl-mounted parking lights, and the first-notch counterclockwise provides low (headlight) beams. The second notch is for the high beams (two-filament bulbs). Standard Fords have their parking lights in the headlamps; the DeLuxe models have them on the cowl. These models also boast two taillights and two horns. The latter are mounted under the headlamps.

"The driver's door has no key entry. The right-hand door must be unlocked, and the driver either scoots across the seat or reaches across and turns a small lever on the driver's door to unlock that side. The doors are extra-wide on the coupe and are hinged at the rear.

"The 1934 coupe was comfortable for four adults. How we ever managed to fit five husky teenagers into the front seat is a mystery. It's impossible in the rumble seat.

"The 85-hp flathead is amazingly quiet and fast. The fact that it eats valve springs is immaterial, as they're not too hard to replace if you have a set of Western Auto socket wrenches. Perhaps a little tendency to overheat should be mentioned. And, the oil consumption could be improved – but what the hey, it's still a beauty!"

Colombian V-8

She's no thing of beauty, this 1936 V-8, but reader Pablo Antonio Porras Chacon, of Bucaramanga, Colombia, hopes to restore her anyway. Chacon, in forwarding the picture, didn't say how he came by the car. Its exterior seems to be in one piece except for the grille and a missing window.

Ford Camp Car

It's called a Ford Camp Car, and the 1933 V-8 owned by Californian David Woodworth was state of the art when built. A side panel folded down to make a table, a water faucet was attached to the back, and a speaker was put on a cord so a radio could be placed outside. Today the vehicle also has pushbutton turn signals and a swivel captain's chair.

The camper is one of 21 recreational vehicles owned by Woodworth. A camping enthusiast, the collector, who may be the only recreational vehicle historian, hopes to build a museum on the history of camping. Of America's most famous motorized campers, Henry Ford, Thomas A. Edison, and Harvey Firestone, who called themselves "The Vagabonds," he says, "They could afford to do anything. But they preferred to travel by RV."

Lucking Out

Rummaging through my files I ran across a four-year-old "lucking out" letter from the late Jim Petrik, Madeira, Ohio.

Petrik, so the story goes, after meeting William Clay Ford's executive assistant, George Haviland, at a 1968 T-Bird convention in Tulsa, asked the executive for a couple of slides. The latter obliged, and Petrik saved an accompanying letter.

In 1972 Petrik bought a '69 Mercury Marauder X-100. By the fall of 1973 its left rear fender had rusted around the gas tank door, a problem common to most, if not all, '69 and '70 Fords and Mercurys. After getting the runaround at a Lincoln-Mercury dealership, Petrik sent photos of his rusted vehicle to Haviland along with a photocopy of the executive's 1968 letter.

Haviland forwarded the complaint to the Factory Service Department. "I suppose," Petrik recalls, "he sent a note on his letterhead, which said 'Office of Vice President, Product Design' and signed it 'Executive Assistant.' "

"You never saw so many monkeys jump so damn high in your life," Petrik continues. "A couple days later when I got home from work, my wife said the zone service manager had called saying that arrangements had been made to fix my car .... I took it in and got it back on a Thursday night. As I was coming through the door, not even having my coat off, the phone rang. Was the repair done in time? Was the job satisfactory? Etc., etc. I was even sent a special card to fill out, no doubt to go back to the main office.

"All this for a four-year-old used car that was not bought new. I guess the '74s were out by then, so this old clunk was five years old. But NO ONE was going to go against the biggies."

I needed Jim's luck in the 1970s when suggesting to Bill Ford that his grandparents' "Honeymoon House" (1889-91) – then facing an uncertain future in Garden City, Mich. – be moved to Greenfield Village. In reply, old friend Haviland, with whom I worked at Ford in the early 1950s, wrote that the village, of which Bill Ford also was board chairman, already was sufficiently stocked with Henry Ford-related buildings. I didn't agree then, and I don't now.

"Father" of the Bird

Frank Hershey, 80, described by the *Houston Post* as the "father" of the Thunderbird, is working on a book on the car's design and development.

Hershey's design career began in 1928, when he joined Pasadena, Calif., coachbuilder Walter M. Murphy. He later joined GM's Art and Colour (design) Section, and styled cars for both Pontiac and Cadillac. He claims credit for designing the Cadillac's famous post-World War II fins. Leaving GM to start his own design business in the late 1940s, Hershey did freelance work for Hudson, Packard, and Ford, joining the latter firm in 1952. He told the *Post* the Thunderbird concept came about in the following manner:

"A friend of mine at GM got a picture of the new Corvette and showed it to me on the QT. I flipped. I had the authority to do anything I wanted to do at that time as long as I stayed within bounds. I thought, 'God, we can't let them get ahead of us.' And, I knew that Ford wasn't geared up mentally to fight.

"So, I had an extra room, which I partitioned off. I got a wooden armature and a couple of clay modelers. Then, I got with Damon Woods, who was my chief designer in the Ford studio. Together we mapped out what we thought the car should be, together with a couple of other people. So, we started on the QT. After we got it pretty well roughed out and set the wheelbase, there was actually very little change. But then, we had a disaster.

"There was a very fine chassis engineer who somehow got into that studio. And, he flipped his lid. So,

Mercury Debut

Two newly-introduced Mercurys and a Lincoln Zephyr, foreground, grace this photo taken in the fall of 1938 at a Spokane dealership. Whitewall tires definitely were "in."

without me knowing about it, he started to lay out a chassis for this thing.

"Then Chief Engineer Earle S. MacPherson, who developed the MacPherson strut and was my boss, came through the engineering department, saw this young engineer working on a chassis, and asked him what he was working on.

"When he responded with 'I'd really rather not tell you,' MacPherson let him know he didn't have a choice.

"So, then he came roaring in to see me, and started to 'read my beads.' When I told him the guy had initiated the work on his own and I hadn't authorized him to work on a chassis, he cooled down. Then he told me to go ahead with the project. 'But let's keep this quiet as long as we can,' he said."

As the face-lift for the 1956 Fords, plus numerous truck and tractor projects began to absorb more of Hershey's time, the stylist assigned William P. Boyer to "keep things rolling" in Ford's embryonic sports car department.

Thunderbird was given its name during a brainstorming session, by stylist Alden R. "Gib" Giberson, according to Hershey. The name derived from Indians of the Southwest who revered the Thunderbird as the spirit controlling violent thunderstorms. Giberson created the original silver-and-turquoise Thunderbird emblem. At a Feb. 9, 1953 meeting, according to Hershey, "Ford's management approved the project, and a prototype was readied for the 1954 Detroit Auto Show. The car was introduced in 1955.

"Another designer working for Hershey, Reese Miller, was responsible for the face-lifts on the '56 and '57 'Birds. While several artists and modelers made their contribution, Hershey, "the master craftsman," in the words of the *Post*, was "there to direct the effort."

Hershey didn't tell the *Post* why he left Ford (he said he left GM because of a disagreement with the corporation over freelance work).

T-Bird Stamp

The 1955 Thunderbird is pictured on a five-cent stamp issued by Tuvalu, an island nation of 10 square miles 2,000 miles northeast of Australia.

Tuvalu's size is smaller than that of all nations except for Vatican City, Nauru, and Monaco; its 10,000 population is smaller than all states except Vatican City and Nauru. Ruled by the British as the Ellice Islands from the 1890s until 1978, Tuvalu is comprised of nine islands, eight inhabitable. One of the islands is named Nanumaga, hence the words "Nanumaga Tuvalu" on the stamp.

The stamp shows a frontal view of the Thunderbird with two palms in the background. The words "Leaders of the World" appear at the bottom of the stamp, and we are left to wonder whether they refer to the T-Bird or Tuvalu.

Insofar as I know, the stamp is the first to honor the Thunderbird.

Thanks to reader Bob Cawley, Kenthurst, New South Wales, Australia, for forwarding a *Sydney Morning Herald* illustration of the stamp.

Buried with T-Bird

American car lover Cliff Tanzell, a Bristol, England supermarket worker, had a dying wish: to be buried with his 1964 Thunderbird. His wish was granted when his car was crushed and buried with his ashes.

A cortege of 30 American cars, flanked by leather-clad rockers astride Harley-Davidson motorcycles, made up the funeral procession. Many mourners wore rocker-style dress and silk blouses bearing logos of their auto appreciation societies which include the Midwest American Auto Club, the Blue Ridge Runners, and Cliff's Club, the Southside Cruisers. Said Cliff's widow, Cherilyn, 47, "It was a fitting tribute to Cliff and I know he would have been very proud."

The story, first appearing in the

Beaulieu T-Bird

A snappy red Thunderbird is among the American cars displayed at Britain's National Motor Museum in Beaulieu. Overheard when I snapped the picture was one English teenager's remark to another, "That's one I'd like to drag along High Street."

Thunderbird Scoop, publication of the Vintage Thunderbird Club International, was forwarded by reader David M. Scott, Wells, Maine, who expressed a view contrary to that of deceased: "How selfish and shortsighted can anybody be!! Why crush a nice car instead of leaving it for someone else to appreciate?"

T-Bird Fifties Symbol

An Arts & Entertainment channel biography of actress Jayne Mansfield cites the Thunderbird, hula hoop, rock 'n' roll music, and Jayne as symbols of the fifties.

Jayne was one of the decade's three buxom blonde bombshells, the others being Marilyn Monroe and Mamie Van Doren. The T-Bird and the bombshells alike evoked shouts of "Hubba hubba," a male warcry of the decade.

T-Bird or Mack Truck?

"If your body and soul were a '65 T-Bird [our new magazine] would be their yardstick for long life and peak performance," says a macho publication, *Men's Health*, written "for the man who realizes that taking care of the physical machine is not something only for wimps, women, and doctors."

Inasmuch as the magazine's first edition emphasizes beer drinking, paunch busting, and he-man foods (buffalo steak), it seems to me that a better automotive role model might be a Mack Truck.

'Bird Flies High

A 1962 Thunderbird perched atop a shaft overlooking Houston's Hard Rock Café, 2801 Kirby, near Westheimer. The 'Bird recently was washed and waxed while atop the shaft, which appears to be 50 to 60 feet high.

The 'Bird serves to advertise the café's Rock 'n' Roll Museum. The cafe specializes in burgers and barbecues, plus "laid-back" service.

McBird

Two all-American names – McDonald's and Ford – were linked in a Hampton, Va., exhibit. McDonald's furnished the setting, above, decorating its dining area in a 1950s motif. A Ford-made 1957 Thunderbird dominated the chrome and neon-filled space. Many restaurant patrons photographed the 'Bird, according to reader Charles D. Edmonson, of Hampton, who forwarded a picture of his 5-year-old son, David, posing with the car.

Continental

The 1956 Continental Mark II was introduced not to outsell the Cadillac, but to top it in elegant overtones, *Tide* magazine reported that year.

"Applicants" for the $10,000 car, the publication added, "would have to submit applications and be screened for financial status and social standing." Ford never confirmed such stories, but did intimate that Lincoln dealers would selectively determine who would and would not get the car in each community. After the car went on sale, dealers reported that 90 of the early buyers paid spot cash.

Cadillac responded to the challenge the following year by asking $12,500 for its top-of-the-line vehicle. Long before its demise in 1957, the Mark II was being sold to anyone willing to buy it, one's social standing being irrelevant.

Edsel TV Spectacular

The television "spectacular" which introduced the Edsel car is available on videotape, writes reader Jack Mueller, Wauwatosa, Wis.

The show, starring Bing Crosby, Frank Sinatra, and Rosemary Clooney (with Bob Hope in a cameo appearance) was aired in September, 1957. It was, according to Mueller, one of CBS' first color spectaculars, and bumped the "Ed Sullivan Show" the night it was presented.

Edsel Yarn

"I want to tell you a little story about the Edsel in '58 when it came out," writes reader Cecil A. Smith, Tucson, Ariz.

"I walked into a showroom in Richmond, Ind. where I then lived. I met a salesman, Bob Gainy, a very nice and pleasant fellow. He said, 'Cecil, I want you to look at this new car – we're the dealership for it.' I was amazed. It was so nice and good-looking. He asked me if I'd like to drive it. Of course.

"We started out on Route 40 east about 10 miles. I turned around and started back to Richmond. We stopped at a light. A hot-looking car pulled up beside me. It was a Henry J. with a hot Chevy engine. Bob said, 'Don't race that car because every cop in town is watching it.' I said, 'I'm not afraid of it.' I knew those two boys and decided to take them. The Ranger had a 405. When the light changed I took them on and beat them. I said, 'Well, Bob, how did you like that?' He had a big smile on his face.

"Although the Edsel was a nice driving car, it was too much for my pocketbook."

Cursed Be Thy Name

Any article on the Edsel is apt to prompt letters from those who were "there" in the late 1950s. A case in point was a recent *Wall Street Journal* article on the car, followed by a letter from an Ashland, Ohio dealer.

"You quoted Ford's old line that the Edsel was the first 'all-new' car from Detroit's Big Three in 18 years," writes Duane Smith, now of Homosassa, Fla., "and that Ford spent $250 million to develop it (Ford's propaganda always said a quarter of a billion – it sounded bigger that way).

"Ford did spend many millions, but mostly on ballyhoo and advertising, and very little on developing an all-new car.

"But the millions did the trick. The public could hardly wait to see this 'innovation.' At my own dealership in Ashland, Ohio, we had a policeman directing traffic for the first two days.

"If the car had been only half as new and great as Ford led us to expect,

Edsel Advertising

This picture postcard of a 1957 Edsel, taken from an advertising illustration, features the rear of the car, rather than the more commonly-shown horsecollar grille. The 1990 illustration, owned by Henry Ford Museum & Greenfield Village, has a setting reminiscent of the view of Detroit from Dieppe Park in Windsor, Ont., across the Detroit River from the Motor City. The skyline is not Detroit's, however.

it might have been a howling success. But this warmed-over Ford/Mercury with a 'toilet seat' grille was soon nothing but a laughingstock.

"Ford Motor showed a profit in 1958, but the buyers got stuck and the dealers lost their shirts."

Not So Good Old Days

Thoughts on the Edsel's failure were recently expressed by a former Edsel dealer, Albert W. "Al" Wagner, now vice president for sales of Toyota Motors Sales U.S.A.

The car was caught in an "in-house squeeze play," says Wagner, as both Ford and Lincoln-Mercury divisions broadened their lines and moved into the Edsel's market niche. Wagner also acknowledges that the Edsel's styling left something to be desired.

"Didn't they do sophisticated consumer clinics on styling?" the ex-dealer was asked. The reply: "The process was a little less scientific back then. Consumer attitudes were sampled by putting up a tent in grand Circus Park in downtown Detroit for a few days. Inside was the proposed Edsel. People walking through the park would be invited to see the car and asked if they liked it."

Wagner lost heavily on his Edsel dealership. He was persuaded to become an Edsel dealer, he said, by the 'Edsel folks' selling job," complete with "a grand tour of the Edsel plant, fancy displays, a sneak preview of the car, and a knock-your-socks-off marketing pitch." Six months after the car's launch, Wagner recalls, "I was so broke I didn't know what I was doing."

Edsel Survivor

The Edsel years were to Edselmen what the Depression years were to most people in the 1930s – rough.

"I saw a lot of grief," retired Ford executive Leo Beebe told Jim Aberts, a contributing writer for *Super Ford*. "We were going one day out to a dealership in Ann Arbor [Mich.] just to get out of the office and call on some dealers. We walked into this one place .... it was quiet. All you could hear as you went into that dealership was somebody hitting a body part in the back. You could hear clang, clang, clang. Otherwise it was silent, nobody around.

"Pretty soon that stopped and this guy walked out and we said to whomever it was, 'where is so-and-so, the owner of the place,' and the guy said 'haven't you heard? He committed suicide.'

"A lot of guys suffered," continued Beebe, "but the company was good with the dealers. They bought back tools and signs; they really did try to help the dealers. Many of them were salvageable. If [the company] could, it would try to get them the Mercury line or maybe merge with the Ford line or something of that nature. There was a tremendous effort made to help the dealers, costly, of course, to Ford."

Beebe was asked to join the Edsel organization for 60 days. "I didn't want to go," he admits, "because I knew darn well what was going on there. I went as assistant general sales manager to try and help out, and of course one thing led to another and I ended up as the Edsel marketing manager, and finally, burying it. That was like going through the valley of the shadow. That's two and a half years, trying to save it. But it was futile; a product couldn't have had more odds against it than that one.

"Starting with timing – timed on the nose with a recession. It was high priced and it was bad quality and it was kind of ugly. At least a lot of people thought so.

"Ford may have made a mistake by setting up an independent dealer organization which didn't have any meat on its bones. And being exclusively Edsel, with the recession and no Edsel sales, these guys were in really sad shape."

Beebe was the last man on the Edsel payroll. "I survived [the Edsel fiasco] very well," he recalls. "Many others did, but some got hurt, that there is no question about."

Retiring from Ford in 1972, Beebe later served as dean of the Administrative Studies Department at Glassboro State College, Glassboro, N.J. He now lives with his wife, Jan, in Ardmore, Pa., near Philadelphia.

Edsels Okay

Were all Edsels bad cars? Not according to a batch of letters recently sent by Edsel owners to Editor Phil Skinner of the *Greenline*, publication of the Edsel Owners Club.

Representative of such letters is one furnished by Charles Kruse, of Lincoln, Neb., who bought a Ranger hardtop on March 7, 1958.

"During the period of time I owned that Ranger," Kruse stated, "I never had any mechanical problems! It was a wonderful car, and with that V-8 engine, did it move out. I would lock the transmission into second by pushing the Low button, and wind it up to 105 mph, then hit Drive and shoot over 120 mph. I did this many a time, always racing with my friend's '55 Cad. He never did beat me.

"I was sick when I heard that the Edsel was being discontinued. I was in my Army coffee line when a friend told me he had heard on the radio that the Edsel was being discontinued. All of my friends knew that I had an Edsel and felt sorry for me."

Although Kruse sold his first Edsel in late 1959, he has owned three others since retiring as an Army chief warrant officer.

Edsel Stories

One never quite knows what will pop up in an Edsel enthusiast magazine, as evidenced by the following tidbits from the *Edseletter* monthly publication of the International Edsel Club.

A letter from Andres M. Flanegin of the Dutch Caribbean island of Aruba, notes that his father bought one of six Edsels sold on the island in 1958. At the time, Andres was eight years old.

"Now I am 40 years old," states Flanegin .... I love the Edsel so much that I decided to give my daughter the name 'Edselyn.' She is now five years old, and I am sure that when she will be 18 she will drive and love our beautiful Edsel."

The same issue reprints a *Super Automotive Service* cartoon which shows the devil and a disbelieving aide standing at the gates of hell, watching new arrivals drive through. "Edsels!" exclaims the aide, "They're all driving Edsels!"

Another issue reprints an *Orlando Sentinel* article on Roy Brown, the Edsel's designer. Brown recalls that his formal presentation of the car to Ford's board of directors inspired Henry Ford to stand and applaud, after which all others present did the same. "It was the first time the board of directors applauded a bloody automobile," recalls Brown. "That was the highlight of my career as a designer. The disaster of it was when the whole thing burst, but you have to take the good with the bad."

The Edsel's famed horsecollar grille can be traced to carwatching by Brown and his five designers on a busy Detroit street in 1955. "We studied all the cars on the road, every one of them, 19 different American makes at the time," says Brown. "They all had a wide mouth. Hell, from a block away you couldn't tell one from another." Brown adds that he has the same impression of today's cars, although he thinks today's styling is much better than it was in the 1950s.

Brown survived the Edsel debacle, being made chief of design for Ford of Britain in 1959. During five years in Europe, he created a new design center and styled the Zephyr, Zodiac, and Cortina. Today, Brown, an architect, painter, and photographer divides his time between Michigan and Florida. He drives two cars, a late-model Lincoln and a white and turquoise 1958 Edsel convertible similar to the car which wowed Ford's directors more than three decades ago.

"Today, when I drive my Edsel people stop me and say, 'What a beautiful car,' " says Brown, who replies, "you're looking at the guy who designed it. Where were you in 1958 when we needed you?"

Edsel Cartoon

The Edsel has been depicted in many political and other cartoons over the years. Among them is a 1994 *Richmond Times-Dispatch* sketch showing President Clinton hunched over the steering wheel of an ambulance bearing the Edsel's horsecollar grille. The words "Clinton Health Care Reform" appear on the side of the vehicle.

Edsel Invocations

"The Edsel car seems destined to endure as a symbol of marketing miscues," the *New York Times* reported recently.

As proof of its statement, the *Times* observed that recent invocations of the Edsel include descriptions of eight-track auto tape as "the Edsel of auto sound," the B1-B bomber as "the Edsel of national defense," remaindered (excess) books as "the Edsels of the world of movable type," and the Newton, Apple computer's new Personal Digital Assistant, as a potential "Personal Digital Edsel."

Edsel, Dinosaur Linked

Billboards picturing a dinosaur and entitled, "75 Million Years Before the Edsel, This was a Dinosaur," advertised a 1995 Detroit News *life-size robotic exhibit on dinosaurs. This billboard is located on a section of the Edsel Ford Freeway traveled by Edsel Ford II on his daily commute between Grosse Pointe Shores and Dearborn. (Photo courtesy Mike Skinner, St. Clair Shores, Mich.)*

The *Times*' discussion of the Edsel was sparked by the recent introduction of a die-cast model of the car by the Franklin Mint. Ford authorized the replica as part of a program to license rights to its products and logos. A Ford spokesman, Bill Collins, opined that the Edsel, because of its "ignominious reputation," has become "a camp or cult classic, like a B-movie."

Edsel References

Press references to the Edsel keep the car in the public eye – some say like a cinder – almost four decades after the vehicle's demise.

"The computers that were state of the art [in 1990] are Edsels today," stated the *New York Times*, March 12, 1998. "Is Cavalier Japanese for Edsel?" ran a headline in the June 24, 1996 issue of *Business Week* in reference to Toyota's 1993 commitment to sell in Japan Chevrolet Cavaliers bearing a Toyota nameplate. "The Edsel of the 1970s" was the subhead of a November

1980 *Harper's* article on the auto industry's decline during the '70s.

Henry Ford II's 1957 declaration to dealers, "The Edsel is here to stay," headlines a 1998 promotional postcard sent to prospective subscribers by the *Economist* [London]. Text accompanying the eye-catching headline suggests that "few things endure as well as the *Economist*."

A fanciful design of how a '99 Edsel SUV might look adorns the cover of *AutoWorld*'s July 1997 edition. The rendering was done by the late automotive designer Larry Shinoda, who, when preparing for his assignment, read Gayle Warnock's book, *The Edsel Affair*, and photographed Edsels at a large all-Ford show at Knott's Berry Farm, Anaheim, Calif.

Shinoda's update of the Edsel captures the car's main design characteristics: the horse-collar grille, split front bumpers, rear side covers, and boomerang tail lamps.

Thanks to reader Mike Skinner, St. Clair Shores, Mich., for bringing the *Economist* card and *AutoWorld* cover to our attention.

Dictionary Omission

"In the 1960s 'Edsel' became a byword for failure," states the Aug. 1, 1997 edition of the *Sydney* (Australia) *Morning Herald*. "The 23rd edition of *Webster's Dictionary* makes it official."

If the Australian version of *Webster's* 23rd lists "Edsel," it varies from its American cousins inasmuch as I have yet to see any *Webster's Dictionary* published in this country that includes the word Edsel, nor does any other dictionary that I have perused.

The word "Edsel" – upper or lower case – should be added to dictionaries because it is repeatedly used by politicians, the press, and others as a synonym for a disaster. Here's a project for the Edsel lobby.

Thanks to reader Bob Cawley, Kenthurst, New South Wales, Australia for forwarding the *Morning Herald*'s story on the Edsel.

Edsel's Swan Song

The text of the telegram informing dealers of the Edsel's discontinuance was published in full in the February 1996 edition of the International Edsel Club's *Edseletter*.

Datelined Detroit and signed by M-E-L [Mercury, Edsel, Lincoln] Division general manager Ben D. Mills, the no-nonsense wire read as follows:

"The company will issue the following statement to the press tomorrow:

"Following introduction by the automobile industry of its 1960 models, including the economy cars, retail sales of the new Edsel have been particularly disappointing and considerably below sales in the periods following 1959 and 1958 model introductions.

"Favorable public response to all other Ford Motor Company lines, however, was immediate. Retail sales of Lincolns, Mercurys, Fords, Falcons, Thunderbirds, and Continentals increased in the first ten days of November more than 40 percent above the same period a year ago. In total, these six Ford Motor Company car lines accounted for 33 percent of all industry retail sales, including foreign imports, for the first ten days of November.

"In view of this high consumer preference for other company lines and the severe decline in the demand for Edsel cars, the continued production of the Edsel is not justified, especially in view of the shortage of steel, the effects of which will extend into 1960s. Even the relatively small amount of steel, manufacturing facilities and related employment used in current Edsel production, when diverted to other company models, will help meet the strong consumer demand for those car lines.

"Accordingly, Edsel production will be halted and the Edsel discontinued as a product of Ford Motor Company.

"In order to assist you in liquidating

your remaining stocks of 1960 and 1959 model Edsels, a special allowance will be granted on all Edsel sales made by you on or after November 19, 1959, as follows:

"1960 Edsel: $400 per unit.

"1959 Edsel: $300 per unit.

"Detailed procedures for submitting claims will be forwarded to you by the district sales office in the near future. The Ford Motor Company will, in the near future, send to all purchasers of new 1960 model Edsels, purchased prior to November 19, 1959, a non-transferable certificate in the name of the original owner which will be worth $300 on the purchase of any domestically produced Ford Motor Company passenger car. Your advance knowledge of this plan should assist you in any dealings with recent Edsel purchasers.

"You will be notified with regard to matters relating to termination of your Edsel franchise in the immediate future. The company will offer to repurchase parts, sign and tools in accordance with the terms of the sales agreement.

"Effectively immediately, the name of the M-E-L Division is changed to Lincoln-Mercury Division."

Just like that, Edsel franchises were snuffed out, dealers' employees lost their jobs, and the Edsel became an orphan. Heads also rolled at Ford Motor Company.

Cheap Lesson?

An illustrated paper cutout of the 1958 Edsel Corsair hardtop, sold by the Henry Ford Museum and Greenfield Village for $1.50, notes that Ford may have gotten off cheaply in losing $350 million on the Edsel.

Quoting leading automotive historian Richard M. Langworth, the text accompanying the photo is as follows:

" 'The aim was right but the target moved.' That's the standard quote about the Edsel, planned during halcyon 1955, sold in recession-year 1958 – at a net loss of $350 million. Ford's famous flop sold 63,110 '58 models – as many as Chrysler, but anything under 100,000 was considered failure.

"Yet the Edsel had a wider significance. It convinced Ford management that a multi-division structure like GM was not feasible. Today, as GM struggles with overlapping divisions producing carbon-copy models, Ford might look upon the Edsel experience as a cheap lesson."

Thanks to reader Mike Skinner, of Dearborn, Mich., for forwarding the cutout. Next to the numbers $350 million, Skinner understandingly writes, "That's cheap?"

Worst Investment

The Edsel car remains "Detroit's single worst investment," according to a recent edition of *Car and Driver*. The magazine says that the Edsel cost the Ford Motor Co. "in the area of $400 million," a figure exceeding the usual estimates of $250 to $350 million. None of these figures takes into account the fact that Edsel-related facilities and equipment were recycled and/or put to good use with the emergence of the Falcon and other vehicles.

Some believe Ford's purchase of Jaguar to be the company's worst investment, considering the inflated purchase price and the large expenditure of money and executive time required to rehabilitate the enterprise. Asked when the investment will pay for itself, one journalist replied, "Never!"

Edsel's Failure

"The principal reason for Edsel's failure," according to Gayle Warnock, the Edsel Division's public relations director, "was the auto industry's failure to recognize the oncoming 'compact' cars.

"Only AMC's George Romney saw the compact coming," stated Warnock, now of Scottsdale, Ariz., in a 1992 letter to me. "But as (Ford chairman) Ernie Breech said when I pointed to American

Motors' success in the small car field, 'We don't pay any attention to Romney.' "

The same attitude prevailed at GM, where I began working in 1959. GM executives regarded Romney as a maverick at best; as an industry traitor at worst. But the success of Romney's Rambler, along with that of VW's Beetle, prompted Studebaker to introduce its Lark, followed by the Big Three's introduction of compact cars in the fall of 1959. Meanwhile, established larger makes were hard pressed to retain market share, and the two-year-old Edsel, wallowing through the 1957-58 recession, was dying on the vine.

The Edsel Affair

A recent letter to the editor of the *Big E*, quarterly publication of the Edsel Owners Club, Inc., caught my eye. It was by an old friend and colleague, Gayle Warnock, an ex-Ford and Edsel public relations executive, and author of *The Edsel Affair*.

"*The Edsel Affair*," writes Warnock, "is out of print and has been for a couple of years. But I want to pass on to *Big E* readers that the book, according to Dave Lewis, auto authority and a professor at the University of Michigan, was sold earlier this year by a dealer for $80. The many Edsel Club members who supported my sales effort by buying a copy will be happy to learn they may have a 'treasure' on their hands, so take care of it. Incidentally, I turned down an offer to go soft cover, so that will keep the hard cover even more valuable."

"As for me," adds Warnock, "I ended up with the book the same way I ended up with my Edsel models. Of the 5,000 books printed, I have one mint copy and a copy in which I have made lots of notes.

Warnock now lives in Scottsdale, Ariz. Although no longer a Ford employee, he continues to serve Ford in a press/public relations capacity in the Southwest.

The Edsel Owners Club, with a membership of 1,330, has eight American, one English, and four Canadian chapters. A cofounder of the 23-year-old club, Edsel Henry Ford (no relation to the Dearborn family), remains active in the organization.

Edsel: A Novel of Detroit

A book entitled *Edsel: A Novel of Detroit*, by Loren D. Estleman, Whitmore Lake, Mich., focuses on the Detroit of the 1950s and blends the car's introduction, business shenanigans, and an assassination attempt on the UAW's Walter Reuther.

The Edsel car, according to the book's dust jacket, "is to compete with Cadillac and make Ford the number one shop in town" (actually, the Edsel competed against GM's midsize Pontiac, Oldsmobile, and Buick).

The book's hero, Connie Minor, an ex-newspaper reporter turned advertising man, is hired to promote the Edsel. Conspiracies abound – personal, corporate, and political. Minor is not sold on the car, and Ford executives are not sold on Minor. Walter Reuther, who actually was shot by a would-be assassin in 1948, threatens the Edsel Division with labor unrest unless the hero can uncover his assailants. Detroit's mob also appears on the scene.

The *Detroit News* unfavorably reviewed the book under a headline describing it as a "clunker." The writing, the *News* states, "all too often falls into thudding pretension, as in this description: 'The sun peered around a corner of the overcast like a beaten serf, drying the mud on the asphalt in crusted patches like dead skin.' " The book, the newspaper concludes, "lives up to its title."

The 291-page novel was published by The Mysterious Press, of New York; it sells for $21.95.

The late David R. Babb, one of the country's foremost Edselites, and U.S. Senator Paul Simon (D-Ill.), upon meeting in May 1987 in Manchester, N.H.

Calling All Edsels

David R. Babb, a former president of the Edsel International Club, has searched for the word "Edsel" in computer data bases which abstract articles from major newspapers.

The data bases, which cover seven or eight years, reveal more than 30 Edsel-related articles. "Subjects," reports Babb, "range from the Susan B. Anthony dollar (an "Edsel") to the rise of Edsel Ford II in the Ford Co.'s ranks. There are many references to Edsel as a symbol for failure, and there are a few happy references to the glory of the Edsel car, and even an occasional mention of Edsel Club members, Texan Shelley Cleaver and Pennsylvanian Hugh Lesley among them."

Babb also has been accumulating Edsel stories through a home service available on CompuServe. This telecommunication service allows him to search for and acquire every Associated Press news story containing the word "Edsel."

"It's surprising how often the word 'Edsel' appears," says Babb. "Sometimes it is used as a derogatory word. Sometimes it involves a member of the Ford family, but, most surprising, it often is the name of an individual, famous or infamous, who just happens to make news."

Among persons named Edsel who are cited in AP stories are Dr. Edsel T. Bucovaz, a University of Tennessee medical researcher; Edsel Jones, Winchester, Ky.'s city attorney; Edsel T. Taylor, warden of MacDougall Youth Correction Center, Ridgeville, S.C.; Lt. Edsel L. Rector, a Bel Air, Md. detention center commander; Edsel Moore, director of Kentucky's Division of Radiation and Product Safety; Margaret Edsel Fitch, an El Reno, Okla. home economist; Fire Chief Edsel McMickle, of Cedar Rapids, Ia.; and Henry Edsel Holmes, of Hialeah, Fla. and Tommy Edsel Holmes, of Opa Locka, Fla., both charged with operating a cocaine-smuggling ring.

Fifties Girl

Pop star Debbie Gibson could afford any car, but prefers to drive a 1957 Ford Fairlane, according to a *Chicago Tribune* profile.

"The '50s is definitely my favorite era," says Debbie. "Everything was so optimistic and fun and upbeat. Even the cars. Today everyone wants to drive around in slick, little cars; and people keep telling me I should buy a new Mercedes. But I just can't see spending $70,000 on a car that isn't a Ford Fairlane.

"I love those big, wide, roomy American cars with huge fins and the whole thing of drive-ins and soda shops. I love all that stuff. One of my favorite things is to pick up all my friends and drive to a burger place in the Ford. You can't have a lot more fun than that."

Mick's Galaxie 500

A 1964 Galaxie 500 convertible once owned by rock star Mick Jagger is featured in a Yorkshire, England car museum. The car, bought new from Britain's Lincoln Cars Ltd., surprisingly has a 1959 Edsel dash.

It also has, according to reader David Hayward, of Southampton, England, "a tear in the roof reportedly caused by a high heel." Bianca's [Mick's ex-wife], we presume.

Father of Mustang's Name

Who named the mustang? Not Lee Iacocca, declares Robert Eggert in a recent issue of *Advertising & Marketing*, an Arizona-based marketing magazine.

"We ran a little contest of suggested names," recalls the ex-Ford marketing research executive. "At that time I was reading about those valiant little horses, the mustangs. It dawned on me that 'Mustang' would be a suitable and descriptive name for a sturdy compact car. 'Mustang' won the contest. I recall that Lee's entry was 'Torino,' after his father's birthplace."

Eggert also discusses his pre-Mustang research findings, which predicted that a million post-World War II "baby boomers" would enter the car market in the 1960s. This influx of young buyers, he reasoned, would favor the development of a sturdy, peppy, inexpensive Mustang-type car.

Although Eggert tends to think of the Mustang as his baby, he gives full credit to Iacocca for selling the concept to Henry Ford II.

"Lee is undoubtedly the best salesman I've ever known," says Eggert. "He is extremely bright – master's degree by age 22 and vice president of Ford by 35. However, with the biggest ego in the country, he can be irritating. I wasn't surprised when he was fired by Henry Ford II, nor when he brought Chrysler back from the grave."

Eggert says the pictures of Iacocca and the Mustang on the covers of both *Time* and *Newsweek* in the same week in April 1964 "led to the sale of an additional 200,000 cars."

A Sedona, Ariz., resident, Eggert, 75, is publisher of the *Blue Chip* newsletter and one of the nation's leading economic forecasters. He owns three Mustangs – a '65, '66, and '68 – and considers the '68 Mustangs to be the best of the breed.

Mustang's Father

Perhaps Ford will find it easier during future Mustang anniversary celebrations to acknowledge Lee Iacocca's shared parenthood of the vehicle. But it did not do so during the company's "carefully staged flogging" of the 25th anniversary of the Mustang in 1988, nor is it doing so in publicity commemorating the 30th anniversary of the product.

In 1988, *Ward's Auto Report* ran a photo of the young Iacocca and the Mustang with: "If you know the identity of the man standing next to this car, please tell the folks at Ford Motor Co. who apparently have forgotten him. Fill them in by writing to: I know Who the Father Is, c/o Ford Public Relations, The American Road, Dearborn, MI 48121."

An accompanying article noted that during the 25th anniversary celebration, the name of Chrysler's chairman was rarely mentioned publicly or in Ford printed material connected with the event. However, Iacocca was Ford's "most visible spokesman for the new car and was proclaimed in the national press as its 'father.' "

During the 25th anniversary, the magazine added, Ford executives, when being interviewed, were told to "keep the focus on the car. When asked about Iacocca's role during a "Today" show interview, Design Vice President Jack Telnack conceded that Lee was around, but quickly returned to discussing the car itself. Ford stopped short of cropping Iacocca out of publicity photographs of the car's launch, instead using photos without his image.

The Mustang, being a great success, had many fathers, of whom Iacocca is most surely one. His main contribution, however, was recognizing an excellent product concept and design, and selling it to a management still reeling from the failure of the Edsel.

Mustang Publicist Dies

Robert W. Hefty, 75, who put Lee Iacocca on the covers of *Newsweek* and *Time* in the same week, died on April 19, 1996 after a fight with cancer.

In 1988 I asked Hefty, an old friend, about the coup, and his response, heretofore unpublished, was as follows:

"That was a coup, but it wasn't entirely of my making. We had been working with Jim Jones of *Newsweek* for a long time on a cover story with Lee (tied to the Mustang). Lee had been traveling quite a bit, and *Newsweek* was following him all over the country, catching snatches of interviews and getting pictures of him in action ...

"Lee was pretty well locked up (for a story) by the time *Time* magazine learned about the Mustang. *Time* came to us and said, 'We're going to do a cover story on Mr. Iacocca and the Mustang.' I said, 'I hope you understand that *Newsweek* is already doing one.' I didn't want to be accused of duplicity. *Time* answered, 'Yes, we know, but we're going to do it anyway.'

"So I went to Jim Jones and said, '*Time* is going to do a story too. I wanted you to know about this in case you didn't want to release your story on the same date.' He replied, 'No, we're going to go ahead.' I think there was a feeling that I had helped undercut *Newsweek*, but I didn't have a choice in the matter ...

"I joined Ford Division as public relations manager in January 1964," Hefty continued, "succeeding Walter Murphy, who was very close to Lee, a real buddy. He had become general marketing manager for Lincoln-Mercury. I was at a tremendous disadvantage, trying to succeed Walter. Lee called me into his office and said, 'I want you to know that I'm going to give you a chance at this, but your job is on-the-line. If you don't do a good job on the Mustang, you're through.'

"*Newsweek* and *Time* both came out the same week featuring Lee and the Mustang .... The day the *Time* and *Newsweek* cover stories appeared, Lee became nationally known. I've been told that the only other time the same person was on the covers of *Time* and *Newsweek* at the same time prior to that involved a new Pope .... But in Lee's book (*Iacocca: An Autobiography*), Walt Murphy got all the credit. Didn't even mention me."

Quite true. Iacocca's autobiography states, "Due to the tireless efforts of Walter Murphy in public relations, the Mustang was featured simultaneously on the covers of both *Time* and *Newsweek*. This was an astounding publicity coup for a new commercial product. Both magazines sensed we had a winner, and their added publicity during the very week of the Mustang's introduction helped make their prediction a self-fulfilling prophecy. I'm convinced that *Time* and *Newsweek* alone led to the sale of an extra 100,000 cars." Nowhere in the book is Hefty mentioned.

"I've never said anything to anybody," Hefty adds, "but I certainly resented it deeply. As a matter of fact, I refused to read Lee's book. I'm told it's so full of holes that it's just abominable anyway. He changed dates and places and people and everything else around to suit his own purposes .... I tell you, my esteem for him fell just like that. I think he overplayed his hand at Ford, and I think Mr. Ford was quite correct in firing him. I admire him tremendously for what he has accomplished at Chrysler, but I can no longer admire the man as a person. When I see him on television commercials, I cut him off."

"You would not buy a car from that man?" I asked.

"No," Hefty replied, "I wouldn't."

Mustang Top Product

The 1965 Mustang was ranked among the nation's top 50 products 1936-86 in *Consumer Reports*' 50th anniversary book, *I'll Buy That!: 50 Small Wonders and Big Deals That Revolutionized the Lives of Consumers*, published in 1986.

Other cars on the list were the '59 Austin-Morris Mini, '42 Jeep, '41 Nash 600, '49 Olds-Cadillac V-8, '66 Oldsmobile Toronado, '84 Plymouth Voyager, '65 Toyota Corona, and '51 Beetle. The Thunderbird did not make the cut. Automatic transmissions are on the list, safety belts are not.

The book states that "the idea of the car as a personal toy came of age with the Mustang." Hardly. Rich men so regarded cars at the dawn of the 20th Century.

Mustang: Durable Image

A 1965 Mustang is shown in a *Time*'s photo montage of durable images of the baby-boomer era.

The montage accompanies an article, "A Generation Takes Power," in the November 16, 1992 issue of the magazine. Other images portrayed include the Beatles, John F. Kennedy, Jr.'s salute to his father's casket, the shooting of Lee Harvey Oswald, and Buzz Aldrin's moonwalk.

Mustang American Classic

The Mustang was among "American classics" depicted in a NBC special, "Made in America." Other classics included the Barbie doll, Louisville Slugger, Avon beauty products, McDonald's restaurants, and Las Vegas.

Part of the show was filmed in the Auto and American life exhibits in Dearborn's Henry Ford Museum. The show's host was Robert Urich, who starred in the "Vegas" TV series, in which he drove a '57 Ford Thunderbird.

Phoniest Muscle Cars

The '76 Mustang Cobra II and '76 Pinto Stallion are ranked as the two "phoniest muscle cars of all time" in the February 1997 issue of *Car Craft*.

"Sure this Pinto-based car was driven by Farrah Fawcett on 'Charlie's Angels,' " the publication states, "but the sclerotic 302 V-8, in its flimsily constructed nose, was rated at only 134 hp. That's less power than a new Dodge Neon packs."

Of the Stallion, the magazine writes, "Painted with a matte-black hood and aggressive stripes and wearing slotted mags, the top engine available in this absurd Pinto was a 103 hp 2.8L V-6 mated to a three-speed automatic. Instead of Stallion, they should have named it Gelding."

Rounding out the list are the '76 Chevrolet Chevette Rally 1.6, '75 AMC Pacer X, '80 Corvette (California), '74 Pontiac GTO, '71 Vega GT, '75 Dodge Charger Daytona, '78 King Cobra, and '79 Hurst Olds.

Thanks to reader Bill Friel, Harwood Heights, Ill., for forwarding the listing.

Mustang Checks

Checks featuring Mustang illustrations are sold by Styles Check Company, Lake Forest, Calif., whose more than 100 check lines also display the "Chevrolet Sport Truck" and scenes from TV's "I Love Lucy" show.

Names and addresses of users and banks also appear on the checks. Two hundred cost $15.95, plus $1.75 for shipping and handling. Phone inquiries should be directed to 1-800-356-0353. If dissatisfied, don't blame me.

Mustang in Puzzle

The Mustang appears in a Great Lakes States puzzle made by White Mountain Puzzles, address not provided on the puzzle.

Surprisingly, the Model T, which

often represents cars or the auto industry in puzzles, pictographs, and maps, is omitted. Michigan places and things shown in the Great Lakes puzzle are the Curved-Dash Olds, Henry Ford Museum, Edsel & Eleanor Ford House, Renaissance Center, Michigan International Speedway, Yankee Air Force, Mackinac Bridge, Andel Museum Center, Taquamenon Falls, a windmill (Holland, Mich.), and skiing.

The puzzle was for sale in the gift shop of Mackinac Island's Grand Hotel in June 1998.

Mustang Miscellany

Prominent entertainers who have owned or own Mustangs were listed in the *Portsmouth* (N.H.) *Herald.*

They include Cher, Jay Leno, Lindsay Wagner, Jackie Cooper, Markie Post, Robert Hayes, Tristan Rogers, Debby Boone, and Sonny Bono. Other prominent owners include baseball Hall of Famer Reggie Jackson and, as everyone must know by now, President Bill Clinton.

The *Herald*, which probably received its information from Ford's External Affairs Staff, also listed Hollywood films in which the Mustang appeared. They are *Goldfinger*, 1967; *Bullit*, 1968; *Diamonds Are Forever*, 1971; *Starman*, 1985; *Coming Home*, 1978; and *Bull Durham*, 1988. Two of the films are James Bond movies.

The article also notes that dealers received 22,000 orders for the Mustang the day it was offered for sale, April 17, 1964. Your commentator remembers that day very well, for it is his late father's birthday. A total of 263,434 Mustangs were sold in 1964, and more than 500,000 were sold in 1965 and 1966.

Love Hath No Bounds

Six weeks after the disappearance of his golden retriever, Abercrombie, distraught David Peterson, 19, of South Pasadena, Calif., offered his 1966 Mustang as ransom for the canine.

Peterson, the Associated Press reports, believes his pet was "dognapped," because Abbie once was missing for two days and managed to return home.

Mustang Musing

What's in a name? Perhaps a lot, as one contemplates the clout of the Mustang nameplate.

Ford, according to the *Detroit Free Press*, had planned to phase out the Mustang at the end of the 1987 model year in favor of a front-wheel-drive replacement to be built at Mazda's Flat Rock (Mich.) Plant.

A howl went up from Mustang devotees, some of whom feel that a Mustang by any other name will not be a Mustang; and also from workers at the old Dearborn Assembly Plant, which builds the car that gave its name to a generation. That howl brought on a disclaimer from Lewis Veraldi, a Ford vice president.

Ford, said Veraldi, had planned to scrap the Ford Crown Victoria, Mercury Grand Marquis, and Lincoln Town Car, but kept them in production in the wake of continuing demand. He added that "the customer is the voice Ford Motor Company is marching to," and that if customers want a Mustang, a Mustang will be produced for them.

How Mini is Mini?

"The *Detroit Free Press* says that 'the Fiesta is the smallest car ever built by Ford Motor Company' " writes reader Ken Willson, of Flint, Mich. "Is that true?"

No. All of Ford's pre-1908 cars, except for the Model K, weighed in at about 1,200 pounds, as compared to the Fiesta's approximately 1,800 pounds. The Model T started at 1,200 pounds, but added weight through the years. Some T models topped 1,800 pounds by 1920, while others remained below

1,800 pounds until production was discontinued in 1927.

The Fiesta, built by Ford of Europe, was imported into America for a few years, starting in 1977. It is not to be confused with another small car, the Festiva, produced by Korea's Kia, which is 10 percent owned by Ford.

Deifying the Fiesta

A Ford Fiesta is depicted in a new stained-glass window in St. Andrew's Church, Essex County, England, home of Ford's big Dagenham Plant. The church, according to the *Wall Street Journal*, wishes to mark its ties to the plant.

The Fiesta is not the first Ford-related stained-glass window. One depicting Henry Ford is in the clerestory of San Francisco's Grace Cathedral. The window, according to a brochure issued by the Cathedral, memorializes endeavors "made possible by the creative and sustaining action of God's grace."

The *Journal* doesn't say precisely why the Fiesta is honored by St. Andrew's, but the memorialization undoubtedly has to do with the thousands of Essex County workers who build Fiestas in Dagenham.

Jaguar Biggest Bomb

Ford's purchase of Jaguar for $2.6 billion in 1990 is described as "the worst" of business acquisitions by Steven Kaplan, professor of finance at the University of Chicago's Graduate School of Business.

Other regrettable acquisitions cited by Kaplan were the following: Quaker Oats of Snapple; A.T.&T. of NCR; Mobil of Montgomery Ward; Coca-Cola of Columbia Pictures; and Sony of Tri-Star Pictures.

Thanks to reader Bill Friel, Harwood Heights, Ill., for forwarding the *Tribune*'s 1997 story on business buys that bombed.

Taurus/Sable Lineage

Corporate mobility was a factor in introducing the aerodynamic styling of Ford's Taurus/Sable, observes auto historian Christopher G. "Kit" Foster, who in a recent letter also traces the cars' lineage.

The cars, says Foster, "have a clear bloodline to Ford of Europe's Sierra ... Most sources seem to give principal credit for the 'smooth' look to Jack Telnack, who served a term as design vice president at Ford of Europe. Apparently [Ford Styling Chief] Gene Bordinat had had some people dabbling at aerodynamics before that, but Telnack's application of the shovelnose to the Mustang/Capri for '79 seems to be the starting point for the present trend. After that, of course, came the 'new' T-Bird and the Tempo/Topaz, each looking successively more 'European.' And all of them owe some homage to the Probe series of show cars from Ford's Carrozzeria Ghia. You also have to factor in Ray Everts, a veteran of Ford of Europe, and British interior designer Trevor Creed.

"But if the Taurus and Sable look 'European' to us and owe their existence to a team which once populated the European design studios can they necessarily be called European designs?" asks Foster. Jean Lindamood, in *Car & Driver*, quoted Telnack as saying, 'I can't say that I or the designers in this building really made it work. We could not have worked those ideas through the corporation if top management wasn't receptive. Why were they receptive? I'd say their conditioning had a hell of a lot to do with it. You've got to bear in mind that all of those guys [Chairman Philip Caldwell, President Donald Petersen, etc.] had European experience.

"I've often wondered what would have happened if these people hadn't been exposed to a similar design approach in Europe. They were comfortable with it. They could understand it. They'd lived with it, driven it on the road, and their only concern was would the U.S. market have a big warm-up period? If all our management were just homegrown Detroit guys, I think it would have been a difficult sell job.' "

"To paraphrase an old saw," adds Foster, "if the guys who designed it say it's European, it's European."

Jellybeans' Parentage

Noting the confusion surrounding the Mustang's parentage (many executives from Lee Iacocca on down claim credit), *Detroit Free Press* columnist Bob Talbert recently asked the Ford Co. to provide "official word" on "who fathered, mothered, midwifed, etc. the company's industry-pacesetting super-hot Taurus and Sable lines."

"The official 'father' of Taurus and Sable," said David Scott, Ford vice president for public affairs, "was Team Taurus, a group of hundreds of men and women who planned and implemented the design, engineering, manufacture, parts supply, production, sales, marketing and service of both cars. The team consisted of hourly, salaried and management employees from just about every function in the company, and from suppliers and dealers.

"The delivery room was filled with fathers, mothers, midwives and nurses in one of the most public pregnancies and births in the company's history."

"How true," says Talbert, "but I think everyone concerned will agree that Ford designer Jack Telnack, who originally stuck his neck out for the jellybeans, is getting the proper accolades for his special role in bringing this hot product to market. But he, too, defers to the team as father."

Tauruses or Tauri

"If a single Taurus is a Taurus," writes reader Jay Vande Velde, of Holland, Mich., "are two of the cars Tauruses or Tauri?"

To get an answer to this singular question, I inquired of a friend of Ford's External Relations Staff. He told me that the company uses "Tauruses," considering Tauri "an affectation."

$60,000 Chariot of Power

Perhaps the catchiest auto ad headline I've seen lately is "Chariots of Power," which appears in an illustrated Jaguar ad. Reader Mike Skinner, of Dearborn, comes close to matching this headline with his own, written atop the ad, "Have You Driven a $60,000 Ford, Lately?" He's referring, of course, to Ford's acquisition of the distinguished marque.

Ford wasted a lot of money trying to teach Americans how to pronounce the name of its European-built Merkur, and some say the car's name contributed to its failure in the States. The company would be well advised to let sleeping dogs lie in the instance of Jaguar, which Americans pronounce "Jagwar," as opposed to "Jag-u-ar," as the British say the word.

Best Convertibles

The 1946-48 Ford Sportsman, 1946-48 Lincoln Continental, and 1955-57 Ford Thunderbird have been rated among the ten best American-produced convertibles of the post-World War II era by Richard A. Wright, a *Detroit News* auto writer.

"When Henry Ford II took over Ford Motor Co. near the end of World War II," says Wright, "he had no time to create a new car, so he ordered up the Sportsman convertible, which was a regular Ford convertible with doors and trunk lid made of wood. Ford owned stands of maple and yellow birch, and it had the needed craftsmen because of its woodie station wagons. It was, and still is, a strikingly beautiful car. Mercury also had a Sportsman convertible in '46 and '47, although only a few hundred were made. Ford or Mercury, an excellent unit will bring $30,000 and up, notes Wright, basing his estimate on *Old Cars Weekly* figures.

"The Lincoln Continental was Edsel

Convertible Police Car

Oh, to have been a member of the North Carolina Highway Patrol in 1935, and cruised the highways and byways in this spiffy 1935 Ford convertible. The vehicle looks as if it could have outrun all but the speediest of moonshiners, and, given its three-inch bulletproof windshield, offers its driver excellent protection from head-on gun blasts and bottles. One might wish for a rollover bar while chasing on mountain roads, but since when have convertible lovers been concerned about such a trifle? The car is displayed in the North Carolina Transportation Museum in Spencer, N.C. Thanks to reader Richard E. Osborne, of Indianapolis, Ind., for forwarding the photo.

Ford's elegant legacy," continues Wright, "and these three years, basically carryovers from the prewar models, were among the best-looking. The Continental was the last American V-12, and was selected as one of eight automotive 'works of art' by the Museum of Modern Art. A perfect specimen brings $29,000, maybe more.

"The 1955-57 Ford Thunderbird, an enormously successful car, was a styling exercise with no sports car pretensions and launched the peculiarly American luxury personal car market .... Good ones command prices up to $21,000."

Other convertibles cited by Wright include the 1952-55 Chevrolet Corvette, 1946-48 Chrysler Town & Country, 1953 Cadillac Eldorado, 1956-57 Corvette, 1949 Chrysler Town & Country, 1955 Chevrolet Bel Air and 1949 Cadillac Series 62.

10 Millionth Ford

How many 10 millionth Fords were there? Perhaps several.

Completed at the company's Highland Park Plant in June 1924, Ford 10 Million led Ford-inspired parades through most of the towns and cities along the Lincoln Highway (New York to San Francisco) and U.S. 66 (Los Angeles to Chicago). Several million people saw the vehicle, which was greeted by the governors and mayors of nearly all of the states and communities through which it passed. A motion picture of the tour, *Fording the Lincoln Highway*, was widely exhibited during the mid-1920s.

Ford 10 Million, or at least one of the Model Ts so designated, now is owned by Alan D. Hathaway, a Davenport, Iowa dentist. Hathaway acquired the car in 1964 from a person who had restored it after finding it in poor condition in a field near Kansas City.

After buying the car, Hathaway duplicated the lettering ("The Ten Millionth New York to San Francisco via Lincoln Highway,") shown in pictures of the right-hand side of the original vehicle. Hathaway has never found a photo depicting the left-hand side of the car.

The dentist and his vehicle have retraced Ford 10 million's 1924 route.

Frank Kulick, left, and William S. Hart, Hollywood's first cowboy star, pose for a "publicity still" with the 1924 Model T designated as the ten millionth Ford. (Photo from the Henry Ford Museum and Greenfield Village.)

"When traveling through East Liverpool, Ohio," he recently wrote, "I was very surprised when a gentleman stepped from the curb and showed me pictures of [the milestone car] that he took in 1924 at the very corner where I was parked. His photos revealed that the right-side lettering had a period after the words 'The Ten Millionth' (my photos and therefore my car did not). Two separate photos printed in 1924 by the East Liverpool newspaper also show the same period.

"I took the car to Greenfield Village to show them my restoration and they claim to have no record of disposition of the '10 millionth' Ford. A retired Army colonel in Evergreen, Colo. wrote an article about his 10 millionth, and I have read of another such claim in Pennsylvania."

"I am of the opinion that more than one Ford 10 millionth existed due to the number of dealerships that displayed the car. It seems impossible that it could have been that many places at once. I have looked for additional early right-side views of Ford 10 Million for 20 years, but have seen none other than the ones I already have. If someone can turn up an authentic right view painted differently from the photos I already have, it will prove my contention of multiple 10 millionth Fords."

Hathaway's address is 2503 Gaines Street, Davenport, IA 52804; phone is 319-323-8649.

So, Who's Counting?

The ten millionth Ford was completed at Ford's Highland Park, Mich. plant in June, 1924, and the vehicle subsequently led Ford-inspired parades through most of the towns and cities along the Lincoln Highway (New York to San Francisco) and U.S. 66 (Los Angeles to Chicago).

But the hoopla, according to a Ford publicist of the day, should have been centered around the "Ten Millionth Motor." "Many thousands of Ford motors that never had a chassis frame or body of their own were included in that total," states W.M. Cunningham, author of *'J8' A Chronicle of the Neglected Truth About Henry Ford, Ford*

D.E. and the Ford Motor Company, published in 1930. "These motors were manufactured for Ford service, to replace motors that had worn out, or were damaged beyond repair."

Good point. But then automakers seldom have been concerned with milestone car technicalities. The one millionth Ramrod Eight, for example, might have been produced at any one of a dozen assembly plants operating on the "Big Day." A plant and a car were chosen for the ceremony, and voilà, a milestone car was born.

Ford 20,000,000

A 1931 Model A Ford owned by Lyn Gentry, a New Zealand orchardist, until recently bore the label "Twenty Millionth Ford."

Gentry bought the car in 1995. While scraping paint in preparation for a new finish, he found the words on the left-side of the car.

Gentry has talked to people who "seem to remember a 1931 tour of a Ford from North Cape to Bluff," according to the *Wellington Dominion*. The thinking is that the sedan may be a replica of *the* Ford Twenty Million, which toured the U.S. in 1931, and, if so, was used for promotional purposes by the New Zealanders. But Gentry has not found a published reference to such activity.

27 Millionth Ford

Seventy-seven-year-old Henry Ford, center, perhaps was of much interest to newsmen as the 27 millionth Ford during Ford Day at the 1939 New York World's Fair. Edsel Ford stands next to the hood. Ford Pavilion Manager Fred L. Black is the balding man just to the right of the word "Car," and to his right is smiling Jimmy Rooney, who drove the car to New York from the Richmond (Calif.) Assembly Plant. I discussed this scene with Rooney and Black, having worked with the former at the Ford Rotunda in the early 1950s and having had Black on my doctoral dissertation committee at the University of Michigan in the late 1950s. (Photo from Henry Ford Museum & Greenfield Village.)

Henry Ford drove the Twenty millionth Ford off the Edgewater, N.J. assembly line on May 22, 1931. In order to generate additional publicity for the car's drive around the nation, arrangements were made for each state through which the vehicle passed to provide License No. 20 000 000. Dealers also set up innumerable receptions at which gifts, ranging from rattlesnake skins and beehives to peace pipes and limestone tablets, were presented to the milestone car's drivers.

Gentry has repainted his car black, and thus has lost the last visible indication that his car may be something more than just another Model A.

Thanks to reader Kevin M. Crowe, of Takapuna, AK, New Zealand, for forwarding the *Dominion*'s article.

C-Series Truck

"Is it true that Ford's C-Series truck was built almost twice as long as the Model T?" writes John Alford, of Omaha.

Introduced in 1956, the C-Series, a low-cost, tilt-cab medium truck, remained in production until 1990, therefore lasted for 34 years, as compared to the Model T's 19. More than a quarter-million C-Series vehicles were made, and for decades they dominated the fire engine, city delivery, public utility and refuse markets. The model was discontinued to move production of the much more modern CF (Cargo) cover from Brazil to the Kentucky Truck Plant.

"I doubt if any truck will ever again achieve the longevity of the venerable C-Series," said Kenneth F. Smith, Ford Heavy Truck general operations manager, at the time of the vehicle's demise.

Perhaps the most visible vocational use for the C-Series was in fire-fighting service. "Firemen," noted fire-fighting historian Wally McCall, "refer to the C-Series as the 'belly-button truck' because virtually every fire station in the U.S. and Canada has one."

The passing of the C-Series marked the "end of the era in fire fighting," McCall added. "No truck on the market is as perfectly matched to the task. Fire equipment makers will have to build their own vehicles in the future."

City delivery was another major application of the C-Series. In 1990, Roadway Express had more than 4,500 of the vehicles in its national fleet. "Cost of ownership was always lowest with the C-Series," a Roadway Express executive stated. "With a design that old, the engineers had worked out all of the bugs long ago. Our technicians loved the Cs, and knew them as well as their own children."

Ford continues to supply parts for the many thousands of C-Series trucks still on the road. Although the "C" was never a glamorous vehicle, it certainly has earned a place in North American trucking history.

Ford Pickups

Money recently cited 99 things that Americans make best. Among them were full-size Ford pickups. No other vehicles were named.

F-Series Gaining

The Model T still holds the record for having been the U.S.'s bestselling model for the most consecutive years – from 1909 through 1926. But another Ford product, the F-Series pickup, is gaining ground, having been the nation's top-selling vehicle since 1981.

The F-Series has had tougher competition from the Chevrolet C/K pickup than the T had from its rivals – until Chevrolet swept by the flivver in 1927. In 1994 Ford sold 646,039 F-Series pickups, Chevrolet 580,445 C/Ks.

Ts and Road Building

A 23-page chapter, "Even Model T Fords Contribute," appears in John L. Butler's 320-page, 1994 book, *First Highways of America*. Approximately two-thirds of the T chapter is devoted to illustrations.

Most Ts used in road building were employed in hauling, according to Butler. Runabouts and coupes were stripped of their turtledecks and fitted with a variety of boxes. One-ton Model TT trucks, bought as bare chassis or without beds, were specially equipped to move materials. Many suppliers provided such equipment as concrete mixers, road graders, maintainers, surfacing implements, dump bodies, shovels, loading equipment, drags, and other devices for installation on the TT and Fordson tractors.

Butler acknowledges that Ts, compared to huge modern equipment, "might appear to be unlikely candidates for road work. However, during the teens and '20s, there was relatively little motorized equipment in use. The major competition for Model Ts were horses and mules. It was the small size, flexibility, and low cost of the Fords that enabled construction companies to adopt, and adapt them."

Many contractors praised their Tin Lizzies highly. "They work like a bunch of ants," typically stated an Indiana builder. "They fly around here and there, the very spirit of industry."

The TT's most unique modification for roadwork, the author notes, was the "Nail Picker," designed to pick up nails before they punctured tires. The equipment consisted of a Model T engine mounted on the bed of a TT truck, the engine powering a dynamo which produced current for a huge electromagnet suspended behind the truck's rear wheels.

The nail picker, created at the suggestion of the New Mexico State Highway Department, was produced by the Spring and Forging Company of Roswell, N.M. Several of the vehicles were used by New Mexico's State Highway Department in the late 1920s and early 1930s, and sales also were made to a number of Southern states and cities, plus Poland's Ministry of Public Works.

Ford, Butler concludes, "bridged the gap between horse and mule power and the large road equipment that became common in the late 1920s. No other manufacturer seemed able to perform this essential function."

The book also discusses "named highways" such as the Yellowstone Trail, Lincoln Highway, Santa Fe Trail, Dixie Highway, Custer Battlefield Highway, and Carrie Nation Highway, among others. Named highways, promoted by business interests along their routes, preceded highway numbering by states and the federal government. During the early 1950s

Louisville Pride

Some plants use billboards to publicize their products. Ford's Kentucky truck plant at Louisville goes one better, displaying a heavy-duty truck on a platform in front of the factory. A sign bearing the Ford and UAW logos and the words, "Built with Quality and Pride by Americans," appears with the truck.

Louisville has had a succession of Ford plants dating to 1913. Its present assembly buildings were opened in 1955 and 1968.

Ford considered the possibility of sponsoring a Henry Ford Highway running from Fairbanks, Alaska through Great Falls, Mont., Denver, and San Antonio to Guatemala City.

Butler, owner of a 1911 Model T and author of many articles in old-car publications, is vice president for academic affairs for Austin Peay State University, Clarksville, Tenn.

Horseless Truck Best

Truck makers were still trying to convince business people of the superiority of the motor vehicle over the horse as late as 1920, according to a Parry Body dealer's advertisement forwarded by reader Leonard Fleshman, Columbus, Ohio.

"Every merchant or manufacturer who adopts motor delivery is helping his customers as well as his own pocketbook," proclaims an ad in a Columbus newspaper. "He helps himself by operating his delivery with greater efficiency, for less money than horse delivery costs. He helps his customers because they receive their goods quicker and in better condition than with a horse delivery system ....

"A Parry Body on a Ford one-ton chassis is a most efficient, economical delivery proposition. The initial expense, and upkeep of both, is small. Call at our salesroom and let us show you what other live businessmen are doing."

This ad uses two words that often appear in pre-1930 advertising – "proposition" and "live." In days of yore, sellers usually made buyers "a proposition" rather than a deal, an offer, or a proposal. But somewhere along the line the word "proposition" came to have a sexual connotation. We no longer use the word "live" in the older context, and one seldom sees "livewire" or "crackerjack" as it would apply to a salesperson. It's also been a while since I've heard "that's a jim-dandy," "he's a pistol," or "that one's a corker." But "it's a doozy" is still around.

English Fordson

A handsome English Fordson truck, recently displayed at a celebration of Dagenham's 60th anniversary by the United Kingdom Section of the Early Ford V-8 Club of America. The oval hood emblem carries the words "Fordson 8 Cylinder." (Photo courtesy of Chris Sanders, Cranham, Upminster, Essex, England.)

Fordson Truck Revisited

Our December 1992 column noted that Ford researcher Ford R. Bryan had run across photos of a Fordson truck, but lacked information on the vehicle.

To the rescue came William F. Grohonski, New Hampton, N.Y., who states that page 64 of James K. Wagner's *Ford Trucks Since 1905* carries pictures of such a truck, and Chris Sanders, president of the United Kingdom's Early Ford V-8 Club, who provides photos and data of English Fordson trucks.

"The Fordson name seems to have been used on all British Ford commercials and tractors from 1936 through 1953," writes Sanders. "The company phased out the name Fordson after 1953, gradually going back to calling them 'Ford.' I enclose a photo of an English 'Fordson 8 Cylinder' known in the U.S.A. as a Model 51." To further illustrate his point, Sanders also enclosed Fordson-filled photostats of pages from an English publication, *Ford Panel Vans*, by Len Cole.

For many years, logging has been regarded as a precarious occupation. This 1920s photo of a log-hauling Fordson and its driver suggests why.

Fordson "Truck"

"In a recent column," writes reader Bob Kennedy, of Klamath Falls, Ore., "you mentioned a Fordson truck. I'm enclosing a picture of a Fordson tractor converted into a truck. It hauled logs in Central Washington state in the 1920s. As a young boy, I personally remember the machine.

"As can be seen from the picture," continues Kennedy, "a frame was added that ran from the radiator back to the rear of the truck. An axle with hard rubber tires also was added. The drive wheels were taken off and replaced with a sprocket, and a roller chain ran from the sprocket to the rear wheels to drive the rear wheels. I have no idea whether this was a Ford factory conversion or one put together in some machine shop. At any rate, judging from the load it is carrying; it must have had a sturdy rear axle.

"The logs were moved from near Cle Elum, Wash. to the Cascade Lumber Co. mill in Yakima, Wash. Many of the logs were yarded directly to the railroad, but when the distances became too great, the hard rubber tired trucks and machines such as this Fordson were used."

Offhand, the driver of this tractor would seem to be in a precarious position, what with that huge load of logs above and behind him. What if he had to drive downhill, or make a quick stop ....?

Fordson Tractor

A *Smithsonian* article on the history of tractors recalls Henry Ford's early tractor activity.

Ford, states the article, named his tractor the Fordson to differentiate it from a lackluster tractor named Ford brought out in 1909 by a Minneapolis company, which had hired a nobody named Paul Ford to capitalize on Henry Ford's automotive success. The Minneapolis Ford had two huge steel wheels in front and a tiny wheel in the rear. It looked like a gigantic wheelchair going backward and worked about as well.

Ford's mass-produced Fordson was frameless, and weighed substantially less than its competitors. The driveline, sealed in oil, was protected. The price, driven down to $395 – was below that of a good team of horses and their harnesses. Parts and service were readily available, thanks to Ford's extensive network of auto dealers.

Even though the Fordson had serious shortcomings, (among them, a tendency to flip over backwards), farmers eagerly purchased them. The vehicle boosted overall tractor sales to more than 160,000 annually by 1920. More Fordsons were sold than all other tractors combined between 1923 and 1925.

Modernized Fordson

A gray Fordson with rubber tires on display at the 1992 Kentucky State Fair. Most Fordsons had cleated metal wheels. However shod, the tractor acquired a reputation for rearing up and toppling over when under stress. This bucking trait became so common that one farm journal suggested that Ford ought to inscribe each machine with a warning in red paint: "Prepare to Meet Thy God." Another magazine ran a list of the names of 136 persons who had been killed or maimed on a Fordson. After hundreds of fatalities and manglings, the company introduced several safety devices, including fenders with rear extensions designed to hit the ground before the tractor could flip over. The tractor was built in the U.S. from 1917 to 1928, when production was shifted to Cork, Ireland and again to Dagenham, England in 1933.

Ford Stories

"I have many memories of Ford cars and tractors extending back over the past 65 years," writes reader Herm Ovind, Yucca Valley, Calif.

"In the farm country of North Dakota where I grew up," states Ovind, "Ford cars were in the majority, followed by Chevys and an occasional Whippet, Essex, Erskine, or Buick. Fords would start in the extreme cold when many other cars would not.

"One of my earliest memories is of my father driving home from town in a shiny new black 1926 Model T touring. With magneto, ignition, and lighting, it had no starter, bumpers or other accessories, and it sold in nearby Wyndmere for $363. Later, my father, with a neighbor's help, winterized the car by installing side curtains ordered from Sears, Roebuck & Co. This neighbor eventually purchased the 'T' from Dad when he bought a new 1929 Ford. The 'T,' being light and a later model, was unusually fast, once making a 150-mile trip in three hours.

"In 1927, my father became one of the first farmers in our area to own a tractor by buying a new Fordson. It was gray in color with red steel wheels. Tractor tires weren't available in those days – the rear wheels had angle iron diagonal lugs, the front wheels a sharp steel ridge encircling the wheel. The engine had a flywheel magneto like the Model T. A unique feature was a water bath air cleaner. Draining it every morning would yield a large quantity of mud, so it must have been effective.

"The Fordson ran boiling hot (normal, according to the owner's manual), so we usually carried a 10-gallon can of water on each of the two rear platforms when going into the field. The clutch, a multiplate affair, was inoperative until everything had warmed up.

"Fordsons were often hard to start by cranking," continues Ovind. "Dad bought a 'Fordson Starter' consisting of an adjustable tumbling rod with a universal joint and a special fitting on each end. One end was bolted to the tractor's crank, the other to the left rear wheel of a spare Model T which we kept permanently jacked up. Spinning the tractor engine via the Model T in high gear produced enough encouragement to the magneto for a quick start. These 'Fordson Starters,' complete with jack stand, sold for about $12.

"The Fordson was intended to run on kerosene – very cheap in those days – and it had a small extra gasoline tank for starting. In spite of its quirks, which included a loud, high-pitched gear whine, it was a reliable worker. It paid for its cost (around $600, I believe) in a few months doing custom work for horse-farming neighbors," Ovind concludes.

HFII Blasts Ferguson

One of Henry Ford II's least favorite persons was Harry Ferguson, the Ulsterman with whom Henry Ford had entered into a "gentlemen's agreement" in 1938 to produce a tractor incorporating the Ferguson System. The system provided a new method for attaching and hydraulically controlling plows and other implements to tractors, thus eliminating the need for wheeled instruments.

Following the agreement, the Ford Company produced 88,933 tractors during 1939-41, taking 20 percent of the market and moving from nowhere to second rank in the U.S. tractor industry. But every tractor was produced at a loss, and the vehicle continued to lose money during World War II. In 1946 Henry II, after several unsuccessful attempts to reach agreement with Ferguson on a better definition of the hazy Ford-Ferguson relationship and to resolve complicated misunderstandings between the two – severed relations between his company and the Ferguson interests. Before making the decision, HFII talked with his grandfather. After the situation had been explained to him, the elder Ford replied, "Well, use your own judgement. Ferguson is a hog anyway, and just keep on building the tractor."

In January 1948 Ferguson, by then the head of his own tractor company, sued the Ford Company, its distribution company, and the officers of both companies for $251 million, alleging that Ford had infringed his patents, sought the destruction of his business, and engaged in unfair acts of competition. In a sharp rejoinder, Henry II termed the charges "ridiculous," adding that "the blunt truth about this relationship is that it made Mr. Ferguson a multimillionaire and cost the Ford Motor Company $25 million in the process." After four years of expensive litigation, the Ford Company settled the suit out of court, giving Ferguson $9,250,000 "in full satisfaction of all claims for patent royalties." In return, Ferguson's charges against all Fordists were dismissed.

In 1985 I asked HFII about his meeting with Ferguson in the immediate postwar era. He replied, "I remember going out to his car, a Rolls-Royce, I believe. He had trouble with his rear end so he sat on a rubber tire when in the car. That's my whole recollection of the meeting. I don't remember any other details. Harry Ferguson was a shit. A plain ordinary shit. There's nothing good I can say about him. Jesus, he took my grandfather [and Ford Motor Company] for a bundle. I mean that episode was terrible. Just awful."

Iron Horse Arrives

When Ford's Thompsonville, Conn., dealer sold 10 Fordson tractors to a nearby tobacco farmer, he was "so proud of the 'deal' that he took before and after photos," writes reader William Nedobity, who forwarded copies of the prints.

Both pictures, above, were taken before "Stable No. 1." One shows the farm's horses, wagons, and farm workers. The second displays the tractors and far fewer employees. A sign placed on the barn (center of tractor picture) by the dealer reads: "Cooley Motor Co./Thompsonville, Conn./Authorized Ford Dealer/The Place of Service/Ask the Man Who Deals with Us," the slogan being a takeoff on Packard's "Ask the Man Who Owns One." Exact location of the Connecticut River Valley farm and the day the pictures were taken are unknown.

Index

In 1976 I asked the publisher of my first book, *The Public Image of Henry Ford*, how to prepare an index. "There are no rules," he said. "Just make sure that you yourself can find whatever you're looking for. That way, your readers will be able to find the same things." So advised, I went through the 489 proof pages, jotted down subject headings and entered numerous subheadings so as to avoid entries such as "Couzens, James," followed by 83 numbers, as in Allan Nevins' *Ford: The Times, the Man, the Company*. Also, some subjects were listed under two or more headings and cross indexed, and page numbers were cited for material appearing "between the lines." As a consequence, *The Public Image* is an "open book," at least for me.

The first and second volumes of Ford Country have similar indexes. Headings for Henry Ford, Henry Ford II, Ford Motor Company, and Model T have 158, 101, 55, and 77 subheadings, respectively. Typically, cigarettes, smoking, and tobacco are separate headings, as are Glasshouse, World Headquarters, and Henry Ford II World Center (all the same building). There are separate listings for charcoal briquets and briquets, charcoal; Depression, Great and Great Depression; Historical markers and Markers, historical; Civil War and War Between the States; and Beetle and Volkswagen, Beetle. Rouge Plant, a subheading under Ford Motor Company, is cited separately with 26 subheadings of its own. England, Scotland, and Wales are cited individually and under United Kingdom, and there is an entry for Great Britain/British as well. Page numbers are entered for such intangibles as Henry Ford's genius, mistakes, vision, and values, although the words themselves may not always appear in the text. Thus the differences between an author-crafted index and one compiled by a professional indexer/computer.

This index follows rules of consistency, yet in the interest of common sense doesn't slavishly obey them. The subheading "mentioned," appearing in many entries, signifies just that. The letters "HF" stand for Henry Ford, "FMC" for Ford Motor Company. Good hunting.

D